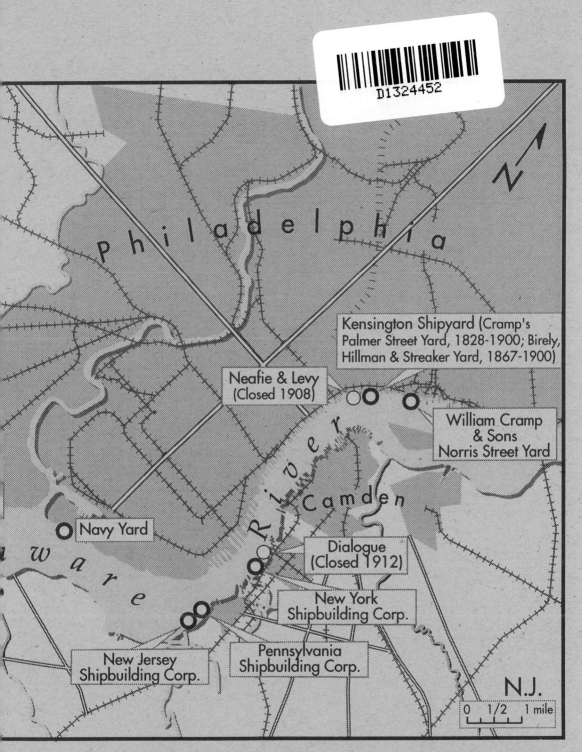

Kensington Shipyard (Cramp's Palmer Street Yard, 1828-1900; Birely, Hillman & Streaker Yard, 1867-1900)

Neafie & Levy (Closed 1908)

William Cramp & Sons Norris Street Yard

Navy Yard

Dialogue (Closed 1912)

New York Shipbuilding Corp.

New Jersey Shipbuilding Corp.

Pennsylvania Shipbuilding Corp.

Philadelphia

River

Camden

Delaware

N.J.

N

0   1/2   1 mile

Ships
FOR THE
Seven Seas

Studies in Industry and Society

PHILIP B. SCRANTON, SERIES EDITOR

Published with the assistance of the Hagley Museum and Library

Ships

FOR THE

Seven Seas

Philadelphia Shipbuilding in
the Age of Industrial Capitalism

Thomas R. Heinrich

The Johns Hopkins University Press

BALTIMORE AND LONDON

© 1997 The Johns Hopkins University Press
All rights reserved. Published 1997
Printed in the United States of America on recycled acid-free
recycled paper

06   05   04   03   02   01   00   99   98   97   5   4   3   2   1

The Johns Hopkins University Press
2715 North Charles Street
Baltimore, Maryland 21218–4319
The Johns Hopkins Press Ltd., London

Library of Congress Cataloging-in-Publication Data will be found
at the end of this book.

A catalog record for this book is available from the British Library.

ISBN 0-8018-5387-7

TO LORIE AND FRITZ

CONTENTS

A C K N O W L E D G M E N T S

The completion of a book, like the launching of a ship, affords an opportunity to thank the many people who have made it all possible.

I wish to thank Philip Scranton and my doctoral advisor Walter Licht, who helped me prepare my doctoral thesis and the book manuscript. Michael Frisch, Michael Katz, Bruce Weindruch, and Jonathan Zeitlin have provided critical support and advice. I have spent many hours with my friends and fellow historians Jeff Kerr-Ritchie, Donna Rilling, and Harold VanLonkhuyzen discussing ideas, draft chapters, and research problems. Lys Ann Shore has been a superb editor and guided the manuscript safely into port. Gerry Krieg and Roger Whiteside helped me prepare maps and illustrations. Special thanks to Rudolf Boch, Jürgen Kocka, Reinhard Koselleck, and Hans-Ulrich Wehler, who apprenticed me to the historian's craft at the University of Bielefeld, Germany. All errors and omissions are mine.

In the course of my research, I received invaluable support from librarians and archivists at the Library of Congress, the National Archives, the Hagley Museum and Library, the Free Library of Philadelphia, the Historical Society of Pennsylvania, the Van Pelt Library at the University of Pennsylvania, the Urban Archives at Temple University, the White Library at Mystic Seaport, and the U.S. Naval Historical Center. I am especially indebted to Ann Wilcox for her help in retrieving the treasures of the Philadelphia Maritime Museum/Independence Seaport Museum's Cramp and New York Ship collections.

I have received personal support from my friends and family, including Lisa Anllo, Annie and Wade Baker, Rose Beiler, Thomas Biene, Tony Ciko, John Delaney, Gottfried and Christel Heinrich, Irene Heinrich, Michael Heinrich, Ken Holston, Peter and Marianne Martz, Sigrid Matzick, Markus Mohr, Frank Rados, Mary Rados, Navenka Rados, Philip Rados, Susan Rados, Volker Schmid, Ulli Sottmar, Marianne and Herman Toewe, and Kerstin Willer. Thanks also to my friends and colleagues at The History Factory, Laurie Bair, Bob Batchelor, Stacey Bender, Nick Einstein, Suzanne Gould, Alden Hathaway, Trey Hiller, Michael Leland, Michael Lesperance, Jack Mullen, Neil Nixon, Debbie Waller, and Brytlin Whalum.

My father Heinz Heinrich (1912–79), pastor at St. Jacob's Evangelical Lutheran Church in Brunsbüttel, Germany, taught me to love history and life. My mother Siglinde Heinrich has given me her precious love and generous support.

I dedicate this book to my wife Lorie Rados Heinrich, whom I met on a cold winter night in Buffalo, New York, nine years ago. I have treasured her love, wit, and sharp mind ever since. This book is also dedicated to our son Fritz Isaac, who has brought immeasurable joy into our life.

Ships
FOR THE
Seven Seas

From these Ways
Shall Go Forth Ships
Embodying the Best Designs
Built with Speed and Pride
By Artisans of Many Trades
To Serve Mankind
In Peace and War
Upon the Seven Seas
                    —Motto of the Cramp Shipyard,
                        Philadelphia Maritime Museum

On November 12, 1894, a crowd of twenty-five thousand flocked to the Philadelphia shipyard district of Kensington to celebrate a launching. Spectators
included President Grover Cleveland and his wife, cabinet members, businessmen, sailors, and workers who thronged the wharves and piers. On the building berth, ship carpenters were busy preparing a big hull for launching. At
1:02 P.M. they sawed through the last shores, 6,000 tons of steel slid down the
ways, and the first lady christened the ship the *St. Louis*. The crowd broke
into cheers and riverboat captains sounded their sirens as the nation's largest
steamship glided into its element.[1]

The *St. Louis* was for the nineteenth century what the space shuttle is for our
own times, the single most sophisticated piece of engineering of the age. Her
engines stood 25 feet tall and developed 20,000 horsepower to give her a speed
of 20 knots. Together with fifty auxiliary engines and six boilers, they were
encased in a 535-foot steel hull made of intricately shaped frames, plates, and
beams; in line with the latest safety standards, bulkheads subdivided the ship
into seventeen watertight compartments. Moreover, the *St. Louis* could have
passed as one of the most exquisite hotels of the day: first-class passengers
dined in a lavishly furnished social hall seating more than two hundred fifty
guests under a glass dome, spent leisure hours listening to concerts and read-

American Line passenger ship St. Louis, *the nation's largest commercial vessel, shortly before launching, 1894.* The American Line, New York to Southampton; The Red Star Line, New York to Antwerp *(New York, 1895)*

ing in the oak-paneled library, and rested in cabins featuring private sitting rooms, closets, and dressing rooms, as well as bathrooms equipped with electrical lighting.[2]

The cradle of the *St. Louis* and her sister ship *St. Paul* was the Cramp shipyard. William Cramp & Sons was the preeminent builder of passenger liners and capital ships in late nineteenth-century America. Cramp belonged to an extensive industrial network of shipyards and engineering works strung along the Delaware River. Contemporaries often referred to this region as "the American Clyde," a modest replica of the great center of British shipbuilding in Scotland. In the 1890s it included Cramp's neighbor Neafie & Levy, specialist in tugboats and elegant yachts; Hillman & Sons of Kensington, like Cramp a veteran builder of wooden sailing ships; and the Philadelphia Navy Yard at League Island, which did not yet build ships but performed extensive overhauls at a big dry dock.

This study examines the history of iron and steel shipbuilding in metropolitan Philadelphia—loosely defined as the city itself plus Camden, New Jersey, and other satellite towns in a ten-mile radius from the center city waterfront—from the Civil War to the 1920s. It explores the industry's beginnings in the age of wooden steamships, the rise of metal construction, and Philadelphia's successes in the Gilded Age. Written for a broad range of readers who find steamships and shipyard engineering fascinating, this book provides detailed descriptions of how "artisans of many trades" built these unique specimens of human ingenuity. It contributes to scholarship on Philadelphia when the city was, in historian Thomas Cochran's words, "the American industrial center."[3]

This study also deepens our understanding of how American shipbuilding, business, labor, and technology related to one another. It contributes to two interesting debates among historians of American industry. One focuses on the significance of "proprietary" versus "corporate" capital in the age of industrialization. In a proprietary organization, owners of the means of production also performed management functions; as owner-managers, they were inti-

Cramp shipyard, c. 1894. The St. Louis *is outfitting at the center. Note the floating derrick, lowering a boiler into the hull: A landmark of the Philadelphia shipbuilding industry, the derrick was one of the most powerful of its kind operated during the 1890s.* Scientific American, *29 December 1894*

mately involved in day-to-day operations on the shop floor while at the same time making long-term production and marketing decisions. They rarely attempted to control demand, which in any case fluctuated wildly for their products. Instead, they tailored production to fit customer orders. The resulting batch-production firms epitomized flexible technology, skilled labor, and rapid response to markets.[4] In corporations, by contrast, shareholders furnished investments and hired professional managers to run day-to-day operations and plot long-range strategy, thus separating ownership and management. The rise of national and international markets for mass-produced consumer items and services induced corporations to standardize output. In the production realm, corporate managers hired small armies of unskilled and semiskilled workers to perform simple, repetitive tasks. Backed by enormous financial resources, some corporations even branched out into marketing, streamlining demand to fit the imperatives of mass production.

How important comparatively were these structures and strategies in nineteenth-century America, and when did the corporate model supersede the proprietary? Alfred D. Chandler, Jr., a leading historian of American business, has argued that proprietorships lost their dominant if not hegemonic position in the nation's economy during the second half of the nineteenth century. By World War I, he concludes, the multi-unit corporation was the "dominant business institution in many sectors of the American economy."[5] Later historians of industrialization have taken Chandler to task for emphasizing progress toward the corporation in American business history. They have put forward instead the significance of an "array of unincorporated formats of capitalist production," which played pivotal roles in American business well into the twentieth century.[6]

A second, related debate concerns the dynamics of technological change. How can the emergence of new technologies and production processes be explained, especially in the nineteenth century, when spinning machines, the Bessemer steel process, and iron shipbuilding contributed to the transformation of the Western world? In the 1960s, when many historians of technology still viewed the work of individual engineers and inventors as the decisive factor, some scholars, notably Thomas Hughes, began to explore technological change in the context of larger economic, social, and political structures. A decade later, the "contextualist" argument that society shaped technology rather than vice versa was refined by David Noble, who posited that new production technologies are the result of social relationships in a capitalist society. Extending this approach, Harry Braverman and the new labor historians explained technological change at the shop-floor level as the outcome of a struggle between workers and managers over control at the point of production. According to this argument, managers used technology to reorganize production processes into minuscule tasks and to wrest control from skilled craftsmen, who still reigned supreme in the nineteenth-century workplace by virtue of their production knowledge. As David Montgomery pointed out, however, this strategy often backfired, since new tools and production processes often enhanced the role of skilled labor. This was the case especially in engineering industries, including shipbuilding, where workers often needed considerable skills to operate new and complicated machinery.[7]

This study builds upon the new labor history and includes detailed point-of-production analyses. I also argue, however, that historians need to look beyond the shop floor to understand the dynamics of technological change. Key factors include the formation of the capitalist market economy, first on a regional and later on a global scale, which generated demand for new products such as iron steamships; interfirm networks composed of batch producers, whose combined efforts led to breakthroughs in shipbuilding technology; and the state, whose contracts for naval warships encouraged private builders to experiment with new designs, materials, and production processes.

Tackling large questions about proprietary/corporate development and the place of the state, labor, and markets in technological change, historians in recent decades have reconstructed the origins and growth of Philadelphia firms, industries, social groups, and capital-labor relations.[8] The scholarly literature on Philadelphia has changed our view of the American system of manufacturing, once commonly associated with the rise of large firms and mass-production technologies pioneered in the textile mills of New England. By contrast, Philadelphia teemed with small and medium-sized custom producers, especially in the textile, apparel, and engineering trades; more complicated firms, such as the Baldwin Locomotive Works and shipyards, were equally and fully engaged in batch production. Philadelphia may not have been an average American manufacturing city; it bore little resemblance to major industrial centers, such as Lowell, Massachusetts, and Detroit. Instead of answering frequent calls for "representative" case studies, however, we might more usefully explore the enormous diversity that characterized the American economy in specific locales and trades and understand the interlacing of industries, regions, and markets.

Few industries lend themselves better to this kind of analysis than shipbuilding. The waterfront was border territory where land and sea, industry and commerce, workshops and the world intersected in unique ways. Philadelphia-built ships, sailing the seven seas in peace and war alike, played a pivotal role in the establishment of America's merchant and naval fleets. Before World War I Philadelphia's yards launched virtually every American transatlantic liner and most deep-sea passenger vessels and freighters. Upon arrival at major ports, such as New York, big ships usually received assistance from Philadelphia-built lightships, pilot boats, ice breakers, and tugs. Beginning with the Civil War ironclad USS *New Ironsides,* Philadelphia and Camden builders supplied the U.S. Navy with its most powerful fighting machines, including the USS *Massachusetts,* the nation's first battleship, and the USS *Saratoga,* the huge aircraft carrier of World War II fame.

Illustrating major trends in the making of industrial America, Philadelphia shipbuilding at the production level demonstrated how and why its yards rose to prominence. Builders laid the groundwork during the first half of the nineteenth century, when wooden steamship construction benefited from the city's deep involvement in steam engineering in general and, in particular, technological spin-offs from stationary engine building. When builders made the transition from timber to iron hulls, Philadelphia yards were especially well positioned to subcontract with the western Pennsylvania iron and steel mills, which during the second half of the nineteenth century formed the throbbing core of the American metallurgy sector. This cluster resembled the regional concentration of shipyards, engineering firms, and iron mills on the Scottish Clyde and made the Delaware Valley the epicenter of American metal shipbuilding in the age of steam, iron, and steel.

Philadelphia's industrial economy combined batch production and skilled labor—critical factors in the rise of iron and steel shipbuilding. Local engineering, metallurgy, and textile firms supplied niche markets with custom-made products; employers required and found the skilled, versatile laborers they needed to keep pace with demand that often changed suddenly and dramatically. Shipbuilding illustrated the Philadelphia system because steamship operators and the navy usually ordered "tailormade" vessels, designed to sail on specific routes or to perform narrowly defined combat tasks. Shipyards rarely built standardized tonnage along the lines of New England textiles, except perhaps during a spectacular but unsuccessful experiment at the Hog Island yard in World War I. In peacetime shipbuilders faced volatile maritime markets. Yards had to survive months and even years without new vessel contracts, a situation that forced them to branch out into nonmarine production. Placing a high premium on versatility, the batch market encouraged builders to hire and train craft workers prepared to build everything from passenger liners and battleships to tugs and barges, even stationary fire engines and electrical locomotives.

A few words about terminology are in order. To avoid confusion between employers and workers, the term *shipbuilders* refers only to yard owners. Employees are identified by their specific trades. The merchant marine includes ships in the foreign trade but not those sailing between domestic ports. As much as possible, the text avoids arcane technical terms used only by shipyard tradesmen, naval architects, and marine engineers. (Naval architecture refers to hull design, while marine engineering pertains to engine and boiler design.) Unlike most industrial products, ships received a christening and were usually referred to by means of the feminine pronoun—a practice followed in this historical study, even though its use today has become outdated. The gesture gave shipbuilding and seafaring at the time a sentimental touch, perhaps to compensate builders, workers, and sailors for the often harsh realities of the maritime world.

"Ship-Building as Much as Possible Advanced": The Rise and Decline of Wooden Shipbuilding, 1640-1870

During the antebellum years, the Philadelphia waterfront presented a lively scene. Downtown, the Delaware River was lined with docks for sailing vessels, wooden steamships, and ferryboats, which took aboard passengers and cargo destined for Camden across the river, other East Coast ports, and foreign countries. Most of these vessels had been built in Kensington, where shipyards were now busy with new craft as well as overhauls. South of center city, the Philadelphia Navy Yard and marine engine builders constructed wooden war-steamers for the U.S. Navy. To the west stretched the city itself, where workshops and factories produced textiles, furniture, sugar granulate, steam engines, chemicals, and footwear—products that were often shipped aboard sailing ships and steam vessels to distant destinations. Philadelphia was the nation's manufacturing center and a leading East Coast port city, where shipbuilding formed an integral part of the economic base.[1]

The first half of the nineteenth century was the zenith of American shipping and shipbuilding. Since the seventeenth century, the maritime economy had evolved from colonial trades into a sophisticated network connecting East Coast merchants and builders with domestic markets and world trade. In this age of wooden hulls and sails, America rivaled Britain as the world's maritime powerhouse whose shipyards built inexpensive tonnage using seemingly inexhaustible supplies of superb ship timber. During the first half of the nineteenth century, American inventors also pioneered steamship technology, which freed shipping from nature's whims—though sometimes less than the inventors believed it would. Philadelphia builders became experts in the construction of wooden screw-steamers, the most advanced vessel type developed by mid-century.

American maritime supremacy came to an end in the Civil War era, when the merchant marine carried a continually shrinking share of the nation's foreign trade. Contemporary observers (and many later industry analysts) often blamed the decline on the conflict itself: Confederate raiders destroyed the North's valuable tonnage, and shippers circumvented high wartime insurance rates by registering tonnage under neutral flags, principally Britain's red ensign. More recent interpretations point to other factors: the rise of British iron shipbuilding since the 1840s, the inability or unwillingness of most American shippers and builders to switch from wood to iron, and the reallocation of investment capital from shipping to other economic sectors. These trends formed the backdrop to the decline of wooden shipbuilding in Philadelphia; their effects were exacerbated by the Civil War. Simultaneously, local and regional economies were developing, and these sustained the remnants of Philadelphia shipbuilding during the difficult postwar era.[2]

The Rise of the American Maritime Economy

In the seventeenth century, shipbuilding and seafaring were decidedly poor men's trades. The centers of maritime activity were Massachusetts and Pennsylvania, which lacked valuable staple goods, such as Virginia tobacco or Connecticut mast timber. Planters and lumbermen had little reason to invest in sailing ships because English merchants deployed virtual fleets to haul these prized staples to Britain. The English traders were less interested in ordinary agricultural goods that formed the mainstay of the Massachusetts and Pennsylvania economies. This situation facilitated the rise of indigenous maritime trades. During the 1640s, when English merchants threatened to cut off supplies unless Massachusetts paid for them, the colonists built a few vessels to transport provisions to the Canary Islands and the West Indies. This trade generated financial resources for colonial trade with Britain, and the crisis passed. During the 1690s Philadelphia colonists copied this strategy and built ships for the West Indies trade, which became the city's stronghold in following decades. At the beginning of the eighteenth century, Philadelphia passed Boston to become America's leading port city.[3]

By the late colonial era shipbuilding had become a vital American industry. British orders for American ships came when English shipowners discovered the considerable cost advantage of colonial vessels over ships built in Britain.

American builders profited from vast colonial timber resources, particularly live oak, which was known as the most suitable ship timber. British builders, by contrast, paid higher timber prices due to intense shipbuilding activity since Elizabethan times. By the 1770s one-third of the English merchant marine consisted of ships built in the colonies. Pondering the benefits of a well-developed shipbuilding industry for the Pennsylvania economy, Benjamin Franklin argued that "a great Advantage it must be to us a Trading Country, that has Workmen and all the Materials proper for that business, to have Ship-Building as much as possible advanced: For every Ship that is built here for the English Merchants, gains the Province her clear Value in Gold and Silver."[4] Other customers included American merchants and riverboat operators who established domestic transportation networks connecting coastal regions with the hinterlands. This created a market for smaller vessels and a home base for colonial shipyards, which increased their output for local customers when foreign demand decreased.[5]

The Revolution reduced American overseas commerce and shipbuilding for more than a decade as the Royal Navy chased American traders from the important West Indies and transatlantic routes. In 1777 England's army struck at the heart of America's maritime economy by occupying Philadelphia and burning dozens of ships during its departure a year later. At the end of the war the English flag disappeared from all American vessels; with it went the privilege of American merchants to trade freely within the English empire, protected by the world's most powerful navy. Independence also hurt the export of American ships because the British Navigation Act excluded foreign-built vessels from English registry until 1849. Although the Revolution impaired the maritime economy in the short term, it had no impact on the great cost advantage of American wooden sailing ships and did not affect the new nation's reliance on waterborne trade.[6]

The newly created federal government cushioned the impact of national independence on shipowners and builders. Article 1, Section 6 of the Constitution gave Congress the authority to "regulate Commerce with foreign Nations, and among the several States." Since most interstate and international commerce was carried aboard ships, the Commerce Clause was in effect a license to formulate federal maritime policy. At the end of the eighteenth century Congress used these powers to erect a protectionist wall whose centerpiece was the Navigation Act of 1792. Like its British counterpart, the U.S. act determined that only U.S.-built vessels were eligible for registry in the American merchant marine and protection by the navy; other legislation de facto excluded foreign ships from domestic trade. On the surface, these policies—which formed the legal framework of American commerce until World War I—favored shipbuilders by forcing owners to buy American-built tonnage, but merchants raised few objections because domestic builders constructed the least expensive ships in the Western world. Shipowners also welcomed the exclusion of foreign (chiefly British) carriers from domestic trade because this gave them a virtual monopoly on the coastwise and river trades.[7]

During the 1790s federal policy turned the liabilities of national independence into major assets. After the passage of the Navigation Act, Philadelphia and Boston merchants ordered new ships to reestablish their old connections with the West Indies. The exotic China trade—hitherto closed to American vessels because British law had given the East India Company a monopoly—was now open to merchants based in Philadelphia, New York, and Baltimore. From 1793 to 1807 the Napoleonic Wars created new opportunities in European commerce for the neutral American carriers. Reflecting the process of nation-state building, the federal government established the U.S. Navy in 1792 and ordered its first ships—among them the frigates USS *Constitution* (built in Boston), USS *Constellation* (Baltimore), and USS *United States* (Philadelphia). These legendary vessels were designed by the Philadelphia builder Joshua Humphreys, perhaps the best naval architect of his time.[8]

Jefferson's embargo and the War of 1812 again slowed maritime growth. In 1807 the Jeffersonian Republicans responded to British attacks on neutral American vessels by invoking the Commerce Clause and closing the nation's export trade until 1809. But the embargo was not rigidly enforced. Also, the coastwise trade absorbed most tonnage previously employed on foreign routes; for example, the number of vessels engaged in Boston's coastwise trade more than doubled between 1807 and 1808, from 1,021 to 2,459.[9]

The first two decades of the nineteenth century marked a period of significant change, as capitalist development transformed urban economic and social structures. Capital accumulation turned many urban craft shops into manufactories and sweatshops, triggering the rise of factories, and also gave rise to putting-out systems in rural areas. These developments went hand in hand with a transportation revolution and an expansion of the banking sector. The shift affected the maritime economy, especially in Philadelphia, where mining, banking, canals, and later railroads offered better investment returns than overseas commerce. The merchant Stephen Girard, for example, who had amassed his fortune in Philadelphia's West Indies and China trades, liquidated some of his maritime assets to buy out the First Bank of the United States and invest in canal bonds and coal mines in northeastern Pennsylvania. Philadelphia merchants also helped finance the Pennsylvania Railroad, founded in 1844. The transportation revolution, by integrating Philadelphia and its rich hinterland replete with potential consumers, facilitated the rise of local manufacturing in light consumer trades, such as textiles and apparel. These developments did not obliterate the city's maritime economy, which continued to grow during the first half of the nineteenth century, though at a slower pace than in other commercial centers. But when Philadelphia emerged as the nation's manufacturing center, it yielded the first rank among port cities to New York.[10]

Nature had endowed New York City with one of the world's most magnificent harbors, where the Hudson and East Rivers provided ample wharfage for large vessels. New York also had access to the northern interior and Long Island Sound, two of the fastest growing regions in nineteenth-century America. Unlike their Philadelphia counterparts, New York merchants had maintained good trade relations with their British business partners after the Revolution; the "English life line," pulled by the rise of British textile manufacturing, triggered the phenomenal rise of New York as America's principal transatlantic port. Its major strength was the cotton trade with England, which accounted for more than half of all American exports during the 1830s. New York shipyards soon built large cargo carriers for this vital trade, which linked southern cotton plantations and English textile mills until the Civil War.[11]

New York consolidated its position as a world center of waterborne trade during the 1820s. In 1818 the Black Ball Line to Liverpool pioneered the American transatlantic packet service in which ships sailed on a regular schedule. On the eastbound trip, packet vessels carried primarily cotton, tobacco, and flour, returning westbound with immigrants and manufactured goods. In the domestic passenger trade, a network of coastwise packets branched out from New York into New England, Philadelphia, and southern ports. Bulk cargoes, such as cotton, coal, and timber, were transported aboard slower craft, which sailed irregularly according to freight offerings at the various ports. In 1826 the Erie Canal connected the Great Lakes to the Hudson River via Buffalo, decreasing freight rates and opening the old Northwest to New York City traders.[12]

The settlement of California, the Gold Rush trade, and Pacific Ocean commerce led to the emergence of clipper ships during the 1840s. These fast and beautiful sailing vessels usually commenced their voyages in New York and carried gold diggers and supplies to San Francisco via Cape Horn. Then they crossed the Pacific to join British clippers in the famous tea race from China to England, which rewarded fast voyages with extra premiums. Outsailing their British rivals in this profitable trade, clippers epitomized the international preeminence of the American sailing ship before the Civil War.[13]

Most clippers were built in New England yards, which also launched coastwise vessels, fishing boats, and whalers. Small-town builders in Connecticut, Massachusetts, and Maine perfected the art of building sailing ships and surpassed their New York City counterparts in vessel output because of lower wages and more abundant timber supplies. In villages such as Mystic, Connecticut, Salem, Massachusetts, and Bath, Maine, which were almost completely dependent on shipbuilding and seafaring, builders employed ship carpenters who had few employment alternatives. By contrast, the big-city yards—McKay in Boston; Webb, Westervelt, and Brown & Bell in New York—often competed with the building and furniture trades for skilled woodworkers and had to pay higher timber prices as well. Although waterborne commerce was centered at New York, New England remained the nation's most important shipbuilding region.[14]

Philadelphia's maritime economy was somewhat sluggish by comparison. The California and China trade booms bypassed the city, which was inconveniently located a hundred miles by river and bay from the Atlantic Ocean. Ice on the Delaware River—an old problem plaguing trade during the winter months—scared away new commerce. Merchants engaged in international commerce usually traded via New York, whose shippers handled half of Philadelphia's imports during the antebellum years.[15]

The city's decline as an international port was to some degree offset by gains in the coastwise trade. On the routes to Savannah and Charleston, southbound ships carried passengers and manufactured goods and returned with cotton for Philadelphia's textile industry. By the 1820s this trade was sufficiently well established to require a degree of regularity; as early as 1827 packets carried more than half of Philadelphia's coastwise trade on schedule.[16]

The 1820s marked the beginning of Pennsylvania's canal age, but the state's canals never generated as much growth as the Erie Canal did in New York state. The least successful canal-building program was aimed at connecting Philadelphia with grain-exporting regions in central and western Pennsylvania. The Main Line canal between Philadelphia and Pittsburgh, for example, included an expensive transshipment point at Johnstown, where cranes lifted canal barges and cargo onto a railway for haulage across a high mountain pass. Although the Main Line canal failed, it inspired the formation of the Pennsylvania Railroad Company, the most important corporately managed enterprise in nineteenth-century America, which connected Philadelphia and Pittsburgh by rail. During the 1850s railroad shipments from Pittsburgh to the East increased mightily and bolstered Philadelphia's coastwise commerce.[17]

Other canal projects linked Philadelphia to one of the greatest assets of the Pennsylvania economy: coal. Despite their proximity to Philadelphia, the state's early mining districts in Schuylkill, Lehigh, and Berks Counties remained relatively undeveloped until the 1820s because of inadequate connections between the city and its hinterland. Reading, the mining center, and

Philadelphia were linked by roads and by the Schuylkill River, but overland transportation of bulk cargo involved prohibitive costs, and the river was unnavigable in most sections. This changed with the completion of the Schuyl-kill Canal, which ran parallel to the river; once the canal was in service, coal shipments to Philadelphia increased in less than a decade from 6,500 tons (1825) to 226,692 tons (1834). The eastern Pennsylvania coal trade also profited from a railroad connection furnished by the Philadelphia & Reading Railroad. The railroad built large depots and wharves at Port Richmond, north of the Kensington shipyard district, where railroad cars dropped their loads into the cargo holds of coal schooners. These unique facilities transmitted the coal to the coastwise trade as shipping companies leased wharves from the railroad company and hauled coal to New England and the South. Independent opera-tors usually had their schooners built in Kensington yards and across the river at Cooper's Point, New Jersey. Links established during the 1840s among Penn-sylvania coal mining, railroads, shipping, and shipyards played a critical role in the development of iron shipbuilding after the Civil War.[18]

Wooden Steamships

American maritime history took a new turn with the arrival of steam technol-ogy, highlighted by the completion of Robert Fulton's paddle-wheeler *Cler-mont* in 1807. Since early steamboats needed firewood and fresh water to produce boiler steam, they usually sailed on rivers lined with bunkering sta-tions. Their need for these supplies made it difficult to introduce the new craft on long-distance saltwater routes. Coal, with its higher calorific value, would have been a better fuel, but it was not widely used until the 1830s because wood remained cheaper. Moreover, early nineteenth-century boilermakers were un-able to make thick boiler iron that would withstand the higher temperatures. When some of these problems had been solved, the New York–Charleston Steam Packet Company established the first coastwise steamship service in 1832. The next decade marked the introduction of paddle-wheel steamships on heavily traveled routes to and from New York, Boston, Philadelphia, Charles-ton, Savannah, and New Orleans. During the California Gold Rush, five steam-ship lines sailing forty-one vessels served the California route via Panama and Nicaragua.[19]

The transatlantic trade remained more elusive. Out of three pioneer North Atlantic steamship operators, two went bankrupt during the 1840s. The sole survivor was Canadian shipowner Samuel Cunard, who established what be-came the most famous line of the nineteenth and twentieth centuries. In 1850 the British Inman Line commenced operations between Liverpool and Philadelphia with an iron steamship. The two decades before the Civil War were a critical era when Britain consolidated its position in the ocean steamer trade, far ahead of all rivals. Although this was in large part due to the rapid development of British marine engineering and iron hull construction, government policy played an important role in establishing an international steamship network on the North Atlantic and elsewhere. Convinced that global commercial hegemony as well as the imperial economy hinged on dependable steamship service, the British government made a strategic decision to subsidize private steamship lines. This began in 1836 with the Peninsular & Oriental Line in the Mediterranean trade, followed three years later by Cunard's transatlantic service. Britain's fairly comprehensive policy sustained a growing network of subsidized lines on major international routes. Moreover, there were well-managed companies, such as the Inman Line, that operated quite successfully without government help.[20]

Given its lack of overseas possessions, the United States had few incentives to subsidize American lines and establish a far-flung steamship network. After years of muddled debates, mostly driven by apprehensions about the "national disgrace" of having the U.S. mails destined for Europe carried by Cunard, Congress finally passed steamship subsidies for the U.S. Mail Steamship Company (commonly referred to as the Collins Line) in 1850. Collins entered into fierce competition with Cunard in the Liverpool–New York trade with large wooden steamers, but it suffered managerial problems, lost two steamers in shipwrecks, and ceased operations shortly after Congress failed to renew its mail subsidy in 1858. As a result of the failure to introduce American steamships on the main transatlantic route, sailing vessels retained a prominent position. For example, sailing ships carried more than 96 percent of all immigrants arriving at New York in 1856.[21]

Paddle-wheel steamers sailed by Collins and other lines were riddled with design problems. Most important, they were uneconomical. When a wheel rotated on the side of the ship, only a few paddles dipped into the water at a given time; a critic estimated that up to "five sixths of the paddle surface of all steamers is constantly out of the water, and in action against the air."[22] Paddle wheels wasted up to 70 percent of engine power as a result of "slipping," defined as "the differential between the mathematically calculated distance moved by the paddle and the actual movement of the vessel."[23] Moreover, navigators found it difficult to steer a paddle-wheel vessel on an even course. In calm seas, both wheels were equally submerged in the water, but heavy weather brought the vessel out of the horizontal position, submerging one wheel deep in the water while exposing the other in midair; when one wheel transmitted engine power while the other did not, the result was "corkscrewing" as the vessel turned left and right. The navy raised its own objections to side-wheel steamers because the large boxes protecting the wheels took up space usually reserved for broadside guns.[24]

The introduction of screw propulsion by the Swedish inventor John Ericsson eliminated some of these problems. Based on ancient Greek technology, a screw propeller featured four curved blades and was attached below the water line to a longitudinal shaft that extended from the engine to the stern of the ship. Early experiments demonstrated its distinct advantages over paddle wheels. The screw propeller was almost completely submerged in the water, transmitted engine power more effectively, and slipped only 20–30 percent of engine power. Propeller steamers also featured better navigational qualities; corkscrewing was not a problem because the engine power was usually transmitted to only one propulsion mechanism. Finally, the navy preferred screw propellers because they were attached aft and did not interrupt broadsides.[25]

In 1841 the navy charged Ericsson with the design of a small screw sloop named USS *Princeton.* Her hull was built at the Philadelphia Navy Yard and her engines by Merrick & Towne, a local engineering firm. The *Princeton's* success was highlighted by a speed race with the fast British side-wheeler *Great Western* shortly after her commissioning. An observer reported that the American sloop "immediately started her engine, gave chase and . . . soon passed [the *Great Western*] with no sails set and the yards square."[26] The triumph of the screw propeller over the paddle wheel seemed assured.[27]

The fate of the *Princeton,* however, tainted that ship and stalled the adoption of screw steamers by the U.S. Navy. The sloop was equipped with a wrought-iron gun named Peacemaker, which had been designed by Ericsson's colleague Robert F. Stockton. On February 28, 1844, Peacemaker exploded during an ordnance trial, killing Secretary of State Abel Upshur, Secretary of the Navy Thomas Gilmer, and three other spectators. The navy blamed the disaster on the *Princeton's* designers and became embroiled in a long controversy with Ericsson that delayed for years the development of screw propulsion.[28]

The USS *Princeton* and other screw steamers also displayed design problems that were related to the new technology itself. First, screw propellers required more revolutions per minute (rpm) than side wheels, causing vibrations that loosened the bolts. Paddle wheels rotated at 10–14 rpm, too slowly to cause serious problems, but screw-propeller engines revolved at 35–60 rpm to generate sufficient thrust. The engine vibrations caused fastenings connecting the engine to the hull to vibrate and dilate timber bolt holes. Unless propeller steamers underwent frequent overhauls to replace worn-out timber, the engine could come loose and cause severe hull damage. Second, very few American engineers had the tools needed to construct reliable engines and drill precision-bored cylinder holes because most American machine toolmakers were unable to supply appropriate production equipment. As a result, many antebellum marine engine builders used no machine tools at all. "So deficient were the facilities of lathes, planers, slotters and drills," a marine engineer recalled, "that 'black[smith] work' of engines . . . was the prevailing finish."[29] Third, long wooden hulls and screw propulsion were not easily matched. Timber hulls were flexible and prone to "hogging" (the drooping of the fore and aft sections relative to the midship segment) when a wave passed underneath the ship. On screw steamers, hogging strained the long shaft that extended from the midship section to the stern.[30]

Discussions among shipbuilders over the merits of screw and paddle-wheel propulsion produced two regional schools of thought. While most New York builders used paddle wheels, Philadelphia builders opted for screw propulsion. Shipbuilder Charles Cramp related that Philadelphia shops, "while not abandoning the paddle-wheel, concluded to take hold of screw-propeller engines also . . . New York interests would not consider any other [propulsion system] but the paddle-wheel with its walking-beam engine." Ignorant "of any other type they loudly and persistently proclaimed its great superiority over all other types, and carried with them the shipowners, shipbuilders, shipping men, mariners, and all others in general, and the screw-propeller was sneered at by them as a low-down Philadelphia idea."[31] One factor explaining the preference of New York builders was local demand for big steamships as yards supplied steamship lines in the long-distance trades with comparatively large vessels exceeding 1,000 gross tons. These vessels featured paddle wheels because long, hogging hulls would have strained longitudinal propeller shafts. Philadelphia yards, by contrast, built smaller craft, such as tugs for towboat companies on the Schuylkill Canal and Delaware River as well as smaller steamers for the regional coastwise trade. One important contract for screw-propelled steamers was issued by the Baltimore Parker Vein Coal Company, which ordered several 450-ton colliers from Philadelphia yards during the early 1850s. Larger Philadelphia passenger vessels that sailed to Boston, Charleston, and Savannah during the 1850s were usually equipped with side wheels.[32]

The introduction of screw propellers in Philadelphia was also a reflection of local industrial development in the engine-building and toolmaking trades. During the first half of the nineteenth century, when the main thrust of the Philadelphia economy turned away from foreign trade and toward manufacturing, local shops developed strong demand for steam engines. (This was partly due to the lack of adequate water power because unlike the rivers along New England's "fall line," the Schuylkill River did not flow fast enough to drive large water wheels.) In 1838, for example, the Philadelphia manufacturing sector employed more than one-third of the nation's stationary steam engine power. The William Sellers machine tool factory, probably the best of its kind in the country, supplied local shops with precision tools that were also necessary to build fast-running engines for screw steamers. This enabled the builders of stationary steam engines, such as Merrick & Towne, to branch into marine work and supply engines for the USS *Princeton* and other small warsteamers. After recovering from the disaster involving the Philadelphia-built sloop, the navy had three additional screw steamers built by the Philadelphia Navy Yard and local engine shops. Meanwhile, Philadelphia engineer Richard Loper designed an improved screw propeller that was manufactured by Reaney & Neafie, a local machine shop. These and other firms defined the Philadelphia steamship-building industry.[33]

The Antebellum Shipbuilding Industry

The construction of wooden steamships required a large variety of firms and trades. At the shipyard, carpenters, caulkers, and joiners built the hull with its intricate arrangement of frames and planks. Blacksmiths and machinists hammered out engine parts, bored cylinder holes, and installed pipes at the engine works. Specialty trades, such as mast-, spar-, rope-, and sailmaking, supplied components for the sail rig. Most firms did not limit their work to shipbuilding but also produced nonmarine items. Machine shops that supplied shipbuilders, for example, usually built stationary steam engines for factories and coal mines as well. Because shipbuilding lacked sharp boundaries with regard to other industries, it is difficult to measure its exact size and shape in the manufacturing economy of the day. This word of caution applies to most quantitative material on shipbuilding, and especially to the federal census of 1850, which provides the background for the following analysis (table 1).

The largest firms were engine shops. Unlike most other businesses, the three major marine engine builders—Merrick & Sons, I. P. Morris, and Neafie & Levy—invested heavily in industrial plants. Their assets averaged more than $160,000 and included forges, brick buildings, punching and planing machines to prepare iron and brass parts, steamhammers, horses and oxen to pull wagons loaded with engine parts, large derricks, and a wharf where hulls were docked to receive engines and boilers. Founded in 1828, Morris of Port Richmond was a specialist in stationary steam engines employed by municipal waterworks. The firm occasionally supplied Pennsylvania iron furnaces with blast engines and also built marine engines for steamboats. Merrick's works in Southwark manufactured not only stationary steam engines but also gas fixtures and sugar-processing equipment. Established in 1835 by John Towne in

TABLE 1
Philadelphia Shipbuilding Industry, 1850

Trade	Number of firms	Average capital investment ($)	Average number of workers per firm	Average raw material input per firm ($)	Average output per firm ($)
Engine building	3	165,000	414.3	92,736	296,667
Ship building	13	12,592	29	19,695	42,992
Mast making	3	7,333	8.3	3,750	9,833
Rigging	19	6,473	12	8,869	15,102
Ship joining	4	3,000	23.3	3,500	20,300
Sail making	8	2,610	6.6	13,818	34,125
Ship smithing	10	1,733	6	3,227	6,719
Boat building	9		4	1,450	4,022

SOURCE: Manufacturing Census 1850.

partnership with Samuel Merrick, the firm thrived during the 1830s when the city introduced gas lighting in a few neighborhoods. Merrick commenced marine engine building in 1839 with a navy contract for the side-wheel engines installed aboard the USS *Mississippi,* the nation's first war-steamer, whose hull was built at the Philadelphia Navy Yard. The firm also built engines for large merchant steamers, such as the *Phineas Sprague,* launched in 1857 at Kensington's Birely & Lynn shipyard.[34]

The history of Neafie & Levy, Philadelphia's third engine-building firm, constitutes a unique chapter in the annals of American shipbuilding because of the firm's record of innovation and the scale and duration of its success. Founder Jacob Neafie was a machinist who became familiar with screw-steamer engines when he served his stint as a journeyman at a Philadelphia shop during the early 1840s. At that time, his employers received an engine contract from the Philadelphia shipowner Thomas Clyde who, inspired by John Ericsson, was one of the nation's first converts to the new propulsion technology. Clyde had his paddle-wheeler *J. S. McKim* converted into a screw-steamer. Neafie worked on these engines and "took an early interest in screw propulsion," Charles Cramp related.[35] In 1844 Neafie entered into a partnership with Thomas Reaney and William Smith and formed a small firm to build fire engines, boilers, and stationary steam engines. Initially, the establishment operated "under almost insuperable disadvantages. The wharf was only rented, and had an area of but fifty by one hundred feet, with scarcely anything that could be called a shop on it. While [Neafie, Reaney, and Smith] were thorough mechanics, their knowledge and acquaintances in society were rather limited."[36] After Smith's death in 1845, Neafie and Reaney were joined by Captain John P. Levy, who brought to the firm his considerable wealth and business connections with steamship operators. Levy was acquainted with the

Reaney, Neafie & Levy engine works and shipyard, 1850s. The tug steaming past on the right is one of the many vessels of this type built at the yard. Historical Society of Pennsylvania

Philadelphia inventor and steamboat operator Richard Loper, who had developed an innovative design for ship propellers. When Loper permitted Reaney, Neafie & Levy the use of his patent, the firm established a thriving business in propeller manufacture. By 1850 Reaney, Neafie & Levy was a respectable firm listing $75,000 in assets, 300 employees, and an annual output of $350,000. In addition to propellers, it built marine engines for wooden steamers whose hulls were constructed by local shipbuilders.[37]

Product specialization in propeller manufacture led the firm to experiment with iron shipbuilding. A propeller required a fast-running engine to generate sufficient thrust, as well as a strong hull to absorb engine vibrations and prevent shaft fractures. These technical requirements led to the introduction of metal hulls, which possessed greater structural strength than wooden shells. Propeller specialists preferred the metal hull because engine bolts did not come loose as easily; moreover, iron hulls possessed greater longitudinal strength and were less prone to hogging. Reaney, Neafie & Levy added shipbuilding facilities to its works and in 1855 launched its first iron ship. This venture was followed by construction of more than 300 vessels at this yard during the next half-century. By 1860 the firm registered $300,000 in assets, employed 300 men, and turned out an annual product worth $368,000. (Thomas Reaney left the partnership in 1859 and established a new iron shipyard at Chester, Pennsylvania.)[38]

Shipyards were the largest firms in the woodworking sector of the economy, employing an average of twenty-nine workers and reporting assets of about $11,000. This surprisingly small amount of capital reflected the fact that most tools were owned by workers, not employers. Reviewing this situation from the perspective of the late nineteenth century, when iron shipbuilding had transformed the industry, a census official observed that in the "wooden-ship yard nearly all the workmen . . . supply their own hand tools." After "the outfit of broad-axes, adzes, saws, bevels, chisels, calking-irons, mallets, rules, etc., is thus provided, little remains for the builder to purchase except a bolt-cutter, a few planking screws, a few large augers for boring bolt and treenail holes, a derrick, and a large cross cut saw. Even if he supplies the yard with steam power, a bevel saw, and a planer, it is hard for him to spend more than $15,000 or $20,000 on his plant, and he can build the largest wooden ships without them."[39]

Like most manufacturing firms in Philadelphia, yards for wooden shipbuilding were owned by proprietary entrepreneurs who performed management functions, designed hulls, and supervised construction. The scions of famous Philadelphia shipbuilding families—the Birelys, Lynns, Vaughans, and Cramps—usually served their apprenticeships at a neighboring yard, spent several years as journeymen, and later joined their fathers as business partners. The Cramp family serves as an example. William Cramp, whose German ancestors had settled in Philadelphia during the eighteenth century, married into the Birely family, operators of several shipyards in Kensington. Upon completion of his apprenticeship, Cramp worked as a journeyman ship carpenter and established his own small yard in 1828. His oldest son Charles graduated from Philadelphia Central High School and commenced his apprenticeship as a ship carpenter with his maternal uncle, John Birely. Along with his five brothers, Charles later worked as a journeyman and designed vessels at his father's yard.[40]

The Vaughans, another distinguished shipbuilding family, entered the trade in the early years of the nineteenth century, when John Vaughan started a large yard at Kensington. In 1833 he admitted his son, Jacob K. Vaughan, as a partner. After John's retirement in 1846, Jacob continued the firm in partnership with Matthew Lynn, whose ancestors had commenced shipbuilding in the early eighteenth century. Yards for wooden shipbuilding often passed through such partnerships, which cemented social and economic ties between shipbuilding families and furnished capital for yard improvements.[41]

Yards for wooden shipbuilding and engine builders sometimes launched collaborative efforts. When Reaney, Neafie & Levy experimented with iron shipbuilding, builders of wooden ships—notably Birely and Cramp—supplied hull designs and supervised workers. Charles Cramp recalled that "the contract with the shipbuilders included the model and mould loft work, superintending the bending of frames, raising them, running the ribbands, shoring and regulating them, building the deck work, and finally launching the vessel."[42] The builders also helped Reaney, Neafie & Levy improve ship iron procurement. When the firm entered iron shipbuilding, it usually ordered square, single-size hull plates from the rolling mills. This resulted in considerable waste because the builders had to cut plates into customized shapes that conformed to the lines of the streamlined hull. Scrap iron plied up at the shipyard, which had no furnace to reprocess it. Charles Cramp suggested that John Levy determine the shape of hull plates from a wooden hull model and order custom-made plates from the mills. According to Cramp, this resulted in the "first order sent to a Pennsylvania mill for tapered plates from a shipyard."[43] Cramp later refined this technique, which was common among British builders and became widely used by Delaware Valley yards during the second half of the nineteenth century.

Marine engine and hull builders depended on extensive subcontracting networks. In the woodworking sector, the most important firms were mast and spar lofts, where carpenters cut large spars from long pieces of straight pine timber that weighed up to 7 tons. Like many entrepreneurs in the woodworking trades, makers of masts and spars hired skilled craftsmen who owned sets of adzes, augers, and other woodworking tools. The employers typically invested less than $8,000 in a derrick to haul timber, a sizable craft shop with a yard for timber storage, and a few large saws.[44]

Shipbuilding also included sailmaking, a branch of Philadelphia's large textile industry. Sail lofts received canvas from local mills and employed workers who, again, supplied their own tools: needles, sail hooks, stitching mallets, and prickers. The trade required physical strength, because sail canvas was the thickest cloth used in the textile industry, and also considerable craft skill, because the canvas had to be cut and sewn into intricate shapes that differed widely according to sail type. Because the work was so labor intensive, the average craft shop owner invested only $3,000. Loft space was inexpensive because sailmaking, which required large uninterrupted floors to spread out the canvas, could take place in attics that were unsuitable for most other trades.[45]

The remaining core trades—rigging, joining, boatbuilding, shipsmithing, and blockmaking—shared the industry's basic characteristics of proprietary capitalism, labor intensity, and limited amounts of fixed capital. In 1850 firms in these trades reported an average capital investment of little more than $3,000 and employed eight to nine men.[46]

Subcontracting interlaced this elaborate urban industrial network. Typically, a shipowner signed three different contracts to build a wooden steamer: the first with a shipyard for the hull, the second with a ropemaker for the rig, and the third with an engine builder for the engine and boilers. These firms, in turn, issued subcontracts to smaller craft shops that supplied specialty items, such as bolts, castings, spars, sails, and anchors. Shipyards also subcontracted so-called "job work," such as hole drilling, which was often performed by small independent work gangs. Once the ship carpenters had launched the hull, it was towed to the engine builder's wharf to receive its engine and boilers. The building of a single wooden steamship usually involved twenty to thirty firms.[47]

Compared to private firms, the Philadelphia Navy Yard developed more centralized shipbuilding methods. This government-owned facility was established during the 1790s and gained national renown when it launched the 120-gun sailing ship USS *Pennsylvania* in 1837. During the 1850s it covered a 16-acre property and employed between 200 and 300 men in a variety of trades. During the construction phase, hulls were sheltered by two massive shiphouses, which had cost the government more than $150,000; to perform warship overhauls, the yard operated a floating dry dock that had cost $831,000. However, these considerable amounts of fixed capital were the only significant difference between the Navy Yard and private yards, because in other respects the navy copied the organization of production in the private sector. The Navy Yard was divided into separate departments that included gun carriage making, plumbing, coppersmithing, sparmaking, blockmaking, and sailmaking. Carpenters and caulkers worked in the two shiphouses. Work remained labor intensive, and craftsmen brought their own tool chests to work. The departments were headed by master workmen and foremen who reported to the yard's naval constructor and the executive officer; administrative affairs were managed by the yard commandant. In effect, the Navy Yard simply crowded a variety of shops into one facility, while private craft shops remained separate from one another.[48]

The Navy Yard was integrated into its own subcontracting networks. In this it resembled other government yards at Portsmouth, New Hampshire; Boston; Brooklyn; Norfolk; Washington, D.C.; Pensacola, Florida; and Mare Island, California. Like those yards, the Philadelphia facility relied on local subcontractors who supplied boilers and engines. Most Navy Yard ships were

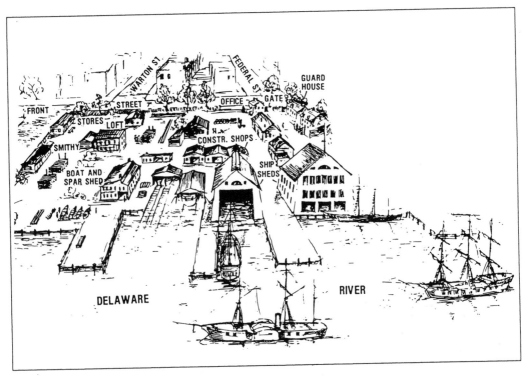

Philadelphia Navy Yard in Southwark, 1850s. Note the large shiphouses (marked "ship sheds") at the center, which were used to shelter hulls during construction. Author's collection

equipped with engines manufactured at Merrick & Sons and I. P. Morris. For its supplies of lumber, spar, and canvas, the yard issued subcontracts to firms in Pennsylvania, Maryland, and New York.[49]

The Philadelphia Navy Yard became the laboratory of the American steam navy during the 1840s, when it built hulls for the pioneer war-steamers USS *Mississippi* and USS *Princeton*. During subsequent years, it launched the side-wheelers USS *Susquehanna* (1850) and USS *Shubrick* (1857), as well as the screw-sloops USS *Lancaster* (1858), USS *Pawnee* (1859), and USS *Wyoming* (1859), all with engines supplied by local shops. On the eve of the Civil War, the Philadelphia Navy Yard and its contractors had gained national fame as innovative builders of war-steamers.[50]

The decade preceding the financial panic of 1857 marked the golden age of American wooden shipbuilding. The nation's shipyards launched trans-atlantic packets, clippers, coastwise sailing ships, steamers, and steamboats. Philadelphia's most active builder in those years was Birely & Son, which launched seven screw-steamers between 1849 and 1853. Cramp built the passenger steamers *General Armero* (1852), *Carolina* (1853), and *Polynesian* (1853), as well as six clippers, representing most of the fast sailing ships of this type built in Philadelphia.

Simultaneously, however, the industry showed some signs of stagnation. Most important, antebellum builders failed to appreciate the significance of iron hulls and screw propulsion, which became the most important steamship technologies of the second half of the century. Although there were a few isolated experiments in Philadelphia and Wilmington (where Harlan & Hollingsworth built its first iron ships in 1844 but stuck to paddle-wheel propulsion), most builders remained committed to sailing ships and wooden paddle-wheelers. Even Delaware Valley yards could not compete with British builders, who by 1844 had launched dozens of large iron vessels, including the 3,000-gross-ton screw-steamer *Great Britain.* At that time, American builders had built exactly fourteen iron ships, none of which exceeded 300 gross tons. Several factors were responsible for this: the lack of adequate shop equipment, the high price of American iron (protected by tariffs), and the low cost of American timber. Moreover, the protectionist Navigation Act made it impossible for American shipowners to sail British-built iron steamers in the nation's coastwise trade or introduce them in the merchant marine. This set the stage for the dramatic decline of American shipbuilding in the Civil War era.

The Civil War Shipbuilding Boom

In spring 1861 business activity along Philadelphia's riverfront and across the city lingered in disarray as the secession crisis hurt the city's important trade with the South. At an emergency meeting, the city's textile manufacturers agreed to operate their works at half-time. In January 1861 Neafie & Levy kept busy with two southern iron-ship contracts, but widely discussed worries about their possible use as naval vessels persuaded the builder to delay delivery. By early April 1861 shipbuilding was suffering along with most other trades in Philadelphia's manufacturing economy.[51]

The attack on Fort Sumter on April 12, 1861, pulled the industry out of the depression. Within days, the Navy Department ordered two vessels into service that had been moored at the Philadelphia Navy Yard for more than a year. In May, when the Navy Department instructed the yard to build two new screw-sloops, master workmen combed Philadelphia's working-class pubs for unemployed ship carpenters, blacksmiths, and riggers. During the following month, private shipyards and engine shops booked government orders for small gunboats.[52]

For the next four years, Philadelphia steam shipbuilding became prosperous as never before. From 1861 to 1865 the yards launched 152 merchant steamships, almost as many as during the entire preceding decade, and almost two dozen naval vessels. In 1861 the nation's active war-steamer fleet consisted of forty-two vessels commissioned for duties from the Mediterranean to the Pacific. Since this force and the increasingly obsolete sailing fleet were unprepared to meet the challenges of Civil War naval operations, such as the blockade of the Confederacy's 3,550-mile coast and 159 ports, the Navy Department issued large warship contracts to private builders. Moreover, the navy and army needed supply vessels, troop transports, and auxiliary warships, which were also built at private yards. Ship carpenters in Philadelphia and elsewhere went to work to build the northern fleet.[53]

The navy's need for vessels for blockade duty resulted in large-scale naval construction programs. In 1861, for example, Congress appropriated emergency funds for seven screw-propulsion sloops-of-war modeled on successful prewar designs. At Philadelphia the *Wyoming* of 1859 was duplicated in the USS *Tuscarora,* whose hull was built in a record time of only fifty-eight days between June and August 1861. In all, the Philadelphia Navy Yard built four of the seven sloops appropriated that year, highlighting the city's status as the nation's center of screw-propeller construction.[54]

In 1862 the shipbuilding boom spread along the Delaware River and across the Union as speculators issued private contracts for ships that were chartered or sold to the government. Philadelphia shipyards built their largest merchant steamers for speculators, including the *Liberty* and the *Thomas A. Scott.* Wartime profiteers reaped handsome returns in this highly speculative market. New York merchant Marshall Roberts, for example, who "bought the 1,750-ton *Empire City* at auction from his old company for $12,000 . . . without counting in his naval charters, received $833,000 for her services to the army alone."[55] The government chartered or bought more than 1 million tons of auxiliary warships from 1861 to 1865. At the end of the war, however, this speculative market collapsed as the government terminated the leases and auctioned off 369 ships to private owners. Predictably, this surplus tonnage sold far below its actual value and oversupplied the private market.[56]

At the height of the boom, from 1862 to 1864, Philadelphia builders also booked contracts from steamship companies. Some lines took advantage of the government's demand for auxiliary war-steamers, sold their ships to the navy or the War Department, and ordered replacements. Henry Winsor's Philadelphia-Boston line, for example, issued contracts to John Lynn at Southwark and to Neafie & Levy. In this case, the renewal program actually enhanced the quality of the Winsor fleet, whose new ships featured composite hulls with iron frames and wooden planking. Unfortunately, few vessel operators grasped this opportunity to introduce new designs.[57]

Philadelphia engine builders thrived on naval contracting. Merrick emerged as one of the navy's major engine suppliers, building engines for six war-steamers whose hulls were constructed at the Philadelphia Navy Yard. Navy Department administrators who held the works in high esteem called it a "patriotic and responsible firm" in an internal memorandum that criticized other engine contractors for wartime profiteering.[58] Merrick's man in charge of naval work was Barnabas H. Bartol, a civil engineer and owner of a large sugar refinery, who was on friendly terms with the chief of the Bureau of Steam Engineering, Benjamin Isherwood. Combined with an experienced work force and a reputation for high-quality work, such contacts also channeled many naval repair contracts into Merrick's coffers.[59]

Cramp attained a similarly prominent position among shipyards and built the ironclad USS *New Ironsides,* the gunboat USS *Wyalusing,* and the monitor USS *Yazoo.* In fall 1863 the Cramp yard also won the contract for the cruiser USS *Chattanooga,* perhaps the most spectacular war-steamer ever launched in Philadelphia. When the northern public panicked over the loss of Union vessels to Confederate commerce raiders, the navy designed a series of seven so-called supercruisers to chase fast, British-built southern raiders. Cramp's *Chattanooga* was part of this program. She featured a 315-foot, 3,045-displacement-ton hull and twin Merrick-built engines. During the construction phase, shipbuilders faced severe labor shortages, forcing Cramp to subcontract large amounts of hull work to several independent gangs of ship carpenters. The navy was impressed with Cramp's efforts to finish the *Chattanooga* within the time frame set by the contract but also noted that labor and supply shortages delayed her completion. In early February 1864, for example, a navy inspector who periodically surveyed progress toward completion reported: "Rapid progress is being made in the construction of this vessel. Her timbers are all up, excepting some few connected with the framework of the stern, where the work has been kept back . . . by the want of a stern post."[60] Similar problems with other supplies forced Cramp to postpone the launching until October 13, 1864. The construction of the *USS Chattanooga* epitomized the difficulties plaguing shipbuilders at the peak of the building boom in wooden steamships and war-steamers.[61]

Many shipbuilders preferred private orders to government work. Articulating a widespread belief, Jacob Neafie argued that the navy was not a reliable customer and that it maintained unrealistic expectations about its contractors' production capacities. Neafie & Levy had built steam engines for the USS

Pawnee before the war, but the navy had failed to make full payments, presumably because the engines had not performed according to contract specifications. In 1862, when the Navy Department inquired about Neafie & Levy's willingness to undertake new contracts, Jacob Neafie responded angrily that "our establishment [is] worked up to Double Capacity and work enough [is] now on hand to last us 12 months . . . has not the *Pawnee* done service enough for us to get the Ballance due us?"[62] The firm refused to deal with the navy and remained busy with private orders for the remainder of the war.

Given these and other difficulties with private contractors, the government built and overhauled many war-steamers at its own yards. By 1863 the Philadelphia Navy Yard had built or outfitted several wooden war-steamers and an ironclad, and had repaired dozens of damaged vessels. Overhauls were crucial to maintain the navy's fighting power. The fleet laid siege to Confederate ports from Virginia to Texas, conquered New Orleans, and helped the Union Army defeat the Confederates along the Mississippi River. Not surprisingly, the ships took a heavy beating in the course of these operations. In 1862 nearly forty warships with cracked engine shafts, leaking boilers, splintered beams and frames, and broken masts limped up the Delaware River to receive repairs. At the peak of its wartime activity, the Navy Yard employed more than 3,000 workers.[63]

The boom ended shortly after Robert E. Lee's surrender, when the navy and army sold their auxiliary warships and troop transports to private owners. But the latter had already replaced some of their old tonnage with newer vessels. As a result, the postwar carrying trades were vastly oversupplied with tonnage. In the meantime, other developments had led to a rapid deterioration of the American maritime economy.

The Crisis of Waterborne Trade

Between 1861 and 1865 northern shippers lost more than 200 vessels to Confederate commerce raiders. At the same time they groaned under the war-related increase in insurance rates for Union tonnage. But the war merely worsened an already precarious situation in the carrying trades. Waterborne trade was weakened by the collapse of the California trade during the late 1850s, when the far West became an independent producer of foodstuffs and was no longer dependent on supplies carried by clippers from the Northeast. During the Civil War the eastbound gold trade declined by two-thirds because shippers feared the capture of transport ships by Confederate raiders; instead, most precious metal was carried overland or diverted into safe British ports. In the postbellum era, waterborne passenger carriers operating between New York and San Francisco via Cape Horn were unable to compete with the Union Pacific Railroad, which completed its overland track in 1869.[64]

During the war, Confederate raiders, such as the famous CSS *Alabama*, played havoc with the northern merchant marine. Their greatest success was not the spectacular sinking of northern tonnage but the less noticeable increase in premiums charged by underwriters who insured cargo transported aboard Union merchant vessels. Freight insurance rates shot up from less than 3 percent of the cargo value (1861) to 9 percent (1863). An English observer commented that "the execution of such exorbitant, although necessary, premiums must cancel the profits of almost any venture."[65] As a result, shipowners "fled" the American flag and reregistered their vessels in Europe to secure the lower insurance rates awarded to neutral carriers. A congressional report claimed that "919,466 tons of American shipping disappeared from our lists during the rebellion. Of this amount, 110,163 tons were destroyed by anglo-confederate pirates, while 803,303 tons were either sold to foreigners or passed nominally into their hands and obtained the protection of their flags."[66] By the end of the war, the American merchant marine in the foreign trade had lost close to one-third of its vessels to British registry, and not one of these ships returned to the American flag. A vindictive Congress wanted to punish "traitors" among vessel owners and hence prohibited the reregistry of outflagged tonnage in the United States. This contributed to a steep decline of American cargo carriers, which transported an ever smaller share of the nation's foreign trade.[67]

Railroads meanwhile tapped the maritime economy for cargo and investment capital. In the Northeast, with its relatively fast-growing regional networks, few waterborne carriers could hold their own in direct competition with the railroads. When the Philadelphia & Reading Railroad entered the eastern Pennsylvania coal trade, for example, the Schuylkill Navigation Company launched an expensive improvement program to accommodate larger barges. This created a considerable debt, which the canal company was unable to retire by collecting higher transit fees from barge operators, who were already losing customers to the railroad's low coal freight rates. The worsening financial situation paved the way for a P&RR buyout in 1870. The railroad gradually reduced canal operations during the postwar era and eventually closed the facility in 1888. A more important shift from waterborne trade to overland transportation was engineered by maritime entrepreneurs who reallocated their investments during the Civil War. For example, America's antebellum steamship tycoon Cornelius Vanderbilt sold most of his vessels to the government and invested the proceeds in the New York Central Railroad.[68]

American transatlantic sailing packets meanwhile saw their trade wither under the double impact of the Civil War and British competition. Most packet lines sold their ships to the government and did not acquire new tonnage because the war interrupted American cotton exports to England as well as the westbound passenger trade. When immigration to the United States returned to prewar levels in 1863, most European travelers preferred neutral British carriers. Moreover, American sailing packets were unable to compete with safe, fast iron steamers operated by British lines. By 1865 the British iron steamers had captured the transatlantic trade, making it impossible for American lines to regain their role in this important route. British operators also captured the lion's share of the transatlantic cotton trade during its postbellum recovery.[69]

The Origin and Growth of British Iron Shipbuilding

The introduction of iron steamships in the British merchant marine secured that country's maritime supremacy until World War I. During the late nineteenth century, British ships carried more than 60 percent of the world's foreign trade. Britain built more metal tonnage than all other countries combined.

Before the introduction of iron ships during the 1840s, British shipbuilding had experienced decades of economic hardship. Large yards were forced to import most of their ship timber from continental Europe and Asia because intense shipbuilding activity had long exhausted domestic supplies. The scarcity of English timber and the expense of importing materials made it difficult for builders to compete with American yards. The American builders enjoyed a 20 percent cost advantage over their British counterparts in the 1830s. In view of the precarious ship timber situation, Royal Navy officials and English merchants even raised doubts about Britain's ability to sustain its status as a world power and to keep up the imperial economy. This concern was partly responsible for the rapid introduction of iron ships in Britain. Another factor was cost: metal tonnage cost 15 percent less than wooden tonnage. By 1870 more than half of Britain's merchant vessel output consisted of iron steamships; in the United States, where timber remained cheaper than iron, this point was not reached until 1902.[70]

Steamship operators discovered other advantages of metal tonnage. First, iron hulls permitted the introduction of powerful propeller engines. Bolts connecting the engine to the hull were inserted into solid iron floors whose bolt holes did not wear out as quickly as timber bolt holes. Second, metal shipbuilding produced longer hulls. Wooden ships whose length exceeded 300 feet hogged and bent under their own weight until the hull broke apart at the bolted joints connecting the timber. Iron frames could be rolled in lengths exceeding that of ordinary ship timber, and riveted joints provided greater longitudinal strength than bolted ones. Third, an iron ship required fewer strengthening pieces and featured more cargo space. In a wooden ship, half the hull timber held the other half in place and consumed interior space. The greater structural strength of iron beams made most supporting pieces super-fluous and thus furnished greater carrying capacity. Fourth, while the natural growth of trees set limits to the curvature of ship timber, iron could be bent into extreme shapes, enabling naval architects to design more streamlined hulls. As a result of all these factors, iron ships were faster and longer, carried more freight, and featured more fluid lines than wooden vessels.[71]

British steamship operators had most of their iron tonnage built in north-east England and on the Scottish Clyde. Some pioneering work was done in the Thames district and at Bristol, but soon the industry clustered on the Tyne, Wear, Tees, and Clyde Rivers outside the traditional centers of wooden ship-building and near the heartland of the British iron and coal industry. When shipyards became part of this industrial network and issued subcontracts for boiler iron, engine castings, plates, angle iron, and ship fittings, many sup-pliers became specialty producers and developed long-lasting relationships with shipyards.[72]

Individual shipyards often concentrated on a few steamship types, a special-ization made possible by the strong, long-term demand for iron steamships for the enormous British merchant marine. Founded at Glasgow in 1847 as a boiler- and engine-building shop, the prestigious J. & R. Thompson yard (later Clydebank) became a specialist for high-performance passenger liners, such as the *Servia* (launched 1881), *City of New York* (1888), *Lusitania* (1906), and Cunard's magnificent *Aquitania* (1913). The Tyne, Wear, and Tees yards built large numbers of so-called tramps, economical cargo ships that served as the workhorses of world trade.[73]

British steamship lines introduced their first iron transatlantic liners at mid-century, when Inman brought in the *City of Glasgow*. The subsequent British takeover of the transatlantic immigrant trade also profited from a passenger-safety law stipulating minimum safety standards aboard English ships. Enacted by Parliament in 1855 in response to several steamship disasters, the law re-quired transatlantic lines to provide more cabin and steerage space as well as better life-saving equipment. It enabled owners to advertise British liners as safe, fast immigrant ships. European emigration to the United States decreased at the beginning of the Civil War—facilitating the withdrawal of many Ameri-can sailing packets from the North Atlantic—but recovered in 1863. At this crucial moment, Cunard and Inman were well prepared to ferry hundreds of thousands of European emigrants across the North Atlantic. Also involved in the trade were Germany's Hamburg Amerika Paket Aktien Gesellschaft and Norddeutsche Lloyd, which sailed British-built steamers. Meanwhile, American sailing packets and steamships were commissioned for blockade duties or busy chasing Confederate raiders. By 1865, when American carriers returned to the immigrant trade with their worn-out wooden ships, British iron steamships had transformed transatlantic shipping and were firmly entrenched in U.S. foreign trade. American packets never regained their foothold in this extremely profitable market, and the U.S. packet lines ceased operations during the 1870s.[74]

The Collapse of Wooden Shipbuilding

In 1865 the United States faced the most serious crisis in the history of shipbuilding. The inflation of vessel supply during the war, a weakened domestic private shipping market, and British competition in the foreign trade together led to a steep decline in construction of wooden ships. The most dramatic collapse occurred in New York. At the end of the war, the Hudson and East Rivers were still lined with twelve yards for wooden shipbuilding, employing thousands of ship carpenters. Among them were such notable firms as William Webb, Westervelt & Co., John English & Son, and Webb & Bell. When vessel orders dried up after 1865, New York experienced its first deindustrialization crisis as shipbuilding virtually disappeared from Manhattan Island in less than a decade. The shipbuilding district at Manhattan Market, birthplace of America's largest sailing packets, was littered with abandoned shipyards, some of which were converted into yards for storing lumber and coal. Thousands of unemployed ship carpenters scrambled for jobs in the building and furniture trades. A few prestigious shipbuilders who had launched luxurious paddle-wheel steamers during the 1850s opened small shops in Brooklyn where they built steamboats and performed repair jobs at the New York Navy Yard and the new Erie Basin Dry Dock.[75]

The postwar shipbuilding crisis assumed a slightly different form in Philadelphia. Because local yards had rarely built ships for transatlantic carriers during the 1850s, they were less severely affected by the rise of the British iron steamship trade. Philadelphia builders depended on steamship customers operating in the coastwise, river, and canal trades. Although these markets were oversupplied with tonnage and suffered from railroad competition, they still generated contracts that helped a few builders survive.

The Philadelphia shipbuilding slump began in summer 1865, when dozens of ships returned from war duties to the Navy Yard to be sold as government surplus. Since most were in deplorable condition, vessel owners submitted very low bids and purchased tonnage at bargain prices. A few Philadelphia towboat operators bought steam tugs, and coastwise lines reacquired the very ships they had sold to the government four years earlier.

The inflated ship market made life difficult for local shipbuilders who were suddenly denuded of contracts. For example, John Lynn, who had been one of the most active builders in wartime Philadelphia, completed his last ships in summer 1865. By 1866, when new contracts were not forthcoming, Lynn supported the formation of the Philadelphia & Southern Mail Steamship Company, founded by merchant Edmund Souder to reestablish the city's coastwise trade with southern ports. At the first shareholders' meeting, Lynn pledged an investment of $20,000, provided that the line ordered a new ship instead of buying government surplus tonnage. Unfortunately, Lynn's maneuver was to no avail, for the Philadelphia & Southern purchased its flagship *Pioneer* at a Navy Yard auction. This left the shipyard without an important contract. In 1866 Lynn's men refused to repair a vessel that had sailed down from New York to avoid a ship carpenters' strike. When the depression lingered, Lynn closed his shipyard in February 1870 and struggled along in a small repair shop for the remainder of his life. This marked the end of a family tradition that had begun in 1717 when Lynn's ancestors had launched their first ship in Philadelphia. Other local shipyards succumbing to the postwar maritime crisis included Vaughan & Lynn (operated by John's brother Robert), Vaughan & Fisher, and James Horne. In wooden shipbuilding, the only survivors were Hillman & Streaker, Jacob Birely, and Simpson & Neil. The proprietors of the first two pooled resources and in 1866 established Birely, Hillman & Streaker, which built ships until the end of the nineteenth century. Simpson & Neil abandoned shipbuilding and specialized in ship overhauls at its floating dry dock in Southwark.[76]

Unlike their New York counterparts, local builders remained active even when shipbuilding reached its nadir. At Cramp, which had switched from wooden to iron construction when it built monitors for the Union Navy, 225 men completed an ice-breaker for the city of Philadelphia, a side-wheeler, and a schooner. Birely, Hillman & Streaker launched a coal schooner. James Simpson built a new wharf at Southwark to dock vessels waiting for repairs at the dry dock.[77]

The Legacy of Two Centuries of Maritime Growth

The rise and decline of the American maritime economy left different legacies in the northeastern states. On the New England coast, the cradle of the American maritime economy, builders had perfected the art of constructing wooden sailing ships since early colonial times. In small towns and villages, the industry was so well entrenched that it survived into the twentieth century, long after the region's great ship-timber resources had been exhausted. New York, after experiencing spectacular maritime growth during the first half of the nineteenth century, suffered the loss of its shipbuilding industry after the Civil War, but it remained the nation's leading port city.

Philadelphia lost its traditional leadership in overseas trade during the first half of the nineteenth century. But two related developments sustained the city as a shipping and shipbuilding center in later decades. First, the port emerged as the main transshipment point for Pennsylvania coal, whose significance for American industrial development increased during the second half of the nineteenth century. Moreover, the coal trade facilitated the rise of Pennsylvania railroad companies, which came to play a pivotal role as customers for shipyard products after the Civil War (see chapter 3). Second, antebellum shipbuilders in Philadelphia banked on screw propulsion, the most advanced steamship drive system of the day. The quest for this technology inspired the search for alternatives to timber hulls, eventually causing engine builders and builders of wooden ships to experiment with iron shipbuilding. These forays continued during the Civil War, when some yards built ironclad warships for the Union Navy.

"A Small Margin": Ironclads and the Transition from Wooden to Iron Shipbuilding

*I*n summer 1865 the navy gathered a large fleet of decommissioned iron-clads south of Philadelphia at League Island. Some of these worn-out ships had bombarded southern forts for months to open the Confederacy for a final assault. In 1864 Admiral David Farragut had led ironclads into one of the most dramatic naval battles of the Civil War at Mobile Bay. Now, after the final shot had been fired and the last rebel fort had surrendered, dozens of the ironclads lay anchored in the Delaware River to rust on League Island's "Monitor Row" for years to come.[1]

Civil War ironclads had a resounding impact on naval warfare. The impressive sight of cannonballs bouncing off the USS *Monitor* and CSS *Virginia* at Hampton Roads precipitated the introduction of iron armor in European navies. Unlike American ironclads, these vessels were oceangoing ships and redefined the parameters of naval warfare. Henceforth, it became virtual suicide for wooden men-of-war to seek battle with a metal-armored vessel.

The effects of ironclad construction on iron shipbuilding are less clear. Maritime historians have concluded that "monitor building," as it was popularly known, had little impact on the development of iron shipbuilding. According to some studies, a strict division of ironclad building into armor plate production performed by subcontracting boiler works and hull construction at shipyards blocked a transition from wooden to iron shipbuilding: "Neither did the boilermakers learn to bend iron to ships' curves nor did the shipwrights learn to work with metal. An excellent opportunity to master already crucial skills was thus lost to the American shipbuilding industry."[2] However, closer examination of the industry reveals that monitor building changed over time. Eventually, it did facilitate the transition from wooden to iron construction. When the navy ordered its first experimental vessels in 1861, shipbuilders learned little about iron as a shipbuilding material because ironclad armor was produced and processed by subcontracting ironworks. But in 1863 some builders retooled their yards, hired metalworkers, and acquired iron shipbuilding capacity to construct second-generation monitors for the Union Navy. This opened a new chapter in the history of Philadelphia shipbuilding as Cramp joined the ranks of Delaware Valley iron shipyards.

The Development of Armored Vessel Technology

Ironclad construction was intertwined with major changes in ordnance. Until the 1820s the armies and navies of the Western world were equipped with guns firing solid shot and shrapnel; cannonballs gained their destructive power from their impact velocity when hitting a target. During the 1820s, however, the French inventor Henri Paixhans developed a shell that contained gunpowder and detonated upon impact. This invention rendered traditional defense systems more vulnerable to artillery hits. The wooden side armor protecting warships, for example, splintered and burned when hit by the new explosive shells. British experiments during the 1840s illustrated that simple iron plating failed to protect warships against modern artillery because shells shattered thin plates and turned them into shrapnel that injured crews. The first real progress was made during the Crimean War, when the Anglo-French allies built floating batteries protected by 4-inch-thick armor plates that resisted explosive shells.[3]

During the late 1850s and early 1860s Britain and France entered into an ironclad arms race. Operating a second-class navy at best, the French built the prototype ironclad *La Gloire,* which featured a wooden hull sheathed with heavy armor plates. In Britain, *La Gloire* inspired fears that a few French ironclads could challenge the entire Royal Navy with its eighty wooden ships-of-the-line. In 1859 the Royal Navy responded to the French project with the first true ironclad, HMS *Warrior.* This vessel epitomized British leadership in naval architecture and marine engineering. The *Warrior* was designed in cooperation between the Royal Navy and John Scott-Russell and Isaac Watts, arguably two of the best engineers of their time. Plans and specifications called for an iron hull throughout, including frames and armor backing—a marked contrast to *La Gloire's* wooden hull. Moreover, while the French hammered together thinner iron plates, British ironclad builders devised a one-piece armor plate made of rolled iron 4½ inches thick. Only British mills were equipped to make iron this thick. In following years the Royal Navy improved this prototype and thereby helped maintain Britain's undisputed control of the seas for the rest of the century. The French-British ironclad rivalry held an important lesson for the American Civil War: that no matter how bold the ironclad initiatives of a growing naval power might be, what counted in the end was the ability to build the better ship.[4]

Across the Atlantic, the Confederacy—a naval power of virtually no significance—first seized upon the new technology to gain a strategic advantage over the Union. When the U.S. Navy abandoned the Norfolk Navy Yard in April 1861, retreating Union officers and sailors burned several warships, including the wooden steam frigate USS *Merrimack*. After seizing the site, the Confederates discovered that the *Merrimack's* hull and machinery had remained intact below the water line. In July 1861 the Confederate secretary of the navy, Stephen Mallory, approved a plan to raise and rebuild the USS *Merrimack* as the ironclad CSS *Virginia*. The Tredegar Iron Works at Richmond, the leading southern foundry, supplied the hammered iron armor.[5]

In July 1861 the U.S. secretary of the navy, Gideon Welles, called attention to the ironclad problem and asked for funds to build a series of experimental vessels. In early August Congress appropriated $1.5 million for this project. The Navy Department soon asked shipbuilders for proposals, received sixteen bids, and appointed a committee to examine them.[6]

The committee consisted of three naval officers who were familiar with wooden ships but admitted that they had "no experience and but scanty knowledge" of iron vessels.[7] Reflecting the typical suspicions of naval traditionalists, their report suggested that armored vessels were useful as floating batteries for harbor operations but that "as cruising vessels . . . we are skeptical as to their advantage and ultimate adoption."[8] Considering the navy's task of entering shallow southern harbors, the officers argued, the Union's ironclad program should emphasize "vessels invulnerable to shot, of light draught of water, to penetrate our shoal harbors, rivers and bayous."[9] In their discussion of armor problems, the officers called attention to the Union's limited industrial capacity to produce thick iron plate. The most desirable armor would consist of rolled plates, tougher than hammered ones, but "we are informed there are no mills and machinery in this country capable of rolling iron 4½ inches thick."[10] They weighed the advantages of buying a complete ironclad in Britain but in the end favored American-made hammered plates.[11]

The officers also evaluated the sixteen construction bids and concluded that only three proposals warranted close attention. They rejected most bids, citing insufficient specifications, exaggerated claims and prices (a naval architect proposed a 6,520-ton ship developing "at least" 18 knots for $1.5 million), as well as freak inventions (one bid suggested a "*rubber-clad* vessel, which we cannot recommend").[12] The more serious proposals included Merrick & Son's plan for a 3,296-displacement-ton, three-masted frigate costing $780,000. "This proposition we consider the most practical one for heavy armor," the officers commented.[13] Next to the Philadelphia monster ship, John Ericsson's proposal looked moderate: The Swedish inventor suggested a floating battery displacing 1,255 tons without a sailing rig at $275,000; its most innovative feature was a revolving turret equipped with two guns. Despite some apprehensions about the vessel's seaworthiness, the board advised that the plan be adopted—USS *Monitor's* first step on the way to the Battle of Hampton Roads. The third experimental ironclad approved by the board was based on another Ericsson design, improved by Bushnell & Co. of New Haven, Connecticut. The Navy Department followed the board's recommendations and signed contracts with the three builders.[14]

Building the USS New Ironsides

When Merrick & Son booked its contract for an ironclad, the firm mobilized the mid-Atlantic manufacturing elite as subcontractors. Merrick's own Southwark works built engines and boilers, and Cramp constructed the wooden hull. Armor plates were forged and hammered at Bailey, Brown & Co.'s Pittsburgh foundry and by the Bristol Forge Co. in Bristol, Pennsylvania. Merrick also enlisted dozens of small Philadelphia machine shops to have armor plates grooved and finished. The contract for the long propeller shaft went to Trego, Baird & Co. in Baltimore; the Phoenix Iron Works in Trenton, New Jersey, furnished heavy gun carriages. The Philadelphia Navy Yard had the only dry dock of sufficient size to take on the enormous hull for coppering. The result of these combined efforts was the frigate USS *New Ironsides*.[15]

The hull contract gave Cramp an opportunity to recover from recent financial troubles. The financial panic of 1857 had forced William Cramp to default on several loans and transfer the firm's management to his sons William M. and Charles H. Cramp (William Cramp, Sr., henceforth served as a shop foreman). By 1861 the yard had built a few steamships, but it still needed a large order to settle old debts.[16]

Merrick and Cramp followed standard procedures of wooden steamship design. Charles Cramp formulated technical specifications in collaboration with Barnabas Bartol, a boiler engineer, sugar manufacturer, and Merrick's superintendent for naval affairs. Cramp, Bartol, and the Navy Department recorded construction details in a booklet that was submitted to the Navy

Department for approval. The USS *New Ironsides* was to measure 232 feet in length and 54 feet in the beam; 2,000 square feet of 4½-inch armor plates would protect her magazines and ordnance.[17]

In October 1861 Cramp advertised in eastern Pennsylvania country newspapers for white oak timber, and farmers in Bucks, Berks, Delaware, and Chester Counties soon began cutting ship timber for the *New Ironsides*. According to Charles Cramp, "These counties were transversed by the North Pennsylvania Railroad, and the various stations from Quakertown down were soon gorged with logs."[18] By January the shipyard had stocked sufficient timber to construct keel and frames.[19]

Hull construction was the domain of woodworkers. Axmen hewed timber into ship-shape, borers drilled holes for bolts and fastenings, ship carpenters assembled and raised frames, joiners built the inside of the hull, and caulkers filled the seams between the planks with oakum and pitch to seal the hull. The only metalworkers involved in wooden shipbuilding were a few smiths who made iron and copper bolts. In the mold loft, Cramp's loftsman copied the construction plans in full size on the floor to determine the lengthwise and crosswise shape of the frames. Ship carpenters then laid thin pine sticks on top of each frame drawing, tacked them together, and handed them to the axmen who hewed timber into the required shapes.[20]

The main hull components included the "backbone" (keel, stem, and stern), the "rib cage" (frames and beams), and the "skin" (outside planks). The 220-foot keel for the *New Ironsides* consisted of long pieces of timber connected by scarfs (angled overlapping joints). Ship carpenters cut a 10-foot scarf into either end of a keel timber and then fastened it to the adjoining scarf of the next timber with four strong copper bolts. They also raised the stem and stern and installed frames, deck beams, and outside planks.[21]

In early spring of 1862 the tall hull towered over the shipyard. The *New Ironsides* drew such crowds of spectators to the Kensington riverfront that Cramp fenced the property to keep visitors out. The shipyard swarmed with 400 workers who completed the hull. Ship carpenters assembled the rudder; joiners built the magazines; dozens of subcontractors worked on ropes, chains, and fittings. In early May the *New Ironsides* was ready for launching.[22]

The christening on May 10, 1862, attracted 20,000 spectators, the largest launching party in memory. The ship was appropriately christened by a veteran navy officer who had served aboard the USS *Constitution* fifty years earlier; during the War of 1812, her crew had nicknamed this famous frigate "Old Ironsides" because no enemy cannonball had pierced her oak timber. At 9:45 A.M. a revenue cutter fired a warning shot to chase vessels cruising on the Delaware River out of the launching path. Ship carpenters sawed through the last shores, and at 10:15 A.M. they were ordered to "clear the ways, haul in the gangway planks."[23] The USS *New Ironsides* slid down the launching ways in 15 seconds. Steam tugs towed the hull downriver to Merrick's Southwark works for further construction.[24]

Armor contractors had already forged iron plates that were now attached to the outside planks. Weighing up to 3 tons apiece, the plates were hammered to the appropriate thickness by blacksmiths who brought long pieces of scrap iron to red heat and forged them with a 2½-ton steamhammer over a large anvil. Because the iron cooled during the process, the plate had to be reheated several times before it reached the required thickness and strength. The mills shipped the plates to Philadelphia, where small ironworks planed and grooved them.[25]

At Merrick's wharf, *New Ironsides* received her engines, boilers, masts, and iron armor. Riggers lifted each plate from the wharf with a large derrick and placed it onto armor bolts protruding from the hull. Blacksmiths attached the lowest row of plates 4 feet below the load line and worked their way upward. Before installing the last plates, Merrick had the ship towed to the Navy Yard for coppering. After the hull was placed securely onto a floating dry dock, heavy steam engines pumped the water out of the tanks that kept the dock afloat, and coppersmiths commenced their work. The ship's underwater body had to be copper-sheathed to prevent the growth of marine zoophytes, which sprouted on wood and iron so abundantly as to slow down the vessel after several years of service; copper was the only cheap metal resistant to mussel growth. Coppersmiths attached the first row of copper plates adjacent to the lowest row of iron plates and worked their way downward to the keel. However, they failed to consider the electrolytic reaction that takes place between copper and iron in saltwater, which oxidized the armor plates. After only two years of service, the lower part of the *New Ironsides's* armor plating showed signs of erosion.[26]

From June to mid-August 1862 Navy Yard workers and Merrick's men completed the armor while the vessel was docked at the Navy Yard's Southwark wharf. Fitted with engines, boilers, and ordnance, the USS *New Ironsides* steamed down the Delaware River for her trial trip on August 21. To civilians, she presented a breathtaking sight that gave rise to wild speculations about her fighting capabilities. The Navy Department was slightly less impressed. Despite claims to the contrary, the ship's draft exceeded 20 feet, her rudder was too small, and her 700-horsepower engine yielded a speed of only 6 knots. But even so, there was nothing afloat in North American waters that the USS *New Ironsides* had to run away from. The Philadelphia builders had constructed the mightiest ship of the Civil War.[27]

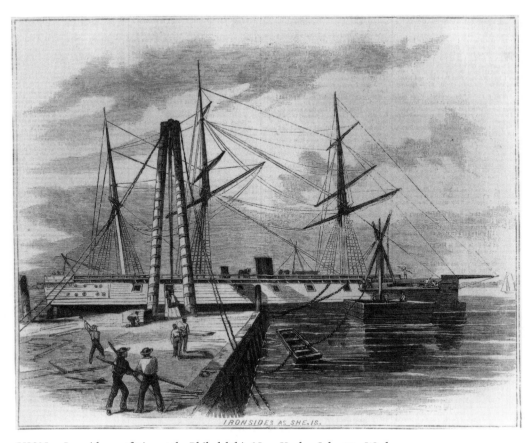

USS New Ironsides *outfitting at the Philadelphia Navy Yard, c. July 1862. Workmen install bow section. Note the shear leg, which was used to lift heavy items.* Harper's Weekly, *August 1862. Library of Congress*

For Cramp the ironclad was a much-needed success. First, the hull contract enabled the firm to restore its credit after netting a $60,000 profit. Brothers William and Charles Cramp soon worked out a plan with the firm's creditors to settle the old debts. Second, the ironclad was a prestigious vessel that boosted Cramp's reputation as a reliable contractor; during the next two years the Navy Department entrusted the yard with a side-wheeler, another ironclad, and the supercruiser USS *Chattanooga*. Third, Cramp made its reputation as an ironclad builder without forging or punching a single plate. Indeed, the contract was probably so profitable mainly because the builders could use the tools and techniques of wooden shipbuilding, instead of launching expensive yard improvements to obtain iron shipbuilding capacity.[28]

From a larger perspective, however, the USS *New Ironsides* illustrated structural problems facing inexperienced builders who ventured into iron construction. Apart from a few designing skills, Cramp and other subcontractors learned little about iron as shipbuilding material, both because the contract was divided into minuscule tasks and because they had no part in the metal processing, which was performed by ironworks. When conventional shipbuilding techniques, such as copper sheathing, did intersect with those of metal shipbuilding, construction mistakes ensued. To master the transition from wooden to iron construction, shipbuilders could not simply enlarge the traditional subcontracting network by drawing forges and ironworks into the orbit of shipyards. Effective ironclad construction required greater familiarity with iron processing techniques among shipbuilders themselves.

The Transition to Iron Shipbuilding

The Union's experimental ironclad program ended prematurely in spring 1862 during a series of dramatic events. On March 8, the CSS *Virginia* steamed out of Norfolk and attacked a Union blockade fleet at Hampton Roads. The Confederate ironclad played havoc with the Union's wooden fleet, destroyed two large warships, and threatened to sink a third. That night, Ericsson's USS *Monitor* arrived at Hampton Roads and positioned herself to protect the Union fleet from the *Virginia,* which returned the next morning. On March 9, 1862, the two vessels slugged it out in the first battle between ironclads in naval history. Neither ship could pierce the other's armor, and the battle ended in a draw. But the *Monitor* prevented the *Virginia* from breaking the Union blockade and steaming north to bombard the capital, as many panicked Unionists had feared. Impressed with Ericsson's vessel, the Navy Department selected the *Monitor* as a prototype for Union ironclads even before the USS *New Ironsides* had been launched.[29]

Charles Cramp was outraged by what he perceived as favoritism and pleaded with naval officials to improve the *New Ironsides's* design. "We recommended that the government build other vessels like her but with twin screws and various other improvements," he wrote later. But "all [our plans] were thrown aside without examination by the navy department."[30] Even the editors of the influential *Army and Navy Journal* could not persuade the navy to build another *New Ironsides.*[31]

The Navy Department proposed several changes to build the next generation of ironclads. In March 1862 a memorandum authored by navy officials John Lenthall and Benjamin Isherwood—respectively, chief of the Bureau of Construction and Repair, and chief of the Bureau of Steam Engineering—asked the secretary of the navy to build a new navy yard for ironclads, so as to construct the entire Union monitor fleet under government auspices. Much to

Lenthall and Isherwood's chagrin, however, Congress blocked the plan because it could not agree on a location (the proposed sites were League Island and New London, Connecticut). The press surmised that private contractors had concocted this deadlock to prevent the nationalization of monitor construction. For the duration of the Civil War, the ironclad navy yard scheme came to naught, and the navy established only a depot for decommissioned monitors at League Island.[32]

With its most ambitious scheme stalled, the Navy Department encouraged private contractors to centralize production. Lenthall informed the secretary of the navy that "selling out or subletting . . . contracts . . . is always to the injury both of the Government, and of the individual interests of the country, by fostering middlemen."[33] The USS *New Ironsides* illustrated that an extreme subdivision of the construction process also caused technical problems. As a result of these and other developments, Congress in July 1862 outlawed unauthorized subcontracting of government orders. Moreover, the Navy Department established a "monitor office" in New York to centralize and supervise ironclad design. This navy "subdepartment," nominally headed by veteran rear admiral Francis H. Gregory and managed by chief engineer Alban Stimers, was located across the hall from Ericsson's design bureau, which supplied general plans and specifications. Navy inspectors at the shipyards supervised contractors and reported every other week to the New York office. Chief Engineer Stimers administered the office and corresponded with contractors, local inspectors, and the Navy Department bureaus for construction, engineering, and ordnance.[34]

The centralization of ironclad design at the New York monitor office had several flaws, internal and external flaws. First, the office was understaffed. Stimers not only supervised its day-to-day operations but also called on workshops and shipyards in New York, Boston, Philadelphia, Chester, and Wilmington during troubleshooting assignments. Moreover, he was an ambitious man bent on reaping credit for designing ironclads and often visited the drawing rooms of the New York office to change plans and specifications. Second, the external coordination between the New York office and the bureaus for construction and steam engineering was insufficient, partly because Navy Department officials viewed it as an unwelcome competitor. Established bureaus rarely answered Stimer's pleas for technical advice. He later recalled, "I always felt that it was a regular fight—that we had to conquer them before we could get anything. On the one side it was a fight with the bureaus, and on the other side it was a fight with the contractors, to make them do anything right. It was a very unpleasant position which I held."[35]

In spring 1863 the secretary of the navy charged the New York office with planning the largest ironclad program of the Civil War, twenty *Casco*-class "Light-Draft Monitors." The Navy planned to use Cascos in the Mississippi River war theater. To operate in shallow waters, the vessels needed a light draft, not exceeding 6 feet, as well as a low freeboard of only 15 inches to present a small target to Confederate guns. Ericsson's initial plans showed a 225-foot hull, an armored upper deck, a revolving turret, and twin screw propellers to give the vessel a speed of 8 knots. This simple but effective design answered the navy's needs for Mississippi River warfare, Ericsson argued.[36]

In planning the new series of ironclads, Ericsson paid special attention to the industrial geography of shipbuilding and iron production. He stressed that the river monitors should be built in the Midwest and not on the Atlantic Coast because light-draft vessels were not equipped to venture on the long voyage from the northeastern shipbuilding centers to the Mississippi River via the dangerous North Carolina coast. (The navy had already lost the *Monitor* in a storm off Cape Hatteras during the attempt to transfer her from Hampton Roads to Beaufort, North Carolina.) At the same time, Ericsson knew that midwestern shipbuilders and iron masters were not nearly so well equipped as their northeastern counterparts. The design, therefore, stressed technical simplicity. He explained, "I conceived the idea of building a plain, oval tank with a flat bottom and upright sides, that could be done in an ordinary establishment in forty days. Around this I attached a raft made of timber, the idea being to give stability and impregnability to this wooden raft."[37]

Before construction began, this design underwent changes that infuriated Ericsson. Chief Engineer Stimers showed the drawings to Admiral Joseph Smith, chief of the Bureau of Yards and Docks in Washington, D.C., who was less hostile toward the New York office than other bureau chiefs. Smith suggested the first alterations to Ericsson's design, recommending that the oval hull be surrounded with large iron tanks that could be filled with water. The additional weight would submerge the vessel further to create a smaller target; if necessary, the water could be pumped out to give the ship a lighter draft. This peculiar design required several auxiliary engines to drive water pumps. Stimers approved of Smith's suggestion and ordered the required changes. The hypersensitive and arrogant Ericsson was so angry about these modifications that he informed the secretary of the navy of his decision to withdraw from the project.[38]

In February 1863 the monitor office asked for bids on the twenty light-draft monitors. It soon signed contracts with shipyards and engine builders across the Union, from St. Louis to Boston. Most of the river monitor contractors were northeastern concerns, because western builders had submitted an insuf-

The light-draft monitor USS Yazoo, *Cramp's first iron vessel. Note the low freeboard that characterized vessels of this class.* Harper's Weekly, *1866. U.S. Naval Historical Center*

ficient number of bids, thereby stifling Ericsson's plan to have the vessels built close to their operational theater. Aggregate costs amounted to almost $8 million, or $395,000 per vessel. Contractors included Reaney & Archbold in Chester, Wilcox & Whitney at Camden, and Harlan & Hollingsworth in Wilmington. Merrick & Sons booked a contract to build engines and boilers for the USS *Yazoo;* Cramp built her hull and the turret.[39]

This subcontract triggered what may have been the single most important development in Civil War shipbuilding: Cramp erected new facilities that included iron-processing equipment. A new facility at the foot of Palmer Street featured a "frame building, 250 feet long and 40 feet wide, and supplied with a powerful engine, driving machines for punching, cutting and planing iron and bending inch plates while in a cold state, to be used in making the turrets etc."[40] Cramp received from iron mills prebent iron plates for hull components, tanks, and the turret. Cramp's workers shaved irregularities off the surface of the plates using the planer, cut the plates into exact shape with a steam-driven shear, and operated a punching machine to pierce them at the rim where they eventually received rivets. To operate these new devices, Cramp hired iron-workers, including blacksmiths, platers, riveters, and machinists. By the summer of 1863, these men had joined Cramp's woodworkers to construct the USS *Yazoo*.[41]

Hull construction began in May 1863. Like the USS *New Ironsides* and other wooden ships, the river ironclad was first laid down full size in the mold loft by ship carpenters. The carpenters copied plans onto the floor and cut wooden patterns for hull components as well as for iron tanks. The patterns were forwarded to blacksmiths, who copied them onto long iron rods by hammering each piece into the required contours. At the point of production, the iron age had begun.[42]

On the berth, the riveters and ship carpenters constructed the hull. Ship carpenters and laborers prepared the building slip by lining up a row of logs, laid the keel, and erected frames that were bolted and riveted by riveting gangs. Plates were precision-bent at Cramp's small foundry; this procedure did not require elaborate shop equipment because the *Yazoo's* hull was almost box-shaped and did not have intricately contoured lines like those of a seagoing ship. Riveters attached plates to the frames and painted them with a zinc layer to prevent oxidation. Ironworkers also assembled and installed Admiral Smith's water tanks and connected them to pipes, valves, and steam-driven water pumps. Cramp cast propeller stuffing boxes at its small foundry and erected them aboard the ship.[43]

Meanwhile, the ship carpenters constructed the wooden raft that encased the iron hull and the water tanks. Made of oak and pine timber, it gave the ironclad additional buoyancy. Like other contractors for the light-draft monitors, however, Cramp used unseasoned timber; one of the contractors recalled that "there was not a ton of seasoned oak in the market suitable for these boats."[44] Unseasoned timber was heavy because it absorbed water. As a result, the *Yazoo's* wooden raft gave the ship less buoyancy than the designers had planned.[45]

The organization of work and the division of labor between ironworkers and woodworkers involved surprisingly few problems. More than half of the 300 men who built the USS *Yazoo* were ironworkers, but there was very little rivalry between them and the ship carpenters. Many woodworkers took the opportunity to learn iron-processing techniques. According to Charles Cramp, "our yard became a sort of kindergarten, as most of the workmen had to be trained to the work and working appliances had to be designed. Most of the members of the old firm could take any part of the building of a ship, from mold loft to launching; and they soon were able to take any iron work, from bending frames to bending plates and designing furnaces and other appliances."[46] Cramp's ship carpenters were more willing to become builders of iron ships than their New England counterparts, who avoided metalwork at any cost. Cramp's experience also contrasted with the situation in Britain and Germany, where journeymen ship carpenters, fearing job losses, launched strikes during the transition from wooden to iron construction. Charles Cramp noted one exception from the relative quiet at the point of production: "Many young ship carpenters and joiners and some fishermen . . . took up all the varieties of the work except riveting, which they did not consider a mechanical occupation."[47] This was probably because riveting represented one of the few mass-production-style jobs in iron shipbuilding and was usually paid by the piece; most skilled workers, by contrast, produced custom-made items and received hourly wages.[48]

At the end of 1863 Cramp and other contractors for the light-draft monitors experienced growing problems due to constant design changes. Stimers and his team of thirty young draftsmen at the New York monitor office added new features to the engines and the turret while the vessels were already being built. A specifications booklet, dubbed the "monitor prayer book" by some builders, contained ninety-two pages of small print. One Boston yard received 83 drawings and 120 explanatory letters from Stimers detailing numerous changes. In the end, each light-draft monitor featured thirteen auxiliary engines and pumps, fancy brasswork where simple cast iron would have been sufficient, and a confusing system of pipes to drain the water tanks. These changes not only cost the government considerable amounts for extra work but also added weight to the light-draft monitors, whose hulls were designed for a freeboard of only 15 inches. The hulls and rafts, which had to carry the additional weight, were the only components that remained unchanged. Together with the heavy water tanks and the unseasoned timber, alterations raised the possibility that the light-draft monitors would not float.[49]

A Boston builder was the first among the twenty contractors who worked his way through the perplexing design changes and finished his vessel, the USS *Chimo*, in spring 1864. At this point, shipyards were already brimming with rumors that something was wrong with the light-draft monitors. Stimers rushed to Boston in May and worked frantically to put the vessel into service. When the *Chimo* embarked on her trial trip, the disaster was complete: Waves washed across the upper deck, and the stern was submerged 3–4 inches. A naval constructor remarked drily that this was a "rather small margin for a man to go to sea with."[50]

In June and July 1864 the "light-draft monitor scandal" rocked the industry and the Navy Department. The press pointed out to the taxpaying public that the USS *Chimo* and her nineteen sister ships had cost close to $500,000 apiece and were entirely useless. The contractors, including Cramp, met at New York and disavowed any responsibility for the mistakes. The mortified secretary of the navy searched for a scapegoat, which he found in Stimers. Welles removed Stimers from his position and placed a team of experienced administrators in charge of the monitor office, including the chiefs of the Bureaus of Construction and Steam Engineering, Lenthall and Isherwood. In cooperation with Ericsson and the contractors, the bureau chiefs tried to rescue the ill-fated ironclad program.[51]

The team redesigned the wooden raft by raising the sides 22 inches to give the vessel greater freeboard. Many pipes and other iron parts had to be lengthened to fit the larger raft. For a cost estimate for the proposed changes, the officials contacted Merrick & Son whose engineers, together with Charles Cramp, also proposed a method of raising the sides at a price of $68,000. Even at this stage, Cramp profited from the doomed monitor program. At Chester, Reaney & Archbold had launched its ironclad, the USS *Tunix,* and reported problems similar to those discovered in the *Chimo.* On her trial trip up the Delaware River, the vessel barely reached a speed of 3½ knots instead of 8, even small waves drenched the upper deck, and her draft was anything but light. The navy, apparently concerned that the *Tunix* might sink on her way back to Chester, kept the vessel in Philadelphia to have the raft rebuilt by Cramp. Lacking a dry dock, Cramp's men, together with dozens of beasts of burden, pulled the *Tunix* out of the river and commenced the alterations in October 1864.[52]

Like many Union ironclads, the light-draft monitors were completed after the Confederate surrender. Without the usual fanfare, Cramp and the other contractors launched their Cascos in spring 1865. They were commissioned as serviceable vessels but never saw any combat; most of them joined the fleet of mothballed ironclads at League Island. On "Monitor Row," the USS *Yazoo* anchored only a short distance from the USS *New Ironsides.*[53]

A few years after the war had ended, the short but momentous story of Philadelphia-built ironclads also came to an end. On a warm summer night in 1870, a watchman discovered a small fire aboard the decommissioned *New Ironsides.* Despite valiant efforts by Philadelphia fire companies, the blaze burned out of control and gutted the big wooden hull. The same year, Cramp completed its last sailing vessel and abandoned wooden shipbuilding to concentrate on iron steamship construction.[54]

THREE

The American Clyde: Corporate and Proprietary Capitalism in the Philadelphia Maritime Economy, 1865-1875

On Monday, May 5, 1873, Cramp's men worked an early morning shift to send the transatlantic passenger liner *Pennsylvania* off on her trial trip. Shortly before 8 A.M. the engineers opened the steam valves, shipyard workers cast the lines, and the ship turned into the river. When the *Pennsylvania* passed downtown, dozens of steamers and factories blew their whistles, calling thousands of working people from their workbenches and offices to the waterfront for a grand celebration of the largest iron steamship of the American merchant marine. As she proceeded through the Delaware Valley toward the open sea, the *Pennsylvania* passed through the heartland of the nation's iron shipbuilding industry, now often called the American Clyde.[1]

Aboard the *Pennsylvania*, captains of industry enjoyed the beautiful spring morning and the excitement ashore caused by the sight of the elegant ship. William Cramp announced that the *Pennsylvania* was the crowning achievement of his shipbuilding career, which had begun on this day fifty years ago when he received his indenture as a journeyman ship carpenter. Among his listeners stood Thomas A. Scott, vice president of the Pennsylvania Railroad, which had financed the construction of the *Pennsylvania*. Cramp, proprietary entrepreneur, and Scott, corporate manager of the world's largest railroad, were fair representatives of Philadelphia's postwar maritime economy.[2]

Proprietary and corporate entrepreneurship intersected during a critical phase in the history of American iron shipbuilding. Most postwar builders

The stately passenger liner Pennsylvania, *steaming past downtown Philadelphia to the cheers of the people. Edward Strahan, ed.,* A Century After: Picturesque Glimpses of Philadelphia and Pennsylvania *(Philadelphia, 1875)*

booked vessel orders from proprietary shipowners who introduced iron tonnage in the harbor and coastwise trades. These contracts triggered modest changes as builders experimented with new types of marine engines and erected a new shop or two. However, these ships remained relatively small, and owners rarely ordered more than one unit. Without larger contracts, builders had little incentive to expand beyond the level of plant development and business organization reached in 1870. Neafie & Levy, for example, received contracts for small freighters, steamboats, tugs, and barges for which the existing shipyard plant was quite adequate. Continuing along these lines during the next two decades, Neafie & Levy remained a rather modest enterprise. Cramp and Roach, by contrast, booked orders for series of large passenger liners and colliers, built extensive additions to their works, and soon rivaled prestigious British yards in terms of plant size and shop equipment. The contracts that precipitated these changes were issued by corporately owned railroads and their steamship subsidiaries.

Surviving the Shipyard Crisis

The years between 1865 and 1870 were a time of crisis in the history of American shipbuilding. The market was glutted with ex–navy ships, so that demand for new ship construction plummeted. Scores of East Coast shipyards closed down. Builders of iron ships were less affected by the depression than their counterparts in wooden shipbuilding, because the navy offered only a few metal steamers at auction. This prompted steamship operators who wanted to sail iron ships to issue new contracts. The Philadelphia & Southern Mail Steamship Company, for example, bought wooden steamers from government surplus but ordered new iron steamers from Reaney & Archbold in Chester and Whitney & Wilcox's National Iron Armor & Shipbuilding Company in Camden. Reaney & Archbold and the Camden firm went bankrupt in 1870, but both were revived by new owners, the former by John Roach of New York and the latter by Dialogue & Wood of Philadelphia.[3]

Neafie & Levy and Cramp plotted an activist approach to postwar survival. In 1866 they founded a small ferryboat company and built the ferry *Shackamaxon*, with a hull constructed by Cramp and engines built by Neafie & Levy. This enterprise enabled both yards to weather the crisis by means of cooperation and self-generated demand. The ferry hull contract was especially important to Cramp because it was the first commercial order after the yard had launched its monitors in 1865 (see chapter 2).[4]

During subsequent years Neafie & Levy obtained an occasional towboat contract and branched out into overhauls. The firm also erected a new workshop to repair the former Confederate raider CSS *Atlanta*, which had been purchased by the Haitian navy. In 1867 the firm suffered a setback with the untimely death of John P. Levy, who had managed the firm for the last two decades. His heir Edmund L. Levy managed the yard together with Jacob Neafie, who grew more conservative with age and became skeptical of changes in established shipyard practice. Gradually, Neafie & Levy passed to Cramp its reputation as one of America's most dynamic shipbuilders.[5]

Cramp was the nation's only shipyard to manage the transition from wooden to ironclad to iron steamship building. Prominent New York and Boston builders tried but failed to accomplish the same feat. William Webb of New York, for example, had constructed wooden transatlantic liners during the 1850s and in the 1860s built the giant ironclad USS *Dunderburg*, but he quit shipbuilding in 1869. Cramp enjoyed advantages lacking in New York and other shipbuilding centers.[6]

Most important, Cramp and other Delaware Valley builders operated at the center of highly developed metal production and engineering industries. The Pittsburgh region boasted an extensive network of iron and coal mines, blast furnaces, and rolling mills whose output was processed in machine shops, locomotive factories, and rail mills in eastern Pennsylvania. A reporter visiting Philadelphia in 1873 felt overwhelmed by the sheer magnitude of its "gigantic . . . array of works, foundries, rolling mills and forges." He learned that "twenty thousand men . . . gain a substantial livelihood in these vast ironworks; and from all I can learn, the manufacturers themselves have no cause to complain that a highly remunerative fragment out of the business sum of their $50,000,000 gross annual sales, does not remain in their pockets as net profit."[7] Prestigious firms included the Disston Saw Factory and the William Sellers machine tool works, which procured rolled and cast iron from local specialty producers, such as Stephen Robbins's Philadelphia Rolling Mill at Kensington or the Vulcan Works at Chester. The latter also produced ship iron for yards in Philadelphia, Camden, Chester, and Wilmington.[8]

From a shipbuilder's point of view, the great advantage of the Pennsylvania iron industry was its location near the shipyards. The proximity of rolling mills, foundries, and shipyards did not necessarily mean that Philadelphia builders paid less for ship iron than shipbuilders elsewhere; iron prices were roughly the same throughout the Northeast. But shipbuilders had to be in daily communication with rolling mills and makers of cast iron to relay specifications for the plates, angle iron, beams, and castings that were custom-made for every vessel. In a widely discussed letter to Rep. William "Pig Iron" Kelly of Pennsylvania, Charles Cramp claimed that "nearly every piece of iron entering into [a metal ship] must be made to special order, and this fact, together with the necessity of rapid delivery, demands that the iron mills should be near the shipyards."[9] These imperatives proved impractical for New York builders because high real-estate prices and other factors impeded the growth of the city's iron industry. But in Philadelphia rolling mills and ironworks were already located near the shipyards, enabling shipbuilders to discuss specifications for customized ship iron with their subcontractors. Indeed, nowhere on the entire East Coast was the iron industry situated so close to a shipbuilding center. Only in Scotland, where most ironworks operated within a small radius of the Clyde, had shipbuilders developed similarly close relationships with metal suppliers. By the early 1870s contemporaries had dubbed the Delaware Valley the "American Clyde."[10]

In 1871 the postwar maritime depression finally gave way to slow economic improvement. Vessel owners by this time had retired their government surplus tonnage. Moreover, waterborne trade was increasing for the first time since the Civil War. This upswing encouraged coastwise steamship operators to update their fleets. Charles H. Mallory of the New York–Galveston steamship line, for example, had previously built wooden steamers at his own yard at Mystic, Connecticut. In 1871 he ordered his first iron vessels from Roach. Likewise, the Clyde Line, owned by Philadelphian William Clyde, in 1870 commenced a four-year fleet modernization and expansion program. Clyde awarded most of its contracts to Cramp, which launched the 1,200-ton iron steamship *Clyde* in July 1870. Her engines were built by Neafie & Levy.[11]

Mallory, Clyde, and other proprietors who issued orders for small and medium-sized iron steamers took exceptional risks at a time when most American vessel operators were still suspicious of the new technology. When large British iron steamers appeared in American ports, conservative trade experts found the new vessel type wanting. Iron steamships were more expensive than wooden sailing ships; they rusted in saltwater; iron hull rivets often cracked; iron hulls were less elastic than wooden ones and sometimes broke apart when "riding" a wave. The critics of iron ships publicized every single accident involving these vessels and strongly advised American shippers to stick to wooden hulls. As a result, iron steamers remained unpopular except among a small minority of harbor and coastwise operators. The latter included Clyde, who was praised by a maritime journal for "doing more, at the present time, to develop the proper and profitable class of coasting steamers than any one in this country. The ideas of this gentleman, in respect to the character and capacity of this class of vessels, are further in advance of and nearer to the mark than the ideas of any one we know of."[12] During the early 1870s this progressive maritime entrepreneur pioneered the introduction of iron steamships as coastwise carriers.[13]

The Clyde contracts gave Cramp an opportunity to experiment with recent developments in marine technology. In 1871 the yard obtained a $200,000 order for the 1,800-gross-ton iron freighter *George W. Clyde* and fitted her with a compound steam engine, the first of its kind installed in an American steamship. A compound engine featured two cylinders: a high-pressure unit received steam directly from the boilers, and a second, low-pressure cylinder received spent steam from the first cylinder and used it as a power source. This new technology was more economical than the single-cylinder system because steam recycling lowered coal consumption. Compound marine engines had been invented by John Elder of Glasgow in 1854, but American builders, who often lacked the necessary precision tools, failed to follow the British lead until Cramp took the initiative in 1871.[14]

Significantly, Cramp built the compound engine for the *George W. Clyde* at the shipyard instead of issuing a subcontract to Neafie & Levy. The integration of hull and engine building was initiated by Charles Cramp, who was convinced that progress in American iron shipbuilding hinged on marine engineering. In 1870 he told a congressional committee that "Great Britain now [has] the advantage of this country in the carrying trade of the world, not because the vessels constructed were superior to ours, but because of the great superiority of their marine engines. The English have built the finest and best marine engines in the world. We have always been inferior to her in that respect."[15] If Americans wanted to compete with British yards, they had to build better marine engines. This meant, in Cramp's view, that shipbuilders had to construct their own engines. The argument had merit: before 1870 most marine engines had been constructed by ironworks insufficiently specialized and motivated to experiment with new marine engine technology. In the antebellum years, only engine specialists and iron shipbuilders—most notably Neafie & Levy—had made significant headway in American marine engineering.[16]

Most Delaware Valley builders, including Roach and Dialogue & Wood, began to integrate marine engine building with hull construction. Only Birely, Hillman & Streaker, which built wooden hulls, continued to subcontract marine engines after 1871. Even this yard usually ordered engines from Neafie & Levy, and not from general engine shops, such as Merrick's Southwark Foundry or I. P. Morris. Such firms lost their foothold in the maritime economy.[17]

During the period of economic recovery, Delaware Valley builders booked contracts for small and medium-sized iron vessels, improved their facilities, and introduced new technologies. Neafie & Levy, the busiest yard, launched twenty-seven vessels for New York customers in 1870 and 1871. In addition to the *George W. Clyde,* Cramp constructed two iron tugs and the three-masted schooner *Bessie Morris,* the last wooden ship built at this yard. Dialogue & Wood of Camden launched iron tugs and ferryboats. John Roach's Delaware River Iron Works at Chester constructed the 1,605-ton *City of San Antonio* for Mallory. Trade experts were soon confident that the "prospects for the future [of the iron shipbuilding industry] . . . look fair."[18] At issue now was whether builders could do more than simply survive. Cramp in particular wanted to emulate prestigious British yards and build large iron steamships in series of three or four. Most American owners, however, lacked sufficient capital for contracts of this magnitude, which involved millions of dollars. Large British lines, especially Peninsular & Oriental, issued these kinds of orders to Clyde yards, such as Caird & Company, which had developed a profitable business in large-scale liner construction since mid-century. American operators occasionally discussed the merits of large iron steamers, but in the end they always shied away from the financial challenges. In the United States, the only customers for big iron ships were corporately owned railroads.[19]

Corporate Capital and the Maritime Economy

Most railroads had roots in the maritime economy. The Pennsylvania Railroad, for example, had been organized in 1844 to connect the eastern and western parts of the state and competed with the Main Line Canal between Philadelphia and Pittsburgh. The Philadelphia & Reading Railroad snatched the coal trade from barge owners who operated on the Schuylkill Navigation Company's canal between Reading and Philadelphia. Both railroads were financed by Philadelphia merchants who channeled their profits from maritime trade into the overland transportation sector.[20]

Although railroads tapped the maritime sector for capital and trade, the relationship between the two was not entirely hostile. The Philadelphia & Reading Railroad invigorated Philadelphia's coastwise coal trade when it built extensive coal wharves at Port Richmond, north of Kensington. Conversely, changes in maritime trade affected the railroads. The Pennsylvania's westbound passenger service, for example, received a boost from the British Inman Line's transatlantic passenger trade, which brought potential railroad customers from Liverpool to Philadelphia beginning in 1850. Seven years later, Inman moved its American terminal from Philadelphia to Manhattan, and the Pennsylvania's passenger trade suffered correspondingly. This inspired the railroad to search for a new transatlantic steamship connection to feed its westward passenger trade at the Philadelphia terminal.[21]

The Pennsylvania was the epitome of nineteenth-century corporate capital. Owned by stockholders, this $400 million company was headed by J. Edgar Thompson who controlled a negligible number of shares but was elected president in 1848. He took control of the Pennsylvania out of the hands of its shareholders and their representatives, the board of directors, created a revolutionary system of management controls, and formulated a policy of corporate expansion. Thompson planned the railroad's future on a national and even international scale, vastly exceeding its original 400-mile track from Philadelphia to Pittsburgh. He bought out competitors and created new subsidiaries. By 1870 he controlled a network of 6,000 miles of railroad track. Thompson also initiated the formation of a transatlantic steamship line to offer integrated passenger service from Liverpool to the Midwest.[22]

The first plan for a transatlantic line evolved in 1863, when Thompson proposed the formation of a steamship company to replace the lost Inman connection. According to this plan, Philadelphia merchants would buy stocks and bonds, the latter of which the Pennsylvania would guarantee to ensure the line's financial viability. The bond guarantee meant that the railroad would fulfill the steamship line's financial obligations if the line proved unable to pay interest on its debt or went bankrupt before the bonds matured. Thompson's plan won enthusiastic support from local merchants but fell through when the city council failed to provide financial support.[23]

In the next five years, the increasing pressures of corporate system building precipitated a revival of the project. After the Civil War, Thompson created a network of subsidiary railroad lines from Pennsylvania to the Midwest. The network needed a transatlantic connection at the Philadelphia hub to compete with a similar railway network radiating from New York. New York railroads had excellent transatlantic feeders, as seven European steamship lines brought thousands of potential railroad passengers each month; the Pennsylvania, by contrast, had no direct overseas links. Philadelphia's mercantile and industrial capital also clamored for a steamship connection between the city and Europe. The lack of a direct overseas connection was especially bothersome to petroleum traders, who were forced to export via New York and pay extra charges to have their barrels transported from Philadelphia to the Manhattan wharves. Moreover, the national press urged capitalists to challenge the growing monopoly of the British merchant marine in American foreign trade. In 1871 the railroad and local investors created the American Steamship Company (ASC), which operated the nation's first postwar transatlantic line.[24]

The ASC organizers included the elite of Philadelphia's railroad, mercantile, and industrial capital. Most important among them were J. Edgar Thompson and Thomas A. Scott of the Pennsylvania Railroad, the merchants Edward C. Knight and Henry Winsor, and Barnabas H. Bartol, owner of Philadelphia's largest sugar refinery. In January 1871 the organizers applied to the Pennsylvania legislature for a charter authorizing the ASC to sell stocks worth $700,000 to the general public. The charter also permitted a $1.5 million bond issue, which was guaranteed by the Pennsylvania Railroad. With this security, the ASC received the highest credit ratings on financial markets. Its securities sold quickly, and the Pennsylvania Railroad bought a large block of stock.[25]

On April 4, 1871, the shareholders convened at the Philadelphia Merchants' Exchange and elected nine members to the board of directors as senior executives. The board included some of the initial organizers, men such as Knight, Bartol, and paint manufacturer Washington Butcher. At the first meeting the board members elected committees on finance, by-laws, and ships. Bartol, who was familiar with marine engineering after his Civil War tenure as Merrick's chief engineer, served as chairman of the committee on ships. The committee recommended the purchase of four iron steamships of 3,000 or more tons to carry 1,000 steerage and 24 first-class passengers at a maximum speed of 11½ knots. These specifications conformed to British standards in the transatlantic liner service, which had recently introduced so-called "Atlantic grey-hounds," such as Inman's *City of Brussels* (3,090 gross tons and 11½ knots). The board of directors approved the recommendation and solicited bids from shipbuilders.[26]

The ASC contract was the largest steamship order of the 1870s. Four eager builders—all Delaware Valley firms—submitted bids: John Roach, Neafie & Levy, Cramp & Sons, and Dialogue & Wood offered to build the vessels at prices ranging from $525,000 to $660,000 apiece. On August 9, 1871, the board of directors examined the proposals and awarded the contract to Cramp, which had submitted the lowest bid.[27]

The Pennsylvania Railroad's system-building efforts also led to the formation of the International Navigation Company (INC), which played an important role in Delaware Valley shipbuilding during subsequent decades. The INC served as the Pennsylvania's transatlantic feeder on the Antwerp-Philadelphia route. It was founded in cooperation between the railroad and James A. Wright of the Peter Wright & Company shipping agency, an old and respected Philadelphia commission house. In 1871 Wright and his junior partner Clement A. Griscom applied to the Pennsylvania state legislature for a corporate charter to issue $1.5 million in stock. In contrast to the ASC, the INC stock was owned not by a large number of investors but by an exclusive circle of railroad managers, including John D. Potts of the Empire Transportation Company, a subsidiary of the Pennsylvania Railroad. Managed by Wright and Griscom, the INC received a $1 million bond guarantee from the Pennsylvania Railroad and ordered four British-built transatlantic liners, which sailed between Philadelphia and Antwerp as the Red Star Line. These vessels were not considered part of the American merchant marine because the U.S. Navigation Acts prohibited the registration of foreign-built vessels in the United States. Instead, the INC registered its vessels in Belgium, where navigation laws permitted the registry of foreign-built liners under the Belgian flag. Moreover, the Red Star Line received a mail contract from the Belgian government. Since the line was controlled by Philadelphia investors, had its ships built in England, and sailed under the Belgian flag, affixing *international* to the company name was quite appropriate.[28]

Other corporate steamship operators included the Philadelphia & Reading Railroad (P&RR), which ordered a series of colliers from Delaware Valley builders and awarded six contracts to Cramp. The P&RR was a vertically and horizontally integrated corporation in the coal trade, whose assets included the Reading coal mines in eastern Pennsylvania, a railroad track from Reading to Philadelphia, extensive coal depots and wharf facilities, steamships, and wholesale dealerships. During the antebellum years the Reading coal mines

An iron steam collier loading coal at the Philadelphia & Reading Railroad coal wharves, Port Richmond. Note the two coal schooners in the background. Edward Strahan, ed., A Century After: Picturesque Glimpses of Philadelphia and Pennsylvania *(Philadelphia, 1875)*

had been owned by small mining companies that shipped coal to Philadelphia via the Schuylkill Canal. In Philadelphia, dockworkers unloaded the canal barges at the Schuylkill Depot, and teamsters hauled coal to the Delaware wharves. When the P&RR built a railroad track from Reading to the Delaware riverfront at Philadelphia in the early 1840s, it literally cut across these junctions. The railroad loaded its cars at Reading; skipped the canal, barges, city teamsters, and wharves; and transported the coal directly to its own docks at Port Richmond on the Delaware. Before the Civil War Reading coal had been sold by independent dealers and transported aboard independently owned schooners.[29]

During the 1860s the P&RR absorbed some of these functions by buying out several coal mines and selling coal directly to large customers. Its next targets were the coastwise schooners. The P&RR first chartered a fleet of vessels during the early 1860s and later ordered small iron colliers from Delaware Valley yards. By 1870 it had amassed an "empire of coal" stretching from Reading to Port Richmond. While the railroad still supplied independent agents with anthracite coal, it also competed with them in the transportation and marketing sectors.[30]

The railroad's encroachments onto the turf of independent entrepreneurs provoked major conflicts between proprietary and corporate capital. Retailers argued that the P&RR charged exorbitant wholesale prices to drive them out of business; schooner operators complained that the railroad undercut agreed-upon coastwise freight rates. In 1873 these conflicts erupted into open business warfare along the Delaware. The P&RR's president Franklin Gowen stated:

[There is an] unusual scarcity of vessels at Port Richmond during many months, caused, it is believed, by systematic attempts on the part of the displaced middle-men to prejudice vessel owners and captains against the Company, under the belief that an inability to procure vessels would induce the . . . Company to withdraw from the trade and surrender it to the hands of the former factors . . . For several months the coal tonnage of the Company was reduced from twenty to forty thousand tons per week, owing to the scarcity of vessels; from 5000 to 7000 loaded cars standing over at Port Richmond at the end of each day.[31]

In response to the boycott, the P&RR enlarged its own fleet and in June 1873 signed a contract with Cramp for six iron colliers. The new vessels were to be 250 feet in length, 37 feet in the beam, and 1,283 gross tons (two similar vessels were built by John Roach).[32]

In addition to the ASC and the P&RR contracts, shipbuilders booked vessel orders from the Pacific Mail Steamship Company, Charles Morgan's Louisiana & Texas Railroad and Steamship Company, the Old Dominion Steamship Company (operated under the joint control of the Norfolk & Western Railroad and the Southern Railroad), and the Camden & Atlantic Railroad. While these corporately owned steamship lines did not replace proprietary entrepreneurs, such as tugboat, ferryboat, and steamship line operators, they did pioneer the integration of the long-distance waterborne trade into the American railroad sector.[33]

The Transformation of Proprietary Capital

In 1871 no American shipyard was sufficiently equipped to build four 3,000-ton iron passenger ships of the kind ordered by the ASC. The largest American metal vessel constructed to that point was the steamer *Wyanoke* of 2,067 tons, launched at Harlan & Hollingsworth in 1870. To build the ASC liners, Cramp needed a major reorganization and new facilities, as well as hundreds of additional workers.

When Cramp received the contract in August 1871, its Palmer Street works were busy with overhauls and the construction of a new steamship for Clyde. Cramp therefore purchased real estate at Norris Street, a few blocks north of the old works, to build a new shipyard. The Norris Street lot alone cost more than $265,000, which was mostly paid for with Cramp family funds and bonds secured by a mortgage on the Palmer Street works. The new works included blacksmith, engine, boiler, and carpenter shops, as well as a 700-foot outfitting wharf. The construction of a shipyard plant from scratch permitted a fairly

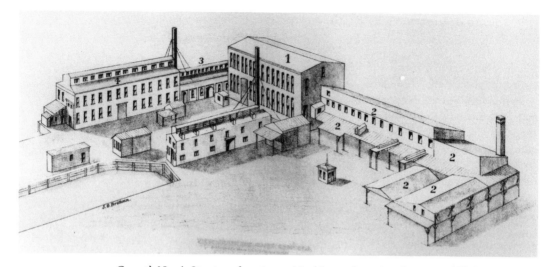

Cramp's Norris Street yard, c. 1872. 1, Machine and erecting shop; 2, mold loft and boat shop; 3, blacksmith shop; 4, boiler shop. Hexamer General Survey, Map Collection, Free Library of Philadelphia

systematic layout of the shops and berths. The important blacksmith shop, for example, where iron parts and plates were hammered into ship-shape, stood in the corner between the boiler shop to the south and the machine shop due west, which received parts and plates from the blacksmith shop.[34]

Cramp also purchased new production equipment. On a recent visit to Britain, Charles Cramp and his superintendent for marine engineering had examined new tools operated by the Thames Iron Works at London and the Thompson, McGregor, and Laird yards on the Scottish Clyde. Charles Cramp related that "this trip was a most useful one . . . [and] gave us an opportunity of examining every method pertaining to hull construction and equipment there, and to discuss all of the problems and methods belonging to it."[35] Upon return from Britain, Cramp selected standard equipment, such as boiler flanges, a punching machine to drive rivet holes, and small forges. Contemporary visitors to the Cramp yard marveled at these "best appliances" and superior "labor saving machinery." But in point of fact, the yard featured only the most basic facilities for iron shipbuilding. Unlike Roach at Chester, for example, Cramp operated no rolling mill because the yard was surrounded by small specialty works that could serve as subcontractors.[36]

The firm transferred some of its employees from Palmer Street to the new yard. Other workers joined Cramp after having worked at Neafie & Levy or one of the local ironworks. Ship carpenter Joseph T. Weaber, hired by Cramp in 1871, had served his stint at Neafie & Levy, where he had learned iron shipbuilding techniques. Moreover, Cramp hired Neafie & Levy's marine engi-

neer, Horace See, who had also worked for I. P. Morris and the National Iron
Armor and Shipbuilding Company in Camden. Marine engineer J. Shields
Wilson was another former Neafie & Levy employee and became Cramp's
expert for compound engines. (Jacob Neafie replaced Wilson with the British
marine engineer Samuel Holmes, a leading advocate of iron shipbuilding in
America during the 1870s.)[37]

In 1872 Cramp applied to the Pennsylvania state legislature for a corporate
charter. The sponsor of Cramp's incorporation bill in the Commonwealth
House of Representatives explained that Cramp's work on the ASC liners "is so
extensive that it is impossible for the firm to get along with it. [The partners]
therefore desire to be incorporated as a company, for the purpose of extending
their privileges and giving them a chance to borrow money and carry on
successfully the building of steamships."[38] With the passage of the incorporation bill, William Cramp & Sons became the William Cramp & Sons Ship and
Engine Building Company. Like the International Navigation Company, the
new firm had no intention of selling shares to the general public; instead,
William Cramp and his five sons converted their existing partnership holdings
into stock. William Cramp and his oldest son Charles each owned $83,400 in
shares, while the four younger partners owned $83,300 each, bringing the total
investment to $500,000.

This corporate form of business organization protected the personal property of the incorporators. In a strictly private firm, each partner's personal
property was liable for the debts of the firm; in a stockholding company, the
incorporators risked only the money invested in shares. Given the considerable risks involved in Cramp's venture into large-scale iron shipbuilding, the
corporate charter provided some measure of protection for personal finances.
Moreover, before the introduction of general incorporation laws during the
late nineteenth century, incorporation was a privilege; at least in theory, state
legislators awarded corporate charters only when the men involved were trust-
worthy individuals. As a result, incorporation amounted to an official confir-
mation that the projected business was sound, assuring financial markets that
it deserved good credit. Cramp needed this kind of assurance because creditors
were somewhat skeptical about the profitability of iron shipbuilding, and they
had noted that Cramp was a bit slow in settling its open accounts. However,
incorporation changed very little in the firm's day-to-day operations; William
Cramp and his sons simply convened annually as shareholders and elected
themselves directors of the company.[39]

The ASC liners were known as the *Pennsylvania* class, after the first such
ship launched. Their plans and specifications showed a vessel of 355 feet in
overall length, with a beam of 43 feet and a weight of 3,104 gross tons. A

compound engine registering 1,400 horsepower drove a single propeller screw, which gave the ship a speed of 11½ knots. This engine resembled that of the British liner *Italy* of similar dimensions, on which Charles Cramp and his supervising engineer J. Shields Wilson had traveled to Britain on their fact-finding mission. During the trip they had conversed at length with the *Italy's* chief engineer W. R. Wilson, discussing compound engine technology, and had then hired him as a consulting engineer.[40]

By early 1872 the construction of the ASC liners was in full swing at Norris Street. The four ships were named *Pennsylvania, Ohio, Illinois,* and *Indiana,* in honor of the four states traversed by the Pennsylvania Railroad network. A work force of 1,000 men laid the four keels and erected more than 200 iron frames on each keel. A newspaper report of February 1872 described a day's work at the nation's busiest yard for iron ships: "The four vessels stand now side by side in the extensive yard with nearly all their ribs in place. . . . The clang of heavy masses of iron as they are lifted and dropped around, added to the shouts of the hundreds of workmen, and the sounds in the blacksmith shops, form a scene of great activity and interest."[41] In the small shipyard office, engineers worked on plans and specifications for ship iron suppliers, such as Seyfert & McManus at Reading and Morris, Wheeler & Company at Pottstown, Pennsylvania. Improving a technique introduced by Charles Cramp during the antebellum years, when he had advised Neafie & Levy to order custom-made plates, Cramp sent wooden templates to the mills to ensure that angle iron and plates needed little correction at the shipyard and could be processed as quickly as possible.[42]

Cramp recruited other subcontractors who supplied specialty items. Subcontracting in the early 1870s differed from antebellum practice because Cramp constructed boilers and engines at the yard itself. The yard ordered plates from the Pottsville Iron Works and other items from Philadelphia suppliers: anchor chains from the Empire Chain Works, forgings from I. P. Morris, and various metal parts from the small shipsmithery, A. H. Stillwell & Brother. The joiner work in saloons and first-class cabins was subcontracted with Smith & Campion, and gas fixtures were made by Thackara, Buck & Company of Philadelphia.[43]

Cramp's subcontracting strategies were criticized by Neafie & Levy's superintendent John S. Lee. Lee told Samuel Randall of Philadelphia, Speaker of the U.S. House of Representatives, that "the Messrs. Cramps were compelled to select a new site for their works and reorganize their whole establishment for the completion of that contract, and notwithstanding all their preparation not one piece of casting that went into these ships was made upon their place, they having no foundry, and all the heavy forgings were made by outside parties."[44]

Although Lee seemed a sore loser because Cramp had underbid his employer for the ASC contracts, his views were shared by critics who considered sub-contracting an outdated and inefficient organization of production. As an alternative, they pointed to vertical integration in the iron and coal industries. Ideally, a company should mine iron ore and coal, ship the material to its own furnaces, produce pig iron, operate integrated rolling mills and cast works, and build ships. In Britain, this strategy was pioneered by Palmer's at Jarrow, which controlled iron mines, a fleet of colliers, engineering works, and a shipyard.[45]

Cramp remained committed to subcontracting because the yard operated in a densely settled urban industrial environment. An integrated shipyard would have required additional real estate to erect large foundries and rolling mills. Further, Cramp had already stretched its financial resources to the limit by purchasing the expensive Norris Street property. Integration made more sense for builders whose plants were located outside urban-industrial centers, such as Roach at Chester or Barrow north of Liverpool. These builders added rolling mills to their plants because there were few ship iron suppliers in the immediate vicinity. Big-city yards, such as Cramp in Philadelphia or Thompson at Glasgow, were surrounded by independent specialty producers and could avoid investing in expensive urban real estate by plugging into networks of "disintegrated" production.[46]

Subcontracting also enabled Cramp to avoid large overhead costs. Small overheads were vital in an industry notorious for extreme market fluctuations. One year, a builder might have his hands full with passenger liners and freighters, while the next year he might build only a few tugboats and barges. Given these well-known conditions, integrated shipyards that consumed large over-heads while contracts dried up were not exactly desirable. These lessons had been learned by leading Scottish yards, such as Thompson's, and formed the basis for Cramp's industrial strategy.[47]

Cramp launched the passenger liners in August and November 1872, and March and June 1873. Contemporaries praised the ASC flagship *Pennsylvania* as the most magnificent ship afloat on the seven seas; she even received an acknowledgment from John Grantham, the doyen of British iron shipbuilding. By British standards, however, the 355-foot, 3,104-gross-ton *Pennsylvania* with her single screw was a fairly average liner, outclassed by the White Star Line's new 437-foot *Adriatic,* a 3,886-gross-ton ship featuring double screws. The ASC liner also experienced some technical difficulties during her maiden voyage when a propeller blade fell off and she had to finish the trip under sail. Fortunately, the passengers took the incident lightly and composed a ditty about it, "Cramp, Cramp, Cramp, the blades are breaking."[48] This must have mortified Charles Cramp, who was proud of Philadelphia's tradition of screw-

Washington Street wharves at Southwark, 1870s. Note the American Steamship Company and Red Star Line docks, and at left the Pennsylvania Railroad Station. The Pennsylvania *is arriving from Liverpool. Library of Congress*

steamer construction. But henceforth, the *Pennsylvania* and her three sister ships performed well and served for more than three and a half decades.[49]

The introduction of transatlantic liners transformed the Philadelphia waterfront. "Those familiar with the appearance of the river front ten years ago," an observer reported in 1875, "would hardly recognize it to-day."[50] To serve its weekly sailings to Liverpool, the ASC built new wharves at the foot of Washington Street in Southwark, supplemented by a Pennsylvania Railroad station across the street. Arriving steamship passengers could disembark, go through customs, and board a westbound train all within one hour. Moreover, the International Navigation Company built extensive wharves at the same location and transferred passengers to the railroad station. These facilities embodied the Pennsylvania Railroad's system-building efforts.[51]

Urban Space and the Limits of Corporate Capital

Upon completion of the ASC contract, Cramp commenced the construction of the six P&RR colliers. Although this $1.3 million contract gave the builders a good opportunity to consolidate their enterprise of iron shipbuilding, Cramp must have viewed this customer with mixed feelings. It was widely assumed that the collier contract would be the last order issued by the P&RR to independent shipyards because the railroad had already announced plans to build its own integrated shipbuilding facility.

The collier contract itself indicated that the P&RR had sufficient production capacity and expertise to branch out into vessel construction. For example, the railroad handed Cramp printed specifications that detailed the construction of the steamers to the last rivet. The specifications had been written by one of the railroad's marine consultants. This differed from the contract negotiations between Cramp and the ASC, which had left ship design to the builders and merely approved Cramp's specifications. The P&RR left almost nothing to the discretion of the builders and even took an active part in procuring vessel components. The railroad delivered boilers, steam pumps, rigging, boats, anchors, chains, and furniture for the officers' quarters; some of these items were made at the P&RR railroad shops in Philadelphia and Reading.[52]

Cramp laid down the iron colliers in fall 1873 after the ASC liners had been launched. Initially, construction proceeded smoothly and helped Cramp weather the business depression that began with the financial panic of 1873. Unlike many other employers, the yard kept almost its entire work force busy through the winter. The contract also improved Cramp's credit rating, when R. G. Dun reported that Cramp was busy during these hard times.[53]

The first collier (named *Harrisburg*) was launched in February 1874. Then, on March 23, 1874, a fire destroyed parts of the machine shop and the engines for the *Pottstown*, another of the colliers. Fortunately, the tight contract between Cramp and the Philadelphia & Reading Railroad had obliged the builders to insure the six colliers during the construction phase. The machine shop had also been insured, so that the financial damage to Cramp was minor. The fire's only effect was that the vessels could not be delivered on schedule. But this, too, was cushioned by the contract, which stipulated that Cramp would pay "the sum of two hundred dollars . . . for each and every day's delay in the delivery of each vessel, unless such delay shall have been occasioned by fire or strikes of workmen beyond the control of the [shipbuilders]."[54] Cramp delivered the colliers in fall 1874.[55]

Meanwhile, the Philadelphia & Reading Railroad pursued its strategy of vertical integration. The company owned fourteen iron colliers (including the six building at Cramp), which required frequent overhauls. In the past the railroad had awarded these repair contracts to Delaware Valley builders, but in 1873 railroad executives decided that growing operations warranted adding ship repair facilities to the company's holdings. Moreover, the P&RR directors discussed a large-scale extension of the collier fleet by no fewer than fifty new vessels, which would be built at the new shipyard.[56]

The railroad purchased a 15-acre lot northeast of its coal wharf facilities in Port Richmond and invested more than $500,000 in the physical plant. Like Cramp's Norris Street yard, the works featured a systematic layout: four building slips, a boiler shop, a tool shop, two pattern shops, a joiner shop, and an outfitting wharf. Unlike the new Cramp yard, however, these facilities also included a shiphouse to protect hulls and workers from rain and snow. Moreover, the railroad erected large furnaces so as to be independent of outside contractors. These facilities were the "most pretentious of any of the kind in the country," the *New York Times* reported.[57] The *Nautical Gazette* surmised: "With their own mines of iron and coal, and their machine shops, the company expects to reduce the cost of iron shipbuilding far below any figure that has heretofore prevailed in the United States."[58]

The centerpiece of the P&RR yard was a projected basin dry dock to overhaul large iron steamships. The port of Philadelphia needed this kind of facility because the existing (floating) dry docks were too small to accommodate big steamers. Private builders had ad hoc arrangements with the Navy Yard, which allowed them to use its large floating dock to repair the transatlantic ocean liners that now frequented the port. Unfortunately, the Navy Yard dock was severely damaged in February 1875 by floating ice while the *Pennsylvania* was docked for an overhaul. The mishap left local builders and operators without sufficient repair capacity.[59]

Since the P&RR shipyard property was too small for the dry dock, the railroad applied to the city council for a permit to buy public property and obliterate a street. For once, however, the P&RR overplayed its hand. The city council was soon confronted with a neighborhood movement that launched a ferocious attack on the project. The protest drew on years of popular discontent with the destruction of housing and public property by railroads, which needed space to lay tracks into the center city and to the waterfront. Despite loud opposition from homeowners and tenants, the city council had time and again issued permits that allowed railroads to build tracks, especially in working-class neighborhoods. Moreover, the P&RR was perhaps the region's most hated corporation before the great Pittsburgh strike against the Pennsylvania Railroad in 1877. During a bitter strike by Reading-area coal-miners in early 1875, the P&RR antagonized independent shippers and agents as well as the miners; the strike found widespread support in working-class Philadelphia. The railroad's dry-dock project provoked neighborhood protests by shopkeepers, small real estate owners, and workers. In a rare display of

Cramp's dry dock, with British steamship Eagle Point *docked for repairs, c. 1900. The caisson closing the dock was built at the shipyard. Library of Congress*

courage in confronting corporate capital, the city council's survey committee heeded the demands and denied the P&RR a permit to build the dry dock on a public street.[60]

Railroad president Franklin Gowen tried to coax the city council into rejecting the committee's recommendation and issuing the permit. He openly threatened to relocate the P&RR coal terminal from Port Richmond to Chester unless the request for dry-dock space was granted. Without the ship repair facility, he claimed, the projected shipyard was almost useless. Gowen further argued that the controversy went far beyond the shipyard matter. He raised the question whether large manufactories could expand at all within the city: "If . . . it is determined by Councils that no large manufacturing or other industrial establishment shall ever be opened to this city unless they can be crowded within the space of one single block . . . it will be necessary for them to remove their business to another locality, where they will not be hampered for room, and where there is some probability of their being able to carry on their works without interference by the authorities of the place."[61]

The protest movement applauded the committee ruling and urged the city council to follow the same course. One protester wrote: "We do intend to stand our rights, as we understand them, though [the railroad men], backed by all the newspapers in the land, howl till doomsday. The interests of our fellow citizens we shall endeavor to protect, and shall not allow Mr. Gowen's company to destroy their business, if we can help it. All honor to the Councilmen who have stood for the right. The Twenty-fifth Ward owes them a debt and will try to pay it, if opportunity shall offer."[62] The city council denied the permit. In the wake of this defeat, the P&RR—also plagued by the business depression after the panic of 1873—abandoned the shipyard, which remained idle for almost a decade.[63]

The Delaware shipbuilders probably breathed a sigh of relief. Experiences among shippers and coal agents had illustrated that the P&RR could overwhelm individual entrepreneurs. Thanks to the protest movement, Cramp, Neafie & Levy, A. L. Archambault, and other Delaware shipbuilders escaped ruinous corporate competition.

Cramp capitalized upon these developments and built its own basin dry dock at Palmer Street in 1875. The new facility allowed the yard to weather the economic depression of the 1870s with repair contracts when orders for new construction declined. Cramp's dry dock cost more than $160,000 and, despite a length of 462 feet, did not interrupt the street grid. The largest steamers frequenting Philadelphia could be towed to the dry dock. After a floating caisson closed the dock, four large steam pumps drained water at a rate of 120,000 gallons a minute, leaving the ship high and dry. For years to come, these works docked the P&RR colliers to conduct annual overhauls.[64]

Workshop of the World: Commerce, Crafts, and Class Conflict, 1875-1885

*I*n 1883 Philadelphia's berths and outfitting docks were crowded with new steamships. Cramp built two large iron vessels for the Hawaiian sugar trade and booked a contract with the Morgan steamship line for three cotton steamers. At Neafie & Levy, shipfitters completed several iron tugs and built engines for wooden hulls launched by Birely, Hillman, & Streaker. The newly established American Shipbuilding Company built a big freighter for the Baltimore-Charleston service at the Philadelphia & Reading Railroad shipyard. This small shipbuilding boom withered in less than two years as builders ran out of contracts and laid off more than 2,000 workers. The American Shipbuilding Company went bankrupt, and the remaining yards struggled along with a few contracts for tugs and yachts. Contrary to established practice, Cramp even built a yacht on its own account to keep a core work force employed, in the hope that a buyer could be found to take the vessel at a bargain price.[1]

Maritime historians have described the late nineteenth century as a "period of decline," a "dark age" of the American carrying trades and shipbuilding. Compared to the British shipbuilding industry, which flourished during the late nineteenth century, the American maritime economy was indeed chronically weak and suffered from technological backwardness. British carriers reigned supreme in foreign trade, while most of what was left of the U.S. merchant marine consisted of outdated wooden ships. The handful of American builders of iron ships, in the Delaware Valley and on the Great Lakes, were unable to match low British steamship prices. These factors, combined with recurring economic depressions after the financial panic of 1873 and the highly volatile demand for commercial tonnage, explain the perpetual instability of late nineteenth-century American shipbuilding. Yet in spite of the grim conditions, some Delaware Valley builders survived and still managed to build iron steamships, arguably the most complicated capital goods produced during the nineteenth century.[2]

Economic Depression and Proprietary Business Strategy

Iron shipbuilding reached its lowest point during the late 1870s. In 1877 Neafie & Levy did not launch a single vessel, while Cramp built only a small tug on its own account. Both yards kept busy with repair contracts and branched out into nonmarine production. Neafie & Levy constructed refrigerating equipment, and Cramp built steam pumps for the Philadelphia Water Works. The small Archambault and Baird & Huston yards abandoned shipbuilding in favor of manufacturing typesetting machinery and other nonmarine products. Pusey & Jones in Wilmington manufactured paper-making machinery and did not build iron ships until the late 1880s.[3]

The shipbuilding crisis reflected the general economic downturn following the panic of 1873, which marked the beginning of the longest depression in the history of American industrial capitalism. The collapse of the railroad bond market, which triggered the panic, soon affected builders of iron ships, who had received some of their most important postwar contracts from railroads (see chapter 3). Moreover, the Pennsylvania Railroad experienced considerable problems with its steamship subsidiary, which frequently called upon the parent company to honor its bond guarantee. In 1874 the board of directors of the American Steamship Company (ASC) explained the annual operating loss of more than $147,000 as follows: "The business of the past year, disastrous as it has been, has been particularly so in the transportation of freight and passengers between this country and Europe."[4] When the ASC proved unable to compete with British transatlantic lines, such as Inman and Cunard, the Pennsylvania Railroad forced the sale of its entire fleet to the International Navigation Company in 1884.[5]

Steamship lines in the coastwise trade suffered setbacks as a result of railroad competition. For example, the Philadelphia & New York Steam Navigation Company, a subsidiary of William Clyde & Son, fought a losing struggle against overland carriers and ceased operations in 1879. Likewise, the Philadelphia & Southern Mail Steamship Company, which sailed large steamers in the general freight and passenger trade between Philadelphia and New Orleans, succumbed to competition. Its board of directors reported as early as 1872 that "the constant extension of railroad facilities to the South and Southwest, and the active competition for freight overland have reduced freights below remunerative rates; and the Board learns that the result of the business of the New Orleans lines from our neighboring ports has not been more satisfactory than our own."[6] Philadelphia & Southern declared insolvency in 1880.[7]

With their prospects in commercial construction dashed, shipbuilders turned to government contracting. Charles Cramp wrote to the secretary of the navy, George Robeson: "Owing to the prevailing depression in business of all kinds, and the number of persons thrown out of employment in this city being *exceedingly* large, causing great privation among the mechanical and operative classes of this community, we think this a good opportunity for government assistance, by commencing work on the new sloops and making the necessary repairs to the other vessels."[8] The Navy Department responded to these calls within the limits imposed by meager naval appropriations. Between 1873 and 1885 Roach booked navy contracts worth almost $4 million; Harlan & Hollingsworth obtained contracts worth $940,000; Cramp, contracts worth $874,000; Neafie & Levy, contracts worth $35,000; and Dialogue's Camden yard, contracts worth $28,000. Although repair work dominated, the navy also issued contracts for four new monitors (disguised as overhauls) to Roach, Cramp, and Harlan & Hollingsworth. Neafie & Levy completed the gunboat USS *Quinnebaug* under contract at the Philadelphia Navy Yard. But as in times past, the navy proved an unreliable customer. Monitor construction ceased in 1877 as a result of insufficient appropriations, and the builders had to keep the unfinished hulls on the berths, where they occupied valuable construction space. The vessels were finally launched in deplorable condition during the early 1880s and remained unfinished for more than a decade.[9]

Naval downsizing also affected the Philadelphia Navy Yard. Several hundred skilled shipyard workers lost their relatively secure government jobs at the height of the depression, when the navy closed the old yard at Washington Street. It failed to develop the new facility at League Island, which remained for the next decade a desolate swamp dotted with a few buildings. As in Civil War years, plans to make League Island the nation's premier Navy Yard for iron and steel shipbuilding were sabotaged by private builders. The builders not only feared the loss of contracts but also the spread of lenient government labor policies into the private sector, because Navy Yard employees worked only an eight-hour day. The first major extensions were built during the 1890s when League Island received a large dry dock for capital ship overhauls, but the yard did not build a new ship until 1913.[10]

Russian cruiser Zabiaca *shortly before launching, 1878. Note the launching ways underneath the hull. This is one of the earliest photographs of a Cramp vessel under construction. Atwater Kent Cramp Collection, Independence Seaport Museum, through the Pew Museum Loan Program*

In spite of the funding limitations of the U.S. Navy, naval construction and conversion sustained the industry during the depression. In 1875 Birely, Hillman & Streaker launched the Haitian gunboats *St. Michel* and *1804*, whose engines and boilers were supplied by Neafie & Levy. In 1878 Cramp secured a larger contract from the Imperial Russian Navy, which was preparing for a war with Britain. In addition to converting three American merchant steamships for service in the Russian fleet, Cramp built the cruiser *Zabiaca* from scratch. Her construction involved many memorable events, which were eulogized in Kensington shipyard yarns. According to one anecdote, a British admiral sneaked into the shipyard, donning a workman's cap and faking an Irish brogue, to spy on the cruiser; he was promptly discovered by William Cramp himself and thrown out of the yard. The jingoistic press, which usually bemoaned the inferiority of America's shipbuilders compared to British builders, relished this tweaking of the lion's tail.[11]

The Russian contracts helped Cramp weather the depression. Charles Cramp called the cruisers "a little manna in the desert of protracted idleness," replenishing the yard's drained shipbuilding account with $1,285,000.[12] According to the press, the Russian contracts also proved "a blessing to the shipwrights and iron workers of Kensington, giving employment to every man who asked for it. Work was pressed ahead night and day on the ships until the war cloud drifted away."[13] The 1878 contracts inaugurated a close relationship between Cramp and the Russian Navy, which ordered a battleship and a cruiser in 1898.[14]

Cramp also helped generate demand for commercial steamers by investing $100,000 in the newly created Iron Steamboat Company (ISBC). This $1 million enterprise, controlled by New York investors, replaced unsafe wooden steamboats with iron steamers in the weekend excursion traffic between Manhattan and Coney Island. The ISBC ordered four large boats from Cramp and two similar vessels from John Roach. At the Palmer Street dry dock, Cramp also performed a good deal of repair work, which contributed to the yard's relatively strong financial performance. In 1881 Cramp expanded this line of business by leasing the Erie Basin Dry Docks in Brooklyn for large ship overhauls.[15]

Charles Cramp, elected president by his four brothers upon their father's death in 1879, initiated this lease and the ISBC investment. Having begun his tenure by steering the firm through the most difficult period in American shipbuilding, over the next quarter-century Charles engineered Cramp's rise to the first rank among the nation's shipyards.[16]

Characteristically, Cramp shared the financial risks of maritime entrepreneurship with other investors. The ISBC, for example, was a joint venture of bankers and shipbuilders to which Cramp contributed only 10 percent of the total investment. Unlike other builders, Charles Cramp steered clear of wholesale integration of shipping and shipbuilding. This was the strategy pursued by John Roach when he founded a steamship line to sail between New York and Brazil. As the sole financier, Roach invested more than $1 million and built three large iron steamships, which kept his Chester yard busy during the depression. The steamship line, however, proved a bottomless money pit. Since American exports to Brazil were insignificant, Roach had to stir interest among American merchants through commercial exhibitions, establish marketing networks in Rio de Janeiro, and personally lobby the Brazilian emperor for steamship subsidies. The venture exhausted Roach's financial resources and was abandoned at a loss of $1 million, which almost led to the collapse of Roach's maritime enterprise. Charles Cramp preferred limited risks, such as the ISBC investment or the leasing of the Erie Basin Dry Docks.[17]

Cramp also became part-owner in vessels built or repaired for Clyde, Philadelphia & Southern, and schooner operators. Although the available data are

TABLE 1
Core Trades of the Philadelphia Shipbuilding Industry, 1880

Trade	Number of firms	Average capital investment ($)	Average number of workers per firm	Average amount of annual wages per firm ($)	Average raw material input per firm ($)	Average output per firm ($)
Ship- and engine building	4	496,250	812	275,953	526,196	879,171
Mast and sparmaking	2	3,500	7.5	3,700	3,500	14,000
Rigging	2	5,000	19.5	8,300	700	10,000
Ship joining	2	3,500	48	8,250	20,000	26,300
Sail making	14	7,860	14.3	4,466	11,895	19,903
Ship smithing	5	27,400	30.2	9,600	14,500	29,800
Boat building	10	2,215	3.8	1,912	1,282	4,203

SOURCE: Manufacturing Census 1880.

not sufficiently detailed to permit definitive conclusions, one may surmise that Cramp took shares in lieu of cash to encourage shipowners to place orders with the yard. This strategy was pursued by several British builders, especially William Denny. Although Denny's investments in shipping were generally unprofitable, they enabled him to form long-term relationships with individual lines, which issued lucrative construction and repair contracts to his shipyard. A similar relationship may have evolved between Cramp and Clyde, who were joint owners of several iron steamships. Until 1907 the Clyde firm placed most of its orders with Cramp.[18]

In addition to repair work and steamboat contracts, Cramp weathered the depression with clever business strategies. As the firm's only shareholders and senior executives, the five Cramp brothers could have derived dividends and salaries from the shipyard. Instead, they transferred dividends into a separate account, which was used exclusively for yard improvements and emergencies. Meanwhile, each partner received a salary that represented his only source of income from the business. When hard times warranted a reduction of expenses, the brothers even slashed their salaries from $15,000 annually (1875) to $7,200 (1879). Such strategies were less common among corporate firms, in which ownership and management rested in different hands.[19]

Jacob Neafie lacked Charles Cramp's ambitions. Neafie had long been a rather conservative businessman who saw no reason to invest in joint ventures or expand into large-scale repair work in the course of the depression. Instead, he adhered to the established practice of taking orders for wooden steamships, building engines at the shipyard, and subcontracting large hulls to builders of wooden ships in Philadelphia, Camden, and Wilmington. This gave Neafie & Levy a secure foothold in the market for wooden tonnage, which remained the backbone of the American merchant marine until the end of the century. Its most important hull subcontractor was Birely, Hillman & Streaker, Philadelphia's only remaining builder of wooden ships. Neafie & Levy also awarded hull contracts to the Bart Hillman shipyard in Camden, operated by a son of Charles Hillman of Birely, Hillman & Streaker.[20]

In May 1880 the federal census took a snapshot of Philadelphia's manufacturing economy, which included a detailed statistical portrait of shipbuilding (table 1). The industry clustered around four yards with an aggregate capital investment of nearly $2 million. These were Cramp; Neafie & Levy; Birely, Hillman & Streaker; and the Simpson repair yard, which specialized in wooden ship overhauls. Small subcontracting firms included boat builders, makers of chain and anchors, and joiner shops, which operated in close proximity to the shipyards. This blend of yards for iron and wooden shipbuilding, repair facilities, and specialty suppliers made Philadelphia the nation's most diverse shipbuilding center of the day.[21]

Neafie & Levy, with $1 million in assets, was still the largest firm, followed by Cramp, which reported $750,000 (table 2). But Cramp produced an output of more than $2.3 million, compared with Neafie & Levy's $819,000. Since there was no significant variation in labor productivity between the two yards, the key factor was Cramp's more productive use of capital. Cramp generated $3.06 in sales for every dollar invested, compared to 82¢ at Neafie & Levy. Cramp's annual return on investment amounted to 15.2 percent in 1880, compared to Neafie & Levy's 7.1 percent. The most important factor explaining Cramp's better performance was its overhaul division with the large dry dock at Palmer Street, run separately from the main shipyard. A census bureau official commented that Cramp's repair division represented "a branch of work which is valued by all iron ship builders as being the most profitable."[22] The dry dock accommodated steamships of up to 450 feet in length and remained busy throughout the census year from June 1879 to May 1880, repairing at least forty-one large steamships. Neafie & Levy, by contrast, operated

TABLE 2
Philadelphia Shipbuilding Firms, 1880

Name of firm	Invested capital ($)	Number of workers	Annual wages ($)	Raw materials ($)	Annual output ($)
Neafie & Levy	1,000,000	500	242,401	505,000	819,000
William Cramp & Sons	750,000	2,300	695,000	1,512,029	2,321,649
A. S. Simpson & Bro.	150,000	300	100,000	20,000	200,000
Birely, Hillman & Streaker	85,000	150	66,412	67,756	176,038
Totals	1,985,000	3,250	1,103,813	2,104,785	3,516,687

SOURCE: Manufacturing Census 1880.

only a marine railway accommodating smaller vessels. During the census year it obtained only three larger repair contracts, which did not involve work below the waterline and hence could be performed at the wharf.[23]

Minor repair jobs were also taken by ship smitheries. The most capital-intensive businesses among smaller firms, smitheries reported an average investment of $27,400 and employed more than thirty workers on average. Their traditional role as shipyard subcontracting firms was somewhat diminished because builders now performed ironwork at their own facilities. A few larger works near the center city waterfront conducted minor overhauls for steamship lines. John Baizley's works near Market Street, for example, was capitalized at $80,000 and employed 110 men.[24]

Shipyards still subcontracted hull fittings and engine parts with a variety of specialty suppliers. These included two anchor and chain manufactories with average assets of $23,500 and thirty-one employees. The larger, Bradlee & Company's Empire Chain Works, the nation's best ship chain manufacturer, operated a metal-testing machine to determine tensile strength of its chains. A maritime journal credited Bradlee for having "about superseded all the chain cable manufacturers in the United States, especially for the large steamers and sailing vessels . . . There is no question but that Bradlee & Co. have won the business by fair competition, and by turning out the very best material and workmanship in the market."[25] Another well-known specialty firm was the Williamson Brothers steering and hoisting gearworks, which supplied many East Coast shipyards.[26]

Sailmaking's traditional dependence on labor-intensive production lessened with the introduction of heavy-duty sewing machines, reflected in increased capitalization from $3,000 (1850) to almost $8,000 (1880) per shop. The most active firm was owned and operated by Charles Lawrence, a former navy sailmaker who had started his first shop in 1865 with an investment of $3,000. During the next fifteen years, he increased his assets to $15,000 and supplied sails to Cramp as well as to local steamship lines. By 1880 Lawrence employed eighteen journeymen sailmakers and held shares in several locally owned schooners. He was also elected president of the Philadelphia Captains' and Vessel Owners' Association and served as a city councilman. Like other sailmakers, Lawrence branched out into tent and awning production, which allowed a smooth exit from shipyard subcontracting when steamship designers dispensed with sail rigging toward the end of the century.[27]

The census takers had barely completed their survey in May 1880 when an influx of new steamship orders signaled the end of the shipbuilding depression. Neafie & Levy booked contracts for freight boats and tugs as well as steamships, including the Clyde steamer *Delaware* for the southern cotton trade. As usual, Neafie & Levy built the engines and subcontracted the 275-foot hull to Birely, Hillman & Streaker. The firm also made engines for the wooden steamships *Maracaibo* and *Fortuano,* whose hulls were built across the river at the Bart Hillman yard in Camden. These vessels were ordered by the Red D Line for service between New York and Venezuela. Cramp received a contract for the Alexandre Line's passenger ship *City of Puebla,* designed for trade between New York and the Caribbean. These orders marked the beginning of a brief shipbuilding boom as the nation's economy recovered from the financial panic of 1873.[28]

International and Domestic Steamship Trade

Growing demand for iron steamships arose from broad changes in the American maritime economy. Steamship lines in the foreign trade acquired iron steamers to carry trade between the nation's industrial centers and agricultural regions in the Western Hemisphere and the Pacific. Interregional trade in raw materials and manufactured goods had been carried on throughout the nineteenth century, but economic development late in the century intensified these transactions through informal imperialism. This involved the establishment of "spheres of economic influence" in different world regions by industrialized nations, aimed at the exploitation of agricultural countries. Unlike colonialism, however, informal imperialism did not entail the formal acquisition of overseas territories. Instead, it involved private entrepreneurs who initiated limited economic development and labor exploitation in regions that were not yet part of the capitalist system. The result was often plantation economies controlled by European or American capital.[29]

The Hawaiian sugar trade, dominated by the San Francisco entrepreneur Claus Spreckels, was perhaps the best example of informal imperialism. Spreckels bought his first plantation in 1875 when the Hawaiian reciprocity treaty removed tariff barriers between the island kingdom and the United States. He subsequently amassed 40,000 acres of agricultural real estate in Hawaii, recruited several thousand Portuguese and Asian workers, and established vast sugar plantations. In 1880 Spreckels founded the Oceanic Steamship Company (OSC) to haul the Hawaiian sugar crop to his San Francisco refinery. He ordered several vessels from the Delaware Valley yards, most important the Cramp-built sister ships *Mariposa* and *Alameda.* In 1885 the OSC expanded the Central Pacific Line to Australia and began importing high-grade wool into the United States. To encourage this trade, the British colonial government awarded an annual steamship subsidy of $187,000 to the OSC. Several thousand miles east, Philadelphia shipbuilders participated in the making of informal imperialism by building its vital instruments.[30]

A similar pattern emerged in the Venezuela trade, where the Red D Line increased that country's coffee exports to the United States. The line was controlled by the Philadelphia merchant house Boulton, Bliss & Dallett (BB&D), which had entered the Venezuelan coffee trade in 1838. Venezuela's notoriously unstable investment climate improved during the late 1870s when Antonio Guzmán Blanco assumed the presidency and introduced a series of agricultural reforms benefiting coffee planters. The BB&D partners became Guzman's principal "economic advisors" and invested heavily in the Venezuelan railroad, steamboat, and plantation sectors. As a result of political changes and infrastructure improvements, Venezuela's export trade with the United States increased from $3 million in 1870 to $13 million in 1888. In 1880 the Red D Line ordered the wooden steamers *Maracaibo* and *Fortuano* from Neafie & Levy, followed by several Cramp-built iron steamships.[31]

The sugar, wool, and coffee trades generated the largest contracts for the Philadelphia shipbuilding industry during the late nineteenth century. Simultaneously, however, U.S. carriers operated under severe disadvantages. For one, American steamship operators paid 25–35 percent more for iron tonnage than their British rivals, a difference largely due to Britain's ten- to twenty-year lead in technology development, yard specialization, lower wages, and cheaper ship iron. Moreover, British shippers enjoyed operating cost advantages because large and diversified steamship lines profited from economies of scale. On the transpacific route, for example, where the OSC sailed two vessels between San Francisco, Honolulu, and Sydney, the Canadian Pacific Steamship Company operated fourteen steamers that served Canadian, American, and Australian ports in conjunction with railroad lines.[32]

The British merchant marine also included so-called tramps, general cargo vessels that sailed on all major trading routes carrying a wide variety of goods. A tramp might haul coffee from Venezuela to Liverpool, then carry British textile machinery to Japan, and leave Yokohama with cotton textiles bound for Canberra. This lucrative but highly competitive trade required inexpensive tonnage that was usually built by tramp specialists in the northeast of England. As a result of high prices for American tonnage, U.S. carriers never gained a foothold in this sector. Until World War I, American steamships were custom-built for specific trades. U.S. builders tried to rationalize this practice by arguing that they would never stoop so low as to build a cheap general-cargo ship because "it would hurt our reputation and we would hear no end of it," as Charles Cramp put it.[33] In reality, however, the lack of tramp steamer construction reflected the inability of American builders of iron and steel ships to supply inexpensive tonnage.[34]

In the protected coastwise trade, iron tramps could not compete with inexpensive wooden sailing ships. Major operators usually sailed custom-built liners serving specific trades on long-distance routes along the East Coast, the Gulf of Mexico, and California. Many lines were linked to railroads that branched out into less developed regions within the United States.[35]

The South had long been a hospitable environment for waterborne commerce because the cotton and sugar trades with the North and Britain required bulk carrying capacities. The cotton trade had declined during the 1860s and early 1870s as a result of wartime devastation and the refusal of many black freedmen to produce what they regarded as a slave crop. Similarly, Louisiana's sugar economy experienced a crisis after 1865 when output dropped to one-tenth of its prewar volume. But southern cotton and sugar production rose once again during Reconstruction in the context of black sharecropping, the commercialization of southern agriculture, and a crop lien system that forced many white upcountry farmers to plant cash crops. Railroads extended their networks into these agricultural regions and hauled crops to the larger ports for shipment north or overseas.[36]

The dominant figure in the southern transportation sector was Charles Morgan, a New York entrepreneur who had pioneered the steamship trade in the Gulf of Mexico during the 1840s. In the deep South, which lacked the extensive railroad system that undercut many northern steamship operators, Morgan established lines radiating from New Orleans to Texas, Alabama, Florida, and Mexico. After a five-year hiatus during the Civil War, he returned to the Gulf Coast trade with eleven iron ships built by Harlan & Hollingsworth. To supplement his waterborne service, Morgan acquired several railroad companies, most important the Houston & Texas Central, which served the cotton region between Houston and Dallas. Shortly before his death in 1878, he consolidated his holdings under the corporate umbrella of Morgan's Louisiana & Texas Railroad & Steamship Company. The company formed a direct steamship connection between New Orleans and New York with the Cramp-built cotton steamer *Chalmette*, Roach's *Louisiana* and *Willamette*, and Harlan & Hollingsworth's *Excelsior*. In 1880 Cramp also booked a Morgan Line contract to convert the side-wheeler *A. L. Hutchinson* into a screw-propelled steamship.[37]

Upon Charles Morgan's death, his managers acted as trustees for the heirs and assumed control of the Morgan Line. In 1883 they sold a large block of shares to the California railroad magnate Collis P. Huntington who integrated the line with his Southern Pacific Railroad Company. Huntington transferred the ships to the newly formed Southern Pacific Steamship Company (SPSSC).

This company also awarded Cramp contracts—for the *Eureka, El Paso,* and *El Dorado* for the cotton trade between New Orleans and New York. Huntington, who controlled several other steamship lines as well, established the Chesapeake Dry Dock Company at Newport News, Virginia, in 1886 as a repair facility for his growing fleet. Unlike the P&RR yard at Port Richmond, this enterprise proved a success. Huntington soon commenced new construction at the yard, which was renamed Newport News Shipbuilding and Dry Dock Company in 1890. Huntington's success epitomized the formation of a New South that sought to detach itself from the domineering influence of northeastern industrial capital. Heretofore, Huntington's steamship conglomerate had ordered tonnage from Delaware Valley builders; after 1890, however, Newport News Shipbuilding not only built steamships for the SPSSC but also competed with Cramp and Harlan & Hollingsworth for commercial and naval contracts.[38]

Unlike the Morgan Line and its successor, some domestic steamship lines remained under the control of proprietary entrepreneurs. Proprietor William P. Clyde, who had moved company headquarters from Philadelphia to New York in 1873, operated ten steamship lines serving the passenger and cargo trade between twenty-one port cities along the East Coast, in partnership with his son Thomas. In 1872 Clyde opened a New York–Charleston line that later became the company's center of activity. In an attempt to avoid the ruinous railroad competition that had crippled his Philadelphia–New York line in 1879, he signed a freight agreement with the South Carolina Railroad Company. The Clyde Line soon emerged as the leading waterborne carrier between the Northeast and the upper South. The firm ordered the Cramp-built iron steamers *Georgia, Seminole, Cherokee,* and *Iroquois* in the 1880s and returned with many follow-up orders during the next two decades. Clyde's wooden steamers *Goldsboro* and *Delaware* were built by Birely, Hillman & Streaker and had engines provided by Neafie & Levy.[39]

Like Clyde, the coastwise steamship lines of the 1880s adjusted to railroad competition. Railroads dominated the passenger market, but transportation of bulk cargo still held opportunities for steamship operators who offered competitive freight rates. Several northeastern coastal carriers left passenger transportation to the railroads and became bulk cargo specialists. The Metropolitan Steamship Company, for example, connected New York and Boston by freighters without passenger accommodations. Founded after the Civil War, the company sailed wooden steamers and switched to iron cargo ships during the 1880s. Metropolitan issued contracts to Cramp for the *H. F. Dimock,* the *Herman Winter,* and the *Henry M. Whitney.*[40]

Other coastwise routes were served by the Merchants' & Miners' Transportation Company, whose lines radiated from its Baltimore hub. The Merchants' & Miners' Line started in the Baltimore-Boston freight trade in 1854. During the 1870s it added service between Baltimore and Savannah, and between Baltimore and Providence. In 1883 it also established a Baltimore-Charleston freight line. Merchants' & Miners' ordered the iron steamers *Alleghany, Berkshire, Chatham,* and *Essex* from Philadelphia builders during the 1880s and returned with additional contracts during the next two decades.[41]

These saltwater carriers were supplemented by bay and river steamers that sometimes operated in conjunction with steamship lines. In the upper South, for example, Clyde controlled a steamboat line connecting Richmond and Norfolk, which sailed the side-wheeler *City of Richmond* built by Birely, Hillman & Streaker. Railroads also operated steamboats to supplement overland transportation networks. The Camden & Atlantic Railroad Company contracted with Neafie & Levy for the iron ferryboat *Atlantic,* which carried passengers from Philadelphia across the Delaware River to the railroad's Camden terminal for transfer to the New Jersey line.[42]

Increasing foreign and domestic steamship traffic generated demand for service vessels: tugs, barges, and pilot boats. Independent entrepreneurs in all major ports operated tugs to perform towing services and salvage operations for steamship companies. Many tugboat specialists also operated two or three barges to transport coal and bulk cargo between wharves. In the late nineteenth century some of them branched out into the coastwise trade. Philadelphia's Lewis Luckenbach Towboat Company, a pioneer in this sector, introduced the tandem system (one tugboat towing a long string of barges). Rival towboat operators and marine insurance companies initially opposed this practice, citing safety hazards, but Luckenbach proved that his system was technically feasible and economically viable. Since tandem towing required larger and more powerful tugs, Luckenbach ordered such vessels as the *Ocean King* of more than 200 tons, which was built by Neafie & Levy in 1884. Luckenbach deployed tugs and barges in the coastwise trade where he eroded the position of collier operators. Unlike colliers, barges were not equipped with expensive propulsion systems and did not require engineers and stokers, resulting in low operating costs. By the turn of the century, when the Philadelphia & Reading Railroad was unable to match Luckenbach's low freight rates, it adopted the barge tandem system for its own operations.[43]

Anatomy of a Shipbuilding Boom

Demand for new steamships reached its climax in 1880–84. The Philadelphia builders closed several important contracts in summer 1880, and in 1881 they launched twelve iron steamers of 11,742 aggregate gross tons. In 1884 they completed eighteen iron steamships aggregating 20,753 tons, almost half the nation's annual output in commercial iron tonnage. A growing number of iron vessels were also built by midwestern yards, which launched large iron ore carriers for the Great Lakes trade.[44]

At first Philadelphia builders were reluctant to improve their facilities in response to the boom. They probably feared that the market would collapse after a few months, as it had done several times during the late 1870s. In spring and summer 1881, for example, Cramp received contracts for three West Coast steamers as well as the Red D Line steamship *Valencia,* yet it erected only a few temporary workshops.[45]

Meanwhile, builders supported local infrastructure improvements, notably the Riverfront Railroad, a branch line of the Philadelphia & Reading Railroad. The new track enhanced material handling along the waterfront and received enthusiastic support throughout the business community. Since it improved the transportation of ship iron from the mills to the shipyards, Jacob Neafie was "strongly favorable to the construction of the road" and the Cramps "[said] that they cannot do without it."[46] Like previous railroad projects, however, the Riverfront Railroad encountered opposition from residents of the Kensington waterfront who did not want to see their neighborhoods intruded upon by a dangerous and noisy railroad. A protest movement rallied around the assistant pastor of St. Ann's Roman Catholic Church on Lehigh Avenue, who declared that the track "will work almost irreparable injury to the interests of the parish. . . . The parochial school of the church contains upwards of a thousand pupils, nearly all of whom will have to cross the tracks going to and returning from school, at the danger of their lives."[47] But this movement, unlike the neighborhood protest against the Philadelphia & Reading Railroad's dry dock in 1875, did not receive support from the business community—because entrepreneurs expected to profit from better transportation facilities. When the protesters filed a suit against the railroad, the judge dismissed their objections, and the project went ahead as scheduled. By 1883 the shipyards received their marine iron and timber via the railroad.[48]

Other infrastructure improvements helped builders cope with the increased demand for steamships during the early 1880s. A harbor improvement program, partially funded by the federal government, deepened the Delaware River to accommodate larger iron steamships. It received support from the Captains' and Vessel Owners' Association and its president Charles Lawrence, the sail manufacturer and maritime entrepreneur. Additional backing came from Charles Cramp in his capacity as a member of the influential Board of Port Wardens.[49]

Cramp during the 1880s. Note the new joiner shop (marked 13) at top left corner and the empty building berths in foreground. Hexamer General Survey, Free Library of Philadelphia

In 1882 Cramp launched facility improvements to handle the growing number of contracts. The Norris Street yard, which had changed little since the construction of the transatlantic steamers and the colliers in the early 1870s, now received new workshops and better tools. Cramp also enlarged the machine shop, built a new shop for boiler and blacksmith work, and erected facilities for joiner and light iron work. To upgrade its capacity to haul heavy plates, frames, and construction tools, Cramp installed railroad tracks inside the yard with a connection to the Riverfront Railroad. As a result, Cramp now had "the facilities for turning out six of the largest steamers built for our flag annually."[50]

In 1884 the yard operated at full capacity and completed three large cotton steamers for the Morgan steamship line, the 2,600-gross-ton passenger vessel *H. F. Dimock* for the Metropolitan Steamship Company, the freighter *San Pablo* of 3,000 gross tons for the Pacific trade, and the oceangoing tug *Relief* for Claus Spreckels's sugar trade. These contracts amounted to six vessels of more than 16,000 aggregate gross tons, the yard's largest annual construction volume between 1873 and 1890.[51]

Neafie & Levy responded more cautiously to increasing demand for new steamships. The only major improvements added a new wharf and better outfitting equipment. The firm maintained its traditional policy of building smaller iron steamships while subcontracting large steamship hulls with other builders. In 1882, for example, Neafie & Levy constructed five small iron vessels and built engines for fifteen wooden steamers.[52]

The local press reported in 1881 that "the demand for ships is at present so great that the builders cannot supply it promptly, and . . . parties desiring to contract for the building of vessels are compelled to wait many months before their orders can be filled."[53] These improving fortunes lured newcomers like

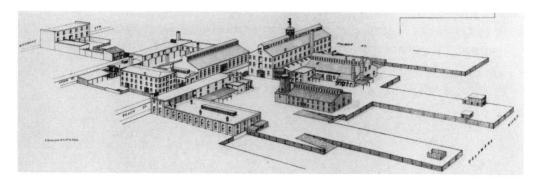

Neafie & Levy during the 1880s. Riffled slopes in foreground indicate location of marine railway. Hexamer General Survey, Free Library of Philadelphia

the American Shipbuilding Company (ASBC), bankrolled by several New York financiers who invested an aggregate $250,000, and managed by Henry Gorringe, a former navy officer. The ASBC leased the idle Philadelphia & Reading Railroad shipyard, procured new shop equipment, and installed electrical lighting. Gorringe claimed that "any establishment that can supply the demand at relatively [low] prices will unquestionably secure all the business that it can undertake, and I propose to start just such an establishment in the Reading yards."[54]

The ASBC plugged into the region's iron shipbuilding network. Gorringe hired experienced foremen who had honed their skills at Roach in Chester, employed 700 craftsmen, and issued subcontracts to local specialty firms, notably to Neafie & Levy, for engines and boilers. The largest ship built in cooperation between the ASBC and Neafie & Levy was the 2,728-gross-ton steamer *Chatham* for the Merchants' & Miners' Line and the collier *Frostburg*. These and other vessel projects employed thousands of skilled shipyard workers.[55]

Shipbuilding at the Point of Production

The transition from wooden to iron construction generally magnified the role of skilled shipyard labor. Ship carpenters no longer worked in hull construction but instead performed important tasks in the mold loft and on the berths. Coppersmiths who had sheathed timber hulls shifted to better paid jobs in pipemaking and pipefitting. New skilled trades included shipfitting, engine building, boilermaking, anglesmithing, and plating. Although riveting, chipping, and caulking were considered less reputable, even these trades required considerable training and several years of helper experience before a worker was ranked as a first-class man.[56]

Shipyard workers received training in a variety of settings. The classic artisanal apprenticeship, in which a boy was introduced to the secrets of the trade by his master, had almost vanished, but several large Philadelphia firms established a new type of industrial apprenticeship system in this period. At Cramp, apprentices in highly skilled trades, such as patternmaking and engine building, were trained for four years by foremen and senior workers. Young journeymen machinists, shipfitters, and ship carpenters were categorized as third-class mechanics. They moved into first-class rank by gathering practical experience at the workplace and sometimes by attending evening classes in arithmetic and geometry at Philadelphia Central High School. In riveting, a teenager first performed ancillary tasks as a rivet boy, then worked as a helper for a few years, and then became a riveter or holder-on.[57]

In the white-collar trades, iron shipbuilding employed naval architects who were responsible for hull design. This occupation dated from the first half of the nineteenth century when builders of wooden ships replaced traditional rules of thumb with more systematic design. Iron shipbuilding precipitated the introduction of precision designs because it involved inflexible construction material. An inaccurately hewn plank could be corrected on the building berth with simple tools like adzes and saws. A warped hull plate, however, had to be hauled back to the blacksmith shop to be rebent with heavy shop equipment. To avoid such problems, builders of iron ships hired professional naval architects who made precision drawings for all basic hull components. When demand for naval architects increased during the shipbuilding boom of the early 1880s, Philadelphia builders hired men trained in American wooden shipbuilding or in Scottish iron shipbuilding.[58]

Marine engineering, another white-collar trade, involved design of main engines, boilers, and auxiliary machinery. The primary task was compound engine design for ships of various sizes. Compound engines had been introduced into American shipbuilding by Cramp and were adopted by most builders during the 1880s. As a result of pioneering work done by Samuel Merrick and John Towne during the antebellum years, Philadelphia had become a leading center of steam engineering. Although general engine builders were no longer involved in shipbuilding, they trained engineers and machinists who were later hired by Delaware Valley shipyards. Marine engineers usually designed so-called Babcock & Wilcox boilers, which had been patented by the New York engineers George Babcock and Stephen Wilcox in 1856. Like naval architects, marine engineers devised precision drawings showing every screw and pin.[59]

Naval architects and marine engineers discussed design problems in technical journals and professional meetings. Cramp's superintending engineer

Horace See, for example, delivered a presentation on the *Mariposa* and the *Alameda* at the March 1883 meeting of the Philadelphia Engineers' Club. The club was a prominent local chapter of the American Society of Mechanical Engineers; at its meetings naval architects, steam engine designers, and inventors discussed technical problems as well as the latest developments in British engineering.[60]

Marine engineers complained that their employers often remained wary of such theoretical discussions and depended too much on traditional handicraft skills. Horace See argued that craftsmen with their rules of thumb constantly interfered with the efforts of the marine engineers to elevate shipbuilding into a modern science. The widespread use of the builder's half-model, for example, which was usually made by a ship carpenter, contradicted the engineers' standards of modern design techniques. The half-model "is called the free hand or mold loft style, in contradistinction to the Draughting Room Tables or 'Mathematical' style."[61] This artisanal method was particularly troublesome because it produced inferior ships, See argued. "Many of the vessels were fearful specimens of naval architecture. It was not due to [the engineer] or his workmanship but to the model, which in many cases was obtained from the ship carpenter, following the uncertain method of whittling and sand papering said model into such shape as pleased the eye, who did not work out the lines on the drawing board."[62]

Employers favored craft labor because they themselves had usually been brought up as skilled artisans, not as scientifically trained engineers. Jacob Neafie had served his stint as a boilermaker apprentice in the 1830s, and Charles Cramp had worked as a journeyman ship carpenter during the 1840s. Even in later decades, these men remained proud of their artisanal skills and discussed vessel plans and construction problems with their craftsmen. They knew that, contrary to the claims of naval architects and marine engineers, many craft skills could not be cast into mathematical formulas. "Shipbuilding is not an exact science," a British observer remarked.[63] Indeed, it was an amalgam of industrial craftsmanship and engineering.[64]

Hull design started after the owner and the builder had agreed on a ship's measurements during the contract negotiations. First, the naval architect sketched plans showing the lengthwise shape of the vessel and a cross-section of the hull. A ship carpenter copied these plans in a wooden half-model to establish the hull's three-dimensional contours. At Cramp, he forwarded the model to the president himself who, according to one account, "hacks into it with fervor. He tapers the bow. He digs away the stern. He shaves the whole model with the nice and dainty touches of a sculptor at work upon a statue . . . The fate of the wooden block alters the figures of the engineer's plans."[65] The revised hull drawings went to the mold loft, where a senior loftsman and his team of patternmakers or ship carpenters copied them in full size on the floor. According to a visitor who observed this practice at Cramp's mold loft, the floor "is a maze of chalk marks, unintelligible to one not brought up to the trade, but each plainly speaking to the experienced craftsman."[66] The patternmakers laid pine sticks over the large drawings and tacked them together to form the patterns showing the shape of each frame.[67]

The builder sent one set of patterns to the rolling mills, which cut angle iron into rough shapes. When the latter arrived at the yard, blacksmiths and anglesmiths placed the pattern on a perforated iron floor in the blacksmith shop and traced its lines with chalk.

The figure having been traced, the men take iron rods resembling huge nails and drop them into the holes nearest to the trace. [A piece of angle iron is heated to red glow] . . . and the men draw near with tongs and hammers . . . [The angle iron] is pushed up against the curving row of blocks sunk in the holes, and one end is fastened with a pin dropped into a hole. Then with their tools the men push and drive the [angle iron] against the blocks. The rosy glow of the hot iron fades away, and the [iron rod] stiffens into its new shape. It is now a rib or frame of the vessel.[68]

To indicate its position in the hull and the exact location of rivet holes, shipfitters marked each frame with white paint. It was then perforated by punchers who pushed the frame through a punching machine. The machine had "enormous jaws and a single canine tooth, bit[ing] a hole through the iron; then another bite, and then another, till the [frame] is punched full of holes."[69] Like many shipbuilding trades, punching was accident-prone because heavy frames sometimes slipped from the machine and crushed workers' legs and feet.[70]

While frames and keel pieces were prepared inside on the shop floor, ship carpenters prepared the building berth for hull assembly, lined up blocks that held the keel, and built wooden platforms for later construction phases. Together with shipfitters, ship carpenters often worked in the erecting gang, which placed the keel on the blocks and raised frames. The "ribcage" was fastened by riveters who placed temporary bolts into the rivet holes. As the skeleton assumed its preliminary shape, alignment was checked and corrected by ship carpenters.[71]

When the framework was even, shipfitters climbed up the stagings and traced lines to make patterns for hull plates. Patternmakers copied these tracings onto wooden templates that were used by platesmiths to hammer and bend flat iron plates into the required shapes. They were installed by riveters who forced plates and frames together by tightening bolt nuts; reamers corrected minor misalignments. This was necessary because "after erecting and

Tracing frame patterns on a perforated iron floor in the blacksmith shop. Like other jobs related to patternmaking, this one required precision skills. Harper's New Monthly Magazine 56 (1878)

bolting, many rivet holes fail to appear perfectly clear due to the fact that the plates have not been punched accurately, or because the two plates do not fit exactly together. Besides enlarging these holes, the reamer tapers, trues up, enlarges and countersinks holes wherever necessary."[72]

This set the stage for the riveting gang. A blacksmith heated the rivet to red glow in a small furnace. A rivet boy picked it up and handed the glowing piece of metal to a helper using a pair of pliers; when the gang worked several feet from the furnace, the boy tossed it into an iron basket held by the helper. Riveting then proceeded as follows: "The riveting gang proper consists of two riveters and a holder-on, that is, the rivet is put in the hole, held in its place at

Bending frames on the basis of pattern drawings. Note the flange at bottom; in later years, it was replaced with hydraulic equipment. Harper's New Monthly Magazine 56 (1878)

Punching a hull frame, one of the less-skilled shipyard jobs performed by workgangs. Harper's New Monthly Magazine 56 (1878)

Keel laying on the berth. Note the ship carpenter (second from left) hewing the timber that holds the keel with an adze, an important holdover from the era of wooden shipbuilding. The workers at right lift a keel plate from the cart. Near the top, a rigger operates the derrick to lift keel plates to their location on the building blocks. At the turn of the century, electrically driven overhead cranes replaced many laborers and beasts of burden, but ship carpenters continued to play an important role in keel laying and hull construction. Harper's New Monthly Magazine 56 (1878)

the back [by the holder-on], and driven by riveters, of whom generally one is right and the other left-handed."[73] This operation was repeated tens of thousands of times and produced the distinct noise of iron shipbuilding, frequently described as "the din of driving rivets" that filled the air in a busy shipyard district. Uneven rivet heads were chiseled by the chipper, who also "trues up all

Bending a stern plate. Featuring multiple curvatures, stern plates were among the most demanding pieces processed in the hull department. Harper's New Monthly Magazine 56 (1878)

irregular plates, cuts off plate edges that are too long . . . and cuts out loose rivets."[74] Finally, caulkers closed the spaces between plates to make the hull watertight.[75]

Once the hull work was complete, ship carpenters launched the vessel—one of the most demanding shipyard jobs. They first placed launching ways underneath the keel and slowly shifted the heavy hull from the building blocks onto the ways, which formed a descending slope toward the river. While the hull was held in place by temporary shores, the ship carpenters greased the launching ways with tallow; the tilt of the ways and the amount of tallow both determined the speed of the hull when it entered the water. The launching speed was a crucial variable because it placed enormous strains on the frame. If the hull slid too fast, it could break apart under its own weight; if the launching ways were insufficiently tilted and greased, the hull would not move at all. During the 1880s the entire operation depended on highly experienced ship carpenters because engineers were unable to calculate the correct relationship between the launching tilt and the amount of tallow. Finally, the ship carpenters knocked away the temporary shores, and the hull slid down the ways.[76]

After launching, the ship was docked at the outfitting wharf to receive its engines and boilers. Making cast iron for engine blocks required close coordination between shipyards and ironworks. Once the marine engineer had completed the drawings, patternmakers built full-size wooden models for every cast-iron engine part. The yard shipped the patterns to a foundry. There, molders packed damp sand around each model to form a hollow pattern and poured molten metal into the sand. When the castings arrived at the shipyard, machinists shaved off irregular surfaces and precision-drilled large cylinder holes. Using lathes, planers, and drills, they also processed hundreds of other metal components and assembled the engine inside the shop. Once they had tested and adjusted the complicated mechanism, machinists disassembled the engine, yard laborers hauled the parts to the outfitting pier, and machinists installed them aboard.[77]

Engines received steam from marine boilers, large drums made by skilled boilermakers. Using detailed blueprints, a boilermaker and his helpers first bent a large sheet of rolled iron into cylindrical shape with flanges. They also made several smaller drums and drilled holes for steam and water tubes, installed them inside the boiler shell, and riveted joints steam-tight. Yard laborers hauled the drums to the outfitting berth, riggers lowered them into the hull using large wooden derricks, and machinists connected boilers and engines.[78]

Other craftsmen worked on hundreds of specialty parts manufactured at the shipyard or by subcontractors. Coppersmiths made engine fittings and copper pipes; pipefitters bent iron pipes and installed steering gear and windlasses; blacksmiths hammered out the intricate contours of the iron screw propeller and made fittings; joiners were responsible for interior woodwork, including furniture and panels; shipfitters installed metal parts, including bulkheads, doors, and porthole fittings. At the end of the outfitting phase, the builder informed the owner that his ship was ready for its performance trial.[79]

During the trial trip, every vessel revealed its own peculiarities, which were the result of variations in design and construction. A ship rarely turned out exactly as the naval architects and marine engineers had planned. Differences were particularly obvious in sister ships that were built on the basis of one set of construction drawings and frame patterns. "One will turn out to be a knot or two faster than the other," a shipbuilder remarked, "and neither the designer nor the builder is able to say why."[80] Such variations underscored the fact that iron shipbuilding was not an exact science in which the quality of the end product was predetermined in the design process. It remained a combination of engineering skills and craftsmanship, which together shaped the character of the ship.[81]

Shipyards and Class Formation

Although iron shipbuilding was a collaborative endeavor, the men involved in it formed sharply divided social groups that were part of an evolving urban class society. The most obvious rift existed between capital and labor. Builders and larger subcontractors belonged to the business class, while most of their employees were members of the working class. Moreover, workers were divided by skill, position in the labor market, and craft unions that organized members by trade. These factors shaped capital-labor relations as well as industrial conflicts that flared up during the early 1880s.

Economically, class distinctions are defined by the control of the means of production. For example, it made little difference that the Cramp brothers were, technically speaking, salaried managers; as stockholders, they owned the firm's shops, machinery, and real estate. They owned the firm to a much larger extent than their father had during the 1850s, for he had employed ship carpenters who owned their own sets of woodworking tools. By the late nineteenth century shipyard workers rarely owned the tools they worked with and usually depended on heavy production equipment furnished by their employers. There were some important exceptions like sailmaking, where workers still owned their needles and mallets, but even there employers increased their control of the means of production with the introduction of heavy sewing machines. Shipbuilding by the 1880s facilitated class formation at the economic level.[82]

Social class formation may be measured by the extent to which employers and employees worked in distinct settings; among workers, social cohesion increased as they shared the same labor market. The Cramp brothers, Jacob Neafie, Charles Hillman, and larger subcontractors usually worked in offices negotiating contracts, balancing account books, and writing technical specifications. In a shipyard, these functions also involved a small staff of clerks, naval architects, and marine engineers, who formed the nucleus of a genuine managerial class. Workers, by contrast, were confined to the shop environment and usually operated heavy machinery under the supervision of foremen. But blue-collar work did not necessarily enhance social cohesion due to a marked increase in occupational diversity compared to the era of wooden ships. During the 1850s the work force had consisted mostly of woodworkers, principally ship carpenters, joiners, and mast makers, supplemented by blacksmiths and sailmakers. Iron shipbuilding added a wide variety of new metal trades, including riveting, shipfitting, and reaming. The integration of engine building and boilermaking brought machinists and boilermakers into shipyards, and subsequent changes in marine technology added electricians and specialists for hydraulic equipment. These craftsmen did not share common labor-market experiences. Differences became especially visible when Philadelphia shipyards laid off workers during a recession. Boilermakers and machinists usually looked for alternative employment in engineering trades, which formed their trade-specific labor market; sailmakers switched into tentmaking, which was part of the local textile industry; ship carpenters traveled up and down the Delaware River or even into the Great Lakes region to find work in other shipyards. Occupational diversity in iron shipbuilding existed to a degree unheard-of in most other industries, such as iron- and steelmaking, and perhaps paralleled only in locomotive building. This diversity impeded social class formation.[83]

Culturally, class formation can be traced in transindividual dispositions and collective organizations, which usually were responses to economic and social conditions. Again, there were pronounced divisions separating employers from workers. Shipbuilders and subcontractors developed collective responses to changes affecting their businesses, as highlighted by their active and undivided support for the Riverfront Railroad during the early 1880s. They also served as members of business organizations, such as the Board of Port Wardens, the Board of Trade, and the Philadelphia Maritime Exchange, to influence commercial and navigation policies. Interestingly, builders did not organize as employers at the local, regional, or national level, as their British counterparts did by forming the Federation of Shipbuilders and Engineers. The federation was formed in 1889 by British shipbuilders to deal with powerful shipyard unions, which did not exist in the United States.[84]

Workers, too, developed shared attitudes and collective organizations. A major concern was the lack of stable employment. Shipbuilding was plagued not only by depressions but also by seasonal unemployment, a frequent topic of discussion at trade union meetings. The most important shipyard labor organizations were the Ship Carpenters and Caulkers Union, with sections in Philadelphia and Camden, and Local No. 19 of the International Brotherhood of Boilermakers and Iron Shipbuilders. Like most labor organizations in the skilled trades, these unions organized workers strictly along trade lines. Structurally, they resembled British shipyard trade organizations, chiefly the United Society of Boilermakers and the Amalgamated Society of Engineers, which admitted skilled workers and excluded less prestigious trades, such as riveting. But while British craft unions could organize thousands of tradesmen in dozens of iron shipyards, their American counterparts operated in a relatively small industry. The prevailing culture of craft unionism was not very well adapted to this industrial environment because it split a limited number of shipyard workers into fragmented organizations.[85]

The consequences became visible in the open conflicts that erupted between capital and labor. As a rule, late nineteenth-century craftsmen launched trade-specific strikes and never attempted to forge industrial movements involving all workers in the shipbuilding trades. In some instances, this reflected the industry's separation into core firms and subcontractors. For example, there was no need to draw shipyard boilermakers into wage conflicts between the journeymen sailmakers and their employers. In other trades, particularly ship carpentry, craftsmen depended on interfirm networks and launched trade-specific strikes at all local shipyards. In 1883, for example, more than 500 unionized ship carpenters walked out in Philadelphia and Camden to gain a wage increase. Significantly, however, the strike failed to close down the iron shipyards because metal tradesmen were not invited and did not attempt to join the walkout. Along with builders of wooden ships, Cramp and Neafie & Levy imported strikebreakers from New England and declared an end to the prevailing closed-shop system in ship carpentry. David Streaker, who served as a spokesman for local builders, declared that "the yards were open to the men to resume work at any time, but they must come prepared to submit to employers' terms. These terms are: The privilege of employing and discharging whom they see fit, whether members of the union or not, and to pay the men what wages they, the employers, consider they were worth."[86] After seven weeks of bitter conflict, the ship carpenters admitted defeat and returned to work under the new rules. Like the new trades in iron shipbuilding, which were only beginning to unionize during this period, ship carpentry became part of an open-shop system that prevailed until World War I.[87]

Builders convinced themselves that shipyard unions were superfluous because workers' interests were taken care of by their paternalist employers who guaranteed high wages and steady employment. Like many other capitalists of that era, shipbuilders argued that wages were threatened not by cost-conscious employers but by free trade. The best safeguard against wage cuts was not unionization but protectionism. Casting his protectionist philosophy in paternalistic terms, Charles Cramp told members of Congress that "I want to be emphatic on the statement that I do not believe in cheapening American labor" by importing foreign-made shipbuilding material.[88]

Paternalism went beyond wage issues and involved special privileges for long-term employees. Apprenticeships formed an important instrument to reward skilled workers. "In our yard we allow every man to put his sons in as apprentices in preference to anybody else from outside. If a workingman is a machinist and wants his son to learn pattern-making, that boy has preference over all others," Cramp related.[89]

Paternalist rhetoric and practice were part of the "Philadelphia system" of fraternal capital-labor relations, which emphasized fair wages, steady employment, and quality work. In the local textile industry, where paternalism was much more pronounced than in shipbuilding, employers often stressed that they shared their employees' background in the skilled crafts and welcomed them into the ranks of small entrepreneurs. Unlike corporate paternalism in company towns, such as Lowell, Massachusetts, the Philadelphia system did not include company-owned housing. Indeed, local employers often touted the city's image as a "city of homes" and the "paradise of the skilled craftsman," where the model tradesman retained a certain degree of personal independence and could buy his own home.[90]

While paternalism undoubtedly shaped capital-labor relations as well as patterns of working-class formation in Philadelphia, shipbuilding lacked one critical ingredient that made paternalism more than mere rhetoric in textiles and other trades: stable jobs. As a result of volatile business cycles in the maritime economy, builders were unable to provide long-term employment for the majority of shipyard workers. When business improved, Cramp increased its work force from fewer than 600 to 1,500 men within months. It fired men at an equally astounding rate at the end of a business cycle. In 1884 Cramp cut its work force from 1,800 to 800 men, while Neafie & Levy cut its payroll from 300 to 50. The ability to expand and contract without having to worry about long-term labor supply was one of the great advantages enjoyed by Philadelphia shipbuilders, who operated in one of the nation's largest centers of skilled labor. At the same time, however, this practice undermined paternalist rhetoric and practice, which hinged on secure jobs and long-term employment.[91]

To be sure, there was a minority of shipyard workers who spent decades with a single employer. One such worker was Benjamin Schaubel, who worked in Neafie & Levy's boiler shop from 1851 to 1901, presumably "without the loss of a single day."[92] In the course of their careers, men like Schaubel came to know a yard and its routines like the palms of their hands, and they were usually prime candidates for better paid positions. John Keen, for example, commenced his apprenticeship in ship carpentry at Cramp shortly after the Civil War, worked as a full mechanic and quarterman (petty foreman responsible for twenty-five workers) for more than twenty years, and became Cramp's foreman ship carpenter during the early 1890s. Machinist Harry Mull was another Cramp apprentice who spent several years as a marine engineer at sea and later served as Cramp's assistant manager. Such stable career patterns, however, were exceptional among shipyard workers, most of whom spent their lives moving from yard to yard and many of whom left shipbuilding to work in less volatile trades.[93]

In this context, the weak status of shipyard labor organizations and the open-shop system were especially problematic. Traditionally, craft unions had served as information agencies for traveling tradesmen looking for work. During the closed-shop era before 1883, the local Ship Carpenters' Union even had a formal arrangement with builders in which the union recruited craft workers who, after a trial period of four weeks, were approved or rejected by the employer. This system disappeared with the demise of the closed shop, leaving shipyard workers without independent job information networks in an era of unstable employment. Although metal-trades unions published job listings in trade journals at the end of the century, this was of little use because Philadelphia builders blacklisted union members. Simultaneously, employers—their rhetoric about fair compensation notwithstanding—made Philadelphia notorious for its low shipyard wages.[94]

As Charles Cramp had pointed out during the panic of 1873, one remedy for the chronic instability of the shipbuilding industry was naval contracting. Although the phrase was not used in these pre-Keynesian times, nineteenth-century builders saw warship construction as a form of countercyclical government intervention to sustain shipyards during commercial depressions. This was one of the few areas where employers agreed with labor activists, who favored naval shipbuilding because it created jobs for their clientele during hard times. Toward the end of the nineteenth century, their demands for warship contracts were echoed by naval officials and foreign-policy makers who called for the construction of an American steel navy.

A Vicious Quality: Cramp and the Origins of the Military-Industrial Complex, 1885-1898

*A*t the height of the Spanish-American War, the U.S. Navy blockaded the Cuban port of Santiago, where it trapped several enemy warships. On the morning of July 3, 1898, a lookout aboard the battleship USS *Iowa* spotted the Spanish fleet under steam as it prepared to break the American blockade and escape to the open sea. The U.S. fleet closed in on the enemy and opened fire. When the smoke cleared a few hours later, hundreds of sailors were dead or wounded, and the Spanish fleet was in shambles. With that battle the U.S. Navy emerged as the principal naval force of the Western Hemisphere. The battle also showed the significance of Philadelphia-built warships: Of the five capital ships that defeated the Spaniards at Santiago de Cuba, three had been built by Cramp.[1]

This demonstration of American naval power reflected a decade of preparation in the course of which the navy had initiated a far-reaching fleet modernization program. The construction of what became known as the new navy involved the creation of an industrial base of shipyards and naval armor works as well as ordnance suppliers concentrated in Pennsylvania. Along with the Carnegie steel plant at Pittsburgh, the Bethlehem Iron works in South Bethlehem, the Midvale Steel ordnance factory at Nicetown, the Roach shipyard at Chester, and the Philadelphia Navy Yard with its new dry dock for capital ship overhauls, Cramp was part of "Fortress Pennsylvania," birthplace of the American steel navy.[2]

The Philadelphia builders and the U.S. Navy became so closely allied that, in Charles Cramp's words, the yard became a quasi-public enterprise: "The shipyard has reached a stage of development at which it is not merely a manufactory in private hands, but the greatest naval arsenal in the Western Hemisphere, universally recognized by the Government, the press and the people as a public institution of the first importance to the sea power of the nation."[3]

This blurring of private and public spheres in weapons procurement was a central characteristic of the military-industrial complex, which had emerged in late nineteenth-century armor production when the federal government helped build up an industrial base of long-term suppliers. The term describes a new quality in state-business relations, shifting the " 'militia theory' of industrial preparedness practiced in the Civil War to an integrated system which was capable of meeting peacetime demands of an expansionist nation functioning in a hostile environment. The needs of the U.S. Navy—like those of navies abroad—became central for stimulating industrial modernization. The U.S. Navy, rather than the army, became the first service to require industrial products more sophisticated than those normally produced by paleo-industry, i.e., rails and farm machinery."[4]

With the birth of the military-industrial complex, naval steel suppliers began to procure specialty production equipment of limited usefulness for commercial manufacturing; for this reason, armor contractors started to demand ever growing naval appropriations. To ensure a steady flow of profitable contracts, they developed close relationships with the Navy Department, opened a revolving door between the public and private sectors by hiring former government officials, and received favorable treatment by a Navy Department bent on maintaining its military-industrial base. The navy often tolerated questionable practices on the part of the armor and later gun contractors, including cartel-like price fixing.[5]

Although builders of warships became dependent on naval construction, their situation was slightly different from that of armor producers. For example, the first clear cases of price fixing among major contractors did not materialize until the late 1920s. Moreover, farsighted builders viewed naval contracting only as a means to sustain shipyards during hard times, while they would return to merchant shipbuilding whenever possible. To bolster commercial construction, they advocated a comprehensive overhaul of federal policy to boost the merchant marine, but these reforms failed. Much to the regret of shipbuilders, shipyards remained dependent on military contracts until the end of the century.

The New Navy and Shipbuilding Technology

Cramp commenced naval construction during the economic downturn of the second half of the 1880s. Like many other businessmen, shipbuilders had increased their production capacities and apprenticed new specialists during the preceding upswing, only to see their new facilities and workers idled by yet another slump. In Charles Cramp's words, "most of the shipyards have gone under on account of periods of depressions, at which time grass and tomato vines grow on the wharves, and at other times there was a gorged condition, then a famine, then a gorge."[6] This pattern of long depressions and short recoveries was especially pronounced in shipbuilding but also pervaded other sectors of the U.S. economy, which experienced cyclical downturns from 1873 to 1879 and from 1882 to 1885.

Most contemporaries believed that chronic instability during the late nineteenth century was related to overproduction and underconsumption in maturing industrial societies. Presumably, production capacity grew much faster than domestic markets. Arguing that overseas market expansion would provide a remedy, imperialists advocated the construction of a powerful navy to open up new markets. One protagonist argued, "At least one-third of our mechanical and agricultural products are now in excess of our own wants, and we must export these products or *deport* the people who are creating them. *It is a question of millions* . . . new markets must be found and new roads opened. The man-of-war precedes the merchantman and impresses rude people with the sense of the power of [the] flag, which covers the one and the other."[7]

Similar demands for state-sponsored imperialism as a solution to domestic economic problems were made throughout the industrialized world and formed the ideological underpinning for the rapid growth of the British and French colonial empires and the establishment of German colonies during the "scramble for Africa" in the 1880s. In the United States the lack of steel warships was a serious impediment for similar ventures, and the dilapidated U.S. fleet with its wooden sloops and Civil War monitors was in no position to conduct gunboat diplomacy or "impress rude people." This changed with the creation of the new navy and the construction of America's first steel warships.

The Navy Department invited shipbuilders' bids when the naval appropriations bill of 1883 funded the construction of two cruisers, a gunboat, and a dispatch vessel. Cramp submitted a proposal but was underbid by John Roach who received the entire batch. Dismayed by what he perceived as blatant favoritism, Cramp asked Secretary of the Navy William Chandler, "Mr. Secretary, are you going to give all these contracts to one man?" Chandler replied, "I don't see how I can help it."[8] Cramp suspected that Roach had submitted an unrealistically low bid: "We got an idea . . . after the bids were opened, that Roach and Chandler were working together so we put in bids lower than it was possible for Roach or anyone else to build the vessels for . . . Roach bid lower yet, and so much lower too, that he cannot begin to do the work according to the specifications."[9]

This suspicion was eventually confirmed: Roach had indeed underestimated his labor and material costs. He later asked the navy to renegotiate the contract, but the new secretary of the navy William Whitney insisted that the vessels be delivered at the original price. The construction of the four ships was also plagued by poor planning, frequent design changes, and material supply problems that resulted in the failure of the first vessel, the gunboat USS *Dolphin,* to perform according to specifications. The affair virtually ruined the shipyard and forced John Roach, the largest shipbuilder of the day, into bankruptcy in 1885—hardly an encouraging beginning for the new navy.[10]

When the navy issued the next round of warship contracts in 1886 and 1887, the memory of Roach's failure was still fresh in the minds of many builders. Several, including Neafie & Levy, John Dialogue, and Pusey & Jones, refused to bid. The small number of competitors led the *Army & Navy Journal* to believe that "Mr. Roach's late experience with the [Navy] Department has certainly not been such as to encourage the shipbuilders to compete with him for its favors."[11] But Cramp, hard pressed for orders because the yard had few commercial contracts, competed fiercely with the Union Iron Works of San Francisco and Harlan & Hollingsworth for three cruiser and two gunboat contracts. Cramp was also interested in a risky "dynamite cruiser" contract that received no other bids. In December 1886 the yard booked the protected cruiser USS *Baltimore,* followed by the protected cruiser USS *Newark,* the "dynamite cruiser" USS *Vesuvius,* the gunboat USS *Yorktown,* and the protected cruiser USS *Philadelphia.* Within ten months the builder had signed five contracts worth a total of $4,728,000, which made Cramp the nation's most prominent warship contractor. Four other vessels were built by the Union Iron Works and the Brooklyn and Norfolk Navy Yards.[12]

The Navy Department signed separate contracts for gun and armor steel with the Bethlehem Iron Company, which, like Cramp, obtained naval contracts to employ idle production capacity. In 1885 and 1886 demand for Bethlehem's steel rails declined, forcing the company to take a $1 million mortgage to maintain its financial viability. A year later the firm bid on a contract for 1,310 tons of gun steel to supply ordnance for warships building in Philadelphia and elsewhere. Bethlehem also obtained a contract for 4,500 tons of armor plates, which were installed aboard armored ships built in Brooklyn and Norfolk. (During the 1880s Cramp built only unarmored cruisers.) Bethlehem made extraordinary efforts to secure these orders, obtained a French steel patent, and upgraded its plant at Bethlehem to manufacture naval steel and ordnance.[13]

Cramp launched facility improvements in preparation for naval construction, procured hydraulic tools, erected a new building for boiler and blacksmith work, and lengthened the machine shop. Charles Cramp related:

> Up to the time the Government promised us these contracts we had no hydraulic boiler-making machinery in our works. We still struggled along with our old devices for bending, flanging, and riveting boiler plates, because we did not have the money to buy new machines . . . As soon as we made [the naval contracts] we knew that by improving our facilities it would be of immense advantage to us and partly pay for itself and thereby help us in future competition . . . We got hydraulic machinery for handling these enormous boilers and riveting the plates. We made a large expenditure, amounting to about $350,000.[14]

Warship construction also facilitated the introduction of new designs when the Navy Department imported hull and engine drawings for the cruiser USS *Baltimore* from England. The engine plans were particularly useful because they provided American builders with detailed information about the new British triple-expansion engine. Unlike the traditional compound engine, which recycled boiler steam only once, the triple-expansion engine recycled it twice, thereby improving fuel efficiency. Cramp had experimented with this new engine type in the yacht *Peerless* in 1885, but the English plans enabled the yard to construct more powerful and compact engines. In his review Charles Cramp thanked Secretary Whitney for making these sophisticated drawings available to U.S. builders: "In procuring these plans you have not only performed a valuable service to the navy but you have also conferred a signal benefit on the shipbuilding interest of the country by laying before them the most elaborate results of the best skills and most approved experience abroad."[15] Capitalizing upon its experience with triple-expansion engines in naval construction, Cramp later introduced the system in merchant shipbuilding.[16]

Charles Cramp believed that although naval work helped yards survive slumps in commercial shipbuilding and experiment with new technologies, in the long run it could not replace more profitable private contracts. Building "men-of-war would simply enable us to perfect our facilities for merchant vessels," he proclaimed. "We must have mercantile ship-owners. We must continue to build mercantile vessels."[17] Government contracting was too complicated and unprofitable to sustain shipyards for any extended period: "No intelligent manufacturer needs to be told that government work alone is not a reliable basis for permanent prosperity. The requirements of the government as to material, workmanship, and performance, are so severe, that there is but little profit in its work as compared with orders for merchant account."[18]

This rather critical view was the result of Cramp's experiences with naval officials who inspected warships during the construction phase and often rejected defective plates and inferior workmanship. As a result of these and other construction problems, the completion of the dynamite cruiser USS *Vesuvius* was almost two years behind schedule.[19]

The USS *Baltimore*, the largest of the five vessels, was ready for her official trial in fall 1889. A trial trip was usually a nerve-racking affair for the contractor because the navy determined afterward whether it would accept or reject the vessel. In 1885 the Navy Department had rejected the USS *Dolphin* due to insufficient speed and other problems, thereby contributing to Roach's downfall. Charles Cramp took some precautions to avoid a similar calamity. During a discussion of the USS *Baltimore* contract, he suggested to Whitney that the navy establish specific penalties for underperformance instead of rejecting the entire vessels. For example, the contract specifications for the USS *Baltimore* called for at least 9,000 Indicated Horse Power (IHP); Charles Cramp related:

I asked Mr. Whitney what would happen if she developed only 8,999 horse-power. After reflection he said he could not accept her under the contract if drawn that way, and invited a suggestion of remedy. I at once proposed the penalty system. That is to say, a system of deducting a certain sum for every unit of power developed short of the guaranty, as was often done in both naval and merchant shipbuilding practice. He assented to this without argument, but said that in order to make the contract entirely equitable there should be a corresponding premium for excess of performance.[20]

Penalties provided a safeguard against the rejection of the vessel after her trial trip, and premiums gave the builder an opportunity to reap extra profits.[21]

The premium system stipulated a bonus of $100 for every unit IHP in excess of the contract specifications. To develop maximum engine power, contractors manned engine rooms with experienced stokers who fed boiler grates with handpicked coal. These efforts paid off handsomely when the USS *Baltimore* developed 1,064.44 excess IHP and earned Cramp a premium of more than $100,000.[22]

The Structure of the American Shipbuilding Industry, c. 1890

Upon completion of most of its naval work in the late 1880s, Cramp recommenced commercial shipbuilding as its old customers for merchant tonnage returned with fresh contracts. Clyde ordered the passenger vessels *Iroquois* and *Algonquin,* and the Red D Line, the *Venezuela* and *Caracas.* Cramp also built the *Henry M. Whitney* for the Metropolitan Line, the *Essex* for the Merchants'

& Miners' Transportation Company, and *El Sol* for the Pacific Improvement Company. In terms of size, building material, and engine type, these vessels reflected Cramp's capacity to build better ships than its competitors. Thanks to its naval construction experience, Cramp built larger hulls and made increasing use of steel, which was 15 percent lighter than equally strong iron. *El Sol* was the first merchant vessel exceeding 4,000 gross tons, and Clyde's *Iroquois* of 1889 was the largest steel vessel of the day. Most Cramp-built merchant steamers were now equipped with triple-expansion engines. These innovations solidified Cramp's position as the nation's leading supplier of large metal steamships.[23]

At the beginning of the 1890s the yard had few competitors for large contracts. Like Cramp, the Union Iron Works had obtained naval contracts for three cruisers and a monitor during the shipbuilding depression. But unlike Cramp, the San Francisco yard had no customer base among leading steamship lines, so that it remained dependent on naval contracting until the second half of the 1890s. Harlan & Hollingsworth had traditionally bid against Cramp on contracts for large iron steamers, but the firm lost its competitive edge when owners ordered ships like *El Sol,* whose length exceeded 400 feet. Operating on the narrow Christiana River in Wilmington, Harlan & Hollingsworth was unable to launch ships of such dimensions. Accordingly, in 1889 the management declared that it would henceforth concentrate on medium-sized vessels and leave larger ships to others. Until Roach's bankruptcy in 1885 his Chester yard had outclassed Cramp in terms of production equipment and vessel output, but as a result of reorganization and financial streamlining by the founder's son, John B. Roach, the yard fell behind. During the late 1890s Collin P. Huntington's Newport News Ship Building & Dry Dock Company became a formidable competitor for large steamship contracts. At the beginning of the decade, however, the company was still relatively inexperienced and lacked Cramp's extensive connections among steamship operators and government officials.[24]

The remaining yards for iron and steel shipbuilding included smaller firms, such as Neafie & Levy, Dialogue, and Pusey & Jones, specializing in tugs, yachts, ferries, and barges of less than 1,500 gross tons. Demand for these ships had declined between 1885 and 1887 but increased in the course of the next half-decade. Neafie & Levy's major customers included the New York, Lake Erie & Western Railroad, which ordered tugs and ferryboats to expand its New York harbor-service fleet. Between 1888 and 1893 Neafie & Levy built twenty-eight small iron steamships and thirty engines for wooden steamers whose hulls were launched at other yards. The firm also capitalized upon its business connections with Central American customers, who had ordered small war-

Neafie & Levy, 1890s. This illustration shows some of the most prestigious vessels built at the yard during this period, including J. P. Morgan's Corsair *at center.* Neafie & Levy Ship and Engine Building Company *(New York, 1896)*

ships and sugar-processing equipment from Neafie & Levy since the 1870s. In 1891 it obtained a contract from the Cuban merchant house of Menendez & Company for the passenger and freight steamer *Antonia Menendez,* followed by the *Purisima Concepcion* in 1893. Neafie & Levy felt confident enough to enlarge its plant with new offices, drafting rooms, and workshops. To mobilize capital for these improvements, Jacob Neafie and Edmund Levy incorporated the firm, which was capitalized at $800,000. As in other closely held corporations, the former proprietors controlled the majority of shares and managed day-to-day operations.[25]

Neafie & Levy's most spectacular vessel was J. Pierpont Morgan's steel yacht *Corsair II,* designed by Morgan's friend J. Frederic Tams. The New York banker handed Tams a stack of blank checks and instructed him to spare no expense for his magnificent toy. In 1890 the Philadelphia yard received the contract to produce the world's largest pleasure vessel. Sporting a clipper bow, a black hull, and a yellow funnel, the 240-foot *Corsair II* was equipped with private cabins and bathrooms, a library, and lavishly furnished social rooms. Morgan struck some of his most important business and political deals during cruises aboard this famous vessel.[26]

Neafie & Levy competed with several newcomers who established yards to build small and medium-sized iron steamships as demand improved during the late 1880s. Local competitors included Charles Hillman and his sons Bart, Josiah, and Jonathan, who had previously built wooden hulls under the auspices of Birely, Hillman & Streaker of Philadelphia and Bart Hillman of Camden. They discontinued the Camden yard and bought out Jacob Birely and David Streaker to establish Hillman & Sons in 1888. Hillman commenced tug engine building in 1889, then switched from wooden to iron construction, and launched its first iron steamer, the Baltimore & Philadelphia Steamboat Company's *Anthony B. Groves,* in 1893.[27]

At the beginning of the 1890s there were signs that American metal shipbuilding could overcome at least some of the problems that had plagued the industry from the start. First, yard specialization increased among established firms. Cramp was the industry leader for larger warships and passenger liners, and the Union Iron Works committed itself to naval construction. Among the second-class yards, Roach and Harlan & Hollingsworth supplied medium-sized passenger vessels, while smaller firms, such as Neafie & Levy and Pusey & Jones, became specialists for tugs, steamboats, and yachts. Second, in spite of its obvious problems, naval contracting during the 1880s had led to the introduction of major new technologies, including triple-expansion engines and steel hulls. Third, and perhaps most important, American builders of metal ships had come within striking distance of British tonnage prices, probably as a result of greater yard specialization. In 1888, despite higher prices for labor and material, U.S. merchant ships cost only 15 percent more than identical British vessels, compared to a gap of at least 25 percent in the early 1880s.[28]

True, the U.S. maritime economy still faced serious difficulties, especially as far as the merchant marine was concerned. There were few U.S. foreign trade carriers, and no American steamship line served the pivotal transatlantic route using American-built tonnage. The bulk of the U.S. merchant marine consisted of outdated wooden sailing ships. European vessels still carried almost 90 percent of U.S. foreign trade. But many builders and shippers were confident that these long-term problems could be alleviated through an overhaul of the nation's merchant marine policy and systematic encouragement of shipowning in the foreign trade.

The Steamship Subsidy Debate

Beginning in the 1880s a maritime reform coalition emerged that included shipbuilders, steamship managers, and the Republican Party. The coalition advocated a government program that would grant subsidies to U.S. ships for each mile sailed in the foreign trade. Reformers argued that this would give the U.S. merchant marine a reasonable chance to compete internationally; equally important, shipyards would be less dependent on troublesome naval contracts. Charles Cramp, a leading spokesman of the reform movement, maintained that the purpose of subsidies was "to promote ship-building and encourage people to own ships . . . They must come to us to build vessels. We do not build vessels to put on our shelves in the open market for sale."[29]

Federal merchant marine policy had long been a divisive issue between Republicans and Democrats in Congress. During the 1870s and 1880s Republicans introduced appropriations bills for the U.S. Postal Service to compensate steamship lines for the transportation of mails, similar to the Collins subsidy of 1850. These postal subsidies were designed to guarantee a fixed annual income to the nation's fledgling foreign trade carriers. Most Democrats were roundly opposed to a federal steamship subsidy because it presumably led to favoritism toward individual carriers. They argued that the real problem of the U.S. merchant marine was the exorbitant price of American-built vessels. Their own reform proposals aimed at making changes in the U.S. Navigation Act to enable American shipowners to buy cheap, foreign-built vessels and register them under the American flag. Republicans countered that the admission of foreign-built vessels to U.S. registry amounted to a death sentence for the nation's shipbuilding industry. The parties remained deadlocked over maritime reform, and Congress passed neither steamship subsidies nor registry law changes.[30]

The Republican victories in the 1888 congressional and presidential elections broke the deadlock. President Harrison and Republican members of Congress, as well as shipbuilders and steamship managers, now formulated a comprehensive policy to revive the nation's foreign trade carriers. It certainly helped that the federal government reported a surplus of $100 million, representing the accumulated customs duties of the protectionist tariff. In response to the Democrats' claim that subsidies to individual lines would involve government favoritism, Republicans amended their earlier schemes by a sweeping proposal to grant federal bounties to *all* American ships engaged in the foreign trade. In 1890 the Senate passed two critical pieces of maritime legislation: the bounty bill, which provided general support to American vessels engaged in foreign trade, and a special subsidy bill supporting express liners. By summer the new merchant marine policy awaited passage in the House of Representatives.[31]

Confident that the legislative package would soon become law, shipbuilders and steamship managers expanded their operations to reap the expected benefits of the government program. Indeed, the anticipated policy change triggered a speculative fever among investors. British bankers and financiers, for example, provided funds to renovate the Roach shipyard at Chester. The press reported that the investors were motivated by the "likelihood of the passage of the Bounty Bill, now favorably before the House of Representatives," which would foster demand for new ships and presumably keep the yard busy for years.[32] Builders also established new facilities, including Maryland Steel's yard at Sparrow's Point near Baltimore.[33]

At the height of the fever, Cramp joined the speculative fray. Previously the company's stock had been exclusively owned by the five Cramp brothers who also served as directors. On June 2, 1890, the firm issued new stocks worth $1,757,500 to the old shareholders, who sold them to outside investors. The latter included some of the titans of American business, such as John D. Rockefeller, Charles Pratt of the machine tool firm Pratt & Whitney, hat manufacturer J. B. Stetson, Wall Street banker Henry Seligman, steamship magnate Clement A. Griscom of the International Navigation Company, and John R. Dos Passos, Philadelphia's most prominent corporate lawyer (father of the renowned novelist). By the stroke of a pen, the firm had been transformed into a corporation of the first order. This development marked the beginning of the end of proprietary capitalism at Cramp.[34]

Significantly, corporate reconstruction did not involve basic changes in Cramp's management. The former owners still controlled more than 30 percent of the shares and served as senior executives for more than a decade. Executive continuity was ensured by an agreement signed by the Cramp brothers committing them "to give their services in the management of the company as heretofore during the next five years for an aggregate compensation of $75,000 a year, to be divided among them . . . [They further] promise and agree not to engage in the business of ship-building nor to permit the use of their names in any such business."[35]

Meanwhile, the merchant marine bills that motivated the speculative fever came under political attack. Democrats and the free-trade press charged that the bounty bill was the tool of "subsidy beggars" among shipbuilders and steamship managers who hoped to rob the federal treasury of its huge surplus. A scathing *New York Times* commentary declared, "The gathering of the subsidy seekers at Washington is not unnatural. They have every reason to look for success in their eager quest. The Republican leaders have declared their sympathy with them. The President has practically invited them. The Secretary of State has been conducting an open campaign in their favor."[36]

Speculation in the shipbuilding industry fueled public suspicion of the bounty bill. As a result of political pressure, the House of Representatives delayed the passage of the merchant marine bills until after the 1890 elections, when the Republicans lost their majority. In March 1891 a lame-duck Congress finally voted on the legislation and defeated the bounty bill. It passed the less important subsidy bill, which provided federal funds to a handful of steamship lines.[37]

The speculative maritime boom collapsed, leaving shipbuilders and other promoters of the bounty bill scrambling for cover. Cramp had purchased prime real estate in South Philadelphia at a cost of $800,000 to erect a new shipyard to build commercial steamships, but the firm now scrapped these plans. Cramp, like other firms, would have enough trouble keeping its existing facilities employed.[38]

Cramp tried to make the best of the steamship subsidy bill passed in 1891. This program provided subsidies on a sliding scale ranging from $4 to $1 per mile traveled on different steamship routes. Unfortunately, only the lower subsidy classes for the Latin American and Pacific routes received a few meager bids from steamship operators; aggregate annual subsidies for these lines amounted to less than $200,000 and yielded few steamship contracts. The subsidy of $4 per mile traveled on the transatlantic route did not receive a single bid. Together with the International Navigation Company (INC), Cramp concentrated its efforts on this highest subsidy class in order to generate at least a few orders.[39]

Founded in Philadelphia at the beginning of the 1870s, the INC sailed British-built steamships under the name Red Star Line between Philadelphia and Antwerp. Performing quite well during the 1880s, it bought out the American Steamship Company and the British Inman line. In 1888 the INC ordered the express liners *City of New York* and *City of Paris* from Thompson at Glasgow and sailed twenty-two transatlantic liners between the United States, Britain, and continental Europe under the British and Belgian flags. When Congress passed the subsidy bill of 1891, the INC could not apply for funds because its British-built liners were ineligible for U.S. registry and steamship subsidies.[40]

This predicament irked INC president Clement A. Griscom, who discussed the subsidy question with former secretary of the navy William Whitney at a dinner party. Whitney suggested that the INC should apply to Congress for special legislation authorizing U.S. registry for its largest ships, the *City of New York* and the *City of Paris*, to render them eligible for the recently passed steamship subsidies. In return for this special favor, Whitney suggested, the INC should issue a large liner contract to an American shipyard. Griscom approved of this scheme, which would yield a $300,000 annual subsidy for the *City of New York* and the *City of Paris* alone.[41]

Since the registry of foreign-built vessels under the American flag was anathema to shipbuilders, protectionists, and Republicans, Whitney's proposal triggered a heated debate. The *Nautical Gazette* proclaimed: "We say, No! . . . For every foreign-built ship that is admitted under American register it is harder for our own shipbuilders . . . [The project] will completely nullify whatever good was expected to be accomplished by the postal subsidy act."[42] Charles Cramp and his brothers, who were not only shipbuilders and protectionists but also staunch Republicans, had long voiced similar criticisms. But when the INC proposed its registry scheme in conjunction with a large contract for American-built liners, Cramp changed his mind: if this contract could only be obtained through compromise on the registry issue, so be it. Charles Cramp actively supported the INC's publicity campaign, traveled overseas to sell the scheme to British investors, and garnered political support in Congress.[43]

As a result of these efforts, Congress passed special legislation enabling the INC to proceed with its plan. American-owned, foreign-built ships exceeding 8,000 gross tons were now eligible for the highest class of steamship subsidies, provided that the owner ordered from U.S. yards "steamships of an aggregate tonnage of not less in amount than that of the steamships so admitted to registry."[44] In 1893 the INC registered the *City of New York* and the *City of Paris* under the U.S. flag and ordered two similar vessels from an American yard.[45]

There was little doubt that the INC's liner contracts would go to Cramp. First, no other builder was so well equipped to construct high-performance vessels exceeding 8,000 gross tons. Second, the steamship company and the shipyard were closely intertwined; the line owned 10 percent of Cramp's stock, and INC president Griscom was a member of its board of directors. Third, Charles Cramp had helped Griscom advertise the steamship scheme in the United States and Britain. In June 1892 the INC and Cramp signed contracts for the transatlantic passenger liners *St. Louis* and *St. Paul.*[46]

These vessels epitomized the enormous problems of the U.S. merchant marine. Nothing less than a change in the Navigation Act was necessary to encourage the construction of American liners. This policy remained an isolated incident and was no substitute for comprehensive merchant marine reforms. Left to its own devices, the merchant marine did not generate sufficient demand for large ships. It was years before Cramp built such vessels once again.[47]

The Transformation of Naval Shipbuilding

While neglecting merchant marine reforms, the federal government developed a far-reaching and expensive program to modernize the U.S. Navy. This nudged yards into naval construction at the expense of commercial shipbuilding. Warships cost the government much more than even a generous bounty to commercial carriers, and naval shipbuilding involved more government intervention into the private sector than subsidies. Warship construction made shipyards more, not less, dependent on government assistance. Despite these contradictions, the opponents of the merchant marine bill applauded Secretary of the Navy Benjamin Tracy's plan for the largest military buildup in the nation's history.

The Tracy program marked the beginning of U.S. battleship construction and involved profound changes in naval strategy and policy. U.S. naval strategy had been based on cruisers of the USS *Baltimore* type, which were designed to destroy an enemy's merchant ships. But cruisers were not equipped to fight other warships, whose artillery could pierce their relatively unprotected hulls. Naval strategy and ship design changed in 1890 following the publication of Captain Alfred T. Mahan's study, *The Influence of Sea Power upon History*, which inspired demands for heavily armored cruisers and battleships. One of the most influential books of the period, Mahan's study argued that a true naval power needed ships that could destroy an enemy's fleet. The book found perceptive readers among the top officials of the new Republican administration, including President Benjamin Harrison, Secretary of State James Blaine, and Tracy. The secretary of the navy devised a program, at a cost of $281 million, to build twenty-three battleships as well as dozens of cruisers, rams, and torpedo boats.[48]

This huge project came under political attack from navy critics, such as Democratic senator William J. Bryan and Populist leader Tom Watson, who charged that battleships were entirely unnecessary for the navy's strategic mission. A naval war with Britain or any European naval power was a remote possibility at best. The nation faced more pressing needs in the civilian sector, the critics argued, including a comprehensive merchant marine policy, agricultural reforms, and Civil War veterans' pensions. All those programs would suffer if the U.S. Navy received expensive battleships. Even Charles Cramp expressed reservations because the shipbuilding industry was not equipped to build armored vessels. In the end Congress passed a scaled-down version of the naval program and appropriated $16 million for three battleships and one protected cruiser.[49]

The Navy Department soon invited bids from shipbuilders and armor manufacturers for the battleships USS *Indiana*, USS *Massachusetts*, and USS *Oregon*, the armored cruiser USS *New York* (appropriated in 1888), and the protected cruiser USS *Columbia*. When they examined the specifications, most builders decided not to submit bids because construction would require considerable investments in production equipment, shops, and berths. Only a handful of ambitious builders tendered proposals. The battleships USS *Indi-*

ana and USS *Massachusetts*, the armored cruiser USS *New York,* and the protected cruiser USS *Columbia* went to Cramp for $12 million. The Union Iron Works of San Francisco obtained the contract for the remaining battleship, USS *Oregon.* The naval program of 1890 solidified Cramp's position as the navy's preeminent contractor for modern warships.

The military-industrial base necessary to proceed with the battleship and cruiser program also included the Carnegie steelworks, which booked naval armor contracts. As early as 1889 Andrew Carnegie had concluded that "there may be millions for us in armor." He upgraded his steelworks for naval steel production, and in 1890 he obtained a $4 millon contract.[50] Cramp's armored vessels received armor made at Carnegie's steel plant in Homestead, Pennsylvania.[51]

The Philadelphia builder prepared its yard for the battleships *Massachusetts* and *Indiana,* the armored cruiser *New York,* and the protected cruiser *Columbia.* The task ahead was stupendous. The *New York Times* reported that "William Cramp & Sons have now on hand the greatest undertaking in the history of American shipbuilding. Four great war ships, the largest vessels ever built in the United States, and designed to be the most powerful fighting ships in the world, must be launched, tried, and turned over to the government in three years' time." Cramp committed its entire resources to this project. "Within the past two months the most important object has been accomplished, namely the clearing of all vessels from the . . . stocks . . . Vast quantities of material of all descriptions must come from different parts of the United States. Manufacturers far and wide will have requisitions made upon them, and directly the magnitude of the work in Philadelphia will be felt throughout the whole country."[52]

Inside the Military-Industrial Complex

The first ship laid down was the armored cruiser USS *New York,* 384 feet long, 64 feet in the beam, and capable of a speed of 20 knots. This was by far the largest and fastest vessel yet contemplated in the history of the U.S. Navy. The outside armor consisted of a 200-foot steel belt protecting the port and starboard sides, an armored conning tower to shield the command center, and armored gun turrets; on the inside, a protective armor deck extended throughout the entire length near the waterline. The main ordnance consisted of six 8-inch guns. As an armored cruiser, the USS *New York* featured only a moderate amount of armor and medium-sized guns. Together with high speed and maneuverability, these technical characteristics distinguished cruisers from battleships, which were slower but better protected by heavy armor.[53]

Cramp and the Navy Department signed the contract for the USS *New York*

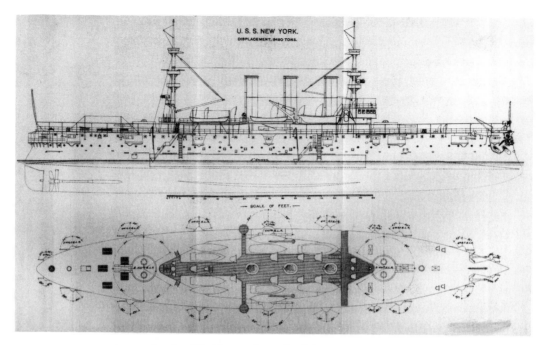

Armored cruiser USS New York, *pride of the new navy, 1893. Note the 200-foot-long side-armor belt near the waterline. Unofficial plan, published in* Transactions of the Society of Naval Architects and Marine Engineers *(1893). U.S. Naval Historical Center*

on August 28, 1890. Significantly, the vessel plans were by no means complete because the Navy Department had developed only a general outline as a basis for Cramp's own construction drawings. Cramp's designers drew detail plans during the construction phase and submitted them to the Navy Department for approval. Individual Navy Department bureaus (chiefly those of construction and repair, ordnance, and engineering) then reviewed Cramp's plans and suggested improvements. Although this was standard practice in naval shipbuilding, it complicated the construction process because bureau chiefs often wanted to include their latest pet technologies in a new vessel and frequently changed specifications. When a shipbuilding firm signed a contract, it had only a general idea of the vessel it was about to build and had to be prepared for major changes. In the case of the USS *New York* and Cramp's other vessels, design changes were numerous because naval technology was changing rapidly while the vessels were under construction.[54]

Despite these looming difficulties, the initial construction phase went according to schedule. The first hull material arrived at the shipyard on September 3, 1890, less than a week after the contract had been signed. On September 30, 1890, Cramp's men laid the first keel plates. The builder ordered steel castings for the bow and stern sections from the Philadelphia steel mill Morris, Tasker & Company, as well as deck beams from Carnegie in Pittsburgh. Despite some technical problems with the production of these components, the construction of the USS *New York* was in full swing by early 1891.[55]

Meanwhile, Cramp improved its facilities to complete the naval contracts. In spring 1891 the firm acquired its old subcontractor I. P. Morris, which produced some of the enormous metal castings installed in the USS *New York* and other warships. The acquisition cost Cramp $450,000. In addition to castings, Morris supplied all sorts of hydraulic tools for the yard's riveting and plate-bending departments. For $118,000, Cramp also acquired the B. H. Cramp Manganese Bronze Works, which was owned independently by a family member who had been a naval contractor since 1888 and had furnished almost all U.S. warships with a new type of bronze screw propeller. B. H. Cramp also operated an ordnance shop, which the shipyard's board of directors considered an important addition to the shipyard's naval construction capacity. "The Gun Plant for manufacture of Guns under patents of Driggs Ordnance Co. is located upon land owned by B. H. Cramp & Co. and the buildings and steam power for operating said Gun Plant were erected and paid for by B. H. Cramp & Co."[56] The acquisition of new facilities did not end subcontracting in naval shipbuilding. For example, the American Ship Windlass Company of Providence, Rhode Island, supplied windlasses; the George Blake Manufacturing Company of New York made air pumps; Williamson & Brother of Philadelphia provided ash hoists; and the Rand Drill Company of New York manufactured air condensers for the torpedo tubes.[57]

The first construction problems arose in August 1891, when Cramp's riveters demanded higher wages and launched a strike. Like other labor conflicts in metal shipbuilding, this one was initiated by the rivet boys, the industry's least skilled workers. The rivet boys received the lowest pay among shipyard employees and worked long hours under dangerous conditions, which made them prime candidates for spontaneous job actions. Often their actions were supported by more skilled workers in the hull department. When the rivet boys struck for higher wages, their "refusal to work threw out the riveters and holders on, who, having no boys to heat the rivets, quit work. After being out for a day the men, riveters and holders on, concluded not to return unless their wages were increased."[58] As Cramp's riveting department closed down, work ceased in other shops as well, even though most workers did not join the strike.[59]

The strike gave Cramp an incentive to begin the mechanization of riveting, which continued over the next two decades. Innovative riveting guns used pneumatic power received through air pipes connected to a central power plant. Cramp's management, which had already discussed the introduction of pneumatic riveting before the strike, refused to raise wages, installed pneumatic riveting tools, and informed the Navy Department that the completion of the USS *New York* and the battleships would be delayed. Unable to hold out against their intransigent employer, the strikers admitted defeat in early October 1891.[60]

The completion of the USS *New York* fell further behind schedule as a result of design changes involving the 3-inch-thick steel deck designed to protect engines and boilers from enemy shot. Initially, the navy's specifications called for ordinary steel plates, made by Carnegie in Homestead. In spring 1891 the mill shipped several plates to the shipyard, where specially trained workers installed them aboard the armored cruiser. But in July the navy discussed plans to replace steel plates with composite nickel-steel plates, the latest development in armor technology. According to the chief of the Bureau of Ordnance, William Folger, recent tests in the United States and Britain had proven its superiority over all-steel plates, as nickel "appears to impart a vicious quality, if such an expression can be used, which eliminates the [plate's] tendency to crack under impact."[61] While the Navy Department argued over Folger's nickel-steel proposal for almost two months, Cramp continued to install all-steel plates aboard the USS *New York*. On September 17, 1891, the navy finally informed the shipbuilder that the all-steel protective deck plates would have to be ripped out and replaced. Although the shipbuilder was annoyed by this change, it had no choice but to have the armor bolts unscrewed and the protective deck removed.[62]

After Cramp had ordered a new set of deck plates, the shipbuilder realized that this type of armor posed unforeseen problems. Charles Cramp informed the secretary of the navy that "nickel steel is very tough and is harder to work than the all-steel."[63] Carnegie's steelworkers clearly agreed: As soon as the contract for nickel-steel arrived in Homestead, they demanded higher wages because forging and rolling the new type of steel proved time-consuming and difficult. Since the old steel wage scale that was in effect between July 1891 and June 1892 did not even include a category for nickel-steel, the Amalgamated Association of Iron, Steel and Tin Workers asked Carnegie to discuss the matter with union representatives. The *New York Times* reported in January 1892 that "it is now the intention of the Amalgamated Association . . . to demand an increase of 200 per cent. over the scale. The indications are that this will be refused and a struggle appears probable."[64] Indeed, Carnegie refused the 200 percent increase for nickel-steel over ordinary steel. The controversy lit the fuse of the most ferocious conflict between capital and labor in the late nineteenth century—the Homestead Strike of 1892.[65]

At Cramp the armor problems accumulated. The USS *New York* was ready for several plates in fall 1891, but the Navy Department, whose bureau chiefs were discussing further design changes, failed to process Cramp's plans and specifications promptly. The builder forwarded stacks of precision drawings for the armored conning tower, side armor, and gun turrets to the Bureau of Construction and Repair, which handed them over to the Bureau of Ordnance. Months passed before Cramp received word that the armor plans and specifications had been approved. The builder submitted plans for the 8-inch gun turrets on February 16, 1891, but the Bureau of Ordnance deliberated for twelve months before ordering the first turret armor. On April 10, 1891, Cramp submitted conning tower plans to the Navy Department, which ordered the plates thirteen months later. The first side-armor plans for the 200-foot belt left the shipyard in July 1891 and were finally approved in January 1892.[66]

These delays caused acute problems at the shipyard. Charles Cramp later recalled how "a large force of special mechanics, trained in the working of armor had to be continued in [Cramp's] service, awaiting daily the receipt of said armor. These mechanics could not be utilized to the same advantage in other lines of work; their pay was higher than ordinary mechanics; yet the contractor could not afford to discharge them, lest their services could not be obtained when the armor etc. was received."[67] These men remained idle for months because the Navy Department did not approve, and Carnegie did not deliver, armor plates according to schedule. In February 1892 Charles Cramp, infuriated, wrote to the secretary of the navy that the armor crisis had "now reached the unendurable stage."[68]

In spring 1892 the department finally sped up the approval of plans and pressed Carnegie to increase armor production for the USS *New York*. The steel company managers proved receptive to the navy's prodding because they wanted to complete most plates before Carnegie's wage contract with the steelworkers' union expired at the end of June 1892. As a result, Carnegie's men worked day and night to turn out steel plates for Cramp's armored cruiser. Although the mill shipped fifteen side-armor plates to Philadelphia in June, it was still working on the turret and conning tower when events took a dramatic turn.[69]

On July 1, 1892, Carnegie's managers declared the Homestead works a non-union shop. This was a carefully planned move inspired by Carnegie's long-standing feud with the Amalgamated Association of Iron, Steel and Tin Workers and his belief that union labor exercised too much control at the point of production. The controversy over the navy's nickel-steel in January 1892 had contributed to this confrontation, which reached its climax when the steelworkers responded to a lockout by taking over the plant. On July 6, 1892, when strikers and Pinkerton detectives slugged it out during the Battle of Homestead, pieces of the USS *New York*'s unfinished armor lay scattered inside the idle shops. The military-industrial complex had crashed to a halt.[70]

Charles Cramp was extremely worried about what he called the "well-known situation at the Homestead Mills." On August 19, 1892, he asked the secretary of the navy whether any provisions "for meeting the pressing requirements of the *New York* have been completed."[71] Arrangements had indeed been made by state authorities and Carnegie's management: On July 12, 1892, the Pennsylvania militia took control of the Homestead plant out of the hands of the steelworkers. The management hired strike breakers, restarted the mills, and resumed armor production in August 1892. Three months later Cramp's inspector at the steel plant reported to Philadelphia: "Two days' observation at the Homestead Mills enables me to say that the general situation there is much better than I anticipated, or than is generally believed to be in the East . . . All the mills are running, some of them on double turn."[72]

These strenuous efforts resolved the USS *New York*'s armor crisis. Once Carnegie shipped the remaining plates, Cramp completed the ship and sent her off on the trial trip in May 1893. She earned her builders a large premium for excess speed and proved one of the navy's most seaworthy vessels. But the construction of the USS *New York* was only a qualified success to her builder: Cramp claimed losses of more than $211,000 as a result of construction delays. These losses were largely offset by the $200,000 speed premium, but the armor delays had wiped out almost all the profit of naval shipbuilding.[73]

These problems paled next to those involving the battleships USS *Massachusetts* and USS *Indiana*. Completion of both ships was delayed by the rivet boys' strike of 1891. More important, each battleship required 2,000 tons of armor steel (four times the amount installed aboard the USS *New York*) whose design and construction posed unprecedented difficulties, starting with the change from all-steel to nickel-steel. Moreover, the specifications called for side-armor plates 18 inches thick, exceeding the thickness of any other steel plate made in the United States. The plates were initially designed with horizontal and vertical curvatures to fit tightly on the hull. But according to Charles Cramp, the steel experts discovered that it "was impossible to bend 18-inch plates to a double curvature, and the vertical warp was dispensed with, thereby rendering the original drawings and templets useless."[74] Moreover, Carnegie realized that the plate shop could not roll 18-inch steel plates because it lacked the necessary equipment. Acting upon a proposal submitted by Charles Cramp, the Navy

Department reshuffled its armor contracts and had the 18-inch plates rolled at the Bethlehem Iron Works instead.[75]

In March 1893, when Bethlehem prepared the first shipment of side-armor plates, the Navy Department decided that nickel-steel had been made obsolete by the so-called Harvey process, which produced subcarbonized steel displaying even more "vicious qualities" than nickel-steel. The secretary of the navy approved the necessary changes in the specifications, canceled the order for 18-inch nickel-steel plates, and signed a new contract with Bethlehem for Harveyized battleship armor for the USS *Massachusetts* and USS *Indiana*. As the steel company commenced production, its managers realized that "the application of the Harvey process, assuming the best rate of progress at all stages, adds about six weeks to the time required for the manufacture of each plate."[76] When the first new steel plates finally arrived in August 1894, further problems arose because the Harvey process had warped the plates unevenly, making it impossible to install them according to plan. "The original standardization was destroyed and each bolt had to be separately measured and trimmed for its particular place [on the hull]," Charles Cramp reported.[77]

As a result of these and other problems, the completion of the USS *Massachusetts* fell two years behind schedule, and completion of the USS *Indiana* was delayed two years and six months. While waiting for an occasional armor shipment, the Cramp firm had to store the unfinished battleship hulls in remote corners of the shipyard. Charles Cramp related: "During this time [1894] the Cramp Company undertook large contracts for the merchant marine [the *St. Louis* and *St. Paul*], and the fact that this vessel [the USS *Indiana*] was still in the yard led to their having to buy new lands, develop new water facilities, and greatly increase the size and expense of their list of employees and of their general organization."[78] Moreover, the company suffered financial losses when the Navy Department delayed its contract installments because construction had made insufficient progress. Combined with the depression of 1893, this pushed the shipyard to the brink of insolvency. According to Charles Cramp, "the company was . . . in dire need of money. It was then carrying more than a million and a quarter of dollars in loans at abnormal rates of interest, with a . . . pay roll of upwards of ten thousand dollars a day, and upwards of five thousand employees, which represented fully twenty thousand persons dependent upon the continuation of work in the company's yard. It was the time of financial panic and to have thrown these men out of employment would have been a calamity to the city and the State."[79] The Cramp firm almost repeated the Roach disaster of 1885, when the navy's most important contractor went bankrupt amid the chaos of the government's naval reconstruction program.

The Ramifications of Military Contracting

Despite its problems with naval construction, Cramp booked contracts for the protected cruiser USS *Minneapolis* (1891), the battleship USS *Iowa* (1892), the armored cruiser USS *Brooklyn* (1893), and the battleship USS *Alabama* (1896). After a fierce bidding contest with British builders, Cramp also received a Japanese contract for the cruiser *Kasagi* in 1896. Cruisers posed fewer construction difficulties and were delivered closer to schedule than battleships.[80]

Cramp's commitment to naval construction was partly a result of the lack of alternatives. The builder would have preferred private contracts because they involved fewer organizational problems and were usually more profitable than naval contracts. But the private market, already weakened by the failure of the bounty bill in 1891, reached a new low when the panic of 1893 curtailed credit for new steamship projects, especially for high-performance ships. During the five years between the Panic and the return of commercial prosperity in 1898, Cramp procured only nine private contracts, including a yacht, a tugboat, and a ferry. This potpourri of high-technology naval construction and low-quality commercial shipbuilding was not terribly efficient. A commentator pointed out that there were "five slips, each capable of building a [passenger liner]; on one was a tug, on another was a battleship, on another was a ferryboat, on another a yacht, and on another a revenue cutter. It is absolutely impossible to practice economies under such circumstances and build the ships so that they would compare favorably in cost with ships built abroad."[81] The sight of ferries, tugs, and barges occupying berth space designed to accommodate passenger liners and capital ships was to become all too common in American shipyards.

Charles Cramp hoped that future naval programs would prove less troublesome as the Navy Department learned from its mistakes, streamlined its contracting procedures, and settled on a standard battleship. At the turn of the century administrative reforms eliminated some of the worst bottlenecks in the Navy Department. But Cramp's demand for standardization, intended to eliminate delays caused by constant design changes, was another matter. Charles Cramp viewed the USS *Indiana* as the best candidate for a standard battleship. "Our very first attempt at capital ship design produced a type which I consider the fairest compromise of all divergent qualities and necessities yet reached anywhere . . . the 'Indiana' class is able to combat any first-rate battleship afloat as to armor and armament; she has as much speed as will ever be needed for manoeuvering purposes, and her coal capacity is sufficient for any cruise that the policy of the United States will ever require in war."[82] He argued that the USS *Indiana* should be duplicated in ten exact copies. Although understandable from the point of view of a contractor who wanted to complete his naval contracts closer to schedule, Cramp's demand for a standard battleship was unrealistic. Warship designers had only begun to explore the possibilities of capital ship technology and already were working on new designs for hulls, turrets, and fire control systems that were to be incorporated in the next generation of capital ships. As a result, the USS *Indiana* became technically obsolete a few years after her commissioning.[83]

In making the transition to naval shipbuilding, builders often suffered heavy financial losses. Barely "saved from threatened bankruptcy," Cramp sued the government for $1.4 million to recoup losses incurred during the construction of the armored cruiser USS *New York*, the battleships USS *Massachusetts* and USS *Indiana*, and the protected cruiser USS *Columbia*. As the case wound its way through the courts, the navy argued that Cramp bore partial responsibility for the delays and had forfeited claims by signing supplemental contracts. The courts granted Cramp only a nominal damage award, which caused financial problems more than a decade after the ships had left the yard. Other contractors fared even worse. Delays during the construction of the torpedo boat USS *McKensie* bankrupted the Hillman shipyard, which was unable to obtain loans when the navy refused to issue contract installments according to schedule. Naval contracting was certainly "not a reliable basis for permanent prosperity," as Charles Cramp had pointed out.[84]

SIX

New Departure: Growth and Crisis, 1898-1914

*T*he year 1900 was one of the most productive in the history of American steel shipbuilding. Cramp, now one of the world's largest shipyards, worked on passenger liners, battleships, and cruisers; Neafie & Levy built high-performance destroyers, yachts, and steamboats; and across the river at Camden, the New York Shipbuilding Company (commonly referred to as New York Ship) developed innovative construction techniques and employed thousands of the skilled tradesmen who still formed the industry's backbone.[1]

The turn of the century marked several departures from nineteenth-century shipbuilding. Changes in production technology and industrial architecture gave rise to enormous plants in metropolitan satellite areas like Camden, where New York Ship operated a yard twice the size of Cramp's Kensington plant. The development of suburban manufacturing districts was less pronounced in Philadelphia than in Boston, Pittsburgh, and Detroit because the relatively large size of Philadelphia County and its industrial base of small and medium-sized specialty firms permitted expansion within city limits. However, there were important exceptions in the capital equipment sector, highlighted by the move of the Baldwin Locomotive Works from Philadelphia to Eddystone near Chester in 1909. In shipbuilding, suburban firms gained a prominent position at the expense of urban yards that were increasingly strapped for space.[2]

Changes also took place at the shop floor level and in industrial relations. With a few notable exceptions, technological change at this time still enhanced the role of skilled labor as shipyards hired specialists to operate new and complicated production equipment. In this increasingly diverse work environment, trade unions continued to organize workers by craft and formed ad hoc coalitions to press demands for a shorter workday. Simultaneously, the trade unions shunned industrial unionism and suffered a series of defeats at the hands of hostile employers who formed a united front against organized labor.

Naval contracting continued to play a problematic role. Like Roach, Cramp, and Hillman during the 1890s, Neafie & Levy and other builders experienced technical and financial difficulties with warship construction. Cramp tried to solve these problems through an ambitious scheme to combine shipbuilding with armor and gun production, part of the trend toward vertical integration in the military-industrial complex. In Cramp's case, this strategy failed in the merger boom in American industry between 1898 and 1903. This disappointment, financial woes, and the rise of New York Ship as a major competitor forced Cramp to surrender its leadership in American shipbuilding. New York Ship became a major player in naval construction and received warship contracts from the U.S. and foreign navies.

Naval and Commercial Demand

At the turn of the century skyrocketing demand for commercial and naval tonnage caused a shipbuilding boom. During an unprecedented period of growth, American output of metal steamships jumped from 65,000 gross tons in 1897 to more than 315,000 in 1902, surpassing wooden construction for the first time in the nation's history. From 1898 to 1906 shipyards also built ninety-one warships aggregating 480,000 displacement tons, which moved the United States from fourth to second rank among the world's naval powers.[3]

Naval construction flourished as a result of a $50 million emergency naval appropriation passed by Congress during the Spanish-American War. In 1904 President Theodore Roosevelt provided a rationale for further naval buildup with his corollary to the Monroe Doctrine. Although builders outside the Delaware Valley, notably Newport News Shipbuilding in Virginia and Fore River Shipbuilding in Massachusetts, received a considerable number of contracts, Cramp, New York Ship, and Neafie & Levy still booked orders for five battleships, four armored cruisers, and three destroyers between 1898 and 1906.[4]

Capital ship construction entered a new era with the completion of the British battleship HMS *Dreadnought* at the Portsmouth Royal Dockyard in 1906. This turbine-propelled vessel featured large-caliber guns and rendered obsolete the so-called predreadnaughts with their reciprocating engines and mixed-caliber ordnance. During the scramble to update its battle fleet, the U.S. Navy ordered twelve dreadnoughts before World War I, including four built by Delaware Valley shipyards.[5]

Commercial shipping was closely intertwined with naval policy. This was especially obvious during the conflict with Spain when the navy invoked a clause in the 1891 subsidy act enabling it to commission mail liners during wartime. Moreover, the navy and army bought merchant steamers aggregating 80,000 gross tons to serve as auxiliary cruisers, troopships, and supply carriers, forcing their owners to order replacement tonnage. "It is easy to see," a federal official commented, "in the light of these purchases, comprising in most cases vessels of the largest and most serviceable type . . . what an abnormal demand for construction has arisen, leading to an unparalleled degree of activity in our shipyards."[6] The war-related withdrawal of commercial tonnage also increased freight rates, improved the profitability of shipowning, and bolstered demand for new tonnage.[7]

In the wake of the Spanish-American War, several steamship lines sailing between the continental United States and new U.S. overseas territories had to order additional tonnage. The decisive factor forcing them to do so was the extension of the Navigation Act reserving trade between the United States and its new territories for American-built steamers. Because commercial interests dependent on inexpensive British tonnage loudly opposed this extension, Congress placed only the Hawaiian and Puerto Rican routes under the protectionist law, leaving the important trade with the Philippines open to foreign carriers.[8]

One line affected by this policy change was Claus Spreckels's Oceanic Steamship Company (OSC). Before 1898 it had sailed two steamers on the San Francisco–Honolulu–Auckland route in coordination with the Union Steamship Company of New Zealand. When the Navigation Act excluded foreign carriers from U.S. trade with Hawaii, OSC had to terminate its cargo-sharing arrangement with the Union Line and replace the latter's British-built tonnage. The resulting contracts for three vessels went to Cramp. Unfortunately, OSC's expansion program coincided with financial troubles in Spreckels's sugar empire, and the line came close to insolvency in 1907. Spreckels laid up the recently built vessels until 1912 when the U.S. government came to the rescue with a steamship subsidy.[9]

Unlike OSC, the new American-Hawaiian Steamship Company that sailed between New York and Honolulu profited from the exclusion of foreign carriers. This line had been established in 1899 by the former clipper operator George S. Dearborn, who sold American-Hawaiian shares to plantation owners. The planters shipped cane sugar to East Coast refineries aboard Dearborn's twenty-six large steamers, which included three built by New York Ship.[10]

In addition to extending the reach of the Navigation Act, maritime reformers campaigned for new steamship subsidies. Most experts agreed that the 1891 Subsidy Act had done little to revive the U.S. merchant marine in the foreign trade. Between 1891 and 1900 only seven vessels eligible for subsidies had been ordered, including the International Navigation Company's passenger liners *St. Louis* and *St. Paul.* INC president Clement Griscom reported in 1900 that his American-flag steamers (the two named as well as the *New York* and *Paris*) represented financial liabilities and "have never made us a dollar."[11] The only beneficiary of the subsidy law was presumably the U.S. Navy, which had sailed the INC's American-flag ships as troop transports during the Spanish-American War. Unless Congress passed a new subsidy law, Griscom argued, the INC would have to transfer its liners to foreign registry and deprive the nation of its most important naval reserves.[12]

Demands for more remunerative mail contracts received support from the Republican Party, which included a steamship subsidy plank in its election platform. In Congress, Republicans introduced several subsidy bills designed to close the gap in operating costs between U.S. and British steamships. Similar to the subsidy bill of 1890, the proposed legislation included a general bounty for all American-flag vessels exceeding 1,000 gross tons as well as a mail subsidy supporting express liners. Mindful of Griscom's complaints, the new bill provided more generous funding than its predecessor: The *Nation* claimed that the INC "would get from the Government in twenty years twice the original cost of each of its fast steamers!"[13]

The subsidy bill triggered speculative shipbuilding on a scale exceeding anything seen during the early 1890s. After sailing British-flag cargo steamers for twenty years, the American-owned Atlantic Transportation Company (ATC) of Baltimore ordered two 13,000-gross-ton ships from Harland & Wolff in Belfast, Ireland, and two more, the *Mongolia* and *Manchuria,* from New York Ship. The INC issued contracts for four transatlantic liners of 12,750 gross tons each to sail between Antwerp and New York; the *Vaderland* and *Zeeland* were launched by Clydebank (formerly Thompson) in Scotland, followed by the Cramp-built *Kroonland* and *Finland.* (The rationale for building sister ships in Britain and the United States was provided by the act granting U.S. registry to the *City of New York* and *City of Paris.* According to this law, foreign steamers exceeding 8,000 tons could obtain American-flag status as long as their owners ordered similar ships from American yards; see chapter 5.)[14]

The subsidy bill also facilitated a reorganization of transatlantic shipping.

Key players were J. Pierpont Morgan of the Morgan Bank and INC president Griscom, who together created a vast fleet to gobble up millions in government subsidies. In 1901 Morgan and Griscom engineered a merger between the INC and ATC, laying the groundwork for the International Mercantile Marine (IMM), the world's largest steamship conglomerate. IMM, capitalized at $150 million, controlled the British White Star, Leyland, and Dominion Lines, ATC, and the INC subsidiaries Red Star Line and American Line; it sailed a grand total of 136 steamers. However, this grandiose speculation collapsed when the all-important subsidy bill died in the House Committee on the Merchant Marine. Like most horizontal mergers formed at the turn of the century, IMM never issued stock dividends. Moreover, financial problems forced ATC to sell its contracts with New York Ship for the *Mongolia* and *Manchuria* to the Pacific Mail Steamship Company. The U.S. commissioner of navigation commented that the construction of these and other transatlantic steamers "is notable as testimony to the skill of our shipbuilders, the excellence of their plants, and to the disposition and resources of our shipowners. It is not evidence of a steady or normal demand, on which our shipbuilders and those identified with them can safely rely for employment thereafter."[15]

In contrast to transatlantic carriers, U.S. steamship lines in the Western Hemisphere prospered with the rise of America's informal empire. In Cuba, U.S. investors expanded their plantation holdings, increased output, and formed new steamship lines or reinvigorated old ones. The United Fruit Company of Boston, for example, established its infamous banana plantations, launched an advertising campaign to introduce the tropical fruit into the nation's diet, and purchased four Cramp-built steamers. Most other plantation companies depended on the New York & Cuba Mail Steamship Company, which had sailed twelve Roach-built steamers before the Spanish-American War. Between 1898 and 1906 the New York & Cuba Mail issued contracts to Cramp for nine vessels totaling more than 50,000 tons.[16]

In the domestic long-distance trade, Clyde was still the largest carrier. During the 1880s it had entered into passenger and freight agreements with railroads and had later applied this strategy to the tourist trade by offering fast through-service from northeastern ports to vacation towns in Florida via the Florida East Coast Railway. Clyde also expanded its traditional stronghold in the East Coast cargo trade, embarked upon a thorough fleet modernization program, and awarded nine contracts to Cramp for passenger and freight steamers.[17]

The growth of coastwise shipping ground to a halt during the panic of 1907. This national financial crisis was partly the result of the collapse of the Consolidated Coastwise Lines (a domestic counterpart to IMM), which had recently acquired Clyde, New York & Cuba Mail, and four other steamship lines. In the wake of the failure, the Consolidated Coastwise subsidiaries were consolidated by Henry Mallory under the corporate umbrella of the Atlantic, Gulf & West Indies Steamship Lines. As a result of this reorganization, Cramp lost the patronage of both Clyde and New York & Cuba Mail—its most important customers for merchant steamships—when Mallory streamlined operations.[18]

Between 1907 and 1914 shipping, like other sectors of the economy, experienced a series of contractions interrupted by spurts of growth. In 1908 the commissioner of navigation predicted that in the aftermath of the recent shipbuilding boom, shipyards would turn out "a diminished product until the demands of trade, international and domestic, has caught up with the great amount of tonnage built throughout the world of late years."[19] Before World War I output oscillated well below the records set in 1902 and 1907.

Erratic demand was reflected in the vessel procurement policies of individual steamship lines. The Pacific Coast Steamship Company, for example, which served ports in California, Washington, Oregon, and Alaska, ordered four large steamships between 1898 and 1907, including two built by New York Ship; between the panic of 1907 and 1914 it issued only one additional contract, which went to New York Ship. The Great Northern Railroad had two large steamships built in 1902 but did not follow up until 1913, when it ordered the passenger liners *Great Northern* and *Northern Pacific* from Cramp.[20]

The only maritime sector posting strong gains throughout the period from the Spanish-American War to World War I was the oil trade between the Gulf of Mexico and the Northeast. Before the turn of the century the U.S. petroleum industry had been dominated by Standard Oil, which operated railroad cars and pipelines. Most of the nation's oil had been extracted, refined, and consumed in the Northeast and the Midwest whose transportation infrastructure did not include seagoing carriers. This situation changed with the rise of the Texas oil industry in the wake of the spectacular strike at Spindletop in 1901; henceforth, many northeastern refineries were supplied by Gulf Refining Company (later Gulf Oil) and the Texas Fuel Company (Texaco), which controlled Texas wells and shipped crude oil aboard tankers on the coastwise route from the Gulf ports to Philadelphia and New York. During the early years of the American tanker trade, Gulf Oil developed a close relationship with New York Ship, which became its principal vessel supplier. Standard Oil followed suit and had tankers as well as oil barges built by Cramp, New York Ship, and Neafie & Levy.[21]

Tankers embodied some of the most radical departures from conventional steamship design. Engines and boilers were positioned aft (instead of amidship as in most other vessels) to reduce the points of contact with the flammable cargo. This unusual feature resulted in hogging as the stern sagged relative to

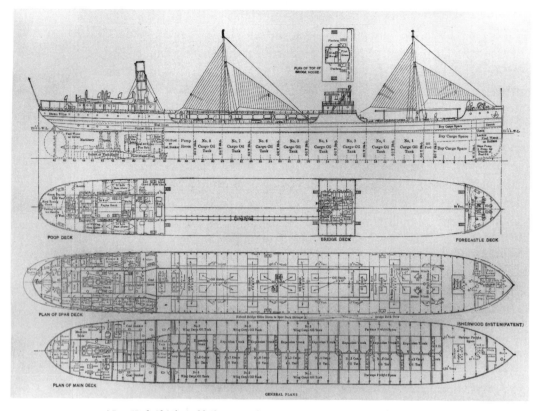

New York Ship's Gulfoil, *1912. The top drawing illustrates the arrangement of tanks, boilers, and engines typical in tanker design.* Marine Engineering *17 (March 1912)*

the midship section. Moreover, the hull had to endure the stresses exerted by the movement of the heavy liquid cargo. Naval architects soon realized that conventional hulls featuring vertical or "ribcage" frames were too weak to sustain these enormous strains, so they adopted instead a British system of longitudinal framing. The first American tanker of this type was the *Gulfoil*, built by New York Ship in 1912.[22]

Boiler design changed with the introduction of oil firing. This became feasible when British and German marine engineers invented reliable valves to spray oil into a fuel-burning chamber that replaced coal grates below the boiler. The advantages of oil firing over coal firing included higher calorific value, quicker and easier storage, and lower operating costs because the new system did not require stokers. The first large American merchant steamer equipped with oil burners was the American-Hawaiian freighter *Nevadan*, launched by New York Ship in 1902.[23]

The advent of marine steam turbines was an even more profound change. Pioneered by Sir Charles Parsons, the steam turbine featured a jacketed rotor with sets of angled vanes. Steam passed through valves onto the vanes and turned the rotor, which was connected to the propeller shaft. This system dispensed with crankshafts, which were necessary in reciprocating engines to transform lateral cylinder movements into rotary motion to turn the propeller. Because large marine turbines had to run at several thousand revolutions per minute (rpm) to operate efficiently, the system included sophisticated reduction gears to turn screw propellers at 125 rpm or less. British builders installed turbine engines in high-performance vessels, such as the battleship HMS *Dreadnought* and the famous Cunard liners *Mauretania* and *Lusitania,* all launched in 1906. The same year, Roach at Chester brought out the first American turbine steamers, *Harvard* and *Yale.*[24]

These changes made life difficult for U.S. builders because unstable vessel markets did not permit product specialization. In Britain strong demand enabled individual builders to concentrate on a few vessel types: Laing on the Wear was a specialist for oil tankers, Thompson/Clydebank usually built fast

Turbine wheels and shaft of Cramp's passenger vessel Old Colony, *the first turbine vessel built by the yard, 1907. This photograph gives a good indication of the precision work involved in turbine construction. William Cramp & Sons Ship and Engine Building Company,* Cramp's Shipyard *(Philadelphia, 1910)*

liners and capital ships, and Yarrow launched fast steamboats and destroyers. In U.S. yards, by contrast, "all types of construction—naval and mercantile, large and small—are contracted for promiscuously," as an engineer told British builders.[25] New marine technologies only increased the bewildering diversity. For example, by 1914 a big yard had to be equipped to build turbines for fast liners *as well as* reciprocating engines for cargo ships. More than ever before, markets and technologies forced U.S. shipbuilders to be jacks-of-all-trades.

Shipyard Architecture and Layout

Rising demand for large merchant steamers and capital ships prompted what Charles Cramp called a "new departure" in American shipbuilding. In order to build steamships of unprecedented size and power like the INC's 12,750-gross-ton passenger liner *Kroonland,* Cramp argued, a builder had to devise a new physical plant. "The sudden augmentation in the size of merchant ships has revolutionized all the methods of work and of manipulating the materials of construction. Man-handling of the materials [for] the mammoth ships now in vogue is out of the question, and the introduction of powerful and newly designed machinery, together with increased yard-space, is imperatively demanded to handle, fashion and work into place the elements of these immense structures."[26]

These changes were also the result of recent developments in industrial architecture as factory designers developed systematic plant layouts to eliminate production bottlenecks and streamline material processing. New industrial plants often featured single-story buildings in which traveling cranes carried production material through sequenced work stations and forwarded semifinished components to the next shop for further processing. This represented a departure from relatively small, multistory factory buildings whose design had been dictated by the limitations on transmission of steam power by shafts and belts. Electrical power enabled factory designers to spread out tools and shops in a less rigid fashion to accommodate fast throughput.[27]

In this context, the most innovative shipbuilder was New York Ship founder Henry Morse, whose unique shipyard plant was designed for a systematic construction sequence from the receipt of material at the railroad yard to the installation of shipfittings at the dock. New York Ship operated on the basis of the so-called template system—Morse's most important contribution to twentieth-century shipbuilding—which improved mold lofting. Traditionally, patternmakers had first made wooden patterns for the keel and frames. Upon completion of the frame, shipfitters would climb up the stagings, trace its contours, and deliver drawings for so-called lifted templates to the mold loft,

Template making in New York Ship's mold loft, showing a set of hull plate templates, Henry Morse's controversial innovation in naval architecture. Fifty Years New York Shipbuilding Corporation Camden, N.J. *(Camden, N.J., 1949)*

where patternmakers would cut plate patterns. This method, which was necessary to ensure a tight fit between frames and plates, often caused construction delays because the shops could not bend plates until the frame was complete. Morse conceived a precision template system in which patternmakers cut patterns directly from blueprints. New York Ship later claimed that the system "did away with the previous practice of 'lifting' templates from work in place before the shop could function. Through accurate mold loft development of templates from plans, the shops are enabled to go ahead with their work for any part of the ship upon receipt of material with the assurance that when a particular part is wanted by the ship erectors, it will fit its appointed place."[28] In theory, plates made on the basis of precision templates were interchangeable parts like those used in sewing machine, bicycle, and later automobile assembly. Indeed, Morse envisioned a "fabricated" ship made of standardized frames, plates, and deck beams.[29]

When Morse commenced his ambitious project in 1898, the forty-eight-year-old engineer already had experience in industrial architecture, civil engineering, and shipbuilding. Born in Poland, Ohio, he graduated from Rensselaer Polytechnic Institute at Troy, New York, in 1871 and commenced a career in bridge and tunnel construction. From 1878 to 1896, Morse served as president of several iron bridge companies and conducted experiments with prefabrication techniques. He then honed his shipyard management skills as president of Harlan & Hollingsworth in Wilmington, resigning in 1898 to launch New York Ship. Morse obtained financial backing for the new company from the Pittsburgh banker Andrew Mellon and Pennsylvania coal magnate Henry C. Frick.[30]

Initially, Morse intended to build the yard on Staten Island (hence the name *New York* Ship), but he finally settled upon Camden, choosing a site less than two miles across the Delaware from Cramp. In addition to low real estate prices, the advantages of the location included the "quality of soil on which depend stability of foundations . . . cost of grading and pile work, depth of water, railway facilities and proximity to a good labor market."[31] Camden was located at the center of the American Clyde, an area with the highest concentration of skilled shipyard workers nationwide. Within the region, U.S. Steel, Bethlehem Steel, and an array of Pennsylvania specialty mills produced ship steel, naval armor, and marine castings, while William Sellers & Co. of Philadelphia specialized in heavy industrial tools and controlled the Midvale Steel Company, which produced naval ordnance at Nicetown. Unlike Philadelphia, where waterfront real estate was expensive and congested, Camden offered cheap land for Morse's colossal plant. In 1899, when he announced the decision to build the yard, Morse inaugurated an era that lasted nearly three-quarters of a century, during which Camden became one of the nation's leading shipbuilding centers.[32]

Morse recruited shipyard managers, engineers, and craftworkers who remained with New York Ship for years to come. His most experienced personnel had previously worked at Cramp and at renowned British yards. General manager De Courcy May, for example, was a native of Baltimore who had emigrated to Scotland during the 1860s to spend several years with the Fairfield yard at Govan. He returned to the United States in 1876, worked as a consulting engineer with the Calumet & Hecla mining company of Massachusetts, was hired by Cramp's subsidiary I. P. Morris as a superintendent, and joined New York Ship in 1899. Chief engineer Luther D. Lovekin commenced his shipbuilding career as a rivet boy at Cramp during the 1880s. Upon completion of a patternmaker apprenticeship, he worked in Hillman's and Cramp's design departments and was hired by New York Ship in 1900. Hundreds of skilled craftsmen formerly employed by Cramp switched to New York Ship in 1899 during a labor conflict at the Philadelphia yard.[33]

The building contractors completed the physical plant in 1900. New York

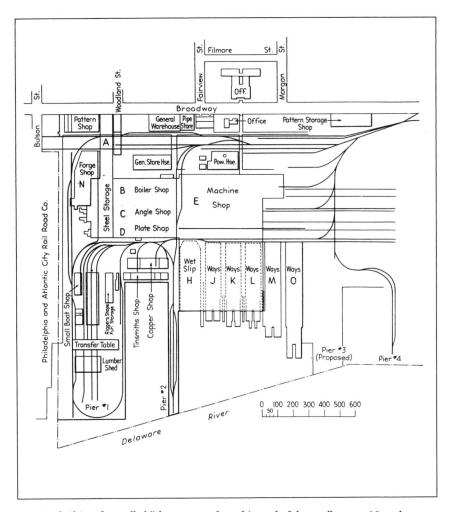

New York Ship, often called "the most modern shipyard of the age," c. 1913. Note the systematic arrangement of railroad facilities, shops, and berths. John Metten, "The New York Shipbuilding Corporation," in Historical Transactions, *ed. Society of Naval Architects and Marine Engineers (New York, 1943)*

Ship's design department, the largest in the American shipbuilding industry, was located on the first floor of a spacious main office building where engineers and draftsmen worked on ship plans and specifications. The specifications were forwarded to acquisition agents who ordered plates, angle iron, and beams from steel mills. Blueprints were processed in the mold loft, where patternmakers constructed wooden templates according to the Morse system.[34]

New York Ship received ship steel at a storage shed, where riggers unloaded railroad cars using cranes equipped with magnetic hoists. Other cranes transferred material to the adjoining plate, angle, and boiler shops, where workers

New York Ship's berth with Argentine battleship Moreno *under construction, c. 1913.*
Note the extensive overhead craning capacity, covered by the giant glass roof that was the
yard's trademark. Marine Engineering *19 (November 1914)*

operated special large tools "for bending, punching and shearing the angles
and shapes. There are two angle furnaces, one for taking a 60 foot angle, and
the shorter for handling a 30 foot angle . . . The long frames are taken from the
bending slab at the furnace to a second slab in the shed, where a special
portable tool is used for setting them to the exact shape."[35] Inside the shops

shipfitters preassembled large vessel components that were "picked up by one of three 10 ton gantries, which run on separate tracks, and [were] carried under the bows of the ships and stored until the time comes for [them] to be erected in place."[36]

In the hull department each berth accommodated either one large hull or two medium-sized units. "Thus six vessels of moderate beam can be laid down at the same time. There are two 10 ton traveling cranes for each of these building bays, the inner end of the cranes being supported by a runway suspended from the roof. These cranes are placed high enough to clear any ship while being built and fitted out after launching. The largest traveling crane in the works, of 100 tons capacity, is here located."[37] This enormous overhead crane capacity enabled New York Ship to haul large engine parts from the machine shop to the berths, where machinists installed them before launching. The berths also received construction material from the engine, forge, joiner, and pattern shops. Most departments used electric, steam, hydraulic, and pneumatic power.[38]

Surveying the plant in 1901, a writer for an engineering magazine reported that such "complete facilities for rapidly and economically handling the work of building ships and marine machinery are to be found in no other yard." Visitors also marveled at the giant glass roof covering the big berths, which gave the yard a distinctive appearance and enabled it to avoid weather-related construction delays. As a result, "the time required to build and completely equip ships of all types will be reduced to a minimum." American and foreign shipbuilders visiting Camden reportedly agreed that "here is found the greatest shipbuilding plant of the age."[39]

Trade experts were less enthusiastic about Morse's precision template system. During the construction of the pioneer vessel *M. S. Dollar,* the builder experienced technical difficulties because many parts did not fit and required corrections. This was particularly the case with hull plates featuring double curvatures to form a ship's streamlined bow and stern sections. Shipyard workers joked that the *M. S. Dollar* was so defective that "the rumor got around the company was going to be arrested for counterfeiting, as they were making 'bad dollars.' "[40] The Morse system produced better results in flat plates for the midship section, which did not require complicated templates. Still, many observers complained that the system was uneconomical. A British trade union representative who visited Delaware Valley shipyards in 1902 pointed out that other builders "turn out a greater tonnage with the employment of three template makers in the loft than the Camden yard can with 50 template makers, and a large array of draughtsmen . . . The equipment is costly, and the returns under the system adopted may be a sorry speculation for the shareholders. [These methods] are certainly those that no level-headed American or British shipbuilder would dream of adopting."[41] Morse nevertheless insisted on the fabrication system and refined his templates. According to naval architect Joseph Powell, "Mr. Morse did a great work, because he proved that a greater proportion of the ship could be fabricated than anyone had believed possible up to that time . . . He tried to do the whole thing and found that he could not, but he did demonstrate how far a ship could be fabricated."[42]

After the Camden firm, the most important new yard was the Fore River Shipbuilding Company at Quincy, Massachusetts, near Boston. Its founders, Thomas A. Watson and machinist Frank O. Wellington, first built engines and boilers, then entered shipbuilding during the late 1890s and erected large new facilities at the turn of the century. Rivaling New York Ship in equipment and construction capacity, Fore River became one of the most prestigious shipyards of the twentieth century.[43]

Among established yards, only the Newport News Shipbuilding Company in Virginia matched these new builders in terms of plant size. A multimillion-dollar facility improvement program enlarged the Newport News works, furnished electrical power in all departments, retooled the machine shop, and provided ample overhead crane capacity throughout the yard. Like New York Ship, Newport News introduced a "continuous, unretarded movement forward of the material from the time it enters the yard in the raw state until it is ready to leave as a part of a completed ship."[44]

For Cramp, the turn of the century marked a critical adjustment period. To compete with new rivals in satellite regions, the builder launched a $2 million yard improvement program that "chang[ed] the plant almost beyond recognition," as *Engineering Magazine* reported.[45] Its centerpiece was a new machine shop measuring 335 by 143 feet, equipped to handle large engine blocks, cylinders, and shafts, and featuring two 50-ton electric cranes and a variety of smaller ones. This equipment was far superior to traditional "pillar cranes, which stood at the center of the iron and steel foundry, and from that position served but a very small part of the floor." Electric shop cranes had "a moveable trolley . . . which covers every square foot of the floor area, takes up no valuable space, and is operated by one man, with a consumption of power only when actually in motion."[46]

Cramp also installed berth overhead cranes to streamline hull construction. Railroad cars carried large engine sections and boilers from the shops to the front end of a building slip, where a crane lifted them up, traveled down the berth, and lowered them for installation. Built by the Brown Hoisting Company of Cleveland, this innovative system replaced the temporary shears and derricks in use before the introduction of fixed berth cranes. At the height of

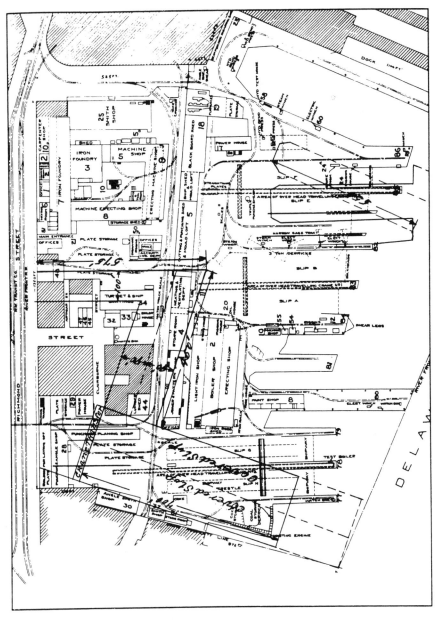

Cramp shipyard, c. 1913. This drawing shows the crowded arrangement of shops and berths. The two large berths shown at the bottom were not built until World War I. Cramp Shipbuilding Co. Collection, Independence Seaport Museum

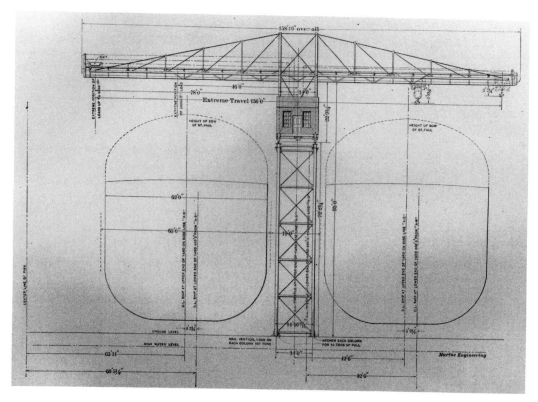

Overhead crane system of Cramp's largest berth. Riffled area indicates electrically powered trolley that moved the long crane arms. In spite of its considerable size, the berth was too small to accommodate the latest class of capital ships. Transactions of the Society of Naval Architects and Marine Engineers *49 (1902)*

the shipbuilding boom, workers would launch a hull, clear the ways, and lay the next keel, all on the same day.[47]

In addition to modernizing the shipyard, Cramp improved its subsidiaries. Most important, I. P. Morris received new tools to build hydraulic turbines. With the completion of a large turbine contract for the Niagara Falls Power Company, Morris became the nation's premier producer of hydraulic equipment, building huge water turbines for power plants in Ontario, Quebec, Colorado, and Washington. Morris and the shipyard received special alloy castings from the Cramp Brass Foundry (formerly B. H. Cramp), which also produced screw propellers, turbine runners, and automobile castings. Independent subcontractors poured steel castings until 1910, when Cramp acquired the Federal Steel Cast plant at Chester, Pennsylvania; Federal Steel Cast also supplied other shipyards as well as customers outside the shipbuilding industry. Cramp's secure foothold in the nonmarine sector made it the most diversified firm in American shipbuilding.[48]

While Cramp, New York Ship, and other major firms launched widely discussed plant improvements, smaller builders, such as Neafie & Levy, made less extensive changes in nineteenth-century shipbuilding practices. Their hull assembly departments, for example, still featured temporary shears instead of traveling overhead cranes. Still, Neafie & Levy spent more than $200,000 on new tools, introduced pneumatic riveting, and lengthened berths to accommodate 400-foot hulls.[49]

Cramp remained the nation's best equipped shipyard, rivaling Britain's Clydebank, Armstrong, Vickers, Fairfield, and Harland & Wolff, as well as other world-class facilities, in terms of equipment and expertise. With six large berths, its construction capacity was more extensive than that of New York Ship, which had three adjustable berths. New York Ship, however, featured larger and more systematically arranged facilities. For example, its machine shop was twice as large as the new Cramp facility and was more conveniently located to receive materials from other shops. Moreover, Cramp lacked New York Ship's direct overhead crane connection between the machine shop and the berths, relying instead on railroad cars that consumed less space but had a lower carrying capacity.[50]

In the congested environment along the Philadelphia waterfront, Cramp was increasingly strapped for space. This was especially obvious when the firm upgraded its overhaul division, which still had the 472-foot dry dock built in 1875, as well as outfitting shops and docks. In 1900 Cramp extended this plant by purchasing the defunct Charles Hillman yard. The *New York Times* reported that "it is the intention of the Cramps to merge the Hillman yard and the dry dock into one of the largest and most thoroughly equipped repair shipyards in the United States. The newly acquired plant includes a marine railway, machine, boiler, and blacksmith shops, which are fitted up with tools of the latest pattern, besides pattern and joiner shops and a mold loft. A new pier built about three years ago, on the end of which are huge hoisting shears, extends to the new Port Warden's line."[51] As *Marine Engineering* pointed out, however, expansion proved difficult because "the head of the dry dock in this yard lies close to a street," making it impossible to enlarge the dry dock.[52] Cramp devised awkward and costly arrangements to repair ships whose length exceeded 470 feet. In 1901, for example, the yard won a contract to overhaul the 560-foot transatlantic liner *New York*. Cramp docked her at the large Erie Basin dry dock in Brooklyn, crafted new engines, boilers, and funnels in Philadelphia, and shipped the sections to Brooklyn aboard barges—a rather clumsy procedure for what purported to be one of "the largest and most thoroughly equipped repair shipyards in the United States." Newport News, with dry docks of 610 feet and 827 feet in length, was much better equipped for this class of work.[53]

The purchase of the Hillman yard due south and a large lot from the Lehigh Valley Railroad to the north increased the Cramp yard from 30 to 50 acres. But Cramp was unable to expand much farther. A manager explained, "Real estate is very costly, and we can not go much farther south, because if we go to the south we go into a rolling mill, and to the north we get into the property of the Reading Railroad Company."[54] Cramp's proximity to Philadelphia's railroad terminals and steel mills, once a major asset, had by now become a liability.[55]

Craft Skills, Work Hours, and the Trade Union Movement

New technologies and production processes transformed workplaces throughout the industry. Some changes were unequivocally positive. For example, new shipyard shops, like many factory buildings erected at the turn of the century, were better ventilated and admitted more light than older structures. Electrical power meant cleaner buildings and workplaces. Job safety improved when builders replaced flimsy wooden derricks with solid steel structures. Cranes allowed shipyards to dispense with horses and mules, which had caused sanitation problems in nineteenth-century yards. Older employees and foreign visitors who were often all too familiar with small, dark, and unsafe facilities appreciated these changes.[56]

The impact of new technologies on skills differed widely from one craft to another. In general, according to a British observer, new tools and equipment still enhanced the role of skilled labor because the typical American shipbuilder introduced labor-saving machinery to replace unskilled workers and "employs his dear labor where thinking is required."[57] The introduction of the overhead crane offers one example: Allowing shipbuilders to dispense with yard laborers who had previously hauled material from one work station to the next using carts or bare hands, cranes required skilled operators and riggers who could lower a heavy vessel component to its precise location in one continuous "lift" without having to adjust the weight numerous times.[58]

Hull-assembly trades, such as drilling, changed with the introduction of electric tools. The impact on skills was usually marginal. For example, although electric drills made the job less physically demanding, they still required a trained operative, as a Harvard study of shipbuilding techniques noted: "It takes some time to learn the proper speeds to be used for the

Cramp's riveters working on the berth. The second worker from right is holding a pneumatic riveting gun. The child standing behind him is probably a rivet boy. Cramp Collection, Philadelphia Maritime Museum

different sizes of drills and different metals so as to drill as fast as possible without overheating or injuring the drill. It is also necessary to hold and control the tool in all manner of places and positions, and this comes only by actual experience."[59] At the same time, drills posed new safety hazards. Because poorly insulated drills charged hull plates, drillers now had to wear rubber boots as protection against electric shocks. For this reason, many builders replaced electric drills with air-powered ones until toolmakers developed more reliable equipment.[60]

Air was also used to power the industry's most celebrated tool, the pneumatic riveter. This hand-held device pushed a rivet into its hole by delivering a series of hammering blows generated by pneumatic power. Handling a pneumatic riveting gun still required considerable training in righthand and left-hand riveting. Some riveting still had to be done manually because many work areas were too narrow to admit large tools; also, some builders doubted whether pneumatically driven rivets provided sufficient strength. As late as 1906, 59 percent of all hull rivets processed by New York Ship were driven by hand.[61]

Other changes in shipbuilding threatened traditional skills. Nineteenth-century riveters had been responsible for setting and bolting hull plates, a task that required physical strength as well as craft skills acquired in years of practical experience. When employers increased the division of labor at the turn of the century, riveters lost this task to specially trained platesetters and bolters. Ship fittings, which traditionally had been crafted by skilled blacksmiths, were now made by semiskilled machine operators who used drop forges, presses, and standardized jigs. Shipyard blacksmiths also lost ground when marine engineers replaced forged engine parts with steel castings.[62]

Shipyard reformers praised these changes. They saw new technologies as means to reduce workers' control at the point of production. Echoing Frederick W. Taylor and other efficiency experts, shipyard reformers claimed that skilled workers exercised too much control over output. They urged production managers to reduce "as far as possible the number of operations which can only be carried out by skilled labor."[63] Specifically, they recommended the elimination of intricately shaped vessel components, the production of which required skilled labor in the bending department, and favored "straight work [which] is much simpler and could be undertaken by cheap or partially skilled labor."[64] Naval architects, however, objected to straight work because most plates required curvature to make a streamlined hull.[65]

A more widely discussed strategy used by employers to deal with production bottlenecks and workers' control was piecework. There were several systems for compensating workers per unit made, from simple payment by the piece to more elaborate task and bonus systems. Piecework rewarded high-quantity output and discouraged slow work. In late nineteenth-century shipyards, only repetitive jobs, such as riveting and caulking, were paid by the piece, but Cramp and a few other builders later introduced the system in skilled trades, such as shipfitting and furnace work.[66]

Like many employers experimenting with pay incentives, Cramp combined piecework with inside contracting, an arrangement by which a senior tradesman agreed to finish a certain job for a fixed price and hired a gang to perform the actual work. Cramp's general manager Harry Mull described the system as follows:

A drawing will come out of the office, for instance, of the keel of a ship. A proposal for bids to erect and assemble this keel is written up by a contract committee, and specifications are made . . . On these specifications there may be 1,000 pieces of work, and [the inside contractor] bids on one, naming the price which he will charge the company for the completed work . . . Then we select from all the bids submitted to us that of the most competent man, with the fairest price, and he receives the job.[67]

Cramp later refined this system with fixed piece-rate tables. Mull argued that this increased output because "every workman becomes his own boss, and it is to his interest to carry out the work and conclude the operation as quickly as possible, because he participates in the profits of the job."[68]

Union organizers and trade experts frequently criticized piecework and inside contracting. Thomas Wilson of the International Association of Machinists wrote, "Piecework takes away from the men the chance to deal with the company collectively and leaves the individuals to the tender mercy of unscrupulous foremen . . . An apprentice becomes not a machinist but a workman who can perform but one single operation, or, in other words, a specialist . . . [He loses] the position in which the American machinist to-day finds himself, where he is competent to fill any position in the shop, either on the floor or on the bench or on the machine."[69] Trade experts argued that piecework encouraged workers to finish a job as quickly as possible and hence was incompatible with good workmanship. It was impossible to place skilled trades "under the piecework system without making the game cost more than the candle," a marine engineer remarked. "When you come to anything that has got to be extremely accurate . . . the way to do [it], I thoroughly believe, is to abandon that very tempting idea of piecework."[70] Cramp's production managers, by contrast, believed that the new system "makes our business more efficient."[71] They had good reason to worry about production efficiency because of Cramp's limited ability to streamline material flows through systematic plant layout. Cramp introduced piecework and inside contracting on a larger scale than most other builders, and in consequence was soon engaged in ferocious conflicts with organized labor.[72]

Another bone of contention was the length of the workday. Nominally, shipyards adhered to the ten-hour day, except in winter when they switched to a nine-hour schedule. But in reality, the industry lacked a standard workday, as some trades had longer hours than others. For example, in 1897 ship painters worked 54.34 hours per week, while patternmakers worked 59.32 hours. Moreover, shipbuilding remained subject to the most volatile business cycles in the U.S. manufacturing sector. When yards that had been idle for months were swamped with fresh orders, tradesmen jumped to action to meet contract deadlines and get hulls off the berths as quickly as possible to make room for the next units. Longer hours meant better pay, but they also meant working night shifts in an accident-prone environment where heavy weights dangled over dimly lit berths. According to a Cramp employee, who exaggerated only slightly, sometimes "there was considerable rush on the ships that were then under construction, and the condition of the work was such that we were compelled to work overtime, although it was dangerous. We worked sometimes thirty-six hours, and twenty-four hours was nothing unusual."[73]

Labor leaders complained that overtime impeded job creation in the wake of the severe depression of the 1890s. Appealing to employers and efficiency experts, they also argued that long workdays fatigued workers and that they would be more productive under the eight-hour system. Perhaps equally important to the rank and file, long workdays often prevented them from participating in the new leisure activities of the day, such as spectator sports and silent movies. Combined with long shifts and piecework, these developments prompted demands for a shorter workday.[74]

The major trade unions spearheading the campaign in Delaware Valley shipbuilding were the International Association of Machinists (IAM) and the International Brotherhood of Boilermakers and Iron Shipbuilders. Like most craft unions affiliated with the American Federation of Labor (AFL), these organizations enlisted many new members between 1898 and 1902 when economic prosperity gave rise to labor activism. In a national organizing drive, the IAM increased its membership from 15,000 in 1898 to more than 40,000 in 1900. At its peak, it listed five locals in Philadelphia and Camden, which recruited machinists at Cramp, Neafie & Levy, New York Ship, the Baldwin Locomotive Works, the Sellers tool factory, and other leading metal trades firms. The boilermakers' union grew from fewer than 2,000 members in 1898 to almost 15,000 in 1901 and listed five locals and two helpers' divisions in Philadelphia and Camden. The unions plotted their own departure from nineteenth-century traditions. "Since the return of good times," a Philadelphia IAM official proclaimed, "organized workers of the whole country have been dreaming of better conditions in the way of shorter hours and better pay."[75]

Shipyard managers remained adamantly opposed to unions and demands for a shorter workday. Charles Cramp argued that the fundamental principle of labor organizations was to bring all workers "down to one level—that is to say, that a workingman of superior skill, diligence, knowledge, and power should be brought down to the level of the most inferior workingman, in so far as rates of wages and working time are concerned."[76] This extreme hostility toward labor organizations transformed conflicts over hours of work into struggles over workers' collective bargaining rights.

In Philadelphia the first confrontation took place in 1899, when four IAM locals tried to introduce the nine-hour workday at Cramp. A union delegation approached the management to discuss the matter but never advanced beyond

Charles Cramp's antechamber. The IAM launched its first strike in the Phila-delphia shipbuilding industry at the end of August 1899. Explaining why the union targeted Cramp, IAM president James O'Connell remarked, "They do not pay as much as other works and have longer hours. They say [to workers] 'you shall not have the right to be represented by committees. You must make known your desires by personal request.' "[77]

Unfortunately for the strikers, the walkout was not well organized and lacked coordination with other unions. During the first three weeks, 300 strik-ing machinists were joined by only a handful of blacksmiths, anglesmiths, and helpers. They failed to close down the yard with its more than 4,000 em-ployees. Moreover, 1,100 workers signed a petition declaring that they were "perfectly satisfied with the time and rates now en vogue."[78] The conflict gained some momentum in early October 1899, when more than 700 boiler-makers, caulkers, fitters, riveters, chippers, and platesmiths joined the strike. Cramp's hull-assembly department closed down because only three out of thirty-seven riveting gangs reported to work. Many strikers took jobs at New York Ship.[79]

At this critical juncture, the trade unions failed to provide decisive leader-ship. Labor organizers were more interested in having their locals recognized by employers as legitimate bargaining partners than in organizing successful grassroots campaigns for shorter hours. When the Cramp strike reached its climax in November 1899, O'Connell of the IAM, AFL president Samuel Gom-pers, and Peter McGuire of the Brotherhood of Carpenters and Joiners rushed to Philadelphia. O'Connell bragged that "in fifteen minutes with Charlie Cramp he could straighten this thing out" and called on the shipyard office to negotiate.[80] But Cramp refused any meeting. At a subsequent rally the labor leaders talked much about the necessity to unionize shipbuilding trades but said very little about the nine-hour day, even though it was the central strike issue. Gompers came closest to addressing the question: "Now I tell you that it is my firm conviction that the movement at Cramps' was a mistake!" he thundered. "Not because you made the movement, but because you asked for nine instead of eight hours . . . The eight-hour day is scientific, practical and based on common sense."[81] Like most craft union leaders, Gompers stressed that shorter hours benefited employers and scientific managers but said next to nothing about rank-and-file union men; from a worker's viewpoint, Gom-pers's call to convince Cramp's shift planners of the efficiency of the eight-hour system was hardly worth risking one's job. The AFL's lack of focus on working-class interests in disputes over hours of work was evident during most labor conflicts at the turn of the century and contributed to a series of stinging de-feats. The Philadelphia shipyard strike of 1899 died a slow death after the mass rally in November failed to broaden the movement's base among Cramp's employees.[82]

The union locals spent the next eighteen months recruiting new members at Cramp, Neafie & Levy, and New York Ship, and at subcontracting firms, such as Williamson Brothers and the John Baizley Iron Works. When the IAM launched a national nine-hour-day campaign in May 1901, it confronted a phalanx of conservative local employers spearheaded by Cramp, New York Ship, and the Baldwin Locomotive Works. Like Charles Cramp two years earlier, Henry Morse of New York Ship refused even to meet with union representatives. Soon after, several hundred machinists and boilermakers at Cramp and New York Ship walked out to join tens of thousands of striking metal-trades workers across the nation to implement the nine-hour day. They failed after weeks of bitter conflict, which left the Delaware Valley union locals defeated and financially exhausted.[83]

Local shipyard labor organizations did not recover for more than a decade. Immediately following the nine-hour-day strike of 1901, Cramp and New York Ship joined other metal-trades employers in an open-shop drive and fired labor activists. "The Cramp Shipyard Company," Gompers told a congressional committee, "has a system of detectives among the men to ascertain who should at any time manifest a desire for a shorter workday."[84] The Camden local of the boilermakers' union reported: "The New York Shipbuilding Company are discharging our members as soon as they find out they carry cards . . . We are of the opinion, and it is pretty well founded, that we have a traitor who is carrying news."[85]

Unions were especially vulnerable to open-shop drives during economic downturns, which were more common in shipbuilding than in any other industry. During maritime recessions, employers sometimes laid off more than 60 percent of their work force, making it difficult for trade unions to establish a permanent presence in shipbuilding. Moreover, Philadelphia's large metal-trades employers in the nonmarine sector agreed with shipbuilders that strikes and unions had to be broken at any cost. The Bement-Miles toolworks, for example, defeated the Iron Molders' Union during a walkout in 1906. The Baldwin Locomotive Works prevailed over metal-trades unions in a major strike four years later. These developments encouraged small engineering firms to end formal wage contracts with trade unions and to launch an open-shop drive organized by the Philadelphia Metal Manufacturers' Association. Among union men, the "paradise of the skilled craftsman" was now often called "scab city."[86]

Facing intractable problems at the point of production, shipyard labor organizations turned to the federal government. In 1892 Congress had passed legislation introducing the eight-hour day on all federal public works, includ-ing naval shipbuilding. In theory, this forced naval contractors to shorten their work hours accordingly, but narrow interpretations by the U.S. Justice Depart-ment and the federal judiciary had rendered the act all but meaningless. At the turn of the century the unions reopened the debate over a federally imposed eight-hour system with a campaign to close the loopholes that allowed Cramp, New York Ship, and other large naval contractors to evade the law. Union men and shipyard managers discussed the issue in a series of congressional hear-ings. Charles Cramp told senators that the introduction of shorter hours on public works "would be so revolutionary and demoralizing that [the contrac-tors] would be compelled either to adopt the eight-hour system in its entirety or abandon contract work for the Government altogether."[87] Agreeing with this assessment, Henry Morse spelled out what he believed to be the conse-quences of building merchant ships under the eight-hour system. Given the inability of American builders to match low British and German tonnage prices even under the prevailing system, it would "be against the interest of the shipowner, the shipbuilder, and the country at large to pass any law which would further increase the cost of ships."[88] Union representatives responded that shorter workdays would improve worker productivity and the compara-tive performance of American shipbuilding.[89]

Union leaders viewed the debate over federal laws regarding hours of work in the larger context of government intervention. Gompers was wary of federal labor legislation because he feared that forceful state action could lead to corporatism and erode the independence of labor organizations as republican institutions. At the opposite extreme, the socialist leaders of the IAM, who saw the state as a potential guarantor of long-term institutional stability of labor organizations, held positive views of labor reform laws. The IAM soon fought a relatively isolated battle for an improved eight-hour law, receiving little support from most AFL unions.[90]

In 1910 the IAM convinced Congress to write an eight-hour clause into the appropriations for the battleships USS *Nevada* and USS *Oklahoma*. (New York Ship built the latter vessel and willy-nilly introduced the eight-hour day in naval construction.) This served as the model for a law passed in 1912 that placed all federal public works contracts under the eight-hour system. Unfortunately for the unions, the U.S. attorney general determined that the clause applied only to work performed on government contracts; after eight hours, a builder could press his men to work additional hours in commercial construction.[91]

Labor's efforts to improve working conditions and to recast relations among workers, capital, and the state failed. Thanks to an improving economy and major organizing drives, the unions recruited new members and challenged employers at the point of production and in Congress. But internal divisions, the unsettled condition of the shipyard labor market, and the open-shop drive made it difficult to translate these initial successes into decisive victories as far as work hours and collective bargaining rights were concerned. It was little consolation to union men that managers faced their own problems when the "new departure" did not work out as planned.

The Demise of Neafie & Levy

At the turn of the century some shipbuilders believed that the perpetual crisis of the U.S. maritime economy since the Civil War had come to an end. Demand for new tonnage increased for years in succession, yards built ships of unprecedented size, and organized labor proved unable to reform the industry in ways deemed detrimental by employers. Simultaneously, however, builders encountered dearth amid the plenty. During prosperous times, most yards were strapped for cash because large-scale shipbuilding required considerable amounts of operating capital. According to established contracting practices, a vessel owner paid the builder in installments as the ship reached various degrees of completion. In the meantime, the builder paid subcontractors and workers out of his own pocket or obtained short-term loans. All too often, this exceeded the means of shipyards both large and small.[92]

Neafie & Levy felt the pinch soon after Jacob Neafie's death in 1898. Neafie's will assigned his shipyard holdings to trustee Matthias Seddinger, who managed the estate for Neafie's daughter Mary G. Whitaker. Seddinger, a Philadelphia real estate broker without much shipbuilding experience, had been elected vice president of the company in 1894 to administer Neafie & Levy's financial affairs. Upon Neafie's death he became president and sold a large block of shipyard shares to marine engineer Sommers N. Smith. Having recently completed a lackluster term as superintendent at Newport News Shipbuilding, Smith now served as Neafie & Levy's vice president and general manager.[93]

Seddinger and Smith promised that Neafie & Levy would "go more extensively for new work in the future than it has for some time past."[94] The yard soon booked contracts for the torpedo-boat destroyers USS *Chauncey,* USS *Barry,* and USS *Bainbridge,* followed by the cruisers USS *Denver* (1901) and USS *St. Louis* (1902), as well as fifty commercial contracts. As in earlier years, much of the commercial work consisted of tugs and ferryboats, but it also included a few larger vessels, such as the passenger steamer *Zulia* for the Red D Line. Neafie & Levy also built three steamboats for Baltimore's Weems Line as well as the *City of Trenton* and *Quaker City* for the Wilmington Steamboat Company.[95]

Unfortunately, Neafie & Levy's shipbuilding record was marred by mishaps involving the three torpedo-boat destroyers. In fierce competition with other builders, the yard had submitted an unreasonably low bid of $374,000 for each of these technically sophisticated vessels. *Bainbridge*-class destroyers featured high-performance, 8,000-horsepower engines weighing 190 tons, which had to be crammed into slim, 245-foot lightweight hulls. Racing at 29 knots, they were designed as the fastest vessels in the U.S. Navy. The first problems arose when subcontractors failed to deliver specialty steel on schedule. Neafie & Levy later told the Navy Department that although "our contract for the forgings called for complete delivery in four to five months, it was nearly two and one half years before delivery of the crank shaft was completed." Even then, Neafie & Levy had to "take the material in its rough state and finish it ourselves at a large increase of the cost to us."[96] A crucial issue was Neafie & Levy's inability to build the USS *Bainbridge*, USS *Barry*, and USS *Chauncey* according to contract specifications because the hulls proved too light to absorb vibrations caused by powerful engines running at 300 rpm. When other contractors experienced similar problems, the Navy Department redesigned the hulls and reduced the speed requirement by one knot. But naval inspectors detected additional problems during the October 1901 trial trip of the *Bainbridge* and recommended further design changes. Before the navy finally accepted her in October 1902, the *Bainbridge* went on more trial trips than any other U.S. warship. As a result of delays and penalties, Neafie & Levy lost approximately $180,000 on the contracts for the three torpedo-boat destroyers.[97]

The yard fared little better with cruiser construction. In 1901 Neafie & Levy won a $2.7 million contract for the armored cruiser USS *St. Louis*, the largest and most expensive vessel it had ever booked. Resembling the slightly smaller USS *New York*, launched by Cramp in 1893, this 426-foot, 9,700-displacement-ton vessel featured light armor plates. Unfortunately, Neafie & Levy did not adhere to the original construction schedule because steel contractors delayed armor deliveries. When the navy refused to honor its contractual obligations because the USS *St. Louis* was insufficiently advanced, Seddinger and Smith obtained loans to finance her completion.[98]

Neafie & Levy's reputation as a first-class shipyard suffered when a boiler explosion ripped through a river steamer it had built, the *City of Trenton*. Her owner, the Wilmington Steamboat Company, wanted to compete with the Delaware River Transportation Company and had asked Neafie & Levy to build a very fast boat. One year after delivery, the *City of Trenton's* port boiler blew up, killing twenty-four passengers in one of the worst steamboat disasters on the Delaware River. The owners charged Neafie & Levy with inferior boiler work and filed a $59,000 damage suit. The firm proclaimed its innocence and argued that the crew had acted irresponsibly by driving the boat at unsafe speeds to attract passengers from the rival line. Although the courts later cleared Neafie & Levy of all wrongdoing, the publicity damaged the yard's standing in maritime and financial circles.[99]

While the firm reeled under financial problems, Seddinger and Smith issued stock dividends totaling $124,000 to themselves. The Pennsylvania Supreme Court, which later declared the dividend illegal, commented: "During the period from 1900 to 1904, the company was engaged in building three torpedo boat destroyers, and a cruiser for the United States Government, and the business was carried on at a loss. The original capital of $800,000 was largely impaired, being depleted by a sum in excess of $760,000, leaving only a nominal amount. *The dividends above referred to were paid, not out of profits, but out of capital* . . . The capital of a company may not lawfully be used for the payment of dividends."[100] The court proceedings also revealed that Seddinger and Smith had used fraudulent bookkeeping methods to justify the payment of dividends at a time when the firm could not afford them.[101]

In May 1903, only three months after having declared and collected the last dividend, Seddinger and Smith obtained a $300,000 loan to finance the construction of the cruiser USS *St. Louis* and several merchant ships. The firm also accumulated a $400,000 uninsured debt to subcontractors. By November 1904 Neafie & Levy was no longer able to service its debts.[102]

A group of friendly creditors initiated receivership proceedings at the Philadelphia Court of Common Pleas in December 1904. Significantly, the creditors (which included I. P. Morris and the American Foundries Company of Chester) believed that Neafie & Levy's problems were only temporary and did not warrant bankruptcy proceedings. The receivership put the repayment of debts on hold and gave the firm time to regroup under a court-appointed management. An editorial pointed out that Neafie & Levy "is only going through the experience of other concerns which have undertaken the carrying out of large Government contracts without ample reserve capital to meet the exceptional conditions attending such work . . . It must be . . . a matter of great satisfaction to Philadelphians to have the assurance that there will be no interruption of work at the great Kensington plant, and that the company will emerge from its present troubles with 'clean books and improved credit.' "[103] Unfortunately, however, the court appointed as receivers the questionable Sommers Smith and the ailing financier John W. Grange, who died a few months later. The court removed Smith from the receivership when the illegal dividends became public, prompting further management changes as the yard went into a tailspin.[104]

By 1906 the creditors were convinced that more drastic steps were necessary to settle their claims. Accordingly, the court ordered a sale of the plant for at least $300,000 to satisfy the mortgage that Seddinger and Smith had obtained in 1903. But an auction brought only a $100,000 bid on the entire plant (which was reputedly worth at least five times that much) and had to be declared void by the court. The newly appointed receiver, Howard E. Cornell, was a competent manager who not only booked a series of vessel contracts under difficult circumstances but also developed a comprehensive plan to put Neafie & Levy's financial affairs in order by branching out into overhauls of large ships. This plan failed because the creditors refused to approve the necessary investments for a new dry dock. In May 1908 Cornell faced the inevitable and had the plant sold for $50,000. The new owners discontinued shipbuilding after Neafie & Levy delivered its last vessel, the steel tug *Adriatic,* in September 1908. Upon removal of the most valuable equipment, the wreckers tore down the buildings and dismantled the berths. The premises were sold to the Immigration Service, which erected a quarantine station where Neafie & Levy had built more than 300 ships and 1,100 marine engines in its seventy-year history.[105]

Neafie & Levy shared some of its problems with other builders. To survive in the competitive market for tugs, barges, and steamboats, firms such as Roach, Harlan & Hollingsworth, and T. S. Marvel frequently submitted low bids and realized slim profits or even losses. Further, the destroyer program of 1898 proved one of the most disastrous projects in the history of American naval shipbuilding, wreaking financial havoc at Neafie & Levy, William Trigg, Harlan & Hollingsworth, Charles Seabury, and Maryland Steel. The navy's review concluded that the "contractors, nearly all of whom were without the requisite skill and experience . . . had great difficulties in obtaining the necessary materials, were encountering additional obstacles in the trial of their boats, and were suffering severe losses under the terms of their contracts."[106]

The Military-Industrial Complex and the Crisis of the Cramp Shipyard

Cramp faced far greater challenges than the small builders did. At the peak of the shipbuilding boom, Cramp worked on vessel contracts worth $24 million and had to finance facility improvements that increased the value of the physical plant to more than $12 million. This required financial restructuring because the firm was somewhat undercapitalized at only $4,448,000. Cramp devised makeshift solutions by issuing bonds and obtaining short-term loans to finance a bulging order backlog.

Between 1898 and 1907 the yard launched twenty-five passenger ships, eight freighters, five battleships, and six cruisers. The most spectacular merchant ships were the INC passenger liners *Kroonland* and *Finland,* whose first-class accommodations featured dining halls for 250 passengers, drawing rooms with green silk tapestry and satinwood tables, and Elizabethan-style smoking rooms paneled with fumed oak. The *Kroonland* and *Finland* were Cramp's last transatlantic liners.[107]

Naval construction included the Imperial Russian Navy cruiser *Variag* and the battleship *Retvizan,* built according to Cramp's own plans and specifications. The U.S. Navy was sufficiently impressed with Cramp's Russian battleship to incorporate most of its features in a new battleship class. The navy awarded Cramp the contract for the lead unit, the USS *Maine,* which carried the name of the famous vessel sunk at Havana in 1898. Cramp also won contracts for the USS *Pennsylvania,* USS *Colorado,* and USS *Tennessee,* its largest (and last) armored cruisers.[108]

Naval construction inspired the most ambitious corporate scheme in the firm's history: Charles Cramp's plan for a merger between the shipyard and a large naval steel producer. Until this time shipyards had obtained only the relatively unprofitable warship hull and engine contracts, leaving the much more lucrative armor and gun orders to steelmakers. As Cramp's naval construction experience had illustrated, separate hull and armor contracts prompted organizational problems, construction delays, and financial woes. A naval concern incorporating shipyards and steel mills could eliminate these problems through systematic coordination of vessel construction and armor production, Cramp argued. He envisioned the construction of "a first-class war ship complete, ready to go into action when delivered, including not only hull, machinery, and equipment, but also armor, guns, and ammunition."[109] Equally important, a merger would raise capital for Cramp's commercial contracts and its costly yard improvement program.[110]

Cramp's role models and potential partners were three British naval conglomerates. The William Armstrong Works at Elswick had pioneered the combination of shipbuilding, armor manufacture, and gun production in 1884. It was followed by the John Brown armor conglomerate, which acquired Thompson/Clydebank in 1897, and the armor and gun manufacturer Vickers' Sons & Maxim, which purchased the Naval Construction Works at Barrow. Since Vickers' Sons occasionally manufactured ordnance for the U.S. Navy and sought a permanent foothold in the booming U.S. warship market, its senior managers lent a sympathetic ear to Cramp's merger proposal. The chief financial expert of Vickers' Sons, Sigmund Loewe, discussed the plan with senior U.S. government officials and received a go-ahead from President William McKinley.[111]

The prospective partners agreed on a double-track strategy. First, Cramp would sell Vickers' Sons a multimillion-dollar stock issue to raise cash for yard improvements and fresh operating capital. Second, Cramp and Vickers' Sons planned to buy an American steel plant to manufacture naval armor and ordnance under patents supplied by Vickers' Sons. The senior executives soon narrowed the field to Carnegie, Midvale, and Bethlehem, which supplied the bulk of U.S. naval steel. Carnegie was unavailable because it had recently merged into U.S. Steel, and this left the Bethlehem Steel works in central Pennsylvania and Midvale Steel at Nicetown near Philadelphia. After a promising start, Midvale bowed out at the last minute, and Cramp and Vickers' Sons concentrated on Bethlehem.[112]

At first glance, Bethlehem was a prime candidate for the merger project. Specializing in steel for navy and merchant ships, Bethlehem had provided Cramp with plates and crankshafts for battleships, cruisers, and passenger liners for more than a decade. However, the partners' enthusiasm was dampened by the discovery of Bethlehem's $8 million debt, which required $500,000 in annual payments. Vickers' Sons insisted on a thorough examination of the account books.[113]

In May 1901 the British executives were satisfied that the merger was feasible. Vickers' Sons would furnish $15 million to buy Bethlehem Steel as well as a $5 million issue of Cramp stocks. To raise additional funds for working capital and plant improvements, Cramp-Vickers-Bethlehem would issue $5 million in bonds, the organizers declared. Together with Cramp's existing capital and Bethlehem's and Cramp's older bonds, the Anglo-American firm would be capitalized at approximately $30 million. Compared with other mergers at the turn of the century—the billion-dollar U.S. Steel or the $150 million International Mercantile Marine—this was a modest undertaking. By the standards of the military-industrial complex, however, Cramp-Vickers-Bethlehem would be a virtual behemoth building hulls, engines, armor, and guns for Britain and the United States, the two fastest growing naval powers of the turn of the century. No other naval concern, including Armstrong and Brown, built capital ships for two world powers. Other foreign orders beckoned as well, because Cramp and Vickers' Sons maintained good relations with naval authorities in Russia, Asia, and Latin America. (In 1901, for example, Cramp booked a Turkish cruiser contract and Vickers' Sons built battleships for the Argentine navy.) In Charles Cramp's words, the projected Cramp-Vickers-Bethlehem company would cease to be shipbuilders and become "navy builders."[114]

The project foundered at the last minute. While Vickers' Sons and Cramp haggled over share prices with Bethlehem's stockholders, the latter suddenly received a more generous takeover bid from Charles Schwab, president of U.S. Steel. Significantly, Schwab had no intention to merge Bethlehem with U.S. Steel because he feared that the U.S. Justice Department would launch an antitrust suit. Instead, he wanted to form a separate naval concern by merging Bethlehem with the recently established U.S. Shipbuilding Company. Schwab's intervention ruined the plans for an Anglo-American naval conglomerate.[115]

This chain of events marked a turning point in Cramp's history because Vickers' Sons abandoned all merger negotiations. The *New York Times* reported that this left the shipyard stranded without badly needed cash to "reimburse the company for capital expenditures, for additions to and improvement of the property during the last few years . . . and to furnish additional working capital."[116] Working capital was the most pressing problem. "The amount of money tied up in the building of ships is large. The material which has to be purchased and paid for, the labor which has to be settled weekly are items which run up when it takes over a year before a ship is completed and the profit realized. For this reason the Cramp Company has often outstanding loans amounting to $2,000,000 and more."[117] A stockholder explained that "contracts representing a prospective income in millions of dollars could be kept alive only by the expenditure of new millions."[118] Problematic contracts included the battleship USS *Maine,* construction of which was months behind schedule as a result of late armor deliveries and strikes. When the navy refused to pay according to schedule because the hull was not sufficiently advanced, Cramp had to borrow money to pay its subcontractors. With Vickers' Sons out of the picture, the firm was on the verge of defaulting on debts of $4 million.[119]

The first day of financial reckoning came in November 1902 when the management used its scarce cash resources to pay interest on loans instead of issuing the scheduled 5 percent annual stock dividend. This caused consternation at the Philadelphia Stock Exchange, where the firm's shares fell from $67 to $61.50 within hours. Financial markets brimmed with rumors that the shipyard was on the verge of a major financial reorganization or even bankruptcy.[120]

Cramp turned to Edward T. Stokesbury of Drexel & Company to obtain a long-term multimillion-dollar loan. Unfortunately, Cramp's cash crisis occurred during the "rich men's panic" of spring 1903, when financial markets contracted in the wake of the preceding five-year merger boom.[121] Stokesbury related that "in all his experiences in the financial world he never had such a difficult time to induce individuals and institutions to advance their money as in the present case. No private parties, banks, or trust companies in New York desired to advance money to the Cramp Company."[122] Cramp's shares fell from $61.50 in November 1902 to $35 in April 1903. At the last minute, Charles Cramp and Stokesbury finally "secured the money from local capitalists through a plea to civic pride."[123] Prodded by Philadelphia bankers, the First National Bank of New York soon joined the rescue operation.

Financial restructuring involved a $5 million loan and a $1.5 million stock issue to settle Cramp's short-term debts, refinance yard improvements, furnish working capital, and compensate the promoters. The bonds were floated by Drexel & Company, the Fourth Street National Bank of Philadelphia, and the First National Bank of New York on the following conditions: "the loan is to be paid off in yearly installments, beginning January 1, 1904, and running in graduated amounts until complete liquidation of the debt shall be effected in July, 1928. It is stipulated that the underwriting bankers shall pay 90 per cent. for the bonds . . . and that they shall receive a bonus of 20 per cent. of the par value of their [bond] subscriptions in stock of the [Cramp] company."[124] Compensating promoters with shares was a sensible strategy, financial experts believed: "It will be much to the interests of the bankers to make this stock valuable and therefore [they] will work to make the company more profitable, not only to pay the interest upon the debt but to restore the stock to the list of dividend payers."[125] However, this scheme fell through because the bankers insisted that interest payments and the retirement of bonds should take priority. Cramp lacked funds for stock dividends until 1917.

During the loan negotiations, the bankers exacted painful concessions and asked for the immediate resignation of the sitting directors, who were held responsible for the hazardous financial strategies of the past. For the time being, Charles Cramp remained president and chaired a new and relatively powerless board whose members "will be directors in name only," the press reported. "They will have no power in directing the company—will simply be figureheads, in fact."[126] Strategic investment decisions were now made by representatives of the underwriters, who established a board of trustees that included Stokesbury of Drexel & Company, Richard H. Rushton of the Fourth Street National Bank, and George F. Baker, president of the First National Bank of New York. "When the trustees take hold," a financial expert remarked, "it will be found that a weeding-out process will begin by which all the dead wood will be cut out."[127] Faced with these unpleasant realities, Charles Cramp submitted his resignation as president in October 1903. The "new departure" had displaced its leading architect.[128]

Cramp was succeeded by Henry S. Grove, who served as president from 1903 to 1917. Born in 1849, Grove had made a fortune in the Philadelphia linseed oil trade. He was later elected president of the Colorado Coal and Iron

Company, vice president of the Continental Cotton Oil Company, and director of the Philadelphia National Bank. The last member of the Cramp family to serve on the board of directors was Charles's son Edwin, who resigned in 1907.[129]

After rescuing the firm from a court-appointed receivership, the new management struggled to keep it afloat. Immediately following the reorganization, Cramp's net surplus fell from $300,397 in 1903 to $188,174 in 1904. Stricter accounting methods revealed that most profits were made by the nonmarine departments. In 1904 Grove reported to the stockholders that "there has been little or no profit in shipbuilding proper. Were it not for our subsidiary companies doing business other than that of building ships we would not have been able to make this showing."[130]

One source of trouble was the battleships USS *Mississippi* and USS *Idaho*. Appropriated by a fiscally conservative Congress in an effort to curb naval expenditures, these 13,000-displacement-ton, 16-knot vessels were smaller and slower than the previous 19-knot battleships of 16,000 tons. When Cramp agreed to take the $6 million contract in January 1904, a manager recalled, the "shipbuilders said that we would not get a new dollar back for an old one spent, and I think they were pretty nearly right."[131] Technical problems loomed large from the beginning because the navy awarded the armor contract for the *Mississippi* and *Idaho* to Midvale Steel, which had no experience in this line of work. As a result, armor deliveries were sporadic and incomplete. The Navy Department itself had little interest in a timely completion of Cramp's stubby battleships, which would presumably spoil the world cruise of the Great White Fleet, a propaganda tour designed to show off America's naval might. Matters were complicated by the destruction of hundreds of plans and models during a shipyard fire. Although the naval establishment breathed a collective sigh of relief when the Great White Fleet departed without the *Mississippi* and *Idaho*, the shipyard management struggled with the financial burdens of numerous construction delays.[132]

Between 1905 and 1911 Cramp's profits went on a roller-coaster ride. The relatively prosperous fiscal year ending on April 30, 1906, yielded substantial gains, followed by a disastrous performance during the next twelve months with a surplus of only $3,407 (table 1). The latter figure, low as it was, was based on the optimistic assumption that the government would finally reimburse Cramp for losses incurred on the USS *Indiana* after nine years of court proceedings. Shortly after the management had issued its annual report for 1907, the U.S. Supreme Court reversed a lower court decision in Cramp's favor and left the firm with an actual net loss of more than $130,000. Thanks to the

TABLE 1
Net Dollar Surplus of William Cramp & Sons, 1901–1914

1901	291,772
1902	385,286
1903	300,397
1904	188,174
1905	314,615
1906	370,972
1907	3,407
1908	242,727
1909	446,153
1910	
1911	6,16
1912	208,108
1913	306,676
1914	847,477

SOURCE: William Cramp & Sons Ship and Engine Building Co., *Annual Report*, 1906–9, 1911–14; *PI; IA.*

good performance of the I. P. Morris division, Cramp posted substantial surpluses in 1908 and 1909, but financial calamity struck again in 1911.[133]

Cramp's financial difficulties were partly the result of its inability to obtain profitable commercial contracts. Most important, the Clyde and Ward steamship companies, which had previously accounted for most of Cramp's passenger liner and freighter contracts, changed their vessel procurement policies after having merged into the Atlantic, Gulf & West Indies Steamship Lines in 1908. Prodded by a new management, both lines abandoned their previous practice of awarding most of their contracts to Cramp without asking other builders for bids. Open competition with New York Ship, the Maryland Steel Shipyard, and Newport News proved a rude awakening for Cramp. The line never issued another ship contract to the Philadelphia builder because other yards tendered lower bids.

One reason for Cramp's inability to book substantial commercial contracts was its expensive design and construction practice, which in turn was a result of extensive naval shipbuilding. Cramp's naval architects and marine engineers were accustomed to drawing minute plans for virtually all vessel components because the Navy Department wanted to inspect blueprints for everything from doors to bathroom sinks. Over the years, these excessive design practices—of questionable value even in naval construction—percolated into merchant ship design. A steamship manager complained that when "we go to [the shipyard draftsmen] to have specifications and bids prepared, they begin to figure on mercantile work as though it was intended for the Government, under Government specifications and inspection, and in consequence the work produced or estimated upon is much better than we ought to have."[134] The only type of commercial tonnage that required the minute plans common

Battleship USS Wyoming, *1912. Note main battery, consisting of five turrets, reduced to four and three in later battleship types. U.S. Naval Historical Center*

in naval shipbuilding was high-performance liners, which American yards rarely built.[135]

From 1907 to 1912 more than two-thirds of Cramp's output consisted of government work. Although most were sand barges ordered by the Panama Canal Commission, there were some outstanding specimens of naval architecture, such as the proto-dreadnought USS *South Carolina,* launched in 1908. Cramp's first real dreadnought was the 27,000-displacement-ton USS *Wyoming,* which set new standards in battleship design. However, the yard did not receive another capital ship order in its remaining years of operation. In 1912 it refused to bid on the battleships USS *Oklahoma* and USS *Nevada,* which had to be built under the eight-hour system; echoing Charles Cramp, the management explained its decision not to compete for the "eight-hour battleships" by pointing out that "the entire plant of the company would have to go on an eight-hour day basis."[136]

Other warships built by Cramp between 1907 and 1914 included a light cruiser and a gunboat for the Cuban government, as well as a submarine and twelve destroyers for the U.S. Navy. After fierce competition with other builders, the yard also obtained the contract for the naval collier USS *Cyclops.* But Cramp submitted a very low bid of $805,000, which was largely responsible for the firm's poor financial showing in 1911.[137]

Cramp survived these lean years in part because its subsidiaries provided technical support for the shipbuilding division. In 1907, for example, the yard booked its first contract for a turbine vessel, the *Old Colony*, whose engines were built by I. P. Morris. Cramp's subsequent success as a builder of turbine vessels was in large part due to Morris's expertise and virtuosity, supplemented by the Cramp Brass Foundry and the recently acquired Federal Steel Cast plant at Chester, which melted the special alloys necessary for turbine production.[138]

Shortly before World War I, Cramp reentered commercial shipbuilding with a series of merchant vessels. A profitable project came along in July 1912, when the yard won a William R. Grace & Company contract for the freighters *Santa Clara*, *Santa Catalina*, and *Santa Cecilia*. In April 1913 Cramp booked a Great Northern Railroad contract for the *Great Northern* and *Northern Pacific*. This marked the firm's return to construction of high-performance liners,

Passenger liners Great Northern *and* Northern Pacific *outfitting at Cramp, November 4, 1914. These vessels, the crowning achievement of Cramp's decade-long experience in liner construction, were equipped with turbines of the type shown earlier in this chapter. Note the three sets of traveling overhead cranes in the background. On the pier in the foreground, note the junk parts of centrifugal pump or steam turbine cases taken out of a vessel undergoing repairs. Although Cramp performed most overhauls at the Kensington Shipyard on Palmer Street, some repair work was also done at the Norris Street facility. Franklin Institute Cramp Shipbuilding Co. Collection, Independence Seaport Museum through the Pew Museum Loan Program*

which required the exceptional attention to detail in which Cramp excelled. Interior hull plans showed every cut in the beautifully designed joiner work; the caulkers, after forcing two hull plates together, went over the seam with a special tool to effect a finish known as "nice work"; in the social halls, painters decorated large windows with panoramic landscapes so that passengers afraid of sea travel could imagine they were dining in rooms overlooking Glacier National Park. Cramp also equipped the 23-knot *Great Northern* and *Northern Pacific* with turbine engines developing 25,000 horsepower, the most powerful propulsion systems installed aboard American turbine vessels before the war.[139]

Cramp's experiences highlighted several trends in shipbuilding and American business at large. First, Cramp's projected merger with Vickers' Sons and Bethlehem reflected a trend toward integrated naval concerns. The initiative usually came from armor producers and not from shipbuilders as in Cramp's case. Following the example set by Vickers' Sons, Armstrong, and Brown, Alfred Krupp, Germany's leading steel producer, bought the Germania yard in Kiel at the turn of the century to build complete warships, and in 1902 Charles Schwab and Lewis Nixon merged Bethlehem Steel with the U.S. Shipbuilding Company. When U.S. Shipbuilding failed a year later, Schwab bought its remnants at bargain prices, closed down the least profitable plants, and created a new naval concern that controlled the armorworks at South Bethlehem, Pennsylvania, the Union Iron Works, Harlan & Hollingsworth, and the Samuel Moore yard in Elizabethport, New Jersey. Following a failed attempt to buy Cramp in 1912, Schwab acquired Fore River, which became Bethlehem's flagship plant.[140]

Second, Charles Cramp's resignation heralded the exit of an entire generation of pioneers from the American shipbuilding scene. Cramp himself spent the remaining ten years of his life as the industry's elder statesman; most of his old rivals had passed away earlier. Jacob Neafie and John Dialogue died in 1898, followed in 1899 by the founder of the Bath Iron Works, Thomas Hyde. Collis P. Huntington of Newport News died in 1900, Irvin Scott of the Union Iron Works in 1903, and John B. Roach in 1908. Dialogue willed his small Camden yard to his son John Dialogue, Jr., but in some cases yards did not survive a proprietor's death. Roach's heirs, for example, refused to continue his "brave effort to keep the business going at the sacrifice of his own means," and the Chester shipyard entered receivership only five months after Roach's death.[141]

New York Ship's Rise to Prominence

Henry Morse died in 1903, shortly after New York Ship had launched its first vessel, and was succeeded by former general manager De Courcy May. The new president inherited a somewhat troublesome order backlog. Completion of the Atlantic Transportation Company freighters *Massachusetts* and *Mississippi*, for example, was delayed by construction problems that prompted a $139,000 damage suit filed by the owners. Other holdovers from the Morse era included the American-Hawaiian Steamship Company contracts for the 8,633-ton cargo steamer *Texan* and the smaller *Nevadan* and *Nebraskan*. Unfortunately, May was unable to win repeat orders from this line because other builders submitted lower bids.[142]

New York Ship's more successful relationship with Gulf Oil dated from 1902, when the yard launched three pioneer tankers. Gulf later issued contracts for the tanker *Oklahoma* and the sister ships *Gulfoil, Gulflight,* and *Gulfstream.* The latter three represented New York Ship's 407-foot class built on the basis of one set of templates for the midship section.[143]

May tried his best to procure similar orders and won a U.S. Lighthouse Department contract for five 114-foot lightships, followed by a five-unit series of slightly larger vessels (including the famous *No. 87 Ambrose Channel* whose light marked the entrance to New York Harbor). The Lighthouse Department also ordered five identical tenders of the 190-foot *Manzanita* class. However, commercial contracts for multiple ships proved hard to secure. In addition to Gulf's 407-foot class, the yard's only series of merchant steamers worth mentioning was Standard Oil's four-unit *Rayo* tanker class, built in 1913. These contracts enabled New York Ship to experiment with prefabrication techniques, but true mass production of oceangoing ships did not take place until World War I. In peacetime the Morse system was ill adapted to the commercial ship market because most owners preferred custom-built tonnage.[144]

New York Ship failed to gain a secure foothold in this market. During May's tenure from 1903 to 1913, the yard obtained only six contracts for passenger liners and rarely secured repeat orders. The Merchants' and Miners' Transportation Company, which ordered the *Ontario* in 1904, returned only once in 1910 with contracts for the *Suwanee* and the *Somerset.* For the Pacific Coast Steamship Company, New York Ship built the *President* and *Governor* in 1907, followed six years later by the *Congress.* One reason for this relatively poor showing may have been bad timing. Since New York Ship was the last of the major yards established near the turn of the century, it had precious little time to accumulate the solid shipbuilding record that steamship company managers wanted to see before they entrusted a builder with valuable liner contracts. Further, during the early years New York Ship's reputation was tarnished by Morse's controversial template system, construction problems, and the delayed completion of the ATC freighters *Mississippi* and *Massachusetts.* When the yard had finally ironed out some of its problems, demand for large

Pacific coast steamship Congress, *one of the few large passenger liners built by New York Ship prior to World War I, at the outfitting pier, c.1913. This photograph provides an exterior view of the yard's famous covered berths; the interior was shown earlier in this chapter. New York Shipbuilding Co. Collection, Independence Seaport Museum*

passenger liners fell off after the panic of 1907, leaving few opportunities to secure repeat orders.[145]

Meanwhile, New York Ship developed a stronghold in warship construction and eroded Cramp's position as the navy's leading contractor for capital ships. Morse secured New York Ship's first naval contract, bidding against Charles Cramp and several other builders for the armored cruisers USS *Tennessee* and USS *Washington* in January 1903. When the Navy Department assigned both ships to Cramp, Morse filed a complaint with Secretary of the Navy William Moody. After a meeting with President Theodore Roosevelt, Moody awarded the USS *Washington* to New York Ship. A few months later, Morse underbid Cramp and obtained a $4,165,000 contract for the battleship USS *Kansas*. May continued Morse's aggressive move into naval construction in 1904 with a very low bid of $3.75 million for the battleship *New Hampshire*, wresting the contract from Cramp, which had submitted the next lowest bid.[146]

New York Ship emerged as the nation's principal battleship builder during the dreadnought era. Its pioneer ship was the proto-dreadnought USS *Michi-*

gan (contract awarded in July 1906) whose twin USS *South Carolina* was built across the river by Cramp. In 1908 May submitted a successful bid of $3.95 million for the dreadnought USS *Utah* and promised to complete her in only thirty-two months. Although New York Ship missed the deadline by six weeks, the construction of the *Utah* established a pre–World War I record for the delivery of dreadnought battleships. In 1909 New York Ship booked the battleship USS *Arkansas,* followed three years later by the USS *Oklahoma.*[147]

In 1910 New York Ship won a subcontract from Bethlehem Steel for the Argentine battleship *Moreno.* This highlighted a move into arms exports that became routine as the military-industrial complex matured. Like Cramp during the 1890s, most naval contractors who upgraded their facilities to build capital ships did not receive sufficient follow-up orders from the U.S. Navy, so they turned to foreign markets. Bethlehem Steel, for example, increased its armor production facilities during the "dreadnought revolution," which failed to produce the anticipated increase in naval appropriations; in 1909 an economy-minded Congress cut President Roosevelt's request for four battleships in half. When the Argentine navy invited bids on two battleships one year later, Bethlehem Steel entered into a fierce contest with British and German builders and received the $21.3 million contract for hulls, engines, and armor amid charges of bribery by its disappointed rivals. Named *Moreno* and *Rivadavia,* the battleships measured 595 feet in length, 98 feet in the beam, and 30,250 displacement tons and were the largest built in the United States before World War I. Since Bethlehem Steel's own shipyards were not yet sufficiently equipped to build dreadnought hulls and engines, the naval concern placed subcontracts with New York Ship and Fore River.[148]

The builders received extensive assistance from the U.S. government, which did its best to facilitate naval arms exports. (The *New York Herald* argued that Bethlehem had won the contract in the first place because President Roosevelt's Great White Fleet had successfully advertised American warships around the world, assuring foreign navies that "American yards deserve the fullest confidence.")[149] In a confidential memorandum discussing the merits of building warships for foreign navies, the chief of the navy's bureau of ordnance argued that it was in the best interest of the government to encourage private "establishments . . . as far as practicable in obtaining foreign orders for the building of ships and the manufacture of war material, especially from those countries affected by the Monroe Doctrine. It is thought that it would result in increasing our available resources in time of war, while adding to our commercial prestige and prosperity."[150] The Navy Department furnished innovative designs for turbines, turrets, and fire control systems, and the government ordnance factory at the Washington Navy Yard supplied underwater torpedo tubes for the Argentine battleships. In return for its support, the U.S. Navy could rest assured that the industrial base necessary to build battleships was kept up to date with foreign contracts even as congressional naval appropriations decreased. The Argentine battleships were also the first vessels built under a policy guaranteeing the U.S. Navy's right to purchase foreign-owned warships from the builder "at any time before delivery in the event of any emergency."[151] The *Moreno* and *Rivadavia* were completed in 1915 after Assistant Secretary of the Navy Franklin D. Roosevelt had settled a minor dispute between the contractors and the Argentine navy. New York Ship celebrated the delivery of the *Moreno* with a banquet featuring President Woodrow Wilson as the guest of honor.[152]

New York Ship's experiences underscored two themes in the history of American shipbuilding. First, New York Ship, Newport News Shipbuilding, and Bethlehem Steel—soon dubbed the Big Three—outclassed Cramp in terms of plant size and construction capacity. This was particularly obvious in capital ship construction: Cramp's largest berth accommodated hulls with a maximum beam of 78 feet, too narrow for the *Moreno,* which measured 98 feet in the beam. Later record-breakers, such as the *Lexington*-class battle cruisers, 888 feet long and 103 feet in the beam, were built by New York Ship and Newport News Shipbuilding. No longer able to compete, Cramp abandoned capital ship construction to concentrate on smaller warships. New York Ship capitalized upon its geographic advantage in the course of plant improvements during World War I and bought additional real estate to build large new facilities in close proximity to the existing plant. Cramp, in contrast, had to tear down valuable buildings to make room for new shops and berths. Most builders who joined the industry in following years emulated New York Ship's geographic strategy and erected shipyard plants in metropolitan satellite areas.[153]

Second, newcomers tried to balance naval construction with large-scale commercial shipbuilding. In this regard, New York Ship was less successful than Newport News and Fore River, which profited from close connections with steamship operators. Newport News obtained contracts from steamship lines controlled by the Huntington heirs, who also held a considerable number of shipyard shares; one of Fore River's stockholders was a director of the United Fruit Company who procured banana steamer contracts for the shipyard. New York Ship lacked similar connections and was hence more dependent on naval contracting. Major commercial orders did not materialize until World War I.

SEVEN

This Machine of War: World War I

During the shipbuilding heyday of World War I, Cramp's restaurant employed a brawny cook named Maggie whose busy schedule included destroyer christenings. According to Kensington shipyard lore, "the ships came tumbling off so fast . . . that there wasn't always time for the big-wigs to come up from Washington to launch them." On those occasions, shipyard president Henry Mull would "grab a telephone and get the restaurant on the wire. 'Send Maggie out here,' he'd yell. 'We're going to launch a ship.' Two minutes later, Maggie would come [running] across the ship-shed yard, wiping flour off hands on an old blue apron. They'd give her a bottle of champagne, and she'd let fly."[1] Across the river, New York Ship celebrated many construction records. In April 1918, for example, the yard laid the keel for the freighter *Tuckahoe*. For the next several weeks, hundreds of shipyard workers raised frames, placed hull plates, and installed beams; one busy gang drove 1,500 rivets in a single shift. Twenty-seven days later, the yard launched this 332-foot ship with engines and boilers already in place.[2]

Although government officials often cited the *Tuckahoe* as a laudable example of how American shipbuilders "beat the Kaiser," few ships were actually built in such record times. Shipyards had suffered neglect during the prewar depression, and builders spent months or even years increasing construction capacity to meet wartime demand. This enormous industrial effort was centered in the Delaware Valley, where builders added new facilities and introduced Henry Morse's fabrication system, which became a fixture of twentieth-century shipbuilding. Capitalizing upon this technique, new yards like Hog Island near Philadelphia also built standardized ships in mass production.

As it did in other industries, World War I marked a transformation of shipyards' capital-labor relations as Delaware Valley builders hired tens of thousands of workers. Combined with the continued suburbanization of shipbuilding, the hiring wave overburdened regional transportation networks connecting urban working-class neighborhoods to outlying areas. In response, employers and the federal government furnished worker housing and developed new labor policies. At the same time shipyard managers and government officials confronted a wave of labor unrest as trade unions launched strikes to wrest long overdue concessions from employers. Building upon a tradition of state intervention, the federal government channeled labor militancy into collective bargaining structures to ensure industrial peace during the wartime shipbuilding effort.

Wartime Shipping

The war created shortages of waterborne carrying capacities on all major trading routes. The chief causes were the commissioning of many English ships for war duties and Britain's decision to concentrate on naval shipbuilding at the expense of commercial work. This policy resulted in a 75 percent drop in British merchant construction during the first year of the war. Commercial shipbuilding rebounded in 1916 when the government realized that replacement of freighters destroyed by German submarines was at least as urgent as the construction of a large naval force to combat Germany's High Seas Fleet. Still, tonnage output remained far below prewar levels until 1919. Meanwhile, the Royal Navy blockaded German steamships in their home ports and in neutral countries, and Germany's shipyards abandoned commercial shipbuilding. The paralysis of the British and German maritime economies effectively removed the world's largest maritime powers from international trade.[3]

The resulting dearth of shipping caused special hardship in the American foreign trade, where British and German ships had played vital roles as passenger and freight carriers. It impaired the agricultural sector, which could not market recent bumper crops despite skyrocketing demand for American foodstuffs and cotton in Europe. This situation formed a sharp contrast to the Napoleonic wars, when the merchant marine was well prepared to carry American goods to Europe and helped create an export boom. Combined with a stock market panic and the liquidation of European investments in the United States, the shortage of shipping caused an economic contraction immediately after the outbreak of hostilities in August 1914.[4]

The Wilson administration responded to the crisis with reforms in U.S. registry policies that had protected the merchant marine since the 1790s. The exclusion of foreign-built ships from American-flag status had changed slightly with the passage of the Panama Canal Act in 1912, which permitted the registry of select foreign-built steamships under the U.S. flag. A registry reform act passed in 1914 abolished most restrictions and enabled shippers to transfer any foreign-built ship to the neutral American flag; these vessels could sail in the U.S. foreign trade but were still excluded from the coastwise routes.[5]

By the end of 1915 more than 500,000 gross tons of foreign shipping—mostly owned by U.S. citizens—had been admitted to U.S. registry. This effectively reversed the depletion of the American merchant marine that had taken place during the Civil War, when northern vessel owners had transferred close to 1 million gross tons to foreign flags. But tonnage registered in the United States after 1914 did not include ships owned by citizens of the belligerents because both the British and German governments sought to prevent a "flight from the flag" through restrictions on outflagging. When it became clear that registry reform had not solved the shipping problem, vessel owners ordered new ships to take advantage of rapidly increasing freight rates. Given the inability of British and German builders to supply commercial tonnage, most of the new vessels were built in the United States, where steel steamship output surged from 143,000 gross tons (1914) to 310,000 (1915) and 1.22 million (1916).[6]

The boom started in the fuel export sector when American operators increased oil and coal shipments to Britain, continental Europe, and non-European markets. U.S. firms benefited from major realignments in the international crude oil and coal trades that had taken place when Britain's imports of petroleum from the Middle East declined as a result of its war with the Ottoman Empire. In addition, wartime restrictions on British coal exports led to fuel shortages in Italy, Greece, and Argentina. These countries turned to U.S. suppliers, which increased production and procured export carrying capacity. In 1915 New York Ship booked orders for four colliers from the Coastwise Transportation Company and also built three tankers for Gulf Oil; in the same year Cramp booked five contracts from Sun Oil and Standard. In response to the oil boom, Sun Oil established an integrated shipyard at Chester. Tanker operators deployed the bulk of their new tonnage on the New York–Liverpool route, where freight rates increased from $4 per ton (1914) to $50 (1917).[7]

Other vessel owners ordered new ships to take advantage of a shipping boom in agricultural products and raw materials. In the Western Hemisphere, American operators assumed a leading role in the Argentine cattle export trade, which switched from British to U.S. carriers in 1915. Similar changes transformed the Chilean nitrate trade, where W. R. Grace & Company replaced British tramp operators and issued eight freighter contracts to Cramp. W. R. Grace also acquired a minority interest in New York Ship and ordered two large cargo and passenger steamers for its Pacific coast service in 1917.[8]

This dramatic revival of the carrying trades went hand in hand with a corporate consolidation of American shipping. Several older steamship companies were reorganized by the American International Corporation (AIC), a $50 million company founded in November 1916. AIC's board of directors included senior executives of the National City Bank of New York, J. Pierpont Morgan, the Boston engineering firm Stone & Webster, and W. R. Grace. In an ambitious attempt to replace European investors in Asia and Latin America, the conglomerate underwrote bonds for U.S. export firms, procured foreign contracts for large construction projects, and invested in shipping, shipbuilding, and machine tool production. AIC acquired the ailing Pacific Mail Steamship Company in partnership with W. R. Grace and transferred its vessels to W. R. Grace and International Mercantile Marine, which was now partly owned by AIC; it also acquired a large interest in United Fruit and New York Ship.[9]

Foreign investors entering the U.S. maritime trades during the shipping famine included European vessel operators who turned to American builders because their home yards were unable to supply the ships they needed. Cunard, for example, issued more than 150 contracts to the Great Lakes Engineering Works at Detroit, the former Roach yard at Chester, and other builders. Like their American counterparts, foreign investors sometimes combined shipowning with shipbuilding to secure a steady supply of new tonnage. The Norwegian ship broker Christoffer Hannevig, for example, acquired Pusey & Jones and bankrolled plant improvements as well as the construction of cargo vessels.[10]

Despite these considerable efforts, American and other neutral steamship operators were unable to relieve the shipping shortage. This alarmed progressives like President Wilson and Secretary of the Treasury William McAdoo, who called for a government-owned merchant marine. Similar demands had been raised by prewar maritime reformers, who had argued that the private sector was unable to halt the decline of the U.S. merchant marine. The wartime crisis increased support for reforms among manufacturers and farmers, who envisioned a federal maritime agency resembling the Interstate Commerce Commission to control freight rates. Steamship operators and their congressional allies, however, claimed that the progressive agenda amounted to a socialist takeover of commercial shipping. They were able to hold up legislation for almost two years. In 1916 Congress finally passed the so-called Shipping Board bill providing $50 million for a government-owned fleet. It created the U.S. Shipping Board, which was authorized to purchase vessels from private owners, issue vessel contracts, operate steamships, and set freight rate schedules for the private sector. In a major concession to conservatives, reformers agreed to end public ownership after five years and then sell or lease Shipping Board tonnage to private shippers.[11]

The Shipping Board was unprepared to meet wartime challenges. Shortly after the bill's passage, freight and marine insurance rates spun out of control due to a marked increase in submarine warfare. This warranted the appointment of competent Shipping Board managers, the swift implementation of comprehensive freight rate schedules, and a shipbuilding program. But President Wilson postponed the selection of senior managers until after the November elections. Then, instead of nominating experienced shipbuilders and steamship men, Wilson used the Shipping Board as a patronage mill to reward political allies. The important chairmanship, for example, went to California lawyer William Denman, who had little experience with maritime issues. Shortly after confirming his appointment, Congress declared war on the Central Powers, appropriated $500 million to build steamships, and authorized the Shipping Board to supervise the nation's entire noncombat vessel program. To administer the building of merchant ships, the Shipping Board established the subsidiary Emergency Fleet Corporation (EFC), chaired by Denman and managed by Major General George Goethals, the former construction supervisor of the Panama Canal project. Against Goethals's advice, Denman approved a bizarre EFC project to construct 1,000 *wooden* auxiliary steamers, several hundred of which were actually built by Denman's friends in the western lumber industry. Open hostility between the two men paralyzed the Shipping Board and the EFC until their departure in July 1917, when they were succeeded by new senior executives.[12]

In summer 1917 the EFC implemented three major policies to meet the wartime emergency. First, it commandeered all commercial steamships exceeding 2,500 tons that were still under construction, financed their completion, and delivered them to the Shipping Board. Between September 1917 and the Armistice in November 1918, the EFC requisitioned more than 3 million gross tons of steel shipping under this program, which created the backbone of the government-owned noncombat fleet carrying U.S. troops and supplies to Europe. Second, the EFC placed new vessel contracts with private shipyards and financed plant improvements. This effort included Denman's infamous wooden ships as well as several hundred steel freighters, tankers, and troopships, most of which were still incomplete at the time of the Armistice. Third, the EFC began mass production of standardized cargo ships at so-called agency yards, new establishments bankrolled by the government and managed by private agents. Although they formed the linchpin of EFC shipbuilding policy and received the bulk of plant construction funds, agency yards failed to deliver a single unit before November 1918.[13]

In addition to the building of noncombat ships, World War I triggered considerable warship construction as the United States inched from neutrality to naval preparedness to war. Before 1914 President Wilson had concentrated on domestic reforms and shown relatively little interest in naval policy. Most of the construction funds in the 1914 naval budget went into three "superdread-naught" battleships, including the USS *Idaho* laid down at New York Ship in 1915. The next two years witnessed Wilson's remarkable conversion to naval preparedness, prompted by the sinking of the *Lusitania* in May 1915 and the Anglo-German stalemate during the naval battle at Jutland in May 1916, which eroded Wilson's faith in British naval supremacy. Arguing that the United States could no longer rely on an invincible Royal Navy to check German naval power, Wilson recommended the largest warship construction program in history: ten battleships, six fast battle cruisers, ten scout cruisers, fifty destroyers, and seventy-seven submarines, tankers, and repair ships. Further appropriations added more than two hundred destroyers to this enormous program.

Revival of the Cramp Shipyard

Burgeoning demand transformed the political economy of the U.S. maritime trades. Prewar recessions had created a buyer's market in which builders had to scramble for contracts to keep their yards employed; this had forced yards to accept low profit margins and accommodate demands for customized designs and specifications. The war created a seller's market, allowing shipbuilders to raise prices and occasionally even to standardize vessel design.

Cramp viewed the war as an opportunity to end the financial crisis that had been looming over the shipyard since its reorganization in 1903. The bankers' board of trustees still made strategic investment decisions, earmarking most profits for the retirement of the $5 million loan and keeping a tight lid on yard improvements. By 1915, however, the trustees were convinced that the shipping shortage would yield profitable future contracts, so they approved an extensive modernization of the physical plant. Cramp added a new machine shop, a marine railway for the Kensington Ship Repair division, additional railroad tracks inside the yard, three large furnaces, and two concrete 810-foot berths. The yard also worked on very lucrative contracts, yielding a whopping $1.08 million net surplus for the year ending in April 1916. Thanks to the improving financial situation, the board of directors accelerated the retirement of long-term bonds from $220,000 to $280,000 annually and, for the first time in the yard's history, accounted for the depreciation of tools and machinery.[14]

Another milestone in Cramp's comeback was the introduction of marine diesel engines and motorships. Invented by Herbert Stuart and Rudolph Diesel, this technology was based on the internal combustion principle and produced higher fuel efficiency than conventional triple-expansion engines. Instead of boiler steam, the diesel system injected heavy petroleum into the cylinder; ignition of the charge by compressed air resulted in rapid expansion, pushing the piston outward. The diesel system required new engine designs because internal combustion produced much higher temperatures and pressures than steam technology; this forced engineers to devise smaller cylinders as well as new metal alloys, cooling systems, and cylinder arrangements. One of the most successful designs for marine diesel engines was developed by the famous Danish engineering firm Burmeister & Wain, which secured European and American patents. In 1916 Cramp obtained a license from Burmeister & Wain and procured new engine construction equipment; in February 1917 it completed the first large American motorship.[15]

The firm's improving fortunes attracted outside investors who vied for 7,000 shares owned by the Cramp estate, which controlled Charles Cramp's holdings after his death in 1913. In June 1915 these stocks were purchased by the Chandler bank of Philadelphia, which also acquired 20,000 shares owned by the First National Bank of New York and other creditors. This takeover facilitated important changes in Cramp's senior management. By 1916 the yard produced substantial profits that were reportedly large enough to have warranted good dividends, but President Henry Grove and the trustees still reserved net earnings for plant improvements and the retirement of bonds. This seems to have irked the Chandler interests that now dominated the board of trustees; they replaced Grove with Cramp's former vice president Harry Hand. During his brief tenure in 1917, Hand declared Cramp's first dividend since 1902. His successor Henry Mull, who remained president until 1927, steered the same course.[16]

In 1917 Cramp devoted itself to the rapid completion of commercial contracts and commenced ship overhauls as well as naval construction. The EFC requisitioned nine merchant ships under construction at Cramp that were worth $12.7 million; most of them were launched and commissioned before the Armistice. From April 1917 to April 1919 Cramp also dry-docked 184 vessels and performed overhauls on more than 560 ships at the repair wharves. The EFC intended to place additional orders for new merchant steamers but had to yield to the Navy Department, which asked Cramp to reserve construction capacity for naval ships. The navy soon issued contracts for five *Omaha*-class scout cruisers as well as forty-six destroyers. Due to the limited availability of berth space, Cramp postponed the cruiser program until 1919 to concentrate on destroyer construction.[17]

The destroyer program was one of the most ambitious projects in the history of naval shipbuilding. In its entirety, it involved 273 flush-decked "four pipers" and produced the world's largest destroyer force. The program began in spring 1917 with the *Wickes* class, measuring 310 feet in length and 1,090 displacement tons and equipped with Parsons turbines; Cramp completed six of these vessels in 1918. During the second stage the yard built forty vessels of the *Clemson* class, with the same hull dimensions but with new ordnance and a different turbine system.[18]

Building vessels of the *Clemson* class required large-scale additions to Cramp's storage and hull engineering departments. These were partly financed by the Navy Department, which provided $4.4 million for plant improvements. Since the old steel sheds were not equipped to store the enormous amounts of material necessary to build at least twenty destroyers at any given time, Cramp erected a steel yard on Petty's Island close to the New Jersey side of the Delaware River. This facility had three storage buildings, plate racks, railroad tracks, wharves, and barges to transport material to the yard. To improve material processing at the shipyard itself, Cramp tore down older buildings and erected a new fabricating shop with a large mold loft, storage space for templates, furnaces, and bending equipment. Modeled on a similar facility at New York Ship, this shop registered a daily output capacity of 150 tons of fabricated material. Like New York Ship a decade earlier, Cramp claimed that "the whole [plant is now] co-ordinated to such an extent that the materials entering the yard as raw material at one end go out of the finishing shops completed and ready to go into place."[19] Although the facility development program improved material flows inside the yard, the inconvenient location of the Petty Island storage facility created new bottlenecks because ship steel had to be loaded onto barges and hauled across the river.[20]

The *Clemson* program also necessitated a remodeling of the foundry to manufacture ship propellers in large quantities for Cramp as well as other destroyer builders. Designed to transmit 14,000 horsepower, each propeller measured 9 feet in diameter and featured three blades that had to be cast, planed, and machined with great skill to produce a well-balanced wheel without secondary vibrations. Propeller castings required special metal alloys, melted and cast at the old foundry. New facilities built specifically for the destroyer program included a new finishing shop where Cramp installed precision tools to machine hundreds of propeller wheels.[21]

Cramp's Propeller Foundry in World War I. This photograph shows destroyer propellers undergoing finishing process in the main bay. Cramp's Shipyard War Activities (Philadelphia, 1919). *Historical Society of Pennsylvania*

Clemson building was a qualified success. Hull construction began in spring 1918. Since each berth accommodated three hulls lined up behind one another, construction had to be well sequenced so that the hull lying closest to the river was the first one to be completed and launched, clearing the ways for the next unit. Cramp launched most hulls according to this pattern, starting with the USS *Chandler* in spring 1919. However, outfitting was less well organized because subcontractors failed to deliver turbine reduction gear according to schedule, delaying commissioning. During speed and endurance trials, naval officials ranked most Cramp boats at the very top of the class along with those built by the Bath Iron Works, the navy's most experienced destroyer builder.[22]

New York Ship

Like Cramp, New York Ship viewed World War I as an opportunity to iron out prewar problems. Designed to build a large series of identical ships, the yard had rarely obtained sufficient contracts to practice ship fabrication on a large scale. This changed after 1914 when rising demand permitted a more extensive use of the Morse system in commercial shipbuilding.

When the first round of wartime contracts was issued in January 1915, New York Ship obtained seven tanker contracts aggregating 66,688 gross tons. The tankers included duplicates of the prewar "407" class whose design produced remarkably durable vessels. The *Gulflight*, for example, was one of the first American ships torpedoed by a German submarine, sustained severe hull damage, and reached port under her own steam with a large hole in her bow.[23]

In 1914 New York Ship booked a contract worth $11.5 million for the "super-dreadnaught" USS *Idaho*—a project that caused major financial losses during the next four years. Shortly after New York Ship agreed to build this 32,500-displacement-ton battleship, wartime inflation wiped out all profits as the yard paid higher prices for ship steel and subcontracted items than expected. The effort to complete the huge ship as soon as possible to avoid the effects of spiraling inflation was abandoned shortly after launching in June 1917, when the navy suspended capital ship construction to free resources for the destroyer program. Although her builders breathed a sigh of relief when she finally left the yard to join the fleet in 1919, the USS *Idaho* became one of the yard's most famous vessels and participated in the World War II battles of Saipan, Iwo Jima, and Okinawa.[24]

In 1916 AIC and W. R. Grace acquired New York Ship. In their attempt to combine shipbuilding with shipping, finance, and international trade, these investors bought out the old stockholders (principally Mellon and Frick) who sold their $6 million in shipyard shares for $15 million. After reorganizing the firm into the New York Shipbuilding Corporation in November 1916, the shareholders elected a new board of directors chaired by George Baldwin, a former public utilities manager and president of the Pacific Mail Steamship Company. Other board members included Charles Stone of Stone & Webster, Philip A. Franklin of International Mercantile Marine, and Joseph P. Grace of W. R. Grace. The board of directors elected Marvin Neeland, a former vice president of U.S. Steel, as chief executive. (His predecessor, Samuel Knox, had been a passenger on the *Lusitania* and suffered mental disorders after barely surviving her sinking.)[25]

During his first year at the helm of the shipyard, Neeland implemented a $1.4 million yard improvement program to provide berth space for the bulging order backlog. At the time of the takeover in November 1916 the yard still featured the original plant with its wet dock and three berths. The Neeland program completed two covered berths, which had been under construction

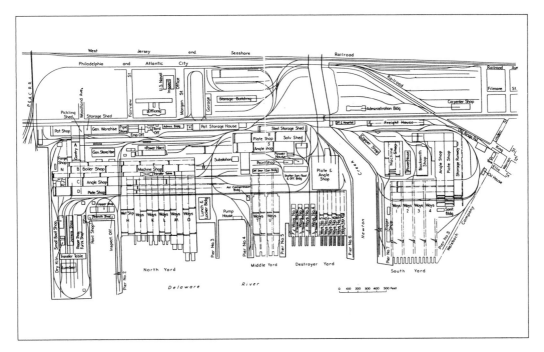

New York Ship in World War I. The entire section east of berth L was built during the war. The Middle Yard had two of the largest berths in the industry. John Metten, "The New York Shipbuilding Corporation," in Historical Transactions, *ed. Society of Naval Architects and Marine Engineers (New York, 1943)*

since early 1916, and added two giant berths accommodating four hulls at the so-called Middle Yard.[26]

As part of the 1916 naval buildup, New York Ship received contracts for the battleships USS *Colorado* and USS *Washington*, the battle cruiser USS *Saratoga*, six *Wickes*-class destroyers, and twenty of the *Clemson* class. Negotiations with the EFC yielded contracts for a nine-unit series of 535-foot troopships and a seven-unit series of 502-foot vessels. All told, New York Ship secured government contracts for forty-five ships while simultaneously working on twenty-three private vessels taken over by the EFC in August 1917.[27]

A key question was how to allocate resources for this large and diverse program. Most existing shops and berths were busy with requisitioned merchant ships for the EFC, including the *Tuckahoe;* although New York Ship managed to cram several destroyers into older berths, there was no room for the *Clemson* vessels. The navy therefore provided $4 million for a new plant built on a property owned by New York Ship. Construction of this Destroyer Yard began on October 17, 1917, and furnished six covered and four open

Aerial view of New York Ship, the world's largest shipyard, c. 1919. Note the original plant at left with a troopship outfitting. Note also the Clemson-*class destroyers outfitting near the Middle Yard. National Archives*

berths, a big plate and angle shop, and extensive facilities to store fabricated material. Completed in a remarkably short time under adverse weather conditions, the Destroyer Yard laid the first keel in December 1917 and became fully operational only five months later.[28]

The EFC pursued a similar strategy of financing plant extensions to build troopships. Adjoining the Destroyer Yard south of Newton Creek, the new South Yard was built on marshland and required extensive dredging and 30,000 wooden piles. The plant operated its own shops for plate, angle, and blacksmith work. There were four berths with cranes specifically designed to serve large troopships. Capitalizing upon past practices, New York Ship installed boilers and engines before launching to prevent overcrowding at the outfitting piers. In a controversial move that fueled widespread suspicion of wartime profiteering, the EFC later sold the yard, which had cost $14.8 million to build, to New York Ship for only $500,000. These additions to its physical plant made New York Ship the world's largest shipyard.[29]

With the destroyer and troopship programs under way in 1919, New York Ship resumed the construction of capital ships and laid keels for the 32,000-displacement-ton USS *Washington* and USS *Colorado.* These battleships were widely regarded as the latest development in marine engineering. Each vessel was equipped with a turbo-electric drive system in which turbines powered two electrical generators that drove four motors connected to propeller shafts. Before the suspension of capital ship construction in 1917 New York Ship had already issued a $2 million subcontract to Westinghouse to manufacture generators and other electrical equipment at its Pittsburgh plant. The USS *Washington* was canceled and scrapped in accordance with a postwar naval disarmament agreement, but her sister ship USS *Colorado* became one of the most powerful battleships of the pre–World War II navy.[30]

The last capital ship built as part of the wartime program was the *Lexington*-class battle cruiser USS *Saratoga,* one of the largest and most powerful vessels ever constructed by New York Ship. Like all battle cruisers, vessels of the *Lexington* class combined heavy battleship ordnance with the speed, performance, and maneuverability of cruisers and were designed to engage enemy scouts before slower and more heavily armored battleships arrived on the scene. The 43,500-displacement-ton *Saratoga* and her five sister ships featured 888-foot hulls and were powered by enormous 180,000-horsepower turbo-electric engines. New York Ship booked the contract in May 1917 but did not lay the keel until 1920. When naval disarmament led to the cancellation of the battle cruiser program in 1922, the builders converted the *Saratoga* into an attack aircraft carrier and completed her in 1927.

Other Delaware Valley Yards

In addition to transforming older firms, the war boom led to a revitalization of abandoned shipyards, the establishment of new plants, and further experiments with ship fabrication. Capitalizing upon the Delaware Valley's vast industrial infrastructure and its long tradition in iron and steel shipbuilding, newcomers opened four plants within a twenty-mile radius of Philadelphia, thereby increasing the region's prestige as a vital center of American and world shipbuilding.

The war brought about a revival of the Roach yard at Chester, which had launched its last ship in 1907. Shortly before 1914 it had been reopened by Charles Jack, a retired navy officer, to convert freighters into tankers. Lacking adequate steel fabrication facilities at the shipyard, Jack conducted an important experiment by issuing subcontracts for hull and tank sections to the American Bridge Company works in Pittsburgh. Mindful of his subcontractor's limited experience with shipyard bending techniques, Jack designed a simple hull and supplied templates for flat plates. American Bridge fabricated plates for tanks and the midship section and shipped them in preassembled sections to Chester, where Jack's men installed them without fitting and rebending. The completion of major hull work by a subcontractor hundreds of miles from the shipyard was a departure from conventional ship fabrication at New York Ship and Cramp, where all hull material was fabricated in yard shops. This innovation formed the basis for the so-called ship assembly system adopted by the EFC for its agency yard program.[31]

In February 1917 Jack's yard was acquired W. Averell Harriman, the young heir to the Edward Harriman railroad empire, who renamed the firm Merchant Shipbuilding Corporation (MSC). Harriman launched a $3 million improvement program to modernize shops and berths. Employing Jack as a consulting engineer and American Bridge as a subcontractor, MSC developed simplified hull designs and built standardized freighters and tankers using fabricated material. "The results of the fabrication in the Bridge Company's mills . . . is beyond criticism," a yard representative reported. "Work is fair, rivet holes require no reaming, and the resulting fit of joints and watertightness is excellent."[32] Like Morse fifteen years earlier, however, MSC discovered that fabricated ships still required a great deal of custom work. The yard had "wherever possible, carried out the idea of duplication and standardization, but very often had to abandon it in the detail."[33]

Other additions to Delaware Valley shipbuilding included Sun Ship at Chester, which opened in 1916. This yard was bankrolled by the Pew brothers, who controlled the Sun Oil Company with its pipeline terminal at Sabine Pass, Texas, and a large refinery at Marcus Hook, Pennsylvania. The Pews invested $3 million to build tankers for Sun's oil export trade. Like most yards built during the war, Sun Ship had a big storage facility receiving ship steel from a railroad branch line, and it processed material in a large fabricating shop that was served by overhead cranes to haul preassembled sections. Hulls were built on five 500-foot berths with traveling overhead cranes and received their outfit at a 500-foot wet dock. The marine engineering department included older shops formerly operated by the Robert Wetherill Engine Company of Chester and bought by the Pew brothers.[34]

Unlike New York Ship and Cramp, Sun Ship was not equipped to perform heavy naval construction, and it specialized in tankers. Its first vessel was the 10,300-deadweight-ton *Chester Sun,* which represented a successful design and was adopted by the EFC as a standard tanker. Employing more than 5,000 men at its peak, the yard also built cargo steamers and tankers for the Luckenbach Steamship Company, Cunard, and Standard Oil, as well as minesweepers for the U.S. Navy.[35]

Two smaller yards were located upriver at Gloucester, New Jersey, a few miles south of Camden. Named Pennsylvania Shipbuilding Company and New Jersey Shipbuilding Company, these works were subsidiaries of Pusey & Jones. Pennsylvania Shipbuilding was managed by Henry Lysholm, who had developed ship fabrication together with Henry Morse and introduced a similar system at Gloucester. One unusual feature was the arrangement of berths, which launched hulls sideways on a narrow river section, a technique common on the Great Lakes but rarely seen on the East Coast.[36]

Across the river at League Island, the Philadelphia Navy Yard underwent a spectacular revival and became the region's largest government-owned facility. Before the war it had operated two large dry docks for battleship overhauls, and it began new construction in 1913 with a transport ship. Among the buildings erected after 1914 was a large propeller foundry that processed large amounts of scrap metal for brass castings. In 1917 the yard received Navy Department orders to build the battle cruisers USS *Constitution* and USS *United States* (sister vessels of New York Ship's USS *Saratoga*), construction of which required a new physical plant. These new facilities were centered on two huge berths measuring 900 feet by 130 feet. There was also a new structural shop, a power plant, and the world's most powerful hammerhead crane with a lifting capacity of 392 tons. Together with other facilities, these additions cost almost $14 million. For an additional $6.3 million, the Navy Yard received Dry Dock No. 3, 1,011 feet long. Together with an identical dock built at the Norfolk Navy Yard, No. 3 "has been called the most complicated piece of mass concrete construction ever built in this country," the Bureau of Yards and Docks reported proudly.[37] Equipped to accommodate the world's largest ships with room to spare, the dock had three centrifugal pumps with a capacity of 14,400 cubic feet per minute that could drain the basin in less than three hours. At its peak, the Navy Yard employed 15,000 workers, many of whom worked on the two battle cruisers. (After the war, both vessels were canceled and broken up for scrap on the berths.)[38]

The creation of new construction and repair facilities in the Delaware Valley reflected the spectacular growth of shipbuilding in wartime America. Between 1913 and 1917 the number of yards increased from 49 yards operating 184 berths to 132 yards with 419 berths; total output rose from less than 200,000 tons deadweight to 3.2 million tons. The Atlantic coast was still the most prominent shipbuilding region in the nation with sixty-six plants, including major new yards, such as Federal Ship at Kearny, New Jersey. Builders on the Pacific coast operated thirty-two yards; those on the Great Lakes, twenty-seven. The war also prompted the establishment of seven shipyards on the Gulf Coast, which until this time had played a marginal role in American steel shipbuilding.[39]

Standardization and the Hog Island Yard

Increased construction inspired debates over the merits of standardization. Before World War I the modest size of the U.S. merchant marine had hampered efforts in this direction because shipyards and subcontractors prized flexibility and built a large variety of customized vessels. A naval officer reported that most prewar builders had "adopted standardization of items such as flanges, fittings, shackles, etc., but few of them [had] attempted the standardization of the entire system such as anchor gear, boat gear, rigging, etc.," let alone whole ships.[40] After 1914 growing demand for new tonnage and the increasing size of the merchant fleet led some shipbuilders to believe that individual yards could specialize in a few standard vessel types.

Standardization required exact duplication of vessel parts. This was the underlying principle of the Morse system, in which precision templates were used to fabricate identical vessel components for sister ships. Prewar experiments had demonstrated that fabrication and preassembly of flat hull parts for square midship sections was feasible. But the technique was not sufficiently accurate to fabricate the more intricately shaped components that formed the streamlined bow and stern sections. These plates still required lifting techniques that defied the standardization principle because every plate had to be bent on the basis of a custom-made pattern.[41]

Swift changes in marine engineering formed another obstacle to standardization as builders introduced new technologies like diesel engines or improved turbine reduction gear. A naval architect who devised standardized specifications for warship fittings reported that "no sooner was the standard issued [when] someone came along with the very urgent suggestion for an improvement, and, in spite of the most vigorous efforts to maintain the standard once issued, changes were made which destroyed the real value of standardization, as any change made in the design carried through in the manufacture. The jigs, fixtures, etc., that had been prepared for the economical manufacture of these standards had to be changed or were of no further use."[42]

Given these limitations, most shipbuilders introduced standardized designs on a fairly modest scale. New York Ship's nine 535-foot troopships, for example, whose outward appearance suggested a large degree of uniformity, in fact differed considerably from one another. The square midship section featured fabricated hull and superstructure plates, but in the bow and stern sections

Troopships outfitting at New York Ship in Newton Creek. Designed to transport U.S. troops to Europe, they were converted into commercial steamers that formed the backbone of the American passenger trade during the 1920s. Fifty Years New York Shipbuilding Corporation Camden, N.J. *(Camden, N.J., 1949)*

where the hull tapered off in double curvatures to facilitate speed and steadiness, the builders used traditional lifting techniques. As a result, the "hulls were practically identical, but even here changes were made to get different oil-fuel capacities; the machinery was built in groups to spread the work to different boiler, turbine, and gear plants, so there was only partial standardization in machinery," an observer commented. "These differences finally resulted in a fleet wherein there were greater and lesser differences in every ship."[43]

Some builders, especially those involved in the *Clemson*-class destroyer program, introduced a greater degree of uniformity. Vessels of the *Clemson* class were built on the basis of general plans supplied by the Bath Iron Works

Destroyer mass production at Cramp, October 1, 1918. Note the boilers on the dock, awaiting installation in the USS Blakely, USS Roper, USS Barney (left) and USS Breckinridge (right). These and other engine parts were made on the basis of the builder's special designs. National Archives

to all contractors, but detail designs for these so-called "mass production destroyers" differed from yard to yard. A project manager recalled that it was "the intention [to] standardize everything possible on board but . . . we ran up against the impossibility of standardizing the engine and boiler fittings as each shipbuilding firm has special rights in engine and boiler construction. We, therefore, allowed a wide latitude in the type of engines and boilers as long as the speed and horsepower were forthcoming. In other words, below the spar deck . . . very little is standardized."[44]

Beyond these limited ventures, the war witnessed efforts to build completely standardized ships in mass production. These projects were inspired by Henry Ford's new automobile plant at Highland Park, Michigan. Their proponents were also impressed with Ford's ship assembly line in Detroit, which "manufactured" 100 *Eagle* submarine chasers for the U.S. Navy. Another attempt to introduce mass production in shipbuilding was undertaken early in the war by the Submarine Boat Corporation, which fabricated and preassembled several hundred wooden submarine chasers for the British Royal Navy.[45]

Plans to fabricate steel freighters in very large series were made in spring 1917. At this time the EFC faced a severe shortage of shipbuilding capacity because most yards worked on private contracts and were pressured by the navy to reserve construction capacity for warships. Moreover, the industry lacked experienced subcontractors for ship steel, castings, and fittings. As a solution, the EFC—drawing upon proposals submitted by private contractors—developed a mass production and ship assembly program. Standardized vessel components should be made by bridge and tank builders not involved in war-essential production; hulls were to be erected in so-called assembly yards, which would also install engines and fittings.[46]

Trade experts disagreed over the technical feasibility of the project. Conceding that structural steelworks without shipbuilding experience could supply simple hull plates, some claimed that nonmarine shops were insufficiently equipped to bend steel for bow and stern sections. In his assessment of the EFC plan to subcontract plates, frames, and beams with firms in the general engineering trades, Joseph Powell of Fore River Shipbuilding predicted: "When they start putting those ships together they are going to find out that the parts will not go together."[47] Other builders were more optimistic. New York Ship general manager George Andrews argued that the project was merely a giant replica of the fabrication system developed by Henry Morse more than a decade earlier. The EFC soon turned to New York Ship's parent company, AIC, with a proposal to build 200 standardized freighters at a new shipyard at Hog Island seven miles south of Philadelphia. It also signed contracts for 60 and 200 ships with Harriman and the Submarine Boat Corporation, respectively.[48]

The ship fabricators tried to solve construction problems foreseen by shipbuilders in the design phase. Radicalizing methods developed by Charles Jack at Chester, AIC designers dispensed as much as possible with intricately shaped parts whose production posed difficulties for subcontracting bridge and tank shops. "We straightened the ship out at every place where we could," an engineer recalled. "We took everything that was bent and made it straight." For example, the designers eliminated the "tumble home," the concave vertical curve that gave a ship steadiness in rough waters: "We straightened that out, because if it was not done . . . we would have had to take every one of the ribs on that boat, which is 400 feet long, and these ribs are only a few feet apart— and we would have had to put them all in the fire and heat them and bend them."[49] The designers also eliminated the slight upward bend in conventional deck beams and plates that allowed spray water to pour off, the deadrise in bottom plates, and numerous small curves in bulkheads, doors, and even furniture. According to detail plans devised by AIC in cooperation with the EFC, the Hog Island ship measured 390 feet in length, 50 feet in the beam, and

7,500 tons deadweight and consisted of 25,000 separate components held together by almost 600,000 rivets. As a result of their peculiar design, AIC stated, fabricated ships do "not look like boats at all, but [more] like a steel frame building lying on its side."[50] Shipyard workers were less fond of standardized ships; putting one overboard, a Delaware Valley tradesman remarked, was "like launching a soap box."[51]

In addition to developing a standard ship design, AIC provided an administrative structure to supervise the Hog Island project. Most important, it created a subsidiary named American International Shipbuilding Corporation (AISBC), which received operating funds from the EFC and was responsible for worker recruitment, subcontracting, quality control, transportation of material within the yard, and ship assembly. Repeating a hiring strategy practiced by new yards since the 1860s, AISBC recruited some of its technical personnel from local builders. Hog Island's superintendent of ship assembly William B. Fortune and shop manager F. B. Gallaher, for example, had held similar positions at New York Ship; material engineer H. I. Toland was a former production engineer at Cramp. But the departure from conventional shipbuilding methods also required new expertise to organize mass production and assist subcontractors in the general engineering trades. R. W. Aitken, head of the employment division, had served a twelve-year stint as a mass production manager with B. F. Goodrich Rubber in Chicago, while Hog Island's structural steel inspector George K. Hoff had worked as a shop supervisor and efficiency expert for the Pennsylvania Railroad.[52]

To furnish 550,000 tons of fabricated material, AISBC enlisted eighty-eight structural steel shops, which received blueprints and templates for hull components. Most of these subcontractors were small and medium-sized firms located far from the Delaware Valley; they included the Crown Iron Works in Minneapolis and the Structural Steel Company in Kansas City, Missouri. These works used shop equipment needed for bridge and tank building to fabricate frames and plates. The EFC built two fabricating plants at Pottstown and Leetsdale, Pennsylvania, to supply beams and angle iron. Project managers also enlisted more than 3,000 subcontractors to supply boilers, propellers, and fittings; the General Electric works at Schenectady, New York, obtained contracts for turbine engines.[53]

The ship assembly plant at Hog Island was designed by the EFC, AISBC, and Stone & Webster. Covering almost 900 acres of land, it was several times the size of the nation's largest shipyard plants. Because subcontractors were fabricating 95 percent of each ship, Hog Island had few production shops and concentrated instead on material handling, storage, hull assembly, and outfitting. Fabricated material arrived on a branch line of the Pennsylvania Railroad

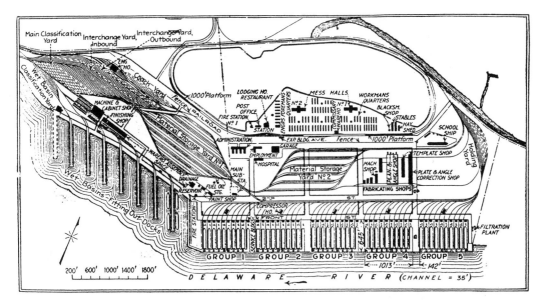

*Hog Island ship assembly yard. Note the railroad connection between material storage
yards no. 1 and 2, a transportation bottleneck responsible for many delays. Note also the
absence of processing shops seen in "normal" shipyards. National Archives*

and was hauled to storage areas along eighty miles of railroad track. While
plates, frames, and anchors were stored in open yards, weather-sensitive material like electrical generators went into roofed warehouses. According to the
initial plant design, components could be tracked through an elaborate inventory system allowing production managers to locate material and process
requests for specific items within hours. Hull assembly was performed on fifty
400-foot building berths designed to accommodate the 390-foot standard hull,
each served by eight cranes.[54]

In September 1917 Stone & Webster commenced the construction of the
physical plant itself, the most chaotic and mismanaged phase of the entire
project. Without formulating a comprehensive schedule, the construction
company ordered vast quantities of cement, structural steel, and timber from
contractors all across the country. Lacking sufficient storage facilities on Hog
Island, Stone & Webster was unable to unload railroad cars stuck in rail traffic
jams miles from the shipyard. (During the national railroad crisis in winter
1917, railroad cars carrying Hog Island construction material clogged the East
Coast railroad network as far south as Norfolk, Virginia.)[55]

In October 1917, shortly after Stone & Webster had laid foundations for
shops and berths, the plant layout underwent major revisions. These were the
result of changes in the original contract between the EFC and AIC for 200

standardized cargo ships of 390 feet length. The revised order called for only 110 units of the original type and 70 troop carriers of 441 feet length. Since the additional standard ship would be larger than the original unit, Stone & Webster had to redesign portions of the hull-assembly department. While these changes were under way, the coldest winter in recent memory further delayed the project; construction workers had to thaw the frozen ground by injecting hot steam before excavation could begin. These and other problems tripled the EFC's plant construction costs from $21 million to $65 million.[56]

As the plant assumed shape, many observers celebrated Hog Island as the most spectacular manifestation of American engineering skill. After visiting the plant, Britain's special ambassador to the United States told AIC: "It is largely upon this machine of war which you are now building that I am founding my hopes of a blow that will strike terrifically at the ambitions of Germany . . . You Americans, when you wake up to things, create something that produces with tremendous rapidity."[57] Such praise proved premature in view of the problems that arose when Hog Island commenced ship fabrication. Whatever its shortcomings, however, the project was an undeniable achievement. In less than a year the contractors had formulated a comprehensive project proposal, furnished detail designs, established a complex management structure, recruited thousands of subcontractors and tens of thousands of workers, and transformed empty marshland into the largest industrial plant built in the United States during World War I. Hog Island stretched its first keel only six months after the EFC and AIC had signed the contract in September 1917.

The ship, a 7,500-ton freighter named *Quistconck,* was laid down on a half-finished building berth. As could be expected, plant construction interfered with ship assembly, so that ship carpenters remained idle for weeks until construction workers had completed the groundwork. Moreover, material inspectors discovered quality problems with some vessel equipment. The *Quistconck's* anchor chains, for example, did not conform to official safety standards. On the positive side, the 25,000 fabricated parts that made up the *Quistconck* did fit together. From a technical viewpoint, the assembly system worked so well that a correction shop where warped fabricated parts could be rebent proved superfluous and served as a warehouse.[58]

The *Quistconck* also revealed unforeseen problems involved in ship assembly. Crucially, the supply and storage divisions descended into chaos because subcontractors failed to deliver material according to schedule. "It is plainly very difficult to cause many thousands of pieces for one ship to come from 88 different fabricating shops, and have them come in their proper sequence, and not have too many of one kind and not enough of another," AISBC reported.[59]

The Quistconck *outfitting at Hog Island, c. 1919. Note the square shape of her superstructure, illustrating the simple design that characterized standardized vessel construction. Library of Congress*

As a result of the uneven flow of material into the yard, the original storage plan unraveled, and thousands of parts piled up in the wrong storage facilities. Electrical equipment arrived ahead of schedule and had to be stored in an open yard for lack of warehouse space; frames and plates that should have been stored near the building berths were stacked in remote corners where material managers spent days searching for parts. As a result of these and other problems, the *Quistconck* was launched in August 1918 and remained incomplete until December, one month after the war ended.[60]

Delivery and storage problems affected the strict construction sequence envisioned by AISBC. In theory, ships were assembled in groups of five units. Ship carpenters laid the first keel and moved to the next berth. They were followed by shipfitters who erected frames and plates. Hull components were riveted by yet another work gang. According to the initial plan, the riveters completed the first hull at the exact time when the ship carpenters had laid the fifth keel and returned to the first berth to launch the ship. In reality, however, the yard swarmed with uncoordinated work gangs scrambling for material and tools; they assembled and launched hulls in random sequences that had little to do with the original schedule. Hull construction time for the first ten ships ranged from 151 days to 277 days and never reached the projected 50-day standard.[61]

In its project evaluation, the EFC argued that the most important problem was the sheer size of the physical plant, construction of which had delayed the start of the shipbuilding program. "Hog Island is laid out [on] too grand a scale. . . . The construction work should have been concentrated on a quarter of the complete plant, so that this quarter might have been immediately available for construction of vessels."[62] Experienced shipbuilders added that any shipyard operating more than a dozen berths would run into intractable managerial problems. The magnitude of the Hog Island program with its fifty berths was "a great shipbuilding mistake," a builder argued. "When you get [to sixteen berths] you have built what is the maximum size of [an] economical shipbuilding unit . . . Sixteen [berths] is too many. Ten is enough."[63]

But a smaller fabrication yard erected by Harriman's Merchant Shipbuilding Corporation twenty-five miles upriver from Philadelphia at Bristol, Pennsylvania, fared little better. Charged with the construction of sixty cargo ships of 8,800 tons deadweight, these works featured only twelve berths. Plant construction required extensive dredging because Bristol bordered a shallow section of the Delaware River where large ships could be launched only with great difficulty. During the preconstruction phase, MSC emulated AIC strategy and issued subcontracts for fabricated material to dozens of engineering firms along the East Coast and in the Midwest. Turbine engines were supplied by a new Westinghouse plant in Essington near Philadelphia, built specifically for the EFC shipbuilding program. When Bristol finally tried to launch its first ship in August 1918, after numerous construction delays caused by material delivery problems, the hull remained stuck on its berth during a launching party attended by 30,000 visitors. By the end of the year, the yard had failed to complete any of the twenty ships whose delivery had been promised by MSC.[64]

The third major assembly yard at Newark, New Jersey, performed slightly better. This plant was operated by the Submarine Boat Corporation, which had gathered some ship fabrication experience before the EFC program, when it built wooden submarine chasers for the Royal Navy. Its contract entailed the construction of 200 cargo ships of 5,000 tons deadweight (later reduced to 150 units) at a thirty-berth yard. Unlike AIC and MSC, Submarine Boat erected the physical plant in summer 1917 before it signed a contract with the EFC in September. Newark also had a more systematic plant layout than Hog Island and covered only 125 acres of land. The first three keels were laid as early as December 1917, and the yard launched its first hull in May 1918. Production problems involving inaccurately made engine parts, however, delayed the completion of this first vessel until December 1918; as late as March 1919 eighteen out of twenty hulls remained incomplete for lack of parts.[65]

One of the most important factors explaining the problems experienced by the three assembly yards was the dispersed organization of production. This defied the regional concentration of steel shipbuilding, viewed by many builders as the industry's "first commandment." During the 1870s Charles Cramp had pointed out that subcontractors should be located in close proximity to the shipyards. This was necessary to coordinate the complicated material flows to build a ship from thousands of subcontracted items. As a result, Delaware Valley yards depended on a regional industrial base and recruited local suppliers whenever possible. The EFC departed from this traditional approach because most Delaware Valley shipyard subcontractors were unavailable for the ship assembly project. But the program designers failed to appreciate the staggering organizational problems accompanying the production of more than half a millon tons of fabricated material by thousands of subcontractors scattered all across the country.

Moreover, Hog Island's location at the center of U.S. shipbuilding overburdened regional labor markets. Even before the assembly yards began operations, the number of Delaware Valley shipyard jobs had increased from fewer than 10,000 in 1914 to almost 50,000 at the end of 1917. To operate at full capacity, Hog Island required more than 30,000 men, and Bristol, 20,000. Because skilled workers were scarce in this tight labor market, the assembly yards had to hire green hands and organize training courses. These difficulties signaled a broader transformation of capital-labor relations in Delaware Valley shipbuilding.[66]

Capital, Organized Labor, and the State

The war effected a dramatic reversal of power relations between workers and employers. For decades, Delaware Valley builders had faced little difficulty hiring skilled craftsmen at comparatively low wages. These conditions changed when the war created unprecedented demand for shipyard labor. "Philadelphia is the shipbuilding center of this country," Homer Ferguson of Newport News Shipbuilding told a congressional committee. "Under normal conditions it is the best place to get shipbuilding labor. Probably under present conditions it is the worst place to get shipbuilding labor, because not only do they have shipbuilding but also munitions manufacturing now."[67] In the scramble for workers, older builders competed with new shipyards as well as major firms in war-related industries, such as the new Westinghouse turbine plant in Essington, the Baldwin Locomotive Works, Midvale Steel, and Lukens Steel.

Labor markets tightened during the early stages of the war as new firms lured experienced shipyard workers from older builders, a practice known as scamping. Cramp's general manager Henry Mull complained in 1916 that shipyard workers were "being taken from the comparatively few shipyards that existed before this new shipbuilding boom was launched upon us." Since new builders like Sun Ship closed vessel contracts later than Cramp and New York Ship, Mull explained, they were "in a position to pay more for their labor than we can afford to pay with contracts of a year and 18 months standing."[68] The Navy Yard experienced similar problems as private builders lured government workers with high wages and other inducements. Scamping resulted in labor turnover as "the new shipyards took labor from the old, and the old yards took labor from each other," an industry analyst observed.[69] Employing 4,500 men in 1916, Cramp reported an annual labor turnover rate of almost 400 percent.[70]

The tight labor market created improved conditions for labor activism. "Men have been induced to join labor unions," Mull reported. "Strikes are constantly taking place—they are almost monthly occurrences—in their efforts to force the wages of shipyards to equal those in the munitions plants."[71] Labor unrest forced Cramp to increase wages by 31 percent in 1916. Regionally, organized labor made further gains when the government increased the work force at the Philadelphia Navy Yard and introduced progressive labor policies formulated by Assistant Secretary of the Navy Franklin D. Roosevelt. Although the Navy Department did not formally recognize unions as bargaining partners, the navy yards under Roosevelt's leadership enacted many policies dear to organized labor, including eight-hour days, higher wages, and the abolition of piecework. Navy Yard workers organized a shipbuilders' council representing tradesmen from a variety of skilled crafts.[72]

The year 1917 marked yet another turning point, when the shipyards hired workers for the enormous naval and EFC programs. New York Ship, for example, increased its work force from 5,150 to 12,372 within a few months. Most new recruits lacked basic shipbuilding experience. "There are no more shipbuilders," New York Ship's general manager George Andrews reported; "in fact, they have been hired three or four times over."[73] At Camden new hires included a large number of unskilled Italian, Polish, and Russian immigrants, who made up one-fourth of the 4,200 workers employed by New York Ship's hull department. This represented a significant change in the ethnic composition of shipyard labor, which had traditionally been a bastion of native-born and British workers, supplemented by a small minority of Germans in specialty trades. Hog Island also hired several thousand women for blue-collar occupations. Unlike many ethnic workers who gained a permanent foothold in the shipyard labor market, however, virtually all the women were discharged after the Armistice.[74]

The hiring wave caused considerable transportation and manpower problems for shipyards in suburban locations. Railroads, streetcars, and ferryboats were notoriously overcrowded, carrying tens of thousands of workers from Philadelphia to the Camden yards, the Navy Yard, Sun Ship, and MSC at Chester. Trolleys operated by a Camden streetcar company, for example, "pass the plant of the New York Shipbuilding Co. and are taxed to the utmost capacity at all times and at rush hours especially. If the trolleys are behind the scheduled time, they will pass the Pennsylvania Ship Building Co. plant without stopping to take any men who are waiting there," a Shipping Board official related.[75] "The other day a car left our yard with 160 people on it, 40 of them hanging outside," Andrews told a congressional committee.[76] Only Cramp reported adequate conditions because the yard was located at the center of Kensington's working-class district where many employees still walked to work.[77]

In cases where employers failed to provide free transportation, shipyard workers had to buy streetcar or ferryboat tickets. As union leaders pointed out, this increased the cost of living, which rose faster than wages. In 1917 American shipyard workers gained wage increases of 15 percent, but inflation caused a 25 percent decline in their real incomes, the highest rate among workers employed in war-related industries. This situation provoked a series of labor conflicts in shipbuilding, which experienced a higher strike rate than most other industries. MSC at Chester, for example, reported seven wage conflicts in 1917, all resulting in pay increases. At Cramp workers launched twenty-one strikes, the highest number in any American shipyard. Tacitly recognizing a drastic shift in power relations, Cramp's management granted wage increases in every single instance.[78]

As part of this offensive, the unions also increased workers' control at the point of production. Most wage strikes were settled through negotiations between shop committees and the management, which willy-nilly recognized unions as legitimate bargaining partners. Moreover, the unions forced Cramp to suspend strict time regulations punishing employees who arrived late for work and to adhere to union work rules. These new realities irked conservative managers who had regularly refused to deal with trade unions in the past. "The present attitude of labor," Grove declared at the end of his presidency in 1917, "is such that I do not care to be the responsible head of an institution dependent upon the loyalty and co-operation of the workingman for its success."[79]

During the strike wave of 1917 the EFC created the Shipyard Labor Adjustment Board (SLAB) to preempt industrial conflicts that threatened the success of the government shipbuilding program. SLAB urged employers and workers to establish so-called joint shop committees staffed by representatives of management and labor. Labor militancy in the Delaware Valley shipyards was a particular target of this reform. A Shipping Board official argued that the region's disproportionate rate of labor militancy resulted from a widespread feeling among workers that employers exploited them

for selfish profiteering reasons, so they see no harm in playing the same game. A shop committee could clear away this atmosphere of mutual distrust. It is suggested that the labor members of such a committee be selected by the unions and the company together in each case, the object being to pick men who will be as fair as possible, impartial, and willing to watch the interests of all concerned. There is no reason why a good union man should not be also a good company man if both sides play the game squarely.[80]

However, SLAB's attempt to form a nonunion collective bargaining mechanism was unpopular among Delaware Valley shipyard locals, which feared that joint committees undermined the existing structure of union shop committees. SLAB committees were introduced at New York Ship, but Cramp dealt with its employees through shop committees organized by the International Association of Machinists, the boilermakers' union, and other unions.[81]

In December 1917 SLAB invited union representatives and employers to discuss wages, piecework, and arbitration procedures. All parties agreed that the industry suffered from a lack of uniformity; every yard maintained its own wage and piece-rate schedules and job classifications. Unions that had long demanded a higher degree of standardization throughout the Delaware Valley were now joined by managers who complained about labor turnover and scamping. Labor turnover, especially rampant among pieceworkers, was aggravated by "rumors that constantly circulated up and down the river causing pieceworkers in some of the yards to feel that they were receiving less than their fellows in other yards, even when as a matter of fact they were receiving as much or more."[82] Unions and managers therefore adopted uniform wage and piece-rate schedules determined by SLAB investigators. SLAB officials also asked employers to compensate workers for transportation to work and to introduce the basic eight-hour day. To placate managers for whom the eight-hour day had long been anathema, the government promised to "reimburse the shipbuilders for any added labor costs occasioned by . . . the decisions of the Board."[83] SLAB formalized its decisions in a Delaware River shipyard labor award, which formed the basis for a national agreement. After consultation with managers and union men, SLAB appointed an arbitration board to settle differences over the interpretation of the award. As a result of SLAB policies and appeals to worker patriotism, labor unrest subsided in 1918.[84]

The federal government also supported worker training programs. Builders such as New York Ship, which introduced company training in 1917, soon realized that they lacked sufficient resources to instruct thousands of recent hires who lacked basic craft skills. The EFC established a school at Newport News where more than 1,000 skilled workers learned teaching techniques; these trade instructors then taught their own courses at New York Ship, Sun Ship, Cramp, and other yards. Tradesmen who had honed their craft skills during years of practical experience, however, never thought much of this type of training. Claims that one could make a shipbuilder "by standing a few plates of iron up and driving a few rivets in it and then having [a trainee] knock the rivets out again [are] so ridiculous that a practical man would never stop to consider [them]," the president of the boilermakers' union argued.[85] Indeed, green hands who received training in hastily arranged courses never attained the productivity rates that had been common in prewar shipbuilding.

Other public policies were aimed at easing the housing and transportation crises plaguing suburban shipyards. In 1918 Congress appropriated $50 million to build homes for shipyard workers in such outlying areas. In Camden, for example, the EFC built 1,600 homes on land owned by New York Ship. Together with schoolhouses and other public buildings financed by the city of Camden, these developments made up the famous shipyard worker neighborhoods of Yorkship Village and Fairview. The EFC built similar housing projects in Haddon Township, New Jersey, Chester, and Bristol. Six hundred fifty family homes, modeled upon the famous Philadelphia brick rowhouse design, were built on Oregon Avenue near the Philadelphia Navy Yard.[86]

These public-private efforts were supplemented by welfare capitalism. Locally AIC pioneered this new system of industrial relations shortly after it took control of New York Ship in December 1916. Industrial relations experts introduced a series of reforms designed to reduce labor turnover, including a group insurance policy covering all employees who worked at New York Ship longer than twelve months; by 1918, 4,000 employees were enrolled in the program. The yard also provided a cafeteria seating 1,800 workers, smoking rooms, locker space, and a company newspaper, as well as recreational facilities where workers played football, soccer, baseball, and tennis. The firm also endorsed associational activities among its employees and supported a worker death-benefit fund with donations.[87]

Welfare capitalism differed from the traditional paternalism that had pervaded the industry during the proprietary era. The new system was no longer rooted in a craft culture shared by workers and employers who had entered their trades as apprentices and sometimes worked together in the shop. Unlike Charles Cramp, for example, New York Ship's president Marvin Neeland had never served a stint as a journeyman ship carpenter. Vestiges of the old regime did survive at Cramp: President Mull had commenced his career as a machinist and had risen through the ranks under Charles Cramp's guidance. Even when the shipyard employed more than 10,000 workers, Mull called many veteran tradesmen by name, knew whose sons and grandsons worked in which department, and was conversant in shop talk. When his college-educated son wanted to work as a bond dealer after graduation, Mull related, "I told him 'Nothing doing.' He went to work at a regular he-man's job" in the shipyard.[88] Prodded by SLAB's industrial relations experts, the yard did experiment with new policies by hiring sports celebrities for senior positions to "inspire" the work force. These efforts received at best a lukewarm response from seasoned tradesmen; some of Cramp's men even walked out because "they objected to baseball players, actors, pugilists, and others inexperienced in shipbuilding being placed over them as bosses." Labor organizers told the press that "there is too much welfare work in the shipyards . . . Privately owned yards, such as Cramps' . . . never had any welfare agents until the Government sent them there at Government expense."[89]

Hog Island hired experts who were responsible for worker recruitment and public relations. Employment managers screened applicants and conducted examinations to determine workers' suitability for shipyard trades. Public relations required close attention because most workers had a less than favorable image of Hog Island itself, which was infested with mosquitoes. Moreover, the yard was located even farther from urban working-class districts than New York Ship, and streetcars carrying more than 10,000 workers from South Philadelphia alone were notoriously overcrowded. AIC and the EFC built barracks for 7,000 workers at the shipyard, but "you could not construct little houses or flats or anything of that kind and get people to live there that cared anything about where they lived," an engineer pointed out.[90] AIC furnished a hospital, a YMCA athletic division, and cafeterias and restaurants, as well as a yard newspaper. Despite these valiant efforts, Hog Island continued to suffer image problems and reported annual labor turnover rates of more than 800 percent.[91]

Long-term Ramifications of Wartime Shipbuilding

World War I accelerated several trends that had been taking shape since the turn of the century. Builders adopted the fabrication and preassembly systems pioneered by New York Ship to maximize plant utilization and reduce hull construction time. Many also copied the locational strategy of the Camden yard and opened plants in metropolitan satellite areas, such as Chester and Bristol, that offered sufficient space for large plants and storage facilities.

Just as in the prewar period, Cramp experienced difficulties pursuing land-intensive production in Philadelphia.

During the wartime emergency, employers soon confronted the infrastructure problems associated with the new industrial geography. Supported by the federal government, employers built housing projects, such as Yorkship Village, and introduced welfare capitalism to attract workers to outlying areas. Although corporate paternalism soon vanished during the postwar depression, suburban worker housing was literally set in stone and became a permanent fixture of America's unique industrial landscape in the twentieth century.

Hog Island illustrated the limits of this new departure. Since shipbuilding remained dependent on a regional industrial base, ship assemblers were unable to solve the organizational problems associated with dispersed production on a national scale. Moreover, workers refused to follow employers into unsuitable locations, and even the most strenuous corporate welfare efforts failed to solve the resulting labor supply problem. Finally, in order to build completely standardized and fabricated ships, naval architects and marine engineers had to ignore established design standards. As the U.S. commissioner of navigation pointed out in 1919, American ships were usually built

with a view to their employment in particular trades, and, while this adds to cost and time of construction, it has made our ships hitherto especially long-lived. . . . It is at least a question whether the fabricated ship[s] . . . are not, from their simple construction handicapped through life by [their] inability to carry the full cargoes of ships constructed in the usual manner . . . The number of shipyard employees could not have been increased about tenfold, and the output increased virtually twentyfold without lowering somewhat American standards of construction.[92]

This was an understatement. Standardized ships contained too many design compromises and were built without any consideration as to their employment in the peacetime carrying trades.

What Next? The Postwar Depression, 1919–1929

On October 4, 1927, Cramp completed the passenger liner *Evangeline*. Workers burnished brass that had already been polished a dozen times, cleaned tidy floors, and kept busy with other odd jobs to delay the awful moment when everything would be done. A whistle finally called them ashore, ropes were untied, and tugs towed the *Evangeline* into the river. Craftsmen gathered on the outfitting pier and watched Cramp's last ship disappear at the riverbend.[1]

Philadelphia's veteran shipyard was the largest casualty of a postwar maritime depression that overwhelmed American shipbuilding. As in the post–Civil War crisis, new vessel construction came to a standstill because wartime building programs had created vast excess tonnage, while at the same time naval construction dried up, depriving builders of a critical source of contracts. The situation during the 1920s, however, did not involve a technologically obsolete industry like post–Civil War wooden shipbuilding. Rather, it affected shipyards that compared favorably with most foreign firms as far as naval architecture and marine engineering were concerned.

Most sectors in the U.S. manufacturing economy slumped into a postwar depression, particularly war-related industries that had increased output and now faced a difficult transition into peacetime production because of excess capacities. But while steel producers and makers of rubber tires, for example, soon recovered thanks to the spectacular growth in automobile production, shipbuilders remained in limbo. This situation was the result of long-term trends in American shipping, exacerbated by the Shipping Board's inept merchant marine policies, and also the drop in naval construction after 1922.

The shipyard crisis had serious effects on metropolitan Philadelphia where the 1920s never "roared." Because shipbuilding had formed a traditional pillar of regional industrial activity, its decline affected subcontractors throughout the region. Moreover, the crisis coincided with the decline of the Baldwin Locomotive Works, which had for more than sixty years been a major regional employer. Already saddled with excess production capacity, Baldwin stuck with steam traction technology at a time when many railroads began introducing diesel and electric engines and hence turned to new suppliers, such as General Electric.[2]

Economic historians have cited similar cases of old industries competing with new ones as one reason for structural weaknesses in specific sectors that paved the way for the Great Depression. Coal mining, for example, which had traditionally supplied electrical power companies, now competed with new suppliers in the natural gas and hydroelectric sectors, leading to overproduction, underconsumption, and severe dislocations during the 1920s and collapse during the Great Depression.[3]

This was not the case in shipbuilding, where old firms introduced new product lines, including marine diesel engines and electrical equipment. Technologically, shipbuilding remained versatile, and leading builders like Cramp pursued sensible diversification strategies. Apart from the wartime legacy, one important factor explaining Cramp's failure to survive the 1920s was ill-conceived corporate strategy, as maritime conglomerates combined shipbuilding with shipping. This drained not only Cramp but also New York Ship of critical financial resources, led to the demise of the former, and pushed the latter to the brink of collapse.

The Postwar Shipping Crisis and Naval Disarmament

By the Armistice the nation's shipyards employed almost 400,000 workers and reported an order backlog of more than 1,400 vessels. Foresighted commentators viewed these statistics with growing apprehension. "Are we not in danger of building too many ships?" an editorial in a trade publication asked as early as September 1918.[4] Shipbuilders voiced similar concerns after Germany's collapse in November 1918 had rendered superfluous the freighters and troopships to supply the American Expeditionary Force in France. In a Cassandra speech delivered in spring 1919, Homer Ferguson of Newport News Shipbuilding recommended a controlled but rapid elimination of excess shipbuilding capacity to ease the transition into what he perceived as an inevitable postwar downturn.[5]

Corporate strategists, by contrast, envisioned a bright future for America's shipyards and foreign trade carriers. Shortly after the Armistice, an official of the American International Corporation proclaimed that world trade needed 35 million to 40 million tons to replace tonnage lost during the war. Moreover, to "take care of the growing commerce, there will, in a few years, be need for fifty-five to sixty million tons" whose construction would keep American shipyards busy for at least eight years.[6] This estimate was grossly exaggerated. World shipping had lost 14 million gross tons during the war, but shipyards had built almost exactly the same amount between August 1914 and November 1918. Although some low-quality wartime tonnage as well as older ships scheduled for scrapping had to be replaced, this would not amount to a postwar boom. The U.S. commissioner of navigation warned in 1919 that "the world's merchant tonnage afloat to-day . . . is greater than ever before, and undoubtedly would more than suffice to conduct the world's diminished foreign commerce consequent upon diminished production and vast national debts."[7]

Federal officials who agreed with the optimistic forecasts made a strategic decision to extend the Shipping Board construction program into the postwar era. This policy derived from the belief that the United States could surpass Britain as the world's leading maritime nation by capitalizing upon wartime gains. During a critical meeting between Shipping Board chairman Edward Hurley and a senior representative of British shipping, the latter predicted (according to Hurley) that "for a year or two shipping of all kinds would have plenty to do with the aftermath of the war; but thereafter surplus vessels would be a [drag] on the market, and the British were planning to curtail their building." Hurley wrongly viewed this as a prevarication to prevent the Americans from exploiting their wartime gains. He "hurried back to his Shipping Board colleagues to urge them to go ahead and build because the British were scared to death of American competition."[8] This argument provided a rationale for the continuation of the Shipping Board program, which included the conversion of New York Ship's troopships of the "502" and "535" class into passenger liners. Moreover, it extended ship fabrication, though on a slightly smaller scale than originally planned: Bristol completed 40 ships out of 60 originally contracted for; Newark, 118 out of 150; and Hog Island, 122 units out of 180. In 1919 and 1920 American yards built more than 5 million gross tons for the government, as well as 1.8 million tons for private owners.[9]

Yet Ferguson and other pessimists were right. Maritime markets became saturated with new tonnage when British steamship output returned to prewar levels in 1919. Hurley's boast notwithstanding, foreign builders had little to fear from American competitors. Despite enormous wartime investment in ship-yard plants and equipment, U.S. builders were still unable to match British tonnage prices. In 1919, for example, the most efficient American yards built ships at $170 per ton, compared to $100 per ton charged by British builders. Assembly yards that presumably reduced construction costs by using mass production techniques proved even less competitive; the Hog Island freighter, for example, cost $210 per ton.[10]

The United States also faced resurgent German competition. Germany had suffered staggering losses when the Peace Treaty of Versailles forced the trans-fer of millions of tons of merchant shipping to Allied powers, but John M. Keynes's observation that its "mercantile marine is swept from the seas" was premature.[11] During an astonishing postwar revival, the government furnished 12 billion Reichsmark to reconstruct the merchant fleet. Determined to regain its prewar status as the world's preeminent steamship line, the Hamburg-Amerika Paket Aktien Gesellschaft (HAPAG) launched a large building pro-gram and returned to the transatlantic trade with an improved fleet.[12]

The U.S. merchant marine lacked big steamship lines like HAPAG or Cunard to sustain shipbuilding during the postwar era. Although W. R. Grace & Company and other specialty carriers had made substantial headway at the expense of European shippers after 1914, operations had been disrupted by the Shipping Board's requisitioning of vessels for government service in 1917. Moreover, these firms could not match leading foreign carriers in terms of capital, diversity, or fleet size. Finally, the Shipping Board charter expired in 1920, eliminating the only management structure capable of operating the enormous array of commercial shipping built during and after the war.[13]

This situation formed the backdrop to the Merchant Marine Act of 1920 (commonly referred to as the Jones Act), designed to reorganize the Shipping Board and bolster the private steamship sector. The Shipping Board became a regulatory agency organizing the transfer of government-owned ships to pri-vate owners and assigning international trading routes to so-called managing operators. The managing operators were private firms that sailed Shipping Board vessels, retained all profits, and were reimbursed for operating losses by the federal government. Reflecting resurgent faith in the merits of competi-tion during the 1920s, the Shipping Board encouraged the formation of small steamship lines and bypassed larger corporations, such as the AIC subsidiary International Mercantile Marine. This policy attracted speculators who lacked the managerial capacity necessary to compete with powerful foreign carriers. The number of operating agents dropped from almost 200 in 1920 to 39 in 1923 as many inexperienced firms went bankrupt. The few successful managing operators included the American Export Lines, which sailed Hog Island steamers between the United States and the Mediterranean during the 1920s. After the passage of a steamship subsidy bill in 1928, American Export ordered four large freighters—known as the Four Aces—from New York Ship.[14]

Another Shipping Board operating agent was W. Averell Harriman, who played a critical role in postwar shipping and Delaware Valley shipbuilding. Convinced that the railroad sector, where his father had made one of the great fortunes in American business, had reached its limits, Harriman turned to what he saw as the most promising growth sector of the postwar era, the maritime economy. He developed a scheme to combine his Merchant Shipbuilding Company at Chester with other shipbuilding firms as well as with coastwise and international steamship lines. This was the most ambitious attempt to create an integrated maritime conglomerate and develop American shipping during the 1920s.[15]

The keystone in Harriman's enterprise was W. A. Harriman & Company, a holding company. It controlled the American Ship & Commerce Corporation, founded in 1919 by the Chandler interests that controlled Cramp and its subsidiaries. Led by the retired general George Goethals and Kermit Roosevelt (Theodore Roosevelt's youngest son), American Ship & Commerce had formed the American Ship & Commerce Navigation Corporation as a shipping division to operate ten vessels owned by the Kerr Navigation Company. In 1920 Harriman bought American Ship & Commerce from Chandler, replaced Goethals as president, and combined the firm with the American-Hawaiian Steamship Company, the Shawmut Steamship Company, and the Coastwise Transportation Company. Harriman soon controlled thirty-nine steamships as well as Cramp and MSC. MSC built new tonnage for Harriman's fleet, including American-Hawaiian's *Californian* and *Missourian,* whose hulls were constructed by MSC and furnished with engines by Cramp.[16]

Branching out into the transatlantic passenger trade, Harriman established the United American Lines (UAL), which purchased the transport USS *De Kalb* from government surplus, converted her for passenger service, and entered the New York–Hamburg trade in December 1920. UAL also ordered the passenger steamers *Mount Carroll* and *Mount Clinton* from MSC and added them to the transatlantic service in 1921. A crucial aspect of the plan was that Harriman's transatlantic operation was a joint venture with HAPAG. According to an agreement signed in 1920, the German line (still without ships) leased its idle steamship terminal at Hamburg to UAL; when it reentered the transatlantic trade with its own vessels, HAPAG used the UAL piers in New York.[17]

Harriman's transatlantic venture faltered due to profound changes in North Atlantic shipping. His *Mount Carroll* and *Mount Clinton,* for example, were

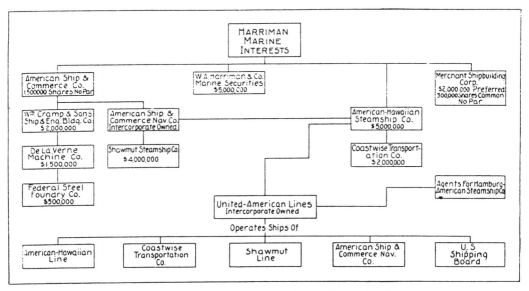

Organization of the Harriman maritime conglomerate. Marine Review 51 (1921)

specifically designed as immigrant carriers featuring comfortable third-class accommodations but no first- and second-class cabins. The third-class trade, however, declined drastically when the Harding administration imposed immigration restrictions, and as a consequence the vessels became so unprofitable that Harriman had them refitted as freighters in 1923. This was no solution because the transatlantic cargo trade also was glutted with excess carrying capacity. Harriman finally sold the *Mount Carroll* and *Mount Clinton* to the Matson Navigation Company, which sailed them in the protected Hawaiian trade.[18]

As replacements, he purchased the large Dutch-built passenger liners *Resolute* and *Reliance,* both of which offered first- and second-class accommodations. But their brief tenure as American-flag steamers was hampered by passage of the Volstead Act that prohibited alcohol aboard U.S. ships. Discovering the disadvantage of sailing "dry" American ships in competition with European and Canadian "wet liners," Harriman transferred both vessels to Panamanian registry—pioneering the use of this "flag of convenience" by American shippers. Eventually, he terminated the venture, the nation's only privately owned steamship line on the North Atlantic. In 1926 Harriman sold UAL to HAPAG, which thereby gained control of the remaining fleet and the valuable docks on the upper west side of New York City. This raised the number of HAPAG's liners in the North Atlantic trade to ten, more than enough to sustain its prominent position in the diminished passenger trade between continental Europe and the United States.[19]

A different set of circumstances troubled Harriman's American-Hawaiian line, which despite its name no longer sailed on its old route between New York and Honolulu. In 1916 the firm had withdrawn most of its vessels from the sugar trade and redeployed them to the North Atlantic to take advantage of higher freight rates in that market. Hawaiian sugar exporters never forgave American-Hawaiian for leaving them stranded without sufficient carrying capacity. Henceforth, they patronized the Matson Navigation Company, which replaced American-Hawaiian in this highly profitable trade. In 1917 American-Hawaiian's first-class freighters had been requisitioned by the Shipping Board as transports; they were not returned to their owners until 1919. American-Hawaiian sailed them on the glutted New York–San Francisco route, where it competed with Shipping Board operating agents for scarce freights.[20]

Harriman's experiences reflected the precarious condition of American and world shipping. Due to unrealistic expectations of a postwar boom, European and U.S. operators had purchased millions of tons of government-surplus vessels and placed premature orders with shipyards. By the end of 1920, however, international trade was dangerously oversupplied with tonnage, a situation exacerbated by the continuation of the Shipping Board construction program. The commissioner of navigation commented that "there can be no doubt that the continued outpour of money from the Federal Treasury upon shipping *after the war had ended* produced results from which immediate recovery cannot be expected."[21] When the wartime shipping famine gave way to excess capacities, freight rates started to fall and dragged tonnage prices along with them. Ships that had cost $200 per ton to build sold for $150 to $170 per ton in 1921 and for $30 per ton in 1922. A year later 9.8 million gross tons, or close to 20 percent of world shipping, was laid up—a figure that included 4.9 million tons owned by the Shipping Board. Many active vessels sailed half-empty. Struggling to maintain a presence on the North Atlantic, the United States established the government-owned United States Lines, which sailed seven converted troopships built by New York Ship, eight Hog Island freighters, and several other vessels. Meanwhile, more than 1,000 ships rusted away at Newport News, Hog Island, and other steamship graveyards.[22]

The depression also affected the tanker market. In 1919 the Shipping Board controlled 119 tankers aggregating 1.1 million tons deadweight; by comparison, *world* tonnage totaled 536 tankers and 3.9 million tons. Expecting a tanker boom during the postwar years, American operators ordered additional tonnage, including eight tankers built by New York Ship, four by MSC, and eleven by Sun Ship. New York Ship even built a tanker on speculation. But demand fell off when British operators and tanker builders returned to markets that soon became saturated with deep-sea carriers. Since most tankers built during and after the war were designed for transatlantic service, there was still some need for light-draft vessels, such as the Standard Transportation Company's *Socony* class, built by New York Ship and Sun Ship for the coastwise routes and the Great Lakes.[23]

Coastwise operators issued contracts for passenger steamers because wartime programs had produced very few vessels in this class. When the growing tourist trade of the 1920s contributed to a small boom, the Eastern Steamship Corporation ordered the *Yarmouth* and *Evangeline* from Cramp, sailed them between Boston and Yarmouth, Nova Scotia, during the summer months, and leased them to Caribbean operators for the winter tourist season. In the shipbuilding industry, however, competition for these prized contracts often resulted in meager profits or even losses.[24]

Builders became increasingly dependent on this small market because demand for warships declined drastically in the aftermath of the Washington Naval Disarmament Treaty of 1922. Signed by Britain, the United States, and Japan, this arms reduction agreement affected vessels exceeding 10,000 displacement tons. It suspended new capital ship construction for ten years, limited the size of warships to 35,000 displacement tons, established a formula determining the number of capital ships allowed each signatory power, and permitted the conversion of two U.S. battle cruisers into aircraft carriers. As a result, the navy scrapped some of its most advanced vessels, as well as older battleships. This provided work for the Philadelphia Navy Yard, which dismantled the battle cruisers USS *United States* and USS *Constitution* on the berths and scrapped the battleship USS *Michigan* (built by New York Ship in 1908). New York Ship and Fore River Shipbuilding kept their yards employed during the so-called "naval holiday" by refitting the battle cruisers USS *Saratoga* and USS *Lexington,* respectively. Because smaller warships remained unaffected by the treaty, Cramp could complete its *Omaha*-class cruisers. The navy issued two contracts for light "treaty" cruisers in 1926, of which one, the 10,000-displacement-ton USS *Salt Lake City,* was awarded to Cramp.[25]

The Contours of the Shipbuilding Depression

The 1920s marked an international shipbuilding crisis. The first casualties were the assembly yards, whose demise could be seen as advantageous because it eliminated inefficient excess capacity. However, the downturn soon affected private builders as well. In Britain, where shipbuilding entered a period of long-term decline, Clydebank teetered on the brink of disaster and Beardmore closed its huge shipyard at Dalumir. The depression also impaired British assembly yards, notably the Furness Shipbuilding Company yard at Haverton

Hill. Although major German yards, such as Blohm & Voss of Hamburg, survived the 1920s fairly well because the reconstruction of the merchant marine generated contracts for them, builders soon abandoned efforts to copy the American assembly system.[26]

In the United States operating agents transferred assembly yards to the Shipping Board, which closed and sold the Bristol and Newark plants. During a somewhat bizarre ceremony to mark the official closing of Hog Island in February 1921, AIC president Matthew Brush presented a 4-foot wooden key to a representative of the Shipping Board, who in return handed Brush a gold key—appropriate though perhaps unintended symbols for the transfer of a useless plant into public hands in return for the $66 million payment AIC had received from the government for building the yard. Lengthy speeches detailing Hog Island's possible conversion into a marine terminal were delivered to an audience of forty patrolmen guarding the property. "Not a workman attended," the press reported.[27] Since no private parties were interested in the unwieldy plant, Hog Island remained under government control and served as a storage facility for laid-up Shipping Board vessels. The government realized $14 million from selling machinery and timber for scrap; what was left standing deteriorated badly. In 1930 the Shipping Board sold the property to the city of Philadelphia, which sent in the wreckers and built the Philadelphia airport on the razed shipyard site.[28]

Private builders made strenuous efforts to survive. This sometimes involved cooperation between yards as they shared vessel contracts. When MSC built the *Californian* and *Missourian,* for example, Cramp received subcontracts for diesel engines, its new specialty. Such cooperation highlighted the benefits of vertical and horizontal integration by distributing contracts generated within Harriman's maritime conglomerate. It remained an isolated incident, however, because Harriman's steamship lines proved unprofitable. Moreover, as Neafie & Levy and Cramp's collaboration after the Civil War had illustrated, contract sharing flourished between independent firms during hard times. In 1926, for example, Cramp awarded New York Ship a subcontract to build twenty lifeboats for the passenger liner *Malolo.*[29]

Yards also developed general labor policies through the Atlantic Coast Shipbuilders' Association, whose members included many Delaware Valley shipyard executives. Predicated on the belief that the "day when a single individual, firm or corporation could stand on its own feet . . . has passed," the association negotiated with the AFL Metal Trades Department on behalf of thirty-four East Coast shipyards.[30] A contract signed with labor representatives in August 1919 formed an extension of the Shipbuilding Labor Adjustment Board awards of 1918, standardized wages, and recognized unions as legitimate bargaining partners. Like most voluntary alliances in crisis-ridden industries, however, the Shipbuilders' Association was plagued by internal conflicts. Some builders "were opposed to any agreement . . . looking toward the perpetuation of [wartime] union conditions."[31] Somewhat surprisingly in view of its past relations with labor unions, Cramp was one of eighteen yards that ratified the labor contract. Some builders also enrolled in the Shipbuilders Council of America, a lobbying group founded in 1920 to influence merchant marine and naval policies.[32]

In spite of these efforts to weather the crisis collectively, however, shipyards were soon engaged in competition. When economic conditions caused them to panic, builders submitted untenable construction proposals only to keep their yards employed and to postpone the evil day when the contract books would be empty. In 1922 the Inter-Island Steam Navigation Company of Honolulu asked for bids on a small steamer. Bidders included Cramp, New York Ship, Bethlehem, and Newport News Shipbuilding, which now competed with new builders, such as Federal Shipbuilding at Newark, Los Angeles Shipbuilding & Dry Dock, and Sun Ship. The last of these submitted the lowest bid and built the vessel at a loss. To compete in a crowded field, established builders soon emulated these unsound practices, including Cramp, which lost substantial amounts on the *Evangeline* and *Yarmouth*.[33]

Given the scarcity and unprofitability of liner contracts, yards often turned to smaller vessels. Cramp obtained three contracts for sand barges in 1922, followed by an order for four carfloats and seven dump barges a few years later. In 1923 New York Ship received a $7 million contract for ten carfloats from the Pennsylvania Railroad. Even apart from the often noted indignity of building dump barges, first-class shipyards were overequipped for this type of work. New York Ship's outfitting division, for example, operated a tall crane with a lifting capacity of more than 200 tons to haul battleship turrets, but certainly not to lift rails onto carfloat decks.[34]

When vessel contracts ran out, some yards entered nonmarine production—another strategy pioneered by Cramp and Neafie & Levy during the post–Civil War era. In spring 1921 MSC had no work after completing the *Mount Carroll* and *Mount Clinton*. It decided to "branch out in general engineering lines, embracing steel construction in general, manufacturing and power plant equipment, machinery and machine work, railroad equipment and material, and plate shop works."[35] If anything, this laundry list indicated the lack of a comprehensive agenda for product diversification. Shipbuilders could no longer select nonmarine product lines at random because unlike their nineteenth-century predecessors, twentieth-century engineering firms had become fairly specialized. Like Cramp, which had entered the hydraulic equipment market at the turn of the century, builders had to concentrate on a few areas and procure specialty production equipment to compete in non-marine markets. Not surprisingly, MSC's diversification effort failed. In 1923 Harriman closed the historic yard whose origins went back to pre–Civil War years and consolidated his shipbuilding operations at Cramp.[36]

Other Delaware Valley builders followed suit. Pusey & Jones entered involuntary receivership shortly after the war because the Shipping Board failed to reimburse it for several wartime orders. Worse, its owner Christoffer Hannevig overburdened his maritime holdings with huge debts piled up in the United States and Norway. Receivers closed Pusey & Jones's subsidiary yards in Gloucester and sold the Wilmington operation to new owners who continued shipbuilding under adverse conditions. Pusey & Jones's old neighbor Harlan & Hollingsworth struggled along until 1926, when its owners closed the shipbuilding division to concentrate on building railroad cars.[37]

The Demise of the Cramp Shipyard

Compared with most other postwar builders, Cramp was in an enviable position. Its five *Omaha*-class cruisers remained unaffected by naval disarmament and kept the yard employed through 1924. At Cramp diversification into nonmarine engineering did not require major adjustments because it formed an element of long-term business strategies that had sustained the shipyard for two decades. In 1919 the firm continued along these lines by purchasing the De La Vergne Machine Company of New York, a specialty producer of oil engines and refrigeration equipment. During a postwar boom in the hydraulic equipment sector, Cramp also acquired the Pelton Water Wheel Company of San Francisco, which henceforth shared this market with I. P. Morris. Moreover, the shipyard had weathered panics, maritime depressions, and structural crises for close to a century, a history that had gained Cramp a reputation as a tough survivor that usually took the right turn at critical junctures.[38]

Shortly after the war Cramp continued its least admirable tradition—union busting. In December 1920 the management posted a notice declaring, "We have decided to discontinue the agreement with the metal trades department of the American Federation of Labor, and to deal directly with our own employees on and after January 1, 1921." This entailed the elimination of union shop committees; henceforth, the management would treat employees as individuals and would expect them "to ignore all laws enacted by labor organizations for the restriction of output." Cramp also reintroduced a time-recording system that had been suspended during the war and asked "our employees to be prompt." Despite claims that "we are indifferent as to whether our employees are members of labor organizations or not," the management soon discharged members of the boilermakers' union who had served as shop committee members.[39]

This open-shop drive occurred in the context of widespread social unrest in postwar America. In 1919, 4 million workers had struck to gain better wages and shorter workdays, and to secure wartime gains, such as employer recognition of shop committees and union work rules. While some employers, such as Bethlehem Steel, had kept strikes at bay through temporary compromises, most had argued that the return to peacetime production required downsizing and the dismantling of wartime labor policies. These actions fueled the great steel strike of 1919, as well as a general strike in Seattle initiated by shipyard workers. To prevent similar strikes on the East Coast, several yards had signed the agreement between the Shipbuilders' Association and the AFL Metal Trades Council. Emboldened by employer victories during the strike wave of 1919 and a beginning economic downturn that weakened organized labor, Cramp launched a full-scale assault on the union shop committees at the end of 1920.[40]

Metal trades unions could not afford to lose the committees, which formed their most important stronghold in the Philadelphia area. During the war many small metal producers had beaten back the unions, while large firms—especially New York Ship with its Shipyard Labor Adjustment Board committees—had introduced employee representation plans to undercut trade unions. Cramp, by contrast, had established shop committees staffed by union members. Many labor organizers saw this, the most advanced form of worker representation, in jeopardy when Cramp fired the committee members. Moreover, since the firm exerted considerable influence (its president Henry Mull was a senior member of both the Philadelphia Chamber of Commerce and the Shipbuilders' Association), the unions were rightly concerned that a successful open-shop drive might unleash similar movements in local industries and other shipyards. The boilermakers' union therefore called a strike on January 14, 1921, to protest Cramp's action. Machinists, blacksmiths, carpenters, painters, engineers, sheet metal workers, foundry laborers, time keepers, clerks, common laborers, and electricians soon joined them. The only tradesmen not participating were the molders, patternmakers, and draftsmen.[41]

The ensuing conflict sparked one of the most violent labor struggles in postwar America. When 7,000 organized workers and nonunion men walked out, Cramp hired strikebreakers to complete the *Omaha*-class cruisers. To convince these replacements to join the walkout, the strikers rented an airplane that dropped leaflets over the plant—an "ultra-modern method of conducting a strike," one newspaper commented.[42] When these efforts proved fruitless, the gloves came off. On their way home from work, scabs were attacked by angry crowds of shipyard workers, assisted by striking textile workers. Cramp's private police assaulted strike organizers; shots fired during these skirmishes killed one man and injured dozens of others.[43]

Philadelphia's mayor soon intervened. After a meeting with union men, he asked Cramp to submit the conflict to arbitration, but the senior management declared, "We don't intend to arbitrate in this strike . . . because there are no questions to be arbitrated."[44] Prodded by a hysterical press that called Kensington a "war zone," the mayor dispatched 1,000 police officers, declared martial law, and closed off streets in the vicinity of the shipyard. Philadelphia police escorted scabs to the plant and clubbed strikers during an All-American parade in April. Evoking images of the Russian Revolution, strikers called the mounted police "cossacks." It was the largest police intervention in a Philadelphia labor conflict since a streetcar operators' strike in 1907.[45]

The fourteen trades participating in the walkout established a central strike committee with one representative from each trade. To ensure unity the committee assumed "sole control over the actions of the various groups. No individual group or trade is permitted to take any action affecting the general welfare of the whole without first getting the consent of the central committee."[46] The committee drummed up support among national trade unions, organized food drives, and conducted daily meetings attended by hundreds of people. The strikers received support from local physicians who volunteered to attend to the sick and wounded, as well as from shopkeepers who refused to sell groceries to strikebreakers. Philadelphia's local Theatrical Stage Employees' Union held a performance at the People's Theatre, attended by thousands, to raise money for Cramp's strikers.[47]

The strike highlighted the structural problems plaguing the postwar trade union movement. A central committee was necessary because unions still organized shipyard workers by craft, often bickering over jurisdictional boundaries. The molders' union had refused to endorse the movement, although some of its members had joined the strike; an organizer declared that "those not returning to their places would be [replaced] by men carrying cards in the Moulders' Union from another city."[48] An advocate of industrial unionism pointed out that "Philadelphia has been blessed (?) or afflicted with three separate organizations having [AFL] Metal Trades Charters, namely: the Delaware River Shipbuilders' Council; the Navy Yard Metal Trades Council, and the council of the trades employed in the manufacturing shops."[49] The efforts of the International Association of Machinists to organize all metal-trades workers in a single industrial union were defeated by craft unions in Philadelphia and nationwide. The Cramp strike fragmented in fall 1921, when several unions decided they could no longer afford to pay benefits and withdrew from the central committee.[50]

The strike fizzled during a severe postwar depression. In 1921 the Philadelphia press reported that more than 80,000 men and women were out of work in textiles, metalworking, and other local industries. Hog Island and Bristol closed that spring, and Pusey & Jones shut down its Gloucester plants. New York Ship began downsizing after the completion of Shipping Board contracts, as did the Westinghouse turbine works at Essington, which announced a 15 percent wage cut. The IAM advised union members to stay away from Philadelphia because "big layoffs have taken place in the Navy Yard and Arsenal, as well as in the shipyards that are still in operation."[51] As a result, Cramp's strikers could not find new jobs as they had during the 1899 walkout. When defeated union men returned to work, they found shop committees abolished and wages slashed.[52]

As the unions had feared, Cramp's tactics encouraged other employers to take a more aggressive stance toward labor unions and workers. A few months into the strike, the Shipbuilders' Association announced general wage cuts of 10–20 percent without consulting the shipyard unions. The unions might have consented to lower wages, but the new get-tough attitude among employers precluded formal negotiations between capital and labor. Upon Henry Mull's election as president, the association joined the open-shop drive and eliminated most union shop committees. The only form of worker representation allowed in shipyards was the former SLAB committees, which were dominated by nonunion representatives and remained on friendly terms with shipyard managers.[53]

Unlike many other employers, Cramp could not argue that its assault on organized labor and the concomitant wage reductions were warranted by the depression. A few days before Mull declared Cramp an open shop, he had reported a $2.1 million net surplus, the largest in the firm's history. Although the strike affected cruiser construction, the subsidiaries worked on profitable nonmarine contracts; I. P. Morris, for example, had a "very satisfactory year with a large volume of work in the shops" and built four 30,000-horsepower turbines for the famous government-owned waterworks at Muscle Shoals, Alabama. During the strike year, Cramp still produced a net surplus of $1.3 million.[54]

Unfortunately, Cramp did not use its considerable resources to ride out the maritime depression together with its employees because Harriman needed money to prop up his ailing shipping operations. In 1921 Cramp's parent company American Ship & Commerce suffered net losses aggregating more than $1 million—an amount that would have been even higher had Cramp not contributed a $600,000 stock dividend. The shipping subsidiaries lost almost $2 million as a result of the disastrous performance of the immigrant passenger service. American Ship & Commerce performed better in 1922, when Harriman sold several vessels, but still lost more than $140,000 in the shipping division. Its profits that year came solely from the shipbuilding and engineering subsidiaries; Cramp issued a *29 percent* dividend aggregating $4.4 million. (American Ship & Commerce earmarked these profits for the purchase of the *Resolute* and *Reliance*.)[55]

Upon completion of the last *Omaha*-class cruiser in 1924, Cramp had no large vessel contracts and kept busy with barges and carfloats. Later that year, however, the yard obtained a $7.5 million contract for the Pacific Ocean passenger liner *Malolo*. Mull believed that this order "places the shipyard in a satisfactory condition, and should the Company be able to book additional shipbuilding work during the year, the operations of the Marine Department will be eminently satisfactory."[56] The yard did receive contracts for the coastwise passenger steamers *Evangeline* and *Yarmouth,* but both vessels produced substantial losses.[57]

The *Malolo* was Cramp's masterpiece. Unlike the Edwardian-style transatlantic passenger vessels of the prewar era, this elegant Art Deco liner sported an inclined bow. A 582-foot, 19,000-gross-ton hull made the *Malolo* the largest merchant vessel yet built in the United States. Her 25,000-horsepower turbine engines were more powerful than those installed aboard the record-breaking *Great Northern.* Construction involved a wide array of subcontractors, including the Hyde Windlass Company of Bath, Maine, which had supplied Cramp since the 1870s, as well as Westinghouse at Essington, the Radio Corporation of America in Philadelphia, New York Ship, and other Delaware Valley firms.[58]

Although this huge contract kept Cramp busy, it failed to produce the anticipated profits. In 1925 the firm posted its first postwar loss aggregating $551,700; actual operating losses were only $74,000, but depreciation added a $477,000 liability. Moreover, Cramp's accumulated surplus account dwindled when Mull issued a $600,000 dividend to American Ship & Commerce. During the next year Cramp was unable to obtain a single commercial contract; the only new business came from the navy, which in June awarded Cramp contracts for the light cruiser USS *Salt Lake City* and for engines for her sister ship USS *Pensacola* (built at the New York Navy Yard). Mull soon realized that he had submitted an unrealistically low bid. He braced for the worst by separating the shipbuilding division from its profitable subsidiaries, which now formed Cramp-Morris Industrials.[59]

On April 16, 1927, Mull issued a statement declaring that Cramp "has de-

Passenger liner Malolo *outfitting at Cramp, April 5, 1927. The largest and most luxurious American passenger liner of her time, the* Malolo *boasted two movie theaters, a swimming pool, and a gymnasium. The De La Vergne Machine Company, Cramp's new subsidiary, supplied turbine reduction gear for each of her two 12,500-horsepower turbines, which ran at 1,500 rpm and had to be geared down to turn the propeller at 125 rpm. To compensate for the lack of alcoholic beverages aboard this Prohibition-era vessel, the builders installed a custom-made soda fountain, where a "bartender" could mix any soft drink imaginable. Franklin Institute Cramp Shipbuilding Co. Collection, Independence Seaport Museums through the Pew Museum Loan Program*

cided to discontinue shipbuilding operations and turn its shipbuilding properties to other uses." Apart from the *Malolo, Evangeline, Yarmouth,* and USS *Salt Lake City,* it had "no other shipbuilding contracts and sufficient shipbuilding business does not appear to be in prospect to justify the continuance of the extended facilities of its shipyards. Work on the above contracts during the past two years, when the company was unable to secure additional shipbuilding contracts, has resulted in very substantial losses."[60] Despite promises that veteran tradesmen would receive jobs in nonmarine production, Mull's statement caused "panic among the approximately 3000 workmen employed [by Cramp] and 2000 or more who have been temporarily laid off for some weeks."[61]

Commentators were flabbergasted at the demise of the legendary shipyard. Trying to explain what had gone awry, *Marine Engineering* pointed to ruinous competition:

Hope fathered the conviction that if any one should be forced to quit it should be some of the less resourceful shipbuilder[s]. As a result most of the old established yards have put up a bitter fight for survival against the keenest sort of competition for the few contracts available and with small hope of profits for the successful bidders. With practically no support from the government from [1920] to this [day] the shipbuilding industry has been slowly starving to a shadow of its former self as one after another of the shipyards has quietly passed out of existence or gone into other lines of work. Such has been the fate of the old Roach yard, the Sparrow's Point, Harlan and Moore plants of the Bethlehem Shipbuilding Corporation and the Bath Iron Works, to mention only a few of the more important ones on the Atlantic Coast, and now Cramp's is added to the list.[62]

This was all the more shocking because Cramp had carried diversification into nonmarine production further than most other builders. "If Cramp's must go," *Marine Engineering* asked, "what next?"[63]

Competition and the lack of an intelligent merchant marine policy were important factors underlying Cramp's demise. In addition, its integration into Harriman's weak maritime conglomerate drained resources during a critical period when Cramp should have accumulated profits in anticipation of hard times. To a certain extent, the yard's fate redeemed Charles Cramp, who had shunned a full-scale integration of shipbuilding with steamship lines. John Roach's forays into shipping during the late 1870s had illustrated that vertical integration in the marine sector was fraught with problems because it combined two unstable economic sectors. These experiences were forgotten during the short-lived postwar boom, only to be repeated in the shipyard depression.

Winding up its affairs, Cramp declared itself in default on the contract for the USS *Salt Lake City,* which was less than 10 percent complete. The

Navy Department readvertised the cruiser in April 1927 and awarded it to New York Ship.

New York Ship and the Resurgence of the Military-Industrial Complex

New York Ship entered the postwar period with a somewhat disappointing performance. At the end of 1918 it reported a huge business volume of almost $72 million but earned only 2.2 percent profit; the largest liability was the USS *Idaho* contract, on which New York Ship lost $1.5 million in 1918 alone. Profits rose during the next few years, as the yard converted sixteen troopships into passenger liners for the Shipping Board, worked on private tanker and freighter contracts, and completed the battleship USS *Colorado*. Throughout this relatively prosperous period, however, financial difficulties loomed because the Internal Revenue Service claimed that New York Ship owed millions in wartime taxes. In 1923 the firm reported only a nominal profit after the navy had canceled the battleship USS *Washington* in accordance with the Washington Naval Treaty and private orders dried up. Its only major contract was the USS *Saratoga*, the battle cruiser turned into an aircraft carrier.[64]

The USS *Saratoga* and her twin USS *Lexington* (built by Fore River Shipbuilding) heralded carrier aviation, perhaps the most profound change in naval warfare and technology since the ironclad warship. Although aircraft had played a marginal role in World War I naval operations, military experts realized that the new technology had far-reaching implications for armed conflict at sea, potentially dooming the battleship. In a dramatic experiment conducted near Norfolk in 1919, a tiny aircraft dropped a bomb on the German dreadnaught SMS *Ostfriesland*, a war prize; the explosion caused the huge vessel to capsize and sink within minutes. Other experiments involving the American pioneer carrier USS *Langley*, a converted collier, demonstrated that aircraft could be successfully launched and landed on a flight deck at sea. To build a larger and more advanced carrier type, the navy decided in 1922 to convert two of the six *Lexington*-class battle cruisers scheduled for scrapping in accordance with the Washington Treaty. At this time, New York Ship had already built the *Saratoga's* exterior hull up to the main deck, but interior work was still incomplete, except foundations for the main turrets. In November 1922 the navy and the shipyard signed a supplemental $23 million contract to turn the battle cruiser into an aircraft carrier.[65]

The USS *Saratoga* conversion was perhaps one of the most challenging jobs in the history of naval shipbuilding, subject to technical as well as diplomatic imperatives. The exterior hull, lower decks, and the 180,000-horsepower turbo-electric drive system remained largely unchanged, but everything else

Battle-cruiser-turned-carrier USS Saratoga *outfitting at New York Ship, 1926. Note the large funnel structure encasing the four separate funnels of the battle cruiser design. Also note the heavy ordnance: Design changes were responsible for construction delays. U.S. Naval Historical Center*

had to be redesigned. Designers eliminated the battle cruiser superstructure and replaced it with a much smaller one on the starboard side of the flight deck. This required a complete redesign of the four funnels, which were moved from the center-keel line to starboard and encased in a large single structure. To hold off smaller warships in surface battles, the *Saratoga* received heavy ordnance. The designers first devised a battery of 6-inch guns, which was considered too light and replaced with 8-inch guns. When the carrier was already under construction, the design of the flight deck underwent significant changes that contributed to construction delays. Finally, the contract fell behind schedule because the navy faced problems in its effort to slim down the 43,500-displacement-ton battle cruiser design to satisfy the provisions of the Washington Treaty, which limited aircraft carriers to 35,000 tons. Although New York Ship removed the turret foundations and some armor plates, and although designers in the Bureau of Construction and Repair reduced weight by eliminating items from the original design wherever possible, the 1926 design still showed the *Saratoga* too large by 3,000 tons. In March the navy decided that detail provisions in the Washington Treaty allowed the extra weight to be retained and ordered the builders to complete the carrier as planned. As a result of frequent design changes, the construction schedule increased from thirty to sixty-seven months, and costs rose from $23 million to

$40 million. New York Ship launched the *Saratoga* on July 7, 1925, and delivered her for commissioning in November 1927.[66]

The USS *Saratoga* was the navy's first true aircraft carrier, and she accumulated an outstanding service record. Thanks to her origins as a 35-knot battle cruiser, she was faster and larger than any other carrier launched until World War II, except the USS *Lexington*. During a fleet exercise in 1929 her successful "strike" against the Panama Canal convinced strategic planners that fast carrier task forces were critical in naval attack operations. This was confirmed in 1942, when the *Saratoga* opened the American assault on Guadalcanal, in the course of which her planes sank the Japanese carrier *Ryuio*. This and other feats, including the disabling of Japanese airfields, shore defenses, and cruisers at Bougainville in 1943, earned her seven battle stars. The USS *Saratoga* ended her career at Bikini Atoll in Operation Crossroads, designed to test the effect of atomic weapons on naval vessels. In a last tribute to its builders, the robust carrier survived a blast that finished off most other vessels and remained stubbornly afloat for more than seven hours after a second nuclear device had been detonated within close range.[67]

During the completion of the USS *Saratoga,* New York Ship entered rough financial waters. Although the carrier contract involved no losses, the yard strained under the burden of corporate policy as parent company AIC compelled New York Ship to issue dividends to cover losses in shipping operations. In 1923, for example, AIC reported losses aggregating $5.6 million; although New York Ship realized a net income of only $90,000, it issued a $200,000 dividend, most of which went to the ailing parent company. Like Cramp, New York Ship paid dividends out of accumulated surpluses from earlier years and thereby depleted emergency funds. Meanwhile, it closed the South, Middle, and Destroyer yards, concentrated all shipbuilding activities at the original plant, and made forays into diesel engineering and nonmarine product lines, such as structural steel. In 1924 it reported a net income of $131,000 but paid out $400,000 in dividends.[68]

One year later, AIC sold its exhausted subsidiary to the Swiss electrical engineering firm Brown & Bovery, which acquired American plants to enter the booming U.S. electrical equipment sector. New York Ship's senior management believed that with "its production diversified through the addition of Brown & Bovery lines, supported by [their] high standing . . . in the electrical manufacturing field, the outlook for the New York Shipbuilding Corporation would appear decidedly improved."[69] Indeed, the new owners made New York Ship the headquarters for their U.S. operations; furnished new production equipment to build electrical transformers, circuit breakers, and locomotives;

and renamed the firm American Brown & Bovery in October 1925. Upon closer examination of their new holdings, however, the Swiss discovered extensive liabilities, including the laid-up oil tanker *Prescilla*, which New York Ship had built on its own account to keep the yard employed. The new management sold the *Prescilla*, had the federal tax liability reduced from $3.8 million to $2.5 million, and completed the remaining contracts, which had shriveled to another tanker built on yard account and Cramp's subcontract for twenty lifeboats.[70]

The shipyard soon hit rock bottom. A chief executive later recalled that the change in management "resulted in serious demoralization . . . of the ship-building operation and . . . in such a falling-off in the quality and character of the work that the corporation and its officers were subjected to very severe criticism . . . by the Navy Department for the work which was then in prog-ress . . . In the ensuing months . . . the financial affairs . . . grew rapidly worse and reached a crisis during the year of 1927."[71] Although the yard scraped by with a contract for thirty-three U.S. Coast Guard patrol boats, there were serious doubts whether Brown & Bovery would continue shipbuilding.[72]

The outlook began to improve in April 1927, when Brown & Bovery submit-ted bids to the Navy Department for two light cruisers. There was little doubt that the yard would receive the readvertised USS *Salt Lake City* because Cramp had already received ship steel and laid the keel; to limit the delays involved in transferring the material to another builder, the navy would have to award her to the Camden yard, the only big plant in the vicinity. Aware of this situation, Brown & Bovery pressured the navy to issue another light cruiser contract as a "bonus" for "taking over that Cramp job."[73] The firm also warned Secretary of the Treasury Andrew Mellon—New York Ship's former owner—that it would lose money if it received only one light cruiser contract. "The recent default of Cramps and the elimination of their engineering talent from shipbuilding is a clear indicant of what we remaining builders will be forced to do if the Navy Department does not support us at this time."[74] Brown & Bovery received the USS *Salt Lake City* as well as the "bonus" cruiser USS *Chester,* realizing profits of more than 33 percent on this $20 million contract. Homer Ferguson, who booked similarly profitable orders for Newport News Shipbuilding, was "per-fectly amazed that we made so much."[75]

These events marked the resurgence of the military-industrial complex that sustained the Big Three. In 1927 Brown & Bovery, Newport News Shipbuilding, and Bethlehem hired lobbyist William Shearer to sabotage the Geneva Naval Disarmament Conference, which would have restricted light cruiser construc-tion along the lines of the capital ship treaty of 1922. The conference failed, and Shearer boasted, though incorrectly, that he was responsible for the later construction of several cruisers. The USS *Indianapolis* went to New York Ship in 1929 (the firm had resumed its old name in 1928). The Big Three also ended competitive bidding on warship contracts through informal agreements on construction bids. These shady activities continued well into the Great Depression and ensured whopping profits in naval shipbuilding.[76]

In the meantime, Brown & Bovery/New York Ship launched aggressive lobbying campaigns to garner federal support for commercial shipping. Lawrence R. Wilder, who had headed the yard during the mid-1920s, practically wrote the Merchant Marine Act of 1928 (New York Ship and other builders reportedly spent $140,000 lobbying for its passage). This measure awarded generous ten-year mail contracts to private carriers ordering fast liners for foreign routes; it also authorized the Shipping Board to issue low-interest loans covering up to 75 percent of construction costs. Thanks to Wilder's efforts, American Export Lines received a $6.6 million loan and in August 1929 awarded New York Ship the Four Aces, fast combination freighters equipped with passenger accommodations. "This is the single largest order for ships in which the Federal Government has participated since the close of the World War period," the *New York Times* commented.[77] Significantly, an informal agreement among the Big Three guaranteed that there were no competitive bids, ensuring handsome profits for New York Ship. The Shipping Board also supported vessel acquisitions by the United States Lines (now in private hands), which ordered the large passenger liners *Manhattan* and *Washington*; again, Newport News Shipbuilding and Bethlehem agreed to let New York Ship have the contract in return for other favors.[78]

These developments enabled the yard to put its financial affairs in order. Between 1927 and 1934, New York Ship increased its assets from $1.3 million to $5 million and earned aggregate net profits of $6 million. "The average income during this period," a former chief executive wrote, "far exceeds that of any similar period in the corporation's existence, with the exception of the period during and immediately after the war."[79] This remarkable performance was achieved at a time when the nation's economy as a whole sank into the Great Depression.

Epilogue

*I*n Philadelphia the Great Depression began earlier and took a greater toll in human suffering than in most other cities. Already weakened by the shipyard crisis, the local economy crumbled after 1929 and threw more than 300,000 people out of work. But shipbuilding was already on its way toward recovery. Prodded by a former assistant secretary of the navy who now occupied the White House, the Public Works Administration poured $238 million into naval shipbuilding in 1933 alone. Through the well-established channels of the military-industrial complex, New York Ship received its share of the resulting contracts, including one for the big cruiser USS *Phoenix*. By the end of the 1930s naval rearmament even brought "the good times back [to] Kensington," as a newspaper cheered when a group of private investors and the navy reopened Cramp to build heavy cruisers.[1] Once again, the American Clyde enjoyed prosperity.

Yet Philadelphia belied comparisons to the Scottish shipbuilding hub. Philadelphia's distinction was American and regional. Handicapped by comparatively high construction costs, Philadelphia yards rarely built vessels for foreign steamship customers. In spite of record-breakers like the *St. Louis*, steamship construction for private *American* operators languished throughout the late nineteenth and early twentieth centuries. The long-term decline of the U.S. merchant marine left Philadelphia shipyards' order books increasingly empty as the twentieth century wore on.

As we have seen, the origins of iron and steel shipbuilding in the Delaware

Valley can be traced to Philadelphia's nineteenth-century strengths as an over-seas port and then as a center of urban manufacturing and railroad trans-portation. Philadelphia created an environment in which artisans and entre-preneurs had to experiment with new technologies, notably steam engines, locomotives, and steamships.

From a macroeconomic perspective, this regional transformation fore-shadowed a national trend. After the mid-nineteenth century the American shipping sector experienced a serious crisis because railroad building drew off capital previously invested in maritime trade. Railroads also cut deep into the quasi-monopoly of waterborne trade on long-distance transportation. Seg-ments of the carrying trades that survived the onslaught often became ad-juncts of the railroad sector. Philadelphia, where railroads branched out into shipping, first experienced this change; it marks the advanced stage of local economic development.

To evaluate our findings in the larger context of American industrial his-tory, we may return to several questions raised in the introduction. How did market demand affect technological change? Shipbuilding supplied the least stable market for capital goods equipment in nineteenth-century America. Aside from fluctuation in demand, customers ordered a wide variety of ves-sel types—passenger liners, freighters, tankers, barges, tugs, and pilot boats among them. Not surprisingly, shipbuilders prized flexible technologies.

One might expect government demand to be an agent of technological change in shipbuilding, as it was in firearms manufacture and armor pro-duction. Here experience left an uneven record. Naval policies generated de-mand for new types of ships, which motivated shipbuilders to introduce new equipment. During the Civil War naval contracting introduced metal technol-ogy to the shipbuilding industry; the relatively simple equipment associated with making ironclads converted easily to the construction of commercial steamships.

Toward the end of the nineteenth century, however, conversion from naval to general commercial construction became increasingly difficult because building warships soon required specialty equipment of limited use in low-technology construction. Encouraged by major government contracts, build-ers of warships erected the huge new berths and installed the expensive ma-chinery required for this type of work. As a result of the growing weakness of the U.S. merchant marine, however, they were unable to procure sufficient high-technology private contracts to allow them to exploit spinoffs in com-mercial construction. The yards had no choice but to build tugs and sand barges on berths that were laid out for battleships and passenger liners. As contemporary observers pointed out—and as most late twentieth-century defense contractors would confirm—building low-technology commercial products with high-technology equipment proved extremely inefficient, impaired a naval contractor's ability to compete in civilian markets, and—when naval disarmament led to a drastic decline in warship construction during the 1920s—pushed the industry to the brink of disaster.

In terms of business organization, proprietary and corporate firms both played pivotal roles in Philadelphia shipbuilding. In the nineteenth century proprietorships reigned supreme. Shipbuilding entrepreneurs mobilized investment for this capital-intensive industry by means of family connections and business partnerships. Although many firms obtained corporate charters or took advantage of general incorporation laws, former proprietors usually retained full control of investments and day-to-day operations in these closely held corporations. Genuine corporations that separated ownership and management flourished in railroading and later in the steamship business, but they rarely made their presence felt in the late nineteenth-century production economy.

The controversy over the relative importance of proprietary and corporate capitalisms should not obscure the fact that they were interrelated. In the maritime economy of the day corporately owned steamship lines issued vessel contracts to proprietary shipyards, contributing to the latter's continued viability. Corporate contracts enabled some builders to expand in the 1870s during a critical period that laid the groundwork for long-term growth. Additional case studies—especially in the history of the locomotive and railroad car industries, where such relationships were even more common than in shipbuilding—will demonstrate the significance of this pattern for the U.S. transportation sector. Other studies may examine the relationship between batch and mass producers in the manufacturing sector, where specialty engineering firms often supplied mass producers with custom-made industrial tools. We may find that industrial development was fueled by a dynamic interaction between proprietary batch producers—dominating significant portions of the capital-equipment and high-quality consumer-goods industries—and corporately owned firms that thrived in the capital-intensive transportation and mass production sectors.

Some proprietorships and closely held corporations separated ownership and management, and thereby evolved into corporations. Yet we should avoid portraying the transition to corporate capitalism as inevitable or as somehow leading to economic maturity. Corporate reconstruction was rarely a "natural" process transforming proprietary larvae into corporate butterflies; more often, it was a crisis strategy designed to save moribund businesses from extinction. At the turn of the century, for example, Cramp embarked upon a dangerous course of expansion and suffered as a result; in that case the advent of the corporation marked retrenchment and financial austerity, not expansion. Similarly, many steel firms suffered from excess capacities and competitive weakness and were rescued by U.S. Steel, which itself began downsizing immediately after its formation in 1901.

Large investment banks, which had concentrated on railroad securities and government bonds but at the turn of the century branched out into industrial financing, played an important role in corporate reconstruction. Like Drexel in Cramp's case, Boston banks reorganized Fore River when the yard's founder, Thomas Watson, was unable to finance a $20 million backlog of orders. Other prominent examples include General Electric, bailed out by J. Pierpont Morgan, and the German Mannesmann steel tube company, rescued by the Deutsche Bank. American and German banks entered industrial financing on an even larger scale by gaining control of large blocks of shares in mergers such as U.S. Steel, International Harvester, and the German Siemens-Schuckert electrical corporation. London banks played a far less prominent role in British industrial financing, where private capital remained the most important source of investments.[2]

Separation between ownership and management paved the way for speculative ventures. Released from proprietary control, shares in industrial enterprises traded on financial markets, where to realize short-term profits, corporate conglomerates such as AIC or W. A. Harriman & Company could and did buy controlling interests in the firms. This pattern was especially noticeable during the World War I boom that turned engineering, shipbuilding, and munitions into highly profitable investments. Corporate capital's often noted genius for formulating long-term business strategies did not, however, pay dividends in shipbuilding. Maritime conglomerates launched questionable ventures—forays into mass production and vertical integration—that contributed directly to the shipbuilding crisis of the 1920s. While much of the blame must be placed on the Shipping Board's doorstep, inept corporate strategy clearly exacerbated the industry's long-term problems.

An intelligent federal policy in the maritime sector, one that established incentives for investment (or offset the disincentives), might have turned the tide and sustained a viable commercial shipbuilding industry. During the second half of the nineteenth century the American carrying trades suffered from a lack of inexpensive metal tonnage. Maritime reforms could have reinvigorated the merchant marine. Republican reform proposals included granting subsidies and admitting foreign-built ships to U.S. registry (with a stipulation that shippers had to buy a certain percentage of their tonnage from American yards). Special legislation placed the *City of New York* and the *City of Paris* under the American flag. Unfortunately, the federal government never formulated an overall merchant marine policy on the basis of this compromise between free trade and protectionism.

A look at German merchant marine policies reveals that well-conceived reforms could make a difference. The nineteenth-century German maritime economy suffered from problems reminiscent of those found in the United States. Wooden shipbuilding continued to play an important role although the technology was obsolete; yards for iron shipbuilding were few and far between; builders were unable to match British prices; and the industry was severely impaired by the recession of 1884, when more than half of all German shipyard workers were laid off. Unlike American steamship lines, however, German carriers, such as HAPAG and Norddeutscher Lloyd (NL), enjoyed the benefits of free registry and sailed British-built tonnage under the German flag. After gaining a stronghold on the North Atlantic (despite fierce competition from British lines), HAPAG branched out into the Latin-American trade and became one of the world's most diversified steamship lines.

In 1886, after the Reichstag passed a maritime reform law awarding subsidies to German-built tonnage, HAPAG and NL ordered their first German passenger liners. Sustained by large customers that still ordered most of their ships in Britain, German shipbuilding gathered momentum during the late 1880s. Yards expanded, and builders gained their first experience in liner construction. Nudged by reformers, German carriers in the course of the next decade switched from British to German builders. By 1898 British yards received contracts only when German builders were too busy to take orders. After the turn of the century, HAPAG became the world's largest steamship line and issued stupendously large contracts to builders such as Vulcan in Stettin and Blohm & Voss in Hamburg. Shortly before World War I Blohm & Voss built three *Imperator*-class passenger liners—bigger (though perhaps less elegant) than anything afloat under Britain's red ensign.[3]

Like its American counterpart, German shipbuilding after the turn of the century received a major stimulus from the naval arms race that eventually led to the catastrophe of August 1914. Unlike Cramp and New York Ship, German builders enjoyed persistent demand for merchant tonnage, which enabled them to balance naval and commercial construction and attain a degree of yard specialization resembling that of British shipbuilding. Blohm & Voss became a specialist in large, high-performance vessels, using its expertise in battle cruiser construction to build fast passenger liners (and vice versa). In the United States, by comparison, weak demand for merchant tonnage left first-class builders at the mercy of government spending and resulted in woeful underutilization of building space. Observers feared for the long-term stability of American shipbuilding.[4]

Extensive yard improvements during the late 1880s did not deceive experienced builders like Charles Cramp, who knew that "government work is not a reliable basis for permanent prosperity" and demanded merchant marine policies to match the naval program. Cramp knew that, above all, he had to continue to build mercantile vessels. During the critical 1890s, however, merchant marine policies led to American orders only on a piecemeal basis. Congress helped widen the noticeable gap between technical capacity and economic performance in American shipbuilding with repeated promises of comprehensive reforms. Repeatedly, however, the resulting periods of hectic activity, when vessel owners placed speculative orders and builders launched plant improvements, ended when legislation was defeated in the House or Senate or died in congressional committees, leaving shipyards with another set of resplendent but often idle facilities.

The lack of a viable merchant marine and commercial shipbuilding had serious implications for the U.S. economy and national security. Although protectionists probably exaggerated the overall effects on the national economy, American businesses did pay British and European carriers up to $100 million annually to serve the nation's foreign trade, an amount that contributed considerably to the negative U.S. balance of payments before World War I. In wartime the withdrawal of foreign tonnage created problems in the export sector, and when U.S. troops were sent overseas, transportation bottlenecks seriously impaired military operations. Swamped with naval orders that took up the bulk of existing construction capacity, older shipyards were usually unable to build sufficient merchant tonnage, which had to be supplied by hastily erected yards.

This sequence was repeated in World War II, when major private builders committed themselves to naval construction. New York Ship built aircraft carriers and battleships, and Cramp, which had been reopened by the navy, specialized in heavy cruiser and submarine construction. Most contracts for noncombat vessels went to new assembly yards, which mass produced 2,708 standardized *Liberty* ships, as well as several hundred *C*-class and *Victory* freighters. In this category, there were marked differences from World War I practice. Concerned about the effects of the vessel design changes that had caused havoc at Hog Island in 1917, the War Production Board opposed any alterations to the *Liberty* ship design long after it had become obsolete. Most ship assemblers in World War II avoided Hog Island's practice of subcontracting major hull-fabrication work. Although Bethlehem's assembly yard at Baltimore received fittings, engines, and steel shapes from subcontractors, the company fabricated standardized hull components in its own large shop fitted with overhead cranes and processing machinery. Members of the Maritime

Commission, responsible for the government program for noncombat vessels, rightly worried about the effects of excess tonnage on the postwar maritime economy and canceled most orders in summer 1945.[5]

In the Delaware Valley the World War II revival proved short-lived. Upon completion of its cruisers in 1946, Cramp closed permanently. Commercial demand was almost nonexistent. The plant was dismantled during the 1960s and the property turned into what urban planners call an industrial park. New York Ship struggled along in the 1950s, when it introduced new marine technologies to build nuclear-powered submarines. Efforts to exploit spinoffs in commercial construction led nowhere, except for the cargo and passenger ship *Savannah,* which accumulated a rather dubious service record and had to be laid up. By the mid-1960s, save for the *Sturgeon*-class nuclear submarine USS *Poggy,* the order books were empty. When in 1967 the navy withdrew the contract because the submarine was insufficiently advanced, New York Ship went out of business, and tugs towed the unfinished *Poggy* to the Philadelphia Navy Yard for completion.[6]

At first the Navy Yard profited from the closure of private yards in the Delaware Valley and hired men (and later also women) who formed the elite of America's shipyard workers. During the early 1930s it commenced capital ship overhauls that allowed it to employ many former Cramp personnel. It built the battleships USS *New Jersey* and USS *Wisconsin* in World War II. When New York Ship followed Cramp into shipyard history, many Camden tradesmen joined the Navy Yard work force, as did former employees of Sun Ship, which closed during the late 1970s when Sun Oil discontinued tanker construction. Although there were rumors that the navy planned to close the Navy Yard, an aircraft carrier overhaul program known as the Service Life Extension Program (SLEP), begun in 1979, reinvigorated the yard and increased its work force from 6,000 to 11,500.[7]

The end was in sight when the Reagan administration curtailed SLEP and poured billions into nuclear-powered aircraft carriers. Unlike most other navy yards, the Philadelphia facility was not equipped to handle nuclear material. In January 1990 the Defense Base Closure and Realignment Commission placed the yard on a "hit list" that was approved by Congress and President George Bush a year later. The closure of the Philadelphia Navy Yard in 1996 marked the end of the American Clyde.[8]

The history of shipbuilding in Philadelphia makes clear how heavy industry first supported the development of a world power and then fell victim to global economic forces.

ABBREVIATIONS

A&NJ	Army and Navy Journal
AN	American Neptune
ARCN	Annual Report of the Commissioner of Navigation
AS	American Ship
BHR	Business History Review
BMISBJ	Boilermakers and Iron Shipbuilders Journal
CG	Congressional Globe
CM	Cassier's Magazine
EFN	Emergency Fleet News
EM	Engineering Magazine
ENR	Engineering News-Record
HM	Harper's Magazine
HNMM	Harper's New Monthly Magazine
HW	Harper's Weekly
IA	Iron Age
ITR	Iron Trade Review
LMS	Log of Mystic Seaport
LT	(London) Times
ME	Marine Engineering
MM	Merchants Magazine
MMJ	Machinists Monthly Journal
MR	Marine Review
NA	National Archives
NAR	North American Review
NG	Nautical Gazette
NYT	New York Times
PB	Philadelphia Bulletin
PI	Philadelphia Inquirer
PL	Public Ledger
PMHB	Philadelphia Magazine of History and Biography
PNASP	Proceedings of the Numismatic and Antiquarian Society of Philadelphia

PP	Philadelphia Press
PR	Philadelphia Record
PUSNI	Proceedings of the United States Naval Institute
RG	Record Group (National Archives)
RGD	R. G. Dun Credit Records, microfilm, Hagley Museum and Library, Wilmington, Del.
SA	Scientific American
SI	Shipping Illustrated
T&C	Technology & Culture
TINA	Transactions of the Institution of Naval Architects
TSNAME	Transactions of the Society of Naval Architects and Marine Engineers
VNEEM	Van Norstrom's Eclectic Engineering Magazine
YN	Yorkship News

Prologue

1. "Launch of the *St. Louis* for the American Line," *SA* 71 (1894): 328; "Launching of the *St. Louis*," *HW* 38 (1894): 1122.

2. *The American Line, New York to Southampton; The Red Star Line, New York to Antwerp* (New York, 1895), pp. 14–26.

3. Thomas C. Cochran, "Philadelphia: The American Industrial Center, 1750–1850," *PMHB* 106 (1982): 323–40.

4. Philip Scranton, *Proprietary Capitalism: The Textile Manufacture at Philadelphia, 1800–1885* (New York, 1983); John Ingham, *Making Iron and Steel: Independent Mills in Pittsburgh, 1820–1920* (Columbus, Ohio, 1991).

5. Alfred D. Chandler, Jr., *The Visible Hand: The Managerial Revolution in American Business* (Cambridge, Mass., 1977), p. 3.

6. See Philip Scranton, "Diversity in Diversity: Flexible Production and American Industrialization, 1880–1930," *BHR* 65 (1991): 35; and Scranton, *Proprietary Capitalism,* p. 7.

7. Thomas Hughes, "British Electrical Industry Lag, 1882–1888," *T&C* 3 (1962): 27–44; see also his seminal *Networks of Power: Electrification in Western Society, 1880–1930* (Baltimore, 1983). See also David Noble, *America by Design: Science, Technology, and the Rise of Corporate Capitalism* (New York, 1977); Harry Braverman, *Labor and Monopoly Capital: The Degradation of Work in the Twentieth Century* (New York, 1974); David Montgomery, *Workers' Control in America: Studies in the History of Work, Technology, and Labor Struggles* (Cambridge, Mass., 1979); Montgomery, *The Fall of the House of Labor: The Workplace, the State, and American Labor Activism, 1865–1925* (Cambridge, Mass., 1987); Michael Nuwer, "From Batch Production to Flow: Technology and Work-Force Skills in the Steel Industry, 1880–1920," *T&C* 29 (1988): 808–38.

8. Studies of Philadelphia industries and capital-labor relations include Bruce Laurie, *Working People of Philadelphia, 1800–1850* (Philadelphia, 1980); Theodore Hershberg et al., eds., *Philadelphia: Work, Space, Family, and Group Experience in the Nineteenth-Century City: Essays toward an Interdisciplinary History of the City* (New York, 1981); Scranton, *Proprietary Capitalism;* Philip Scranton and Walter Licht, *Work Sights: Industrial Philadelphia 1890–1940* (Philadelphia, 1986); and John K. Brown, *The Baldwin Locomotive Works, 1831–1915: A Study in American Industrial Practice* (Baltimore, 1995).

One: "Ship-Building as Much as Possible Advanced"

1. Philip C. F. Smith, *Philadelphia on the River* (Philadelphia, 1986).

2. For a historiographical overview, see Jeffrey J. Safford, "The Decline of the American Merchant Marine, 1850–1914: A Historiographic Appraisal," in *Change and Adaptation in Maritime History: The North Atlantic Fleets in the Nineteenth Century,* ed. Lewis Fischer and Gerald E. Panting (St. John's, Newfoundland, Canada, 1985), pp. 53–85. The most prominent study blaming the decline of the American maritime economy on the Civil War is Frank L. Owsley, *King Cotton Diplomacy: Foreign Relations of the Confederate States of America* (Chicago, 1931). For analyses of long-term causes, see David B. Tyler, *Steam Conquers the Atlantic* (New York, 1939); and John Hutchins, *The American Maritime Industries and Public Policy, 1789–1914: An Economic History* (Cambridge, Mass., 1941).

3. For this and the following paragraphs, see Joseph A. Goldenberg, *Shipbuilding in Colonial America* (Charlottesville, Va., 1976); Charles L. Chandler, *Early Shipbuilding in Pennsylvania, 1683–1812* (Princeton, N.J., 1932), pp. 16–17; James F. Shepherd, *Shipping, Maritime Trade and the Economic Development of Colonial North America* (Cambridge, Mass., 1972), pp. 159–63.

4. Benjamin Franklin, "A Modest Inquiry into the Nature and Necessity of a Paper Currency" (1729), quoted in Simeon J. Crowther, "The Shipbuilding Output of the Delaware Valley, 1722–1776," *Proceedings of the American Philosophical Society* 117 (1975): 90.

5. Julian D. Fischer, "Shipbuilding in Colonial Portsmouth: The *Raleigh,*" *Historical New Hampshire* 42 (1987): 1–35.

6. K. Jack Bauer, "The Golden Age," in *America's Maritime Legacy: A History of the U.S. Merchant Marine and Shipbuilding Industry since Colonial Times,* ed. Robert A. Kilmarx (Boulder, Colo., 1979), p. 27.

7. Hutchins, *American Maritime Industries,* pp. 249–50.

8. Bauer, "Golden Age," pp. 28–32; William A. Fairburn, *Merchant Sail, Vol. 5* (Center Lovell, Maine, 1955), pp. 2764–65; James D. Phillips, "The Salem Shipbuilding Industry before 1812," *AN* 2 (1942): 278–88.

9. Robin D. Higham, "The Port of Boston and the Embargo of 1807–1809," *AN* 16 (1956): 189–210.

10. James W. Livingood, *The Philadelphia-Baltimore Trade Rivalry, 1780–1860* (reprint, New York, 1970); Diane Lindstrom, *Economic Development in the Philadelphia Region, 1810–1850* (New York, 1978), pp. 28–40. On Girard, see *The National Cyclopedia of American Biography, Vol. 7* (New York, 1897), pp. 11–12.

11. George R. Taylor, *The Transportation Revolution, 1815–1860* (New York, 1950), pp. 126–27; Robert G. Albion, *The Rise of New York Port, 1815–1860* (reprint, New York, 1970), pp. 95–121.

12. Albion, *Rise of New York Port,* pp. 38–43, 55–94; Taylor, *Transportation Revolution,* pp. 32–36, 105–31; Hutchins, *American Maritime Industries,* pp. 101, 214.

13. Hutchins, *American Maritime Industries,* pp. 264–69.

14. Samuel E. Morison, *The Maritime History of Massachusetts, 1783–1860* (reprint, Boston, 1979), pp. 314–64; Ray Brighton, *Clippers of the Port of Portsmouth and the Men Who Built Them* (Portsmouth, N.H., 1985); U.S. House Select Committee, "Report of the Select Committee on the Causes of the Reduction of American Tonnage," 41st Cong., 2nd sess., House Report No. 28, p. xii (hereafter cited as Lynch Report).

15. Lindstrom, *Economic Development*, pp. 30–34.

16. Taylor, *Transportation Revolution*, p. 107.

17. Ibid., pp. 44, 54; Livingood, *Philadelphia-Baltimore Trade Rivalry*, pp. 81–97; Bauer, "Golden Age," p. 47; James A. Ward, *J. Edgar Thompson: Master of the Pennsylvania* (Westport, Conn., 1980), pp. 68–109.

18. *MM* 31 (1854): 258–59; *MM* 33 (1855): 498; James L. Holton, *The Reading Railroad: History of a Coal Empire, Vol.1: The Nineteenth Century* (Laury's Station, Pa., 1989), pp. 85–110; Barbara Fisher, "Maritime History of the Reading, 1833–1905," *PMHB* 86 (1962): 162–70.

19. *MM* 43 (1860): 110–11; Hutchins, *American Maritime Industries*, pp. 328–32; Cedric Ridgley-Nevitt, *American Steamships on the Atlantic* (Newark, N.J., 1981), pp. 18–24, 73–80; Frederick M. Binder, "Pennsylvania Coal and the Beginnings of American Steam Navigation," *PMHB* 83 (1959): 420–45.

20. Hutchins, *American Maritime Industries*, pp. 336–43; see also A. G. Course, *Ships of the P & O* (Gillingham, England, 1954).

21. Francis E. Hyde, *Cunard and the North Atlantic, 1840–1973: A History of Shipping and Financial Management* (London, 1975), pp. 27–45; Hutchins, *American Maritime Industries*, pp. 348–58.

22. *MM* 39 (1858): 281.

23. Donald L. Canney, *The Old Steam Navy, Vol. 1: Frigates, Sloops, and Gunboats, 1815–1885* (Annapolis, Md., 1990), p. 26.

24. Ibid., p. 17; Charles Cramp, "Evolution of Screw Propulsion in the United States," *TSNAME* 17 (1908): 155; Hutchins, *American Maritime Industries*, p. 331.

25. Cramp, "Evolution of Screw Propulsion," passim; Canney, *Old Steam Navy*, p. 17; Ridgley-Nevitt, *American Steamships*, p. 187.

26. Robert F. Stockton to Secretary of the Navy, 2 October 1843, cited in Canney, *Old Steam Navy*, p. 24.

27. Canney, *Old Steam Navy*, pp. 23–24.

28. U.S. House Committee on Naval Affairs, "Report on Ericsson's Steam Battleship," 29th Cong., 1st sess., reprinted in *The New American State Papers: Science & Technology, Vol 9: Military Technology*, ed. Thomas Cochran et al. (Wilmington, Del., 1973), pp. 318–64.

29. Charles H. Haswell, "Reminiscences of Early Marine Steam Engine Construction in the United States of America," *TINA* 40 (1898): 105; see also Cramp, "Evolution of Screw Propulsion," p. 145.

30. Hutchins, *American Maritime Industries*, p. 443; Ridgley-Nevitt, *American Steamships*, p. 188.

31. Cramp, "Evolution of Screw Propulsion," pp. 152, 154.

32. Ibid., p. 156; Tyler, *Steam Conquers the Atlantic,* pp. 184–85; Eric Heyl, *Early American Steamers, Vol. 3* (New York, 1964), pp. 235–36, 269–70, 319–20, 347–48; Heyl, *Early American Steamers, Vol. 4* (Buffalo, N.Y., 1965), pp. 141–42.

33. *PL,* 30 July 1873; *NG,* 4 September 1902; Charles Robson, *The Manufactories and Manufacturers of Pennsylvania of the Nineteenth Century* (Philadelphia, 1875), pp. 15–18; Canney, *Old Steam Navy,* pp. 45–89; Ridgley-Nevitt, *American Steamships,* pp. 187–207.

34. Edwin Freedley, *Philadelphia and Its Manufactures: A Hand-book Exhibiting the Development, Variety, and Statistics of the Manufacturing Industry of Philadelphia in 1857* (Philadelphia, 1858), pp. 316–18, 326–28; Robson, *Manufactories and Manufacturers,* pp. 24–26, 443–45; *The National Cyclopedia of American Biography, Vol. 13* (New York, 1906), pp. 333–34.

35. Cramp, "Evolution of Screw Propulsion," p. 149.

36. Edgar M. Levy, "Memoirs of Captain John P. Levy (with Family Sketches)," manuscript, Historical Society of Pennsylvania, Philadelphia, Society Collection, p. 21.

37. U.S. Bureau of the Census, Manufacturing Census (1850), microfilm, NA, "Schedule 5: Products of Industry in the County of Philadelphia, State of Pennsylvania, During the Year Ending June 1, 1850." (This and other editions of the U.S. Manufacturing Census are hereafter cited as "Manufacturing Census" with the year.) *The Neafie & Levy Ship and Engine Building Company* (New York, 1896), pp. 5–7.

38. Manufacturing Census 1860; Manufacturing Census 1870; RGD, Pennsylvania vol. 131, p. 495. Thomas Reaney to Jacob Neafie and John Levy, 18 November 1859, Marine Historical Association, Mystic Seaport, Conn., Howard E. Cornell Papers, Box 2; Leonard Swann, Jr., *John Roach, Maritime Entrepreneur: The Years as Naval Contractor, 1862–1884* (Annapolis, Md., 1965), pp. 51–53.

39. Henry Hall, *Report on the Ship-Building Industry of the United States* (Washington, D.C., 1882), p. 199.

40. Augustus C. Buell, *The Memoirs of Charles H. Cramp* (Philadelphia, 1906), pp. 39–50.

41. David W. Gauer, *Vaughan Shipwrights of Kensington: Their Van Hook and Norris Lineages and Combined Progeny* (Decorah, Iowa, 1982), pp. 74–75; Manufacturing Census 1850. For further examples of antebellum shipbuilding clans and business strategies, see Robson, *Manufactories and Manufacturers,* p. 485; RGD, Pennsylvania vol. 140, p. 104; *PI,* 23 March 1861.

42. Cramp, "Evolution of Screw Propulsion," p. 156.

43. Ibid., p. 158.

44. RGD, Pennsylvania vol. 140, p. 24; Hutchins, *American Maritime Industries,* p. 78.

45. On Philadelphia's textile industry, see Philip Scranton, *Proprietary Capitalism: The Textile Manufacture at Philadelphia, 1800–1885* (New York, 1983). On technology and labor process, see M. V. Brewington, "The Sailmaker's Gear," *AN* 9 (1949): 278–96; R. A. Salaman, *Dictionary of Tools Used in the Woodworking and Allied Trades, c. 1700–1970* (New York, 1975), pp. 401–4.

46. On shipsmiths, see RGD, Pennsylvania vol. 139, p. 77; RGD, Pennsylvania vol. 140, p. 150. On joiners, see RGD, Pennsylvania vol. 142, p. 37.

47. Vaughan & Lynn, Charles Hillman, Specifications Book, Historical Society of Pennsylvania, Philadelphia, Society Collection; Cheney, "Industries Allied to Shipbuilding," p. 114; Hutchins, *American Maritime Industries*, pp. 393–94.

48. Henry M. Valette, "History and Reminiscences of the Philadelphia Navy Yard," manuscript, Philadelphia Maritime Museum; U.S. House, "Evidence Taken before the Board of Navy Officers," 36th Cong., 1st sess., Executive Document No. 71, pp. 135–82; *PI*, 4 April 1861, 4 October 1862; *CG* 40(4) (1861–62): 2895.

49. Lenthall to DuPont, 4 April 1861, NA, RG 19, Entry 54, vol. 2.

50. Canney, *Old Steam Navy*, pp. 32–35, 66–67, 72–74, 84–87, with examples; James L. Kauffman, *Philadelphia's Navy Yards, 1801–1948* (New York, 1948), pp. 12–15; Freedley, *Philadelphia and Its Manufactures*, pp. 327–28.

51. J. Matthew Gallman, *Mastering Wartime: A Social History of Philadelphia during the Civil War* (Cambridge, Mass., 1990), pp. 266–71; *PI*, 25 March 1861, 18 April 1861.

52. DuPont to Lardner, 24 April 1861, NA, Mid-Atlantic Region, Philadelphia, RG 181; *PL*, 15 April 1861.

53. Bern Anderson, *By Sea and by River: The Naval History of the Civil War* (New York, 1962), pp. 9–10, 15–17; Canney, *Old Steam Navy*, pp. 91–94.

54. Lenthall to DuPont, 17 April 1861, 3 June 1861, both NA, RG 19, Entry 54, vol. 2; Lenthall to Welles, 2 July 1862, RG 19, Entry 49. *PI*, 10 June 1861, 24 August 1861, 16 November 1861, 24 April 1863; Canney, *Old Steam Navy*, pp. 72, 109–20; Paul H. Silverstone, *Warships of the Civil War Navies* (Annapolis, Md., 1989), pp. 58–66.

55. Robert G. Albion and Jennie B. Pope, *Sea Lanes in Wartime: The American Experience, 1775–1945* (reprint, New York, 1968), p. 149.

56. Henry Winsor & Co. to Lenthall, 7 November 1862, NA, RG 19, Entry 71, Box 2; Samuel Bowen to Lenthall, 27 June 1864, NA, RG 19, Entry 71, Box 4. *PL*, 16 June 1865, 13 September 1865, 12 October 1865; *PI*, 21 June 1865, 8 August 1865; Henry Hall, *American Navigation, with Some Account of the Causes of Its Recent Decay* (New York, 1880), pp. 59–60.

57. *PL*, 11 June 1862; Heyl, *Early American Steamers, Vol. 4*, pp. 221–22, 287.

58. Wood to Gregory, 8 July 1864, NA, RG 19, Entry 64, Box 5.

59. Isherwood to Merrick, 30 July 1862, 15 August 1862, 9 September 1862, 5 February 1863, 23 June 1863, 22 December 1863, 16 June 1864, 28 July 1864, 5 December 1864, NA, RG 19, Entry 968; RGD, Pennsylvania vol. 134, pp. 320BB; *PL*, 1 July 1861, 30 November 1861, 28 July 1862, 7 September 1863.

60. Thomas to Gregory, 2 February 1864, NA, RG 19, Entry 64, Box 3.

61. On hull subcontractors, see affidavits by Charles M. Thompson, Henry Butler, and James Welde, all 4 March 1864, enclosed with Stribling to Smith, 11 March 1864, NA, RG 71, Entry 5, Box 238; Charles H. Cramp, "Certain Incidents in the Evolution of the Modern Warship," *PNASP* (1904–6): 120–25; Canney, *Old Steam Navy*, pp. 121–44. On independent shipyard gangs, see also Nathan Lipfert, "The Shipyard Worker and the Iron Shipyard," *LMS* 35 (1983): 76.

62. Neafie to Isherwood, 28 July 1862, NA, RG 19, Entry 973.

63. Log of the Philadelphia Navy Yard 1860–62, NA, Mid-Atlantic Region, Philadelphia, RG 181.

64. *MM* 45 (1861): 62; Tyler, *Steam Conquers the Atlantic*, p. 293; Hutchins, *American Maritime Industries*, p. 321.

65. Frederick M. Edge, quoted in George W. Dalzell, *The Flight from the Flag: The Continuing Effect of the Civil War upon the American Carrying Trades* (Chapel Hill, N.C., 1910), p. 239; see also Lawrence Allin, "The Civil War and the Period of Decline," in *America's Maritime Legacy*, ed. Kilmarx, pp. 66–67.

66. Lynch Report, p. ix.

67. Albion and Pope, *Sea Lanes in Wartime*, pp. 157–58; Dalzell, *Flight from the Flag*, pp. 247–62; Kenneth J. Blume, "The Flight from the Flag: The American Government, the British Caribbean, and the American Merchant Marine," *Civil War History* 32 (1986): 44–55.

68. Wheaton J. Lane, *Commodore Vanderbilt: An Epic of the Steam Age* (New York, 1942), pp. 153–83.

69. Tyler, *Steam Conquers the Atlantic*, p. 293; Hutchins, *American Maritime Industries*, p. 321.

70. Sidney Pollard and Paul Robertson, *The British Shipbuilding Industry, 1870–1914* (Cambridge, Mass., 1979), pp. 9–11; Fred M. Walker, *Song of the Clyde: A History of Clyde Shipbuilding* (Cambridge, 1984), pp. 17–19; Hutchins, *American Maritime Industries*, pp. 398–443.

71. *NG*, 20 January 1872; Hutchins, *American Maritime Industries*, p. 444.

72. Pollard and Robertson, *British Shipbuilding Industry*, pp. 89–92.

73. Ibid., pp. 84–86.

74. Hyde, *Cunard and the North Atlantic*, pp. 27–30; Tyler, *Steam Conquers the Atlantic*, pp. 247–60.

75. *PL*, 16 October 1866; John H. Morrison, *History of the New York Shipyards* (New York, 1909), p. 162.

76. *PL*, 28 July 1865, 22 November 1865; *An Act to Incorporate the Philadelphia and Southern Mail Steamship Company* (Philadelphia, 1866). On Lynn, see RGD, Pennsylvania vol. 140, pp. 103–4.

77. *PL*, 12 and 19 November 1868.

Two: "A Small Margin"

1. *PI*, 19 June 1865; *PL*, 11 and 31 July 1865. On Civil War ironclad operations, see Bern Anderson, *By Sea and by River: The Naval History of the Civil War* (New York, 1962), pp. 156–77, 233–50.

2. Lawrence C. Allin, "The Civil War and the Period of Decline," in *America's Maritime Legacy: A History of the U.S. Merchant Marine and Shipbuilding Industry since Colonial Times*, ed. Robert A. Kilmarx (Boulder, Colo., 1979), p. 67.

3. James P. Baxter, *The Introduction of the Ironclad Warship* (reprint, Hamden, Conn., 1968), pp. 17–32, 37, 69–91.

4. Andrew Lambert, *Warrior: The World's First Ironclad Then and Now* (Annapolis, Md., 1987), pp. 12–26; HMS *Warrior* still exists and can be visited at Liverpool.

5. Edward Miller, *U.S.S. Monitor: The Ship That Launched a Modern Navy* (Annapolis, Md., 1978), pp. 17–18; Walter Millis, "The Iron Sea Elephants," *AN* 10 (1950): 16.

6. Frank M. Bennett, *Steam Navy of the United States: A History of the Growth of the Steam Vessel of War in the U.S. Navy, and of the Naval Engineer Corps* (reprint, Westport, Conn., 1972), pp. 266–71; Baxter, *Introduction,* pp. 247–52; Augustus C. Buell, *The Memoirs of Charles H. Cramp* (Philadelphia, 1906), p. 61.

7. Report text reprinted in Bennett, *Steam Navy,* p. 264.

8. Ibid., p. 265.

9. Ibid.; Baxter, *Introduction,* p. 284.

10. Bennett, *Steam Navy,* p. 267.

11. Baxter, *Introduction,* pp. 204–8.

12. Bennett, *Steam Navy,* p. 271 (emphasis in original).

13. Ibid., p. 270.

14. William N. Still, *Monitor Builders: A Historical Study of the Principal Firms and Individuals Involved in the Construction of USS* Monitor (Washington, D.C., 1988); Millis, "Iron Sea," p. 16; Buell, *Memoirs of Charles Cramp,* p. 62.

15. "The U.S.S. Armored Frigate *New Ironsides,*" *Journal of the Franklin Institute* 53 (1867): 76–81; *PI,* 25 February 1862; *PL,* 8 August 1862; Buell, *Memoirs of Charles Cramp,* p. 69.

16. RGD, Pennsylvania vol. 141, p. 70, and vol. 140, p. 150; Gail F. Farr and Brett F. Bostwick, *Shipbuilding at Cramp & Sons: A History and Guide of the William Cramp & Sons Ship and Engine Building Company (1830–1927) and the Cramp Shipbuilding Company (1941–46) of Philadelphia* (Philadelphia, 1991), p. 8. Davidson to Hoover, 17 March 1862, NA, RG 71, Entry 5, Box 236; Augustus C. Buell, *Memoirs of Charles Cramp,* pp. 45–49; Charles Robson, *The Manufactories and Manufacturers of Pennsylvania of the Nineteenth Century* (Philadelphia, 1875), pp. 20–21; *PL,* 14 March 1861; Cramp to Lenthall, 8 January 1862, NA, RG 19, Entry 61, Box 2.

17. Barnabas H. Bartol, *A Treatise on the Marine Boilers of the United States* (Philadelphia, 1851); "The Building of the Ship," *HNMM* 24 (1862): 610. Specifications of the USS *New Ironsides:* NA, Architectural and Cartographic Division, Alexandria, Va., RG 19, NARS 107-9-12 A–F, I–K.

18. Buell, *Memoirs of Charles Cramp,* p. 64.

19. On Pennsylvania ship timber, see also *Thirtieth Annual Report of the Philadelphia Board of Trade* (Philadelphia, 1863), pp. 73–79. A more general work is Virginia S. Wood, *Live Oaking: Southern Timber for Tall Ships* (Boston, 1981).

20. "Building of the Ship," pp. 609–16; Jean Boudriot, *The Seventy-Four Gun Ship: A Practical Treatise on the Art of Naval Architecture, Vol. 1: Hull Construction* (Annapolis, Md., 1986), pp. 39–47; Wood, *Live Oaking,* p. 92.

21. Theodore Wilson, *A Series of Ten Lectures Delivered to the Second Class of Cadet Midshipmen on the Practice of Building, Launching, Docking and Fitting of U.S. Naval Vessels* (Annapolis, Md., 1872), pp. 3–9; Boudriot, *Seventy-Four Gun Ship, Vol. 1: Hull Construction*, pp. 78–79; James Dodd and James Moore, *Building the Wooden Fighting Ship* (New York, 1984), pp. 58–65.

22. Buell, *Memoirs of Charles Cramp*, p. 67; *PL*, 26 April 1862; *PI*, 5 April 1862; Wilson, *Series of Ten Lectures*, pp. 53–54; "Building of the Ship," p. 614.

23. *PI*, 12 May 1862.

24. Ibid.; *PL*, 12 May 1862.

25. "*New Ironsides*—Specifications," pp. 1–2; *PL*, 30 November 1861, 14 February 1862, 14 March 1862; *PI*, 2 May 1862; "U.S.S. Armored Frigate," pp. 78–79.

26. *PL*, 30 May, 5 and 10–12 June, 1862; "New Ironsides—Specifications," pp. 1–2, 13; Lenthall to Hull, 6, 8, 11 August 1864, NA, RG 19, Entry 54, vol. 2.

27. Paul H. Silverstone, *Warships of the Civil War Navies* (Annapolis, Md., 1989), p. 15; Baxter, *Introduction*, pp. 268–69.

28. RGD, Pennsylvania vol. 141, p. 70.

29. John Taylor Wood, "The Battle Was a Drawn One," and S. Dana Greene, "We Thought We Had Gained a Great Victory," in *Battles and Leaders of the Civil War*, ed. Ned Bradford (reprint, New York, 1956), pp. 97–108, 111–18.

30. Charles H. Cramp, "Certain Incidents in the Evolution of the Modern Warship," *PNASP* (1904–6): 117.

31. *A&NJ*, 26 September 1863; U.S. Congress, *Report of the Joint Committee on the Conduct of the War at the Second Session Thirty-Eighth Congress, Vol. 3* (Washington, D.C., 1865), p. 100 (hereafter cited as Joint Committee Report); Buell, *Memoirs of Charles Cramp*, p. 72.

32. Lenthall and Isherwood to Welles, 17 June 1862, NA, RG 19, Entry 49; *PI*, 8 September 1862, 3 February 1863, 16 and 30 December 1863, 13 February 1864, 23 March 1864, 11 April 1864, 9 May 1864, 15 December 1864, 19 June 1865; *Thirtieth Annual Report*, 29–34, 72–90; *Thirty-First Annual Report of the Philadelphia Board of Trade* (Philadelphia, 1864), pp. 10–15; *CG* 40(4) (1861–62): 2894–96, 3245–48, 3263–66; U.S. House Committee on Naval Affairs, "Navy Yard at League Island," 37th Cong., 3rd sess., Executive Document No. 45.

33. Lenthall to Welles, 23 July 1863, NA, RG 19, Entry 49.

34. Millis, "Iron Sea," pp. 22–26; Joint Committee Report, pp. 52–53; Buell, *Memoirs of Charles Cramp*, pp. 79–81.

35. Joint Committee Report, p. iv; see also Edward Sloan, *Benjamin Franklin Isherwood, Naval Engineer* (Annapolis, Md., 1966), p. 68.

36. Bennett, *Steam Navy*, p. 484; Buell, *Memoirs of Charles Cramp*, p. 81.

37. Joint Committee Report, p. 69.

38. Sloan, *Isherwood*, p. 69.

39. Silverstone, *Warships*, p. 12, with a list of contractors. Charles Cramp held an unfavorable view of his fellow contractors for the light-draft monitors: "The fact is, that none of the bidders except Harlan & Hollingsworth and ourselves were ship-

builders" (quoted in Buell, *Memoirs of Charles Cramp*, p. 82). Cramp overlooked
Reaney & Archbold in Chester, another firm of experienced shipbuilders, but the
general criticism of the contractors is corroborated by other evidence, e.g., Joint Committee Report, p. 13. One of the vessels was built at Pittsburgh; William F. Trimble,
"From Sail to Steam: Shipbuilding in the Pittsburgh Area, 1790–1865," *Western Pennsylvania Historical Magazine* 58 (1975): 165.

40. *PL*, 9 June 1863.

41. Thomas to Stimers, 13 May and 17 November 1863, NA, RG 19, Entry 68, Box 1;
PL, 17 and 25 March 1863, 22 April 1863, 13 May 1863.

42. Thomas to Stimers, 13 May 1863, NA, RG 19, Entry 68, Box 1.

43. "The American Clyde," *HNMM* 46 (1878): 650; Thomas to Stimers, 27 May 1863,
30 September 1863, 23 November 1863, all in NA, RG 19, Entry 68, Box 1. See also *PL*, 23
September 1863; *A&NJ*, 3 October 1863.

44. Joint Committee Report, p. 42.

45. Ibid., pp. 38–39, 42.

46. Charles Cramp, "Sixty Years of Shipbuilding on the Delaware," *PNASP* (1904–
6), pp. 179–80.

47. Ibid., p. 180.

48. On New England, see Nathan Lipfert, "The Shipyard Worker and the Iron
Shipyard," *LMS* 35 (1983): 75–87; on Germany, see Marina Cattaruzza, *Arbeiter und
Unternehmer auf den Werften des Kaiserreichs* (Stuttgart, 1988), pp. 103–8.

49. Joint Committee Report, pp. 31–37; Sloan, *Isherwood*, pp. 72–73; Cramp, "Certain Incidents," p. 118.

50. Joint Committee Report, p. 5; on Stimers's efforts, ibid., pp. 12–19, 75.

51. *NYT*, 24 July 1864; Gideon Welles, *Diary of Gideon Welles, Secretary of the Navy
under Lincoln and Johnson, Vol. 2: April 1, 1864–December 31, 1866* (Boston, 1911), pp. 52–
53, 81–82, 108; Joint Committee Report, p. 75; Buell, *Memoirs of Charles Cramp*, p. 83.

52. Wood to Gregory, 8 July 1864; Wood to Merrick, 29 June 1864; Wood to Betts, 29
June 1864; Merrick to Wood, 7 July 1864; Betts to Wood, 7 July 1864; all in NA, RG 19,
Entry 64, Box 5. Cramp, "Certain Incidents," p. 118; *PI*, 12 July 1864; Gregory to Lenthall,
19 October 1864, NA, RG 19, Entry 64, Box 6; *PL*, 25 October 1864, 4 May 1865.

53. James L. Mooney, ed., *Dictionary of American Naval Fighting Ships, Vol. 8*
(Washington, D.C., 1981), p. 523; *NYT*, 9 and 20 May 1865.

54. *PL*, 17 June 1870.

Three: The American Clyde

1. *NG*, 17 May 1873; *PL*, 6 May 1873.

2. *NG*, 17 May 1873; *National Cyclopedia of American Biography, Vol. 13* (New York,
1906), pp. 334–35.

3. Philadelphia & Southern Mail Steamship Company, *First Annual Report of the
Board of Directors of the Philadelphia & Southern Mail Steamship Company to the
Stockholders, May 1st, 1867* (Philadelphia, 1867); *PI*, 15 and 21 May 1866; *PL*, 25 January

1866, 11 and 15 November 1866, 4 March 1867, 4 August 1870, 14 January 1871, 20 April 1871; Leonard A. Swann, Jr., *John Roach, Maritime Entrepreneur: The Years as Naval Contractor, 1862–1886* (Annapolis, Md., 1965), p. 52; William A. Baker, "Commercial Shipping and Shipbuilding in the Delaware Valley," paper presented at Society of Naval Architects and Marine Engineers' Spring Meeting, Philadelphia, 1976; see also David B. Tyler, *The American Clyde: A History of Iron and Steel Shipbuilding on the Delaware from 1840 to World War I* (Wilmington, Del., 1958), pp. 26–27.

4. *PI*, 28 May 1866, 26 July 1866; *PL*, 25 May 1866, 12 June 1866; *The Neafie & Levy Ship and Engine Building Company, Penn Works* (New York, 1896), p. 13.

5. *PL*, 28 May 1866, 20 May 1869; "Record of Metal Vessels Built in the United States," NA, RG 19, Entry 129; RGD, Pennsylvania vol. 131, p. 495.

6. U.S. House Select Committee, "Report of the Select Committee on the Causes of the Reduction of American Tonnage," 41st Cong., 2nd sess., House Report No. 28, p. 167 (hereafter cited as Lynch Report); *NYT*, 16 September 1869, 20 November 1869; John Hutchins, *The American Maritime Industries and Public Policy, 1789–1914: An Economic History* (Cambridge, Mass., 1941), p. 451.

7. *NYT*, 3 February 1873; see also *PL*, 4 February 1873.

8. William T. Hogan, *Economic History of the Iron and Steel Industry in the United States* (Lexington, Mass., 1971), pp. 27–51. On Philadelphia ironworks, see Charles Robson, *Manufactories and Manufacturers of Pennsylvania in the Nineteenth Century* (Philadelphia, 1875), pp. 15–18, 24–26, 236–37, 334–35, 390–95, 509–10; Bruce Laurie and Mark Schmitz, "Manufacture and Productivity: The Making of an Industrial Base, Philadelphia, 1850–1880," in *Philadelphia: Work, Space, Family, and Group Experience in the Nineteenth Century*, ed. Theodore Hershberg (New York, 1981), pp. 56–61. For a vivid contemporary description of the industry, see *NYT*, 3 February 1873.

9. William Cramp & Sons to William Kelley, 15 January 1872, printed in *Bulletin of the American Iron and Steel Association* 6 (1872): 154. Cramp's argument that the ironworks should be located near the shipyards for effective industrial organization is corroborated by the history of German iron shipbuilding during this era. German yards imported most of their ship iron from Britain and neglected the development of a local subcontracting industry. As a result, German iron shipbuilding faced constant supply problems and remained insignificant until the 1880s. See Günter Leckebusch, "Der Beginn des deutschen Eisenschiffbaues 1850–1890," in *Moderne deutsche Wirtschaftgeschichte*, ed. Karl E. Born (Cologne, 1966), pp. 183–84.

10. Lynch Report, pp. 27–29; Augustus C. Buell, *The Memoirs of Charles H. Cramp* (Philadelphia, 1906), pp. 108–9. On industrial geography, see Sidney Pollard and Paul Robertson, *The British Shipbuilding Industry, 1870–1914* (Cambridge, Mass., 1979), pp. 49–69; *PL*, 14 March 1870, 4 and 22 August 1870; *NG*, 9 December 1874; Robson, *Manufactories*, pp. 20–21, 91–92, 261–62, 443–45.

11. Swann, *John Roach*, pp. 77–79. On the Mallory Line, see *NG*, 12 December 1873; Erik Heyl, *Early American Steamers, Vol. 1* (Buffalo, N.Y., 1953), p. 91. On the recovery of the American maritime industries at the beginning of the 1870s, see *PL*, 18 July 1871; *NG*, 26 August 1871, 6 January 1872.

12. *NG*, 27 April 1872.

13. For criticism of iron hulls, see *NG*, 2 March 1872, 6 April 1872, 15 February 1873; *Mechanics' Magazine*, 13 March 1863; *SA* 2 (1860): 217. On Clyde, see "The Clyde Steamship Company," in *The City of Philadelphia as It Appears in the Year 1894*, ed. Frank H. Taylor (Philadelphia, 1894), p. 114; *NG*, 29 July 1871, 13 July 1872; *National Cyclopedia of American Biography*, Vol. 20 (New York, 1929), pp. 57–58; *PL*, 14 July 1870, 26 June 1872. On the growth of the Philadelphia coastwise trade, see *NG*, 28 December 1872.

14. Heyl, *Early American Steamers, Vol. 1*, p. 175; *PL*, 18 July 1871, 9 January 1872; *NG*, 23 March 1872; Charles E. Hyde, "The Modern Marine Engine," *CM* 12 (1897): 445–49; Fred M. Walker, *Song of the Clyde: A History of Clyde Shipbuilding* (Cambridge, 1984), pp. 25–26.

15. Lynch Report, pp. 156–57.

16. Manufacturing Census 1870, "Schedule 3. Manufactures. Products of Industry in the County of Philadelphia, State of Pennsylvania, During the Twelve Months Beginning June 1, 1869, and Ending May 31, 1870, District 53, Ward 18," p. 7. On other builders, see William H. Collins, "History of Bethlehem's Wilmington Plant, Formerly the Harlan & Hollingsworth Corporation," in *Historical Transactions, 1893–1943*, ed. Society of Naval Architects and Marine Engineers (New York, 1945), pp. 208–9. On British marine engineering, see Walker, *Song of the Clyde*, pp. 24–25; Lynch Report, p. 121.

17. Hyde, "Modern Marine Engine," pp. 441–58; Charles H. Cramp, "Evolution of the Atlantic Greyhound," *TSNAME* 1 (1893): 4–5; *PL*, 18 July 1871, 14 December 1872, 11 January 1873, 10 September 1874; *NG*, 20 January 1872, 13 April 1872. Dialogue & Wood of Camden pioneered the use of compound technology in small steamships; *PL*, 6 June 1874.

18. *NG*, 26 August 1871 (quotation); Lorin Blodgett, "Ship-Building and the Tariff," *Penn Monthly* 4 (1873): 38–39; Swann, *John Roach*, p. 239; *NG*, 15 July 1871, 16 and 23 September 1871, 4, 11, and 18 November 1871, 12 December 1871. In contrast to the activity along the Delaware River, "things are very quiet among the New York ship builders. There are quite a number of new vessels *talked* of, but nothing is definitely decided upon" (*NG*, 9 September 1871).

19. *NG*, 30 September 1871; Lynch Report, p. 26.

20. Barbara Fisher, "Maritime History of the Reading, 1833–1905," *PMHB* 86 (1962): 169; James A. Ward, *J. Edgar Thompson: Master of the Pennsylvania* (Westport, Conn., 1980), p. 190; Wheaton J. Lane, *Commodore Vanderbilt: An Epic of the Steam Age* (New York, 1942), pp. 153–83.

21. James L. Holton, *The Reading Railroad: History of a Coal Empire*, vol. 1: *The Nineteenth Century* (Laury's Station, Pa., 1989), p. 106; *MM* 31 (1854): 258–59; *Twenty-Eighth Annual Report of the Philadelphia Board of Trade* (Philadelphia, 1861), pp. 13–14.

22. Alfred D. Chandler, Jr., *The Visible Hand: The Managerial Revolution in American Business* (Cambridge, Mass., 1977), pp. 148–59.

23. *PI*, 24 March 1863, 9 May 1863, 14, 27, and 30 January 1864, 9 February 1864, 2 June 1864; *NG*, 18 April 1874.

24. Philadelphia Board of Trade, *Thirtieth Annual Report of the Philadelphia Board of Trade* (Philadelphia, 1863), pp. 19–21, 29; *NYT*, 7 June 1865, 24 December 1871; *NG*, 16 October 1872.

25. American Steamship Company (ASC) Minute Book, 1871–76, Urban Archives, Temple University, Philadelphia, Pennsylvania Railroad Collection, Box 89, pp. 1–7; RGD, Pennsylvania vol. 154, p. 110; Pennsylvania General Assembly, *Journal of the Senate of the Commonwealth of Pennsylvania for the Session Begun at Harrisburg on the Third Day of January, 1871* (Harrisburg, Pa., 1871), pp. 183, 189, 240, 359, 515, 667; *An Act to Incorporate the American Steamship Company of Philadelphia* (n.p., 1870). On the board of directors, see *PL*, 9 January 1873.

26. ASC Minute Book, pp. 8–19; *PL*, 5 April 1871, 2 May 1871; Cramp, "Evolution of the Atlantic Greyhound," pp. 23–29.

27. ASC Minute Book, pp. 29–33; *PL*, 10 August 1871.

28. RGD, Pennsylvania vol. 154, p. 264; "Clement Acton Griscom: Head of a Great Steamship Line," *HW* 35 (1891): 246; "The International Navigation Company," in *City of Philadelphia*, ed. Taylor, pp. 112–13. On Empire Transportation Company, see Chandler, *Visible Hand*, pp. 127–28; *NG*, 17 and 24 June 1876; *Report of the Investigating Committee of the Pennsylvania Railroad Company* (Philadelphia, 1874); Edward N. Wright, "The Story of Peter Wright & Sons, Philadelphia Quaker Shipping Firm, 1818–1911," *Quaker History* 56 (1967): 72.

29. Philadelphia Board of Trade, *Thirtieth Annual Report*, p. 40; Fisher, "Maritime History of the Reading," pp. 169–71; Holton, *Reading Railroad*, pp. 99–104.

30. Contract No. 434, 16 September 1869: Contract of the Philadelphia & Reading Railroad Company with Reaney, Sons, & Co. [for building three iron steam colliers]; and Contract No. 437, 28 September 1869: Contract of the Philadelphia & Reading Railroad Company with Harlan & Hollingsworth [for building one iron steam collier]; both in Hagley Museum and Library, Wilmington, Del., Philadelphia & Reading Railroad Company Collection, Contracts, Box 3. Swann, *John Roach*, pp. 52–53; Fisher, "Maritime History of the Reading," pp. 172–73.

31. *Report of the President and Managers of the Philadelphia & Reading Railroad Company to the Stockholders, January 12, 1874* (Philadelphia, 1874), p. 18.

32. On the conflict between the railroad and the coal agents and shippers, see *Joint Committee Appointed to Inquire into the Affairs of the Philadelphia & Reading Coal and Iron Company and the Philadelphia & Reading Railroad Company. Proceedings of the Legislative Investigating Committee* (Philadelphia, 1875); *NG*, 1 March 1873. Collier contracts: Contract No. 590, 18 June 1873: Contract of the Philadelphia & Reading Railroad Company with the William Cramp & Sons Ship and Engine Building Company [for six iron steam colliers], Hagley Museum and Library, Wilmington, Del., Philadelphia & Reading Railroad Company Collection, Contracts, Box 4 (hereafter cited as Contract No. 590); see also *NG*, 14 February 1880.

33. Joint Industrial Commission, *Report of the Industrial Commission on Transportation, Vol. 2*, 57th Cong., 1st sess. (Washington, D.C., 1901), p. 443; Swann, *John Roach*,

pp. 78–92; James P. Baughman, *Charles Morgan and the Development of Southern Transportation* (Nashville, Tenn., 1968), pp. 208–35.

34. *PL*, 18 July 1871, 29 February 1872; *NG*, 30 September 1871, 7 October 1871, 2 December 1871, 3 February 1872, 6 June 1872, 22 February 1873; Minute Book of the William Cramp & Sons Ship and Engine Building Company, 1872–92, Philadelphia Maritime Museum, Cramp Collection, p. 32A (hereafter cited as Cramp Minute Book). On shipyard layout, see Pollard and Robertson, *British Shipbuilding Industry*, pp. 108–15.

35. Buell, *Memoirs of Charles Cramp*, p. 116.

36. Ibid., pp. 113–15; *PL*, 29 February 1872; *NG*, 18 November 1871, 12 April 1873. On British iron shipyard equipment, see Walker, *Song of the Clyde*, pp. 160–62.

37. *PL*, 14 April 1874; "See, Horace," in *Mechanical Engineers in America Born prior to 1861: A Biographical Dictionary*, ed. American Society of Mechanical Engineers (New York, 1980), pp. 271–72; *NG*, 17 May 1873. On Shields Wilson, see Buell, *Memoirs of Charles Cramp*, p. 112. On Samuel Holmes, see *PL*, 10 May 1873; *NG*, 13 January 1875. Holmes wrote a series of articles defending iron steamships against builders of wooden ships: *NG*, 20 January 1872, 23 March 1872, 20 April 1872, 18 May 1872, 20 July 1872, 19 October 1872, 18 and 25 January 1873, 15 November 1873.

38. *The Legislative Journal Containing the Debates and Proceedings of the Pennsylvania Legislature for the Session of 1872* (Harrisburg, Pa., 1872), p. 872.

39. Cramp Minute Book, pp. 34–37; RGD, Pennsylvania vol. 141, p. 70; *The Legislative Journal Containing the Debates and Proceedings of the Pennsylvania Legislature for the Session of 1872* (Harrisburg, 1872), p. 872.

40. Cramp, "Evolution of the Atlantic Greyhound," p. 4; Buell, *Memoirs of Charles Cramp*, pp. 112–13; ASC Minute Book, pp. 62–63.

41. *PL*, 29 February 1872.

42. Ibid.; *NG*, 5 July 1873.

43. *NG*, 27 December 1873; *NYT*, 3 February 1873; Cramp Minute Book, p. 40; Robson, *Manufactories and Manufacturers*, pp. 24–27.

44. Lee to Randall, 15 December 1874, NA, RG 19, Entry 72, Box 1.

45. *NG*, 3 January 1876.

46. Swann, *John Roach*, p. 59; Pollard and Robertson, *British Shipbuilding Industry*, pp. 90–91. On the relationship between urban space and industrial production, see Stephanie Greenberg, "Industrial Location and Ethnic Residential Patterns in an Industrializing City: Philadelphia, 1880," in *Philadelphia*, ed. Hershberg, pp. 204–32. For a further discussion of subcontracting, "production linkages," and "disintegrated production," see Philip Scranton, *Proprietary Capitalism: The Textile Manufacture at Philadelphia, 1800–1885* (Cambridge, Mass., 1983), pp. 83–87, 207–8, 334; Scranton, "Diversity in Diversity: Flexible Production and American Industrialization, 1880–1930," *BHR* 65 (1991): 35–36.

47. Pollard and Robertson, *British Shipbuilding Industry*, pp. 27–29, 90–91.

48. *PL*, 18 June 1873.

49. *NG*, 17 August 1872, 21 September 1872, 9 November 1872, 25 January 1873, 29 March 1873, 14 June 1873, 5 and 26 July 1873; *PL*, 16 August 1872, 26 March 1873; Charles Cramp, "Evolution of the Atlantic Greyhound," pp. 1–5.

50. *NG*, 29 September 1875.

51. *PL*, 5 April 1873. On improvement of the port of Philadelphia, see *NG*, 17 May 1873, 22 July 1874, 26 August 1874; *PL*, 10 and 24 May 1873; Philadelphia Board of Trade, *Forty-Second Annual Report of the Philadelphia Board of Trade* (Philadelphia, 1875), pp. 27–28, 31–37.

52. Contract No. 590.

53. RGD, Pennsylvania vol. 141, pp. 66, 70.

54. Contract No. 590.

55. *NG*, 16 August 1873, 21 February 1874, 28 March 1874, 4 April 1874, 16 May 1874, 15 July 1874, 12 August 1874. On the construction of the colliers, see *PL*, 16 February 1874, 24 and 25 March 1874, 5 May 1874, 6 June 1874, 28 August 1874.

56. *NG*, 2 November 1872; Fisher, "Maritime History of the Reading," p. 174.

57. *NYT*, 3 December 1885.

58. *NG*, 15 May 1873 (quotation); *PL*, 20 August 1873, 14 August 1874; Philadelphia & Reading Railroad Company, *Report of the President and Managers of the Philadelphia & Reading Railroad Company to the Stockholders, Jan. 8, 1877 for the Year Ending November 30th, 1876* (Philadelphia, 1876), p. 20.

59. Lacking an adequate dry dock, Philadelphia shipbuilders sometimes even beached a large iron steamer to conduct repairs: *PL*, 30 April 1874. On the private use of the Navy Yard dry dock, see *PL*, 8 July 1874, 25 December 1874, 11 February 1875; Hanscom to unknown correspondent, 14 October 1874, NA, RG 19, Entry 50, vol. 3; Hanscom to Cramp & Sons, 2 July 1873, NA, RG 19, Entry 60, vol. 1.

60. *PL*, 12 December 1874, 17 May 1875, 6 June 1875. *Report of the President and Managers of the Philadelphia & Reading Railroad Company to the Stockholders, January 10, 1876, for the Year Ending November 30th, 1875* (Philadelphia, 1876), pp. 16–17, on strikes and popular discontent with the railroad. On earlier conflicts between the railroads and neighborhood movements over the uses of urban space, see Michael Feldberg, "The Crowd in Philadelphia History: A Comparative Perspective," in *American Workingclass Culture: Explorations in American Labor and Social History*, ed. Milton Cantor (Westport, Conn., 1979), pp. 83–84.

61. *PL*, 11 June 1875.

62. *PL*, 19 June 1875.

63. *NG*, 14 June 1879; Marvin W. Schlegel, *Ruler of the Reading: The Life of Franklin B. Gowen, 1836–1889* (Harrisburg, Pa., 1947), pp. 51–52, 227.

64. Cramp Minute Book, pp. 56–68; *NG*, 29 September 1875, 5 January 1876, 17 May 1876, 7 June 1876. The dry dock was built by James E. Simpson of Boston (not related to Adam S. Simpson, who owned and operated a floating dry dock at Philadelphia). RGD, Pennsylvania vol. 154, p. 165; Lynch Report, pp. 147–49. Cramp hired a New York representative to obtain repair contracts there: *NG*, 28 April 1875.

Four: Workshop of the World

1. *NG*, 10 May 1883, 7, 14, 28 June 1883, 12 and 26 July 1883, 2 April 1885; *PL*, 4 May 1883, 16 June 1883, 3 August 1883, 8 November 1884.

2. Lawrence C. Allin, "The Civil War and the Period of Decline," in *America's Maritime Legacy: A History of the U.S. Merchant Marine and Shipbuilding Industry since Colonial Times,* ed. Robert A. Kilmarx (Boulder, Colo., 1979), p. 65.

3. *PL*, 21 March 1878, 2 and 10 September 1878; RGD, Pennsylvania vol. 140, p. 24.

4. American Steamship Company, *Fourth Annual Report of the American Steamship Company of Philadelphia to the Stockholders, April 5, 1875* (Philadelphia, 1875), p. 9.

5. American Steamship Company, *Ninth Annual Report of the American Steamship Company of Philadelphia to the Stockholders, April 5, 1880* (Philadelphia, 1880), pp. 8–9. On ASC's annual losses for 1874, see *NG*, 31 March 1875. On its loss of financial credit, see RGD, Pennsylvania vol. 154, p. 110; *LT*, 16 May 1878; *NYT*, 20 March 1884, 16 and 18 October 1884, on the sale to the International Navigation Company; also Frederick E. Emmons, *American Passenger Ships: The Ocean Lines and Liners, 1873–1983* (Newark, Del., 1985), p. 22.

6. Philadelphia & Southern Mail Steamship Company, *Sixth Annual Report of the Board of Directors of the Philadelphia and Southern Mail Steamship Company to the Stockholders, May 1, 1872* (Philadelphia, 1872), p. 7.

7. *NG*, 28 June 1879; *PL*, 9 February 1881, 24 December 1881, 4 April 1882.

8. William Cramp & Sons to Secretary of the Navy Robeson, 6 November 1873, NA, RG 19, Entry 72, vol. 1.

9. *PL*, 29 September 1875, 23 March 1883.

10. A. R. Ritter, "A Brief History of the Philadelphia Navy Yard from Its Inception to December 31, 1920" (1921), manuscript, Philadelphia Maritime Museum, pp. 1–5.

11. *PL*, 1 and 19 July 1875, 8 August 1875; *NYT*, 21 October 1878; Augustus C. Buell, *The Memoirs of Charles H. Cramp* (Philadelphia, 1906), pp. 206–26.

12. U.S. House, Committee on Merchant Marine and Fisheries, "American Merchant Marine in the Foreign Trade," 51st Cong., 1st sess., House Report No. 1210, p. 126 (hereafter cited as Farquhar Report).

13. *PL*, 7 July 1879.

14. Buell, *Memoirs of Charles Cramp,* pp. 227–38.

15. William Cramp & Sons, Minute Book, Philadelphia Maritime Museum, Cramp Collection, p. 85 (hereafter cited as Cramp Minute Book). On ISBC, see *NYT*, 28 and 29 September 1880, 10 March 1881, 5 May 1881, 16 June 1881; *PL*, 26 October 1880; *NG*, 2 April 1881; Iron Steamboat Company, Minutes of the Board of Directors, 1880–85, New-York Historical Society. The Cramp-built excursion steamers were riddled with technical problems that embarrassed their builders: *NG*, 22 July 1882, 19 August 1882.

16. On early Cramp biography, see Buell, *Memoirs of Charles Cramp,* pp. 39–57. For other examples of family succession, see Philip Scranton, *Proprietary Capitalism: The Textile Manufacture at Philadelphia, 1800–1885* (New York, 1983), pp. 273–75.

17. Leonard Swann, Jr., *John Roach, Maritime Entrepreneur: The Years as Naval Contractor, 1862–1884* (Annapolis, Md., 1965), pp. 95–124.

18. Cramp Minute Book, passim; Paul Robertson, "Shipping and Shipbuilding: The Case of William Denny and Brothers," *Business History* 16 (1974): 36–47.

19. Cramp Minute Book, pp. 55, 76; Scranton, *Proprietary Capitalism*, pp. 222–23.

20. On Neafie & Levy, see Charles Robson, *The Manufactories and Manufacturers of Pennsylvania of the Nineteenth Century* (Philadelphia, 1875), pp. 443–44. On Birely, Hillman & Streaker's role as subcontractor, see *NG*, 31 May 1879; see also RGD, Pennsylvania vol. 140, p. 104.

21. Manufacturing Census 1880, "Schedule 3. Manufactures. Products of Industry in the County of Philadelphia, State of Pennsylvania, During the Twelve Months Beginning June 1, 1879, and Ending May 31, 1880." For analysis and context of the 1880 manufacturing census material on shipbuilding, see Henry Hall, *Report on the Shipbuilding Industry of the United States* (Washington, 1882).

22. Hall, *Report on the Shipbuilding Industry*, p. 203.

23. On Cramp's dry-dock business during the census year, see *NG*, 7 June 1879, 7 and 26 July 1879, 6 September 1879, 22 November 1879, 13 and 20 December 1879, 24 January 1880, 21 February 1880, 6 March 1880, 10 April 1880.

24. Manufacturing Census 1880; *AS*, 16 August 1879; *NG*, 21 February 1880, 13 March 1880.

25. *NG*, 12 April 1883.

26. *PL*, 28 July 1880; *NG*, 6 May 1882, 26 June 1884.

27. RGD, Pennsylvania vol. 138, p. 849; vol. 140, p. 395; vol. 141, pp. 111, 425. *NG*, 4 January 1883; *PL*, 1 April 1874, 23 May 1878. See also Mark Hirsch, "Sailmakers: The Maintenance of Craft Traditions in the Age of Steam," in *Divisions of Labour: Skilled Workers and Technological Change in Nineteenth Century England*, ed. Royden Harrison and Jonathan Zeitlin (Brighton, U.K., 1985), pp. 87–113.

28. On Clyde's *Delaware*, see *AS*, 6 December 1879, 17 January 1880. On *Maracaibo* and *Fortuano*, see *PL*, 17 June 1880, 16 April 1881. On *City of Puebla*, see *PL*, 21 October 1881; Emmons, *American Passenger Ships*, pp. 115–16. The plans for the *City of Puebla*, one of the most complete sets of drawings of a Gilded Age steamship, are held at the Philadelphia Maritime Museum, Cramp Collection.

29. Edward P. Crapol and Howard Schonberger, "The Shift to Global Expansion, 1865–1900," in *From Colony to Empire: Essays in the History of American Foreign Relations*, ed. William A. Williams (New York, 1972), pp. 137–39, 157–58; Eric Hobsbawm, *The Age of Empire, 1875–1914* (New York, 1987), pp. 56–83.

30. *NG*, 19 August 1882, 10 May 1883, 26 July 1883, 9 October 1883; *NYT*, 27 December 1908; Hans-Ulrich Wehler, *Der Aufstieg des amerikanischen Imperialismus: Studien zur Entwicklung des Imperium Americanum, 1865–1900* (Göttingen, 1974), p. 238; Ralph S. Kuykendall, *The Hawaiian Kingdom, Vol. 3, 1874–1893: The Kalakaua Dynasty* (Honolulu, 1963), pp. 59–61, 104; Emmons, *American Passenger Ships*, pp. 54–55. For interesting conceptual suggestions on the relationship between agriculture and shipping, see Gaddis Smith, "Agricultural Roots of Maritime History," *AN* 44 (1984): 5–10.

31. *NYT*, 27 July 1916; *NG*, 29 April 1882, 2 April 1885, 12 November 1885; Winthrop Marvin, *The American Merchant Marine: Its History and Romance from 1620 to 1902* (New York, 1910), p. 382; Henry C. Taylor, "American Maritime Development," *TSNAME* 3 (1895): 3–4; Benjamin A. Frankel, "Venezuela and the United States" (Ph.D. diss., University of California at Berkeley, 1964), pp. 218–28, 250; Judith Ewell, *Venezuela: A Century of Change* (Stanford, Calif., 1984), p. 14; Emmons, *American Passenger Ships*, pp. 76–77.

32. John Hutchins, "History and Development of the Shipbuilding Industry in the United States," in *The Shipbuilding Business in the United States of America*, ed. F. G. Fasset (New York, 1948), p. 45; Sidney Pollard and Paul Robertson, *The British Shipbuilding Industry, 1870–1914* (Cambridge, Mass., 1979), passim.

33. Farquhar Report, p. 107.

34. Sarah Palmer, "The British Shipping Industry," in *Change and Adaptation in Maritime History: The North Atlantic Fleets in the Nineteenth Century*, ed. Lewis Fischer and Gerald Panting (St. John's, Newfoundland, Canada, 1985), p. 109; Pollard and Robertson, *British Shipbuilding Industry*, p. 20; "Tramps or Tramp Vessels," in René De La Pedraja, *A Historical Dictionary of the U.S. Merchant Marine and Shipping Industry since the Introduction of Steam* (Westport, Conn., 1994), p. 605.

35. Hutchins, *American Maritime Industries*, pp. 544–45, 565–66.

36. Eric Foner, *Reconstruction: America's Unfinished Revolution, 1862–1877* (New York, 1989), pp. 54, 392–94, 537; Steven Hahn, *The Roots of Southern Populism: Yeoman Farmers and the Transformation of the Georgia Upcountry, 1850–1890* (New York, 1983).

37. James P. Baughman, *Charles Morgan and the Development of Southern Transportation* (Nashville, Tenn., 1968), passim; *NG*, 20 September 1870, 2 and 29 November 1879; *PL*, 2 July 1879, 29 January 1880; Emmons, *American Passenger Ships*, pp. 138–39.

38. *NG*, 29 September 1879, 31 July 1884, 2 October 1884; John H. Morrison, *History of American Steam Navigation* (New York, 1903), p. 462; William Tazewell, *Newport News Shipbuilding: The First Century* (Newport News, Va., 1986), pp. 46–47.

39. U.S. Senate, Committee on Merchant Marine and Fisheries, "Report of the Merchant Marine Commission, Together with the Testimony Taken at the Hearings," 58th Cong., 3rd sess., Senate Report No. 2755, 1:5–35; Morrison, *American Steam Navigation*, pp. 447–48; Emmons, *American Passenger Ships*, pp. 129–30; "Clyde Line," in De La Pedraja, *Historical Dictionary of the U.S. Merchant Marine*, p. 126.

40. *American Syren and Shipping*, 7 March 1903; *NG*, 25 October 1883.

41. U.S. Congress, Joint Industrial Commission, *Report of the Industrial Commission on Transportation*, Vol. 2, 57th Cong., 1st sess. (Washington, D.C., 1901), p. 413; *NG*, 24 April 1880, 25 December 1880, 11 August 1904; Hutchins, *American Maritime Industries*, pp. 568–69; Emmons, *American Passenger Ships*, pp. 125–27.

42. *NG*, 14 February 1880; Morrison, *American Steam Navigation*, p. 463.

43. *NG*, 27 November 1890, 13 July 1905, 23 August 1906; *National Cyclopedia of American Biography*, Vol. 35 (New York, 1949), p. 158; "Luckenbach, Edgar F.," in De La Pedraja, *Historical Dictionary of the U.S. Merchant Marine*, p. 321.

44. On the start of the shipbuilding boom, see *AS*, 13 March 1880.

45. *NG*, 26 March 1881, 29 April 1882; *PL*, 21 June 1881, 12 July 1881, 21 October 1881.

46. All quotations from *PL*, 23 July 1881.

47. *PL*, 22 July 1881.

48. *PL*, 24 September 1881, 21 October 1881, 1 February 1882, 10 July 1882, 4 April 1883. On the extension of the railroad track into the shipyard, see E. Hexamer, "Wm. Cramp & Sons, Ship and Engine Building Company, Surveyed July 31, 1883," Hexamer Insurance Records, Free Library, Philadelphia, Philadelphia Volume, pl. 1685 (hereafter cited as Hexamer Records).

49. *PL*, 23 February 1880.

50. Hexamer, "Wm. Cramp," pl. 1686, Hexamer Records; *NG*, 20 December 1883. In addition to the growing number of commercial contracts, these yard improvements may have been inspired by naval rearmament, as Cramp positioned itself to bid on the first vessels of the new steel navy; see chapter 5.

51. *NG*, 6 March 1884, 26 June 1884, 31 July 1884, 2 October 1884, 6 November 1884; Hutchins, *American Maritime Industries*, p. 448.

52. Neafie & Levy Construction Ledger, Howard E. Cornell Papers, Marine Historical Association of Mystic Seaport, Conn., Collection 84; E. Hexamer, "Penn Works, Neafie & Levy, Surveyed March 13, 1885," pls. 1903–4, Hexamer Records; *PL*, 10 May 1882, 1 August 1882.

53. *PL*, 1 September 1881.

54. *NYT*, 20 February 1883 (quotation). For illustration and description of the yard, see E. Hexamer, "The American Ship Building Co. Works, Surveyed Feb. 4, 1884," pls. 1821–22, Hexamer Records; also *NG*, 8 March 1883, 19 April 1883. For a description of Reading Railroad yard before modernization, see *NG*, 6 June 1879.

55. *NG*, 11 January 1883, 15 March 1883, 26 April 1883, 31 May 1883, 7 June 1883, 12 and 26 July 1883, 2 August 1883, 27 September 1883; *PL*, 6 June 1883.

56. The most detailed account of workplace skills involved in metal shipbuilding is Roy W. Kelly and Frederick J. Allen, *The Shipbuilding Industry* (New York, 1918), pp. 115–99; although written during World War I, it describes many techniques that were common during the nineteenth century. I have checked it against *YN*, 1919–20; "The American Clyde," *HNMM* 56 (1878): 641–53; [Pennsylvania] Department of the Interior, "Ship-Building on the Delaware," in *Annual Report of the Bureau of Industrial Statistics (for 1891)*, Part C, pp. 100–111 (hereafter cited as Cheney Report). See also A. M. Robb, "Ship-Building," in *A History of Technology*, vol. 5: *The Late Nineteenth Century, c. 1850 to c. 1900* (Oxford, 1958), pp. 365–69; Keith McClelland and Alastair Reid, "Wood, Iron and Steel: Technology, Labour and Trade Union Organization in the Shipbuilding Industry, 1840–1914," in *Divisions of Labour*, ed. Harrison and Zeitlin, pp. 151–84.

57. William Cramp & Sons Ship and Engine Building Company, Book of Apprentices, 1882–1919, Franklin Institute, Philadelphia.

58. *NG*, 7 June 1879, 7 February 1880; Henry West, "The Problem of Steamship Design," *CM* 12 (1897): 319–40; Kelly and Allen, *Shipbuilding Industry*, pp. 104–9.

59. Kelly and Allen, *Shipbuilding Industry*, pp. 109–11; Farquhar Report, p. 126;

Edgar C. Smith, *A Short History of Naval and Marine Engineering* (Cambridge, 1937), pp. 309–10.

60. "Engineers' Club of Philadelphia, Regular Meeting March 3rd [1883]," *VNEEM* 28 (1883): 345, on See's presentation; for other presentations of marine engineers at the Philadelphia Engineers' Club, see "Engineers' Club of Philadelphia [Meeting 18 November 1882]," *VNEEM* 28 (1883): 79; "Engineers' Club of Philadelphia, Records of Regular Meeting, Nov. 15th, 1884," *VNEEM* 22 (1885): 81; also *PL*, 21 December 1880.

61. [Taylor Gause], *Harlan & Hollingsworth* (Wilmington, Del., 1886), p. 366.

62. "Discussion," *TSNAME* 17 (1908): 161.

63. William H. Rideing, "The Building of an 'Ocean Greyhound,'" in *Ocean Steamships: A Popular Account of Their Construction, Development, Management and Appliances,* ed. F. E. Chatwick et al. (New York, 1891), p. 93.

64. On artisanal careers of Jacob Neafie and Charles Cramp, see Robson, *Manufacturers and Manufactories,* p. 444; Buell, *Memoirs of Charles Cramp,* p. 47; Julian Ralph, "Building of a Great Ship," *HW* 37 (1893): 1128–29.

65. Ralph, "Building of a Great Ship," p. 1129.

66. *PL,* 23 March 1880.

67. On models, plans, and patterning, see Lewis Nixon, "Building of a Ship," *CM* 12 (1897): 387; Rideing, "Building of an 'Ocean Greyhound,'" pp. 97–98.

68. "The American Clyde," *HNMM* 56 (1878): 646.

69. Ibid., pp. 645–46.

70. Nixon, "The Building of a Ship," p. 403; Rideing, "Building of an 'Ocean Greyhound,'" pp. 98–101; Ralph, "Building of a Great Ship," p. 1129. On accidents, see *PL*, 29 January 1881.

71. Rideing, "Building of an 'Ocean Greyhound,'" pp. 101–2; Cheney Report, p. 101; *YN,* March 1920, p. 22. In later decades, bolting was performed by specially trained bolters; during the nineteenth century, it was still done by riveters. See *YN,* November 1920, p. 21.

72. Kelly and Allen, *Shipbuilding Industry,* p. 141.

73. Nixon, "Building of a Ship," p. 395.

74. Kelly and Allen, *Shipbuilding Industry,* p. 141.

75. Nixon, "Building of a Ship," pp. 389–96; Rideing, "Building of an 'Ocean Greyhound,'" p. 103. On piecework among riveters, see *PL*, 28 August 1891; Cheney Report, p. 103; Farquhar Report, p. 134.

76. Robert Caird, "The Launching of a Ship," *CM* 12 (1897): 341–50.

77. Nixon, "Building of a Ship," pp. 399–401; Kelly and Allen, *Shipbuilding Industry,* pp. 157–59.

78. Kelly and Allen, *Shipbuilding Industry,* pp. 161–64; Nixon, "Building of a Ship," pp. 401–3.

79. Kelly and Allen, *Shipbuilding Industry,* pp. 164–77.

80. Rideing, "Building of an 'Ocean Greyhound,'" p. 93.

81. *NG,* 10 May 1883, 26 July 1883.

82. This and the following paragraphs are based on a theory of class formation

formulated by Ira Katznelson, Jürgen Kocka, and others; see especially Ira Katznelson, "Working-Class Formation: Constructing Cases and Comparisons," in *Working-Class Formation: Nineteenth-Century Patterns in Western Europe and the United States* (Princeton, 1986), pp. 3–41. As indicated, the theory distinguishes among economic, social, cultural, and political class formation, refining the somewhat schematic Marxist notion of "classes in themselves" (objective class structure as defined by the control of the means of production) and "classes for themselves" (subjective class consciousness/ideology).

83. Farquhar Report, p. 126; *Report of the Proceedings of the Thirteenth Annual Convention of the International Brotherhood of Boiler Makers and Iron Shipbuilders* (Chicago, 1893), p. 78 (hereafter cited as Boilermakers Report).

84. On builders' activities in Board of Trade, Maritime Exchange, and Board of Port Wardens, see *PL*, 5 February 1878, 19 April 1878, 17 December 1878, 4 October 1880, 3 March 1881, 21 June 1881.

85. On the ship carpenters' and caulkers' union, see *PL*, 10 and 15 June 1872, 10 July 1874. On Boilermakers Union Local 19, see Boilermakers Report, p. 39; Pollard and Robertson, *British Shipbuilding Industry*, pp. 156–69.

86. *PL*, 2 June 1883.

87. *PL*, 13, 17, 19, 27, and 28 April 1883, 1, 3, 4, 7, 8, and 28 May 1883, 7 June 1883.

88. Farquhar Report, p. 116.

89. Ibid., p. 113.

90. Philip Scranton, "Varieties of Paternalism: Industrial Structures and the Social Relations of Production in American Textiles," *American Quarterly* 36 (1984): 241–42.

91. *PL*, 3 November 1884. This argument has been made by Alastair Reid, "Employers' Strategies and Craft Production: The British Shipbuilding Industry 1870–1950," in *The Power to Manage? Employers and Industrial Relations in Comparative Historical Perspective*, ed. Steven Tolliday and Jonathan Zeitlin (London, 1991), pp. 35–51.

92. *PI*, 17 May 1901.

93. U.S. Senate, Committee on Education and Labor, "Eight Hours for Laborers on Government Work," 57th Cong., 2nd sess., Senate Document No. 141, pp. 336, 355–56.

94. On hiring practice, see *PL*, 21 May 1883.

Five: A Vicious Quality

1. S. A. Staunton, "The Naval Campaign of 1898 in the West Indies," *HNMM* 48 (1899): 183–90. The fleet proper at Santiago consisted of the battleships USS *Indiana*, USS *Iowa*, USS *Oregon*, and USS *Texas*, and the cruiser USS *Brooklyn*. All these vessels, except the *Oregon* and *Texas*, were built by Cramp. Of two auxiliary warships participating in the battle, one was J. P. Morgan's converted yacht *Corsair*, built by Neafie & Levy. Two other Cramp-built vessels, the battleship USS *Massachusetts* and the cruiser USS *New York*, had just left their stations in front of the port and did not take part in the Battle of Santiago.

2. This phrase is borrowed from Roger Lotchin, *Fortress California, 1910–1961: From*

Warfare to Welfare (New York, 1992). Pennsylvania was California's pre–World War I counterpart as the nation's center of high-tech weapons production.

3. U.S. House, Industrial Commission, "Report of the Industrial Commission on the Relations and Conditions of Capital and Labor Employed in Manufactures and General Business, Vol. 2," 57th Cong., 1st sess., House Document No. 183, p. 397 (hereafter cited as Industrial Commission Report).

4. Benjamin F. Cooling, *Gray Steel and Blue Water Navy: The Formative Years of America's Military-Industrial Complex, 1881–1917* (Hamden, Conn., 1979), p. 13.

5. Stephen Rosen, ed., *Testing the Theory of the Military-Industrial Complex* (Lexington, Mass., 1973); Mary Kandor, *The Baroque Arsenal* (New York, 1981); Benjamin F. Cooling, *War, Business, and American Society: Historical Perspectives on the Military-Industrial Complex* (Port Washington, N.Y., 1977); Paul A. Koistinen, *The Military-Industrial Complex: A Historical Perspective* (New York, 1980).

6. Industrial Commission Report, p. 415.

7. Robert W. Shufeld, "The Relations of the Navy to the Commerce of the United States" (1878), reprinted in *Creating an American Empire, 1865–1914*, ed. Milton Plesur (New York, 1971), pp. 36, 38 (emphasis in original); see also Edward Crapol and Howard Schonberger, "The Shift to Global Expansion, 1865–1890," in *From Colony to Empire: Essays in the History of American Foreign Relations*, ed. William A. Williams (New York, 1972), p. 140; William A. Williams, *The Roots of the Modern American Empire: A Study in the Growth and Shaping of Social Consciousness in a Marketplace Society* (New York, 1969), pp. 236–68, on the relationship between the overproduction thesis and overseas expansion; Hans-Ulrich Wehler, *Der Aufstieg des amerikanischen Imperialismus: Studien zur Entwicklung des Imperium Americanum, 1865–1900* (Göttingen, 1974), pp. 24–37.

8. Quoted in Leonard Swann, Jr., *John Roach, Maritime Entrepreneur: The Years as Naval Contractor, 1862–1886* (Annapolis, Md., 1965), p. 179.

9. Baltimore *American*, 18 July 1883, quoted in Swann, *John Roach*, pp. 180–81.

10. Ibid., pp. 185–234.

11. *A&NJ*, 25 September 1886.

12. The navy initially consulted with Pusey & Jones, John Dialogue, and Neafie & Levy, but these and other builders did not submit bids. J. E. Walker, Circular of the Board on Additional Vessels, 10 March 1886, NA, RG 19, Entry 247, vol. 1. On the "dynamite cruiser" contract, see *NYT*, 4 November 1886. There were rumors that the shipbuilders "boycotted" the Navy Department: *NG*, 6 October 1886, 1 December 1886.

13. *NYT*, 15 April 1887; *NG*, 6 April 1887; William H. Jaques, "Description of the Works of the Bethlehem Iron Company," *PUSNI* 15 (1889): 531–40; Cooling, *Gray Steel*, pp. 66–76.

14. U.S. House, Committee on Merchant Marine and Fisheries, "American Merchant Marine in the Foreign Trade," 51st Cong., 1st sess., House Report No. 1210, p. 129 (hereafter cited as Farquhar Report). Cramp's yard improvements are described in *NG*, 6 June 1887. The naval programs of the 1880s also facilitated plant improvement at other yards, notably the Union Iron Works of San Francisco; see John Hutchins, *The*

American Maritime Industries and Public Policy, 1789–1914: An Economic History (Cambridge, Mass., 1941), pp. 457–58.

15. Charles Cramp to William Whitney, 28 June 1886, reprinted in *NG,* 21 July 1886; on procurement of British warship plans, see also *NYT,* 12 and 31 July 1886.

16. On the triple-expansion engine for *Peerless,* see Gail E. Farr and Brett F. Bostwick, *Shipbuilding at Cramp & Sons: A History and Guide of the William Cramp & Sons Ship and Engine Building Company (1830–1927) and the Cramp Shipbuilding Company (1941–46) of Philadelphia* (Philadelphia, 1991), p. 27, with references; see also Edgar C. Smith, *A Short History of Naval and Marine Engineering* (Cambridge, 1939), pp. 238–53.

17. Farquhar Report, p. 130.

18. Charles H. Cramp, "American Shipbuilding and Commercial Supremacy," *Forum* 12 (1891): 391.

19. On construction delays see *NG,* 8 August 1887. Material on USS *Vesuvius:* contract, 11 February 1887, enclosed with William Whitney to Wilson, 15 July 1887, NA, RG 19, Entry 74, Box 174; report on problems and delays, Wilson to Whitney, 8 May 1888, NA, RG 19, Entry 74, Box 181; *NYT,* 18 May 1888; "Failure of the Dynamite Cruiser *Vesuvius,*" *SA* 65 (1891): 368.

20. Charles Cramp to Hilary Herbert, 16 October 1893, reprinted in U.S. House, Committee on Naval Affairs, "Premiums Paid to Contractors of War Vessels for the Navy," 53rd Cong., 2nd sess., House Report No. 407, p. 107 (hereafter cited as Premium Report).

21. On Roach's trial trip problems with the USS *Dolphin,* see Swann, *John Roach,* pp. 197–203.

22. Benjamin Tracy to W. Cramp, 15 October 1889, NA, RG 19, Entry 74, Box 197; William S. Schley, "Official Report on the Behavior of the U.S.S. Baltimore," *PUSNI* 18 (1892): 234–49.

23. On the recovery of the steamship trade, see *NG,* 8 August 1890. *Algonquin* is described in *NYT,* 29 September 1890. For a description of *El Sol,* see *NYT,* 27 September 1890, 7 December 1890; *NG,* 12 December 1890.

24. Hugo P. Frear, "History of Bethlehem's San Francisco Yard," in *Historical Transactions, 1893–1943,* ed. Society of Naval Architects and Marine Engineers (New York, 1945), p. 239; William Tazewell, *Newport News: The First Century* (Newport News, Va., 1986), pp. 53–56.

25. *The Neafie & Levy Ship and Engine Building Company* (New York, 1896), pp. 6–8; *NG,* 19 November 1891.

26. Ron Chernow, *The House of Morgan: An American Banking Dynasty and the Rise of Modern Finance* (New York, 1990), p. 60.

27. Vaughan & Lynn, Charles Hillman, Specifications Book, Historical Society of Pennsylvania, Philadelphia, Society Collection; *NG,* 3 March 1892, 29 December 1892, 2 March 1893, 31 August 1893.

28. U.S. Senate, Committee on Education and Labor, "Eight Hours for Laborers on Government Work" (1903), 57th Congress, 2nd session, Senate Document 141, p. 381.

29. Ibid., pp. 129–30.

30. *NG*, 2 January 1890; Hutchins, *American Maritime Industries*, pp. 527–34; Lawrence Algin, "The Civil War and the Period of Decline, 1865–1913," in *America's Maritime Legacy: A History of the U.S. Merchant Marine and Shipbuilding Industry since Colonial Times*, ed. Robert Kilmarx (Boulder, Colo., 1979), pp. 81–82.

31. On bounties, see Nelson Dingley, Jr., "How to Restore American Shipping," *NAR* 148 (1889): 687–96. On subsidies, see E. P. North, "American Shipping—The Disease and the Remedy," *NAR* 146 (1888): 566–79; Ray B. Smith, "Subsidies to American Shipping," *New Englander and Yale Review* 55 (1891): 133–63. On passage of bills in the Senate, see *NG*, 17 July 1890. See also "Ocean Mail Act of 1891," in René De La Pedraja, *A Historical Dictionary of the U.S. Merchant Marine and Shipping Industry since the Introduction of Steam* (Westport, Conn., 1994), p. 452.

32. *NG*, 3 July 1890.

33. *NG*, 18 September 1890. The Maryland Steel yard integrated shipbuilding with steel production, a strategy harshly criticized by Charles Cramp; see *PR*, 3 October 1891.

34. William Cramp & Sons, Minute Book, 1872–95, Philadelphia Maritime Museum, Cramp Collection, pp. 115–24 (hereafter cited as Cramp Minute Book).

35. Ibid., p. 124.

36. *NYT*, 2 February 1890.

37. Hutchins, *American Maritime Industries*, pp. 534–35. For a survey of editorial opinions on the subsidy issue, see "The Question of Subsidies," *Public Opinion* 8 (1890): 357; also *NG*, 2, 19, and 26 February 1891, 5 March 1891.

38. On the proposed new shipyard, see Cramp Minute Book, p. 127; *PR*, 6 June 1890; *NG*, 3 July 1890.

39. The steamship subsidy law is reprinted in *NG*, 5 March 1891; see also *NG*, 5 May 1891, 4 June 1891, 29 October 1891; Algin, "Period of Decline," p. 90.

40. On the American Line purchase, see *NYT*, 3 March 1884, 16 and 18 October 1884. On the Inman Line purchase, see *NYT*, 10 and 20 October 1886. On the history of the INC during the late nineteenth century, see RGD, Pennsylvania vol. 154, p. 264; also Vivian Vale, *The American Peril: Challenge to Britain on the North Atlantic, 1901–1904* (Manchester, England, 1984), pp. 36–37.

41. Industrial Commission Report, p. 409.

42. *NG*, 26 March 1891.

43. Farquhar Report, p. 112; Charles H. Cramp, "Our Navigation Laws," *NAR* 158 (1894): 433–45.

44. The bill is reprinted in *NYT*, 3 May 1892.

45. *NYT*, 28 January 1893, 9 March 1893, 22 June 1893; "Naturalization of the *New York*," *HW* 37 (1893): 193, 211; "Raising the Flag on the Steamship *New York*," *SA* 68 (1893): 136–37; Algin, "Period of Decline," p. 92.

46. On the organizational and financial relationship between Cramp and the steamship line, see Cramp Minute Book, p. 127; also Premium Report, p. 149, on the alleged political power of the two companies. On advertising, see *NG*, 17 December 1891.

47. Maritime reformers saw the INC registry scheme as a blueprint for a maritime policy permitting the registry of foreign-built ships in the United States as long as

shippers ordered an identical vessel from American builders; see Eugene T. Chamberlain, "A Present Chance for American Shipping," *NAR* 158 (1894): 277–82. Unfortunately, this plan failed.

48. Alfred T. Mahan, *The Influence of Sea Power upon History, 1660–1783* (1890; reprint, New York, 1987); Benjamin F. Cooling, *Benjamin Franklin Tracy, Father of the Modern American Fighting Navy* (Hamden, Conn., 1973), pp. 73–76.

49. On Charles Cramp's views, see U.S. House, Committee on Naval Affairs, *Vessels of the New Navy* (Washington, 1890), 51st Cong., 1st sess., p. 18. On the final version of the 1890 naval program, see Cooling, *Gray Steel*, p. 90.

50. Quoted in Paul Krause, *The Battle for Homestead, 1880–1892: Politics, Culture, and Steel* (Pittsburgh, 1992), p. 281.

51. Ibid.

52. *NYT*, 14 December 1890.

53. The USS *New York* is described and analyzed in Ivan Musicant, *U.S. Armored Cruisers: A Design and Operational History* (Annapolis, Md., 1985), pp. 15–26.

54. U.S. House, Committee on Claims, "William Cramp & Sons Ship and Engine Building Company," 54th Cong., 1st sess., House Document No. 68 (hereafter cited as Herbert Report).

55. Delivery of first material, John Hanscom to Theodore Wilson, 3 September 1890; first keel plates laid, Hanscom to Wilson, 30 September 1890; order to Morris, Rowland to Cramp, 20 October 1890; order to Carnegie, Wilson to Tracy, 9 October 1890; all in NA, RG 19, Entry 74, Box 233. On forgings, see Russel W. Davenport, "Steel for Marine Forgings," *CM* 12 (1897): 513–30.

56. Cramp Minute Book, p. 133.

57. *NG*, 4 April 1891. On B. H. Cramp, see *NYT*, 27 and 30 December 1889, 2 and 8 February 1890, 4 and 30 April 1890, 4 and 25 May 1890; *NG*, 7 July 1890; F. Meriam Wheeler, "The Auxiliary Machinery of an American Warship," *CM* 12 (1897): 483–512; R. M. Watt, "Novelties in Ship Fittings," *TSNAME* 7 (1899): 217–28.

58. *PL*, 22 August 1891.

59. Ibid.; Cramp to Secretary of the Navy [Tracy], 23 September 1891, NA, RG 19, Entry 74, Box 259.

60. *PL*, 22 September 1891, 8 October 1891. On delays on the battleship USS *Indiana*, see Cramp firm to Secretary of the Navy [Tracy], 14 October 1891, Cramp to Hanscom, 15 October 1891, Hanscom to Wilson, 15 October 1891; all in NA, RG 19, Entry 74, Box 259. For a summary of strike-related construction delays on the armored cruiser USS *New York*, see Cramp to Secretary of the Navy [Tracy], 1 February 1893, NA, RG 19, Entry 74, Box 352.

61. William Folger to George Dewey, 31 July 1891, NA, RG 19, Entry 74, Box 274.

62. On the protective deck, see Wilson and Folger to Tracy, 23 March 1891, NA, RG 19, Entry 74, Box 273; and Musicant, *U.S. Armored Cruisers*, pp. 22–23. On the Navy Department's deliberations, see Folger to Tracy, 24 July 1891, Cramp to Hanscom, 6 August 1891, Green to Hanscom, 17 August 1891, Tracy to Wilson, 16 September 1891, Wilson to Hanscom, 16 September 1891, Wilson and Folger to Tracy, 19 September 1891;

all in NA, RG 19, Entry 74, Box 274. On Cramp's work, see Cramp to Hanscom, 10 December 1891, NA, RG 19, Entry 74, Box 311. On all-steel versus nickel-steel tests, see Davenport, "Production in the United States," pp. 81–82.

63. Charles Cramp to Hanscom, 10 December 1891, NA, RG 19, Entry 74, Box 311.

64. *NYT*, 7 January 1892.

65. The relationship between the Homestead strike and the nickel-steel question has been hinted at in Cooling, *Gray Steel*, p. 103.

66. Charles Cramp to Tracy, 18 February 1891, 21 January 1892, 12 February 1892, printed in Herbert Report, pp. 7–11.

67. Herbert Report, pp. 5–6.

68. Charles Cramp to Tracy, 28 February 1892, printed in Herbert Report, p. 11.

69. Studies of the Homestead Strike of 1892 have overlooked this relationship between Carnegie and naval shipbuilding at Cramp. Sources on the frenzied pace of armor production for the USS *New York* at Homestead during the spring of 1892 include Brummett to Wilson, 25 March 1892, Folger to Tracy, 16 April 1892, Millard Hunskey to Wilson, 20 April 1892, Wilson to Hanscom, 7 May 1892, Folger to Wilson, 7 and 9 May 1892, Hanscom to Wilson, 11 May 1892, Green to Hanscom, 20 June 1892; all in NA, RG 19, Entry 74, Box 312. See also Cooling, *Gray Steel*, p. 103.

70. *NYT*, 7 July 1892.

71. Charles Cramp to Tracy, 19 August 1892, printed in Herbert Report, p. 17.

72. "Report by Contractor's Representative on Condition of Armor at the Mills," 12 October 1892, printed in Herbert Report, p. 15.

73. Herbert Report, pp. 1–5.

74. Charles Cramp to Hilarary Herbert, 30 September 1896, printed in Herbert Report, p. 41.

75. Cramp to Herbert, 31 August 1896, printed in Herbert Report, p. 77; see also Norman Friedman, *U.S. Battleships: An Illustrated Design History* (Annapolis, Md., 1985), pp. 25–27.

76. Memorandum, 24 October 1894, printed in Herbert Report, p. 92.

77. Charles Cramp to Herbert, 31 August 1896, p. 77.

78. Ibid.

79. "Affidavit of Mr. Charles H. Cramp," 10 August 1907, printed in U.S. Senate, Committee on Claims, "To Pay Judgement in Favor of William Cramp & Sons for Building U.S.S. Indiana," 60th Cong., 1st sess., Senate Report No. 239, p. 12.

80. *NG*, 12 January 1893, 17 August 1893; Friedman, *U.S. Battleships*, pp. 29–30; Musicant, *U.S. Armored Cruisers*, pp. 46–62.

81. George W. Dickie, "Can the American Shipbuilder under Present Conditions Compete with the British and German Shipbuilders in the Production of the Largest Class of Passenger and Freight Steamers?" *TSNAME* 8 (1900): 195.

82. Charles Cramp, "Sea Power of the United States," *NAR* 159 (1894): 141–42.

83. Friedman, *U.S. Battleships*, pp. 27, 32–38.

84. On Hillman, see *MR*, 20 February 1902.

Six: New Departure

1. *MR,* 14 November 1901, 26 December 1901, 9 January 1902.

2. Philip Scranton, "Large Firms and Industrial Restructuring: The Philadelphia Region, 1900–1980," *PMHB* 115 (1992): 424–25. Scranton argues that because of the inclusion of territory into Philadelphia County in 1854, the city was "long immune from witnessing the placement of most new regional factories beyond its political boundaries in separate jurisdictions" (p. 425). On the suburbanization of manufacturing in Detroit, see Olivier Zunz, *The Changing Face of Inequality: Urbanization, Industrial Development, and Immigrants in Detroit, 1880–1920* (Chicago, 1982), pp. 293–309.

3. "Record of Metal Vessels Built in the United States," NA, RG 19, Entry 129.

4. Robert G. Albion, *Makers of Naval Policy, 1798–1947* (Annapolis, Md., 1980), pp. 211–13, 324–38.

5. Ibid., pp. 216–17. See also Benjamin F. Cooling, *Gray Steel and the Blue Water Navy: The Formative Years of America's First Military-Industrial Complex, 1881–1917* (Annapolis, Md., 1979), pp. 164–65.

6. Alexander R. Smith, "Shipbuilding," in *Census Reports Vol. X. Twelfth Census of the United States Taken in the Year 1900. Manufactures, Part IV: Special Reports on Selected Industries* (Washington, D.C., 1902), p. 212.

7. Ibid.; *ARCN* (1900), p. 26; Ronald Hope, *A New History of British Shipping* (London, 1990), p. 338.

8. René De La Pedraja, *The Rise and Decline of U.S. Merchant Shipping in the Twentieth Century* (New York, 1992), pp. 23–38.

9. Ibid., pp. 17–18; *NG,* 12 July 1907, 7 July 1908; *Report of the Merchant Marine Commission, Together with the Testimony Taken at the Hearings, Vol. 3,* 58th Cong., 1st sess. (Washington, D.C., 1905), pp. 1202–5.

10. De La Pedraja, *Rise and Decline of U.S. Merchant Shipping,* pp. 23–29; Thomas C. Cochran and Ray Gibger, "The American-Hawaiian Steamship Company, 1899–1919," *BHR* 28 (1954): 343–65.

11. Quoted in *NG,* 1 January 1900.

12. Ibid.

13. *Nation,* 10 August 1899.

14. *MR,* 21 February 1901; Bernard Baker to Joseph Chamberlain, 17 October 1901, printed in *ARCN* (1902), p. 70. See also *ARCN* (1901), pp. 22–25; Charles Cramp, "The Merchant Marine and the Subsidy Bill," *Independent* 53 (1901): 130–32.

15. *ARCN* (1903), p. 13. See also Vivian Vale, *The American Peril: Challenge to Britain on the North Atlantic, 1901–1904* (Manchester, 1984). Vale gives a superb analysis of the IMM in the framework of the merger movement in American business and the rivalry between Britain, Germany, and the United States in the transatlantic steamship trade.

16. *NG,* 6 and 12 January 1898, 8 June 1899, 19 April 1900, 25 April 1901, 15 June 1905, 2 November 1905, 5 May 1906, 18 October 1906; Frank J. Taylor, "Early American Steamship Lines," in *Historical Transactions,* ed. Society of Naval Architects and Marine

Engineers (New York, 1945), pp. 51–52; De La Pedraja, *Rise and Decline of U.S. Merchant Shipping,* pp. 34–41.

17. *NG,* 4 April 1901, 20 June 1901, 1 September 1904; *SI,* 28 November 1903, 3 January 1907; *MR,* 13 September 1906.

18. *NG,* 8 August 1907, 31 October 1907, 6 February 1908.

19. *ARCN* (1908), p. 8.

20. *NG,* 2 November 1905; John Hutchins, *The American Maritime Industries and Public Policy, 1789–1914: An Economic History* (Cambridge, Mass., 1941), p. 575.

21. *NG,* 24 July 1902, 7 August 1902, 11 December 1902, 2 March 1905; *MR,* 14 November 1901; Mike Ratcliffe, *Liquid Gold Ships: A History of the Tanker* (London, 1985), pp. 53–93.

22. Ratcliffe, *Liquid Gold Ships,* pp. 83–85.

23. Andrew Laing, "Oil Burning aboard Ship," *CM* 32 (1907): 141–50; Edgar C. Smith, *A Short History of Naval and Marine Engineering* (Cambridge, 1937), pp. 285–87.

24. Smith, *Short History,* pp. 271–302; R. J. Walker, "Recent Developments in the Marine Steam Turbine," *CM* 32 (1907): 197–207. For a critical assessment of the new technology, see "Steam Turbines," in René De La Pedraja, *A Historical Dictionary of the U.S. Merchant Marine and Shipping Industry since the Introduction of Steam* (Westport, Conn., 1994), pp. 593–94.

25. William A. Fairburn, "Fitting-out Wharf Crane Service in American Shipyards," *TSNAME* 65 (1903): 153.

26. Charles Cramp, "The Steamship Merger and American Shipbuilding," *NAR* 175 (1902): 14–15.

27. Daniel Nelson, *Managers and Workers: Origins of the New Factory System in the United States* (Madison, Wis., 1975), pp. 17–25.

28. *Fifty Years, New York Shipbuilding Corporation, Camden, N.J.* (Camden, N.J., 1949), p. 16.

29. Sidney H. McLane, "Practical Mold Work in Shipyards," *ME* 8 (1903): 526–28.

30. *NG,* 24 January 1901; *ME* 8 (1903): 376.

31. "The Works of the New York Shipbuilding Company," *ME* 6 (1901): 499–500.

32. On subcontracting firms, see *NG,* 6 June 1901, 16 October 1902; *MR,* 11 July 1901. See also Tjark Schwarz and Ernst von Halle, *Die Schiffbauindustrie in Deutschland und im Auslande, Vol. 1* (Berlin, 1902), pp. 140–44.

33. *NG,* 12 July 1900.

34. "Main Office Building of the New York Shipbuilding Co., Camden, N.J.," *ME* 5 (1900): 188–93.

35. "Works of the New York Shipbuilding Company," pp. 503–4.

36. Ibid.; see also Schwarz and von Halle, *Schiffbauindustrie,* p. 147.

37. "Works of the New York Shipbuilding Company," p. 504.

38. *NG,* 12 July 1900, 25 October 1900, 1 November 1900; Schwarz and von Halle, *Schiffbauindustrie,* p. 149; Sidney Pollard and Paul Robertson, *The British Shipbuilding Industry, 1870–1914* (Cambridge, Mass., 1979), p. 128.

39. "Works of the New York Shipbuilding Company," p. 509.

40. *YN*, March 1920, p. 6.

41. "Report by Mr. D. C. Cummings, of the Iron and Steel Shipbuilders and Boiler Makers' Society," in *Mosely Industrial Commission to the United States of America, Oct.–Dec., 1902* (Manchester, 1903), p. 80.

42. U.S. Senate, Committee on Commerce, *United States Shipping Board Emergency Fleet Corporation: Hearing before the Committee on Commerce . . . Part 5*, 65th Cong., 2nd sess. (Washington, D.C., 1918), p. 1402.

43. *MR*, 5 September 1901; see also David Palmer, "Organizing the Shipyards: Unionization at New York Ship, Federal Ship, and Fore River, 1898–1945" (Ph.D. diss., Brandeis University, 1990), pp. 47–52.

44. Waldon Fawcett, "The Ship-Building Yards of the United States," *EM* 19 (1900): 498; see also William Tazewell, *Newport News Shipbuilding: The First Century* (Newport News, Va., 1986), pp. 68–69.

45. Fawcett, "Ship-Building Yards," p. 503.

46. Joseph S. Schultz, "Shipyard Cranes and Their Function in Marine Construction," *EM* 29 (1905): 62.

47. *NG*, 6 June 1900; James Dickie, "Overhead Cranes, Staging, and Riveter-Carrying Appliances in the Shipyard," *TSNAME* 7 (1899): 189–92.

48. *Cramp's Shipyard: The William Cramp & Sons' Ship and Engine Building Co, 1830—The I. P. Morris Co., 1828—The Kensington Shipyard Co., 1900* (Philadelphia, 1910), pp. 67–116; *IA*, 24 March 1910.

49. Fawcett, "Ship-Building Yards," p. 666; *NG*, 3 January 1901.

50. Harland & Wolff faced similar spatial problems in Belfast; like New York Ship, Vickers's Naval Construction Works at Barrow-in-Furness emphasized streamlined material throughput. See Pollard and Robertson, *British Shipbuilding Industry*, pp. 111–14.

51. *NYT*, 24 March 1900.

52. *ME* 6 (1901): 424.

53. *NG*, 5 April 1900, 24 May 1900; *ME* 8 (1903): 266–71; Tazewell, *Newport News*, p. 60.

54. U.S. House, Committee on Labor, *Eight Hours for Laborers on Government Work*, 60th Cong., 1st sess. (Washington, D.C., 1908), p. 119.

55. *NG*, 5 April 1900, 24 May 1900; Schwarz and von Halle, *Schiffbauindustrie*, p. 140. See also Nelson, *Managers and Workers*, p. 23; Pollard and Robertson, *British Shipbuilding Industry*, p. 109.

56. "Report by Mr. Alexander Wilkie, of the Associated Shipwrights' Society," in *Mosely Industrial Commission*, p. 93; Schwarz and von Halle, *Schiffbauindustrie*, pp. 144–45; Nelson, *Managers and Workers*, pp. 25–29.

57. G. R. Dunell, "The Prospective Expansion in American Ship-Building," *EM* 17 (1899): 113.

58. *YN*, March 1921, p. 9; U.S. Senate, Committee on Education and Labor, "Eight Hours for Laborers on Government Work" (1903), 57th Cong., 2nd sess., Senate Document No. 141, pp. 321, 331–36; Schwarz and von Halle, *Schiffbauindustrie*, p. 151.

59. Roy W. Kelley and Frederick J. Allen, *The Shipbuilding Industry* (Boston, 1918), pp. 141–42.

60. *YN*, August–November 1921, p. 9.

61. Kelley and Allen, *Shipbuilding Industry,* pp. 143–46; *MR,* 1 June 1905; *YN,* November 1920, p. 9. See also George Dickie, "Can the American Shipbuilder under Present Conditions Compete with the British and German Shipbuilders in the Production of the Largest Class of Ocean Passenger and Freight Steamships?" *TSNAME* 8 (1900): 181–82; Pollard and Robertson, *British Shipbuilding Industry,* p. 122.

62. *YN,* March 1921, p. 4; R. S. Hubbard, "Shipyard Economies (Part I)," *ME* 9 (1904): 13.

63. Hubbard, "Shipyard Economies (Part I)," p. 13.

64. Ibid.

65. Dickie, "Can the American Shipbuilder Compete," passim.

66. David Montgomery, *The Fall of the House of Labor: The Workplace, the State, and American Labor Activism, 1865–1925* (Cambridge, 1987), pp. 148–54; Palmer, "Organizing the Shipyards," pp. 55–56.

67. "Eight Hours for Laborers on Government Work" (1903), p. 357.

68. Ibid., p. 361. See also U.S. House, Committee on Labor, *Hours of Labor for Workmen on Public Works,* 56th Cong., 1st sess. (Washington, D.C., 1900), p. 54; William Cramp & Sons Ship and Engine Building Co., *Angle Furnace Piece-Work Rates* (Philadelphia, 1905).

69. *MMJ,* March 1903, p. 185.

70. Dickie, "Can the American Shipbuilder Compete," p. 188.

71. "Eight Hours for Laborers on Government Work" (1903), p. 365.

72. Watson introduced a similar system at Fore River; see Palmer, "Organizing the Shipyards," pp. 68–69.

73. "Eight Hours for Laborers on Government Work" (1903), p. 319; statistics calculated from *Nineteenth Annual Report of the Commissioner of Labor, 1904,* 58th Cong., 3rd sess. (Washington, D.C., 1905), pp. 354–56.

74. David R. Roediger and Philip S. Foner, *Our Own Time: A History of American Labor and the Working Day* (London, 1989), pp. 145–62.

75. *MMJ,* October 1899, p. 631. On shipyard labor organizations, see U.S. House, Industrial Commission, "Reports of the Industrial Commission on Labor Organizations, Labor Disputes, and Arbitration, and on Railway Labor Vol. XVII," 57th Cong., 1st sess., House Document No. 186, pp. 217–22, 228–31.

76. *Hours of Labor for Workmen on Public Works* (1900).

77. *MMJ,* November 1899, p. 692. See also *PI,* 30 August 1899. Similar strikes occurred at Fore River; see Palmer, "Organizing the Shipyards," pp. 90–92.

78. "Eight Hours for Laborers on Government Work" (1903), p. 370.

79. *PP,* 1, 2, 3, 12, 13, 14, 21, and 22 September 1899, 3 and 4 October 1899; *NG,* 12 July 1900.

80. "Eight Hours for Laborers on Government Work" (1903), p. 384.

81. *MMJ,* November 1899, p. 695.

82. *BMISBJ*, March 1900, pp. 83, 86.

83. *PI*, 19, 20, 21, 22, 29 May 1901, 20 June 1901; *BMISBJ*, May 1902, p. 168.

84. "Eight Hours for Laborers on Government Work" (1903), p. 331.

85. *BMISBJ*, March 1903, p. 121.

86. *BMISBJ*, October 1904, pp. 655–56; *BMISBJ*, October 1906, p. 631; *MR*, 10 March 1904; Palmer, "Organizing the Shipyards," pp. 57–58, 83–84; Howell Harris, "Employers' Collective Action in the Open-shop Era: The Metal Manufacturers' Association of Philadelphia, c. 1903–1933," in *The Power to Manage? Employers and Industrial Relations in Comparative Historical Perspective*, ed. Steven Tolliday and Jonathan Zeitlin (London, 1991), pp. 117–46.

87. U.S. Senate, Committee on Education and Labor, *Hours of Labor for Workmen, Mechanics, Etc. Employed upon the Public Works of the United States*, 55th Cong., 1st sess. (Washington, D.C., 1898), p. 24.

88. Morse to L. E. McComas, 9 December 1902, printed in "Eight Hours for Laborers on Government Work" (1903), p. 294.

89. *MR*, 29 December 1901; Marion C. Cahill, *Shorter Hours: A Study of the Movement since the Civil War* (New York, 1932), pp. 68–77.

90. Christopher Tomlins, *The State and the Unions: Labor Relations, Law, and the Organized Labor Movement in America, 1880–1960* (Cambridge, Mass., 1985), pp. 60–95.

91. *NYT*, 24 July 1910, 23 December 1910, 12 May 1912; *ITR*, 22 December 1910; Cahill, *Shorter Hours*, pp. 77–82.

92. On contracting, see "Eight Hours for Laborers on Government Work" (1903), p. 382.

93. *PI*, 12 December 1904; Tazewell, *Newport News*, pp. 48, 58.

94. *ME* 2 (1898): 37.

95. *NG*, 1 March 1900, 14 March 1901.

96. "Torpedo Boat Destroyers *Bainbridge, Barry,* and *Chauncey*" (Brief 1902), Howard E. Cornell Papers, Marine Historical Association of Mystic Seaport, Conn., Manuscript Collection, Box 2, Folder 2.

97. Ibid.; *MR*, 7 March 1901, 15 August 1901, 23 January 1902, 27 March 1902. See also U.S. Senate, Committee on Claims, "Relief of the Bath Iron Works and Others," 58th Cong., 2nd sess., Senate Document No. 112; "Trials of the United States Torpedo-Boat Destroyers *Bainbridge, Barry,* and *Chauncey*," *ME* 7 (1902): 545–48.

98. *MR*, 20 February 1902; L. E. Baldt, "Trial Performance of the United States Cruiser *St. Louis*," *ME* 11 (1906): 294–302.

99. *NG*, 14 March 1901; *MR*, 5 and 17 September 1901, 16 October 1901.

100. *Cornell, Appellant v Seddinger*, 237 Pennsylvania, pp. 394–95 (emphasis added).

101. Ibid., pp. 396–97.

102. Howard C. Johnson, "Bill [in the Case of S. B. Vrooman v. Neafie & Levy]," NA, RG 21, U.S. District Courts, Eastern District of Pennsylvania, Bankruptcy Cases, 1898–1924, Box 380, Case File No. 2122.

103. *PI*, 11 December 1904.

104. *PL*, 10, 11, and 13 December 1904.

105. *PL,* 26 September 1906; *NG,* 2 and 23 August 1906, 4 October 1906.

106. John Long to George Foss, 25 April 1902, reprinted in "Relief of the Bath Iron Works and Others," p. 141.

107. "New Steamship Kroonland," *ME* 7 (1902): 430–43.

108. *NG,* 29 June 1899, 18 October 1900, 2 May 1901, 8 and 29 August 1901, 24 October 1901, 9 September 1902, 30 April 1903, 8 December 1904; Norman Friedman, *U.S. Battleships: An Illustrated Design History* (Annapolis, Md., 1985), pp. 38–41; Ivan Musicant, *U.S. Armored Cruisers: A Design and Operational History* (Annapolis, Md., 1985), pp. 74–210.

109. U.S. House, Industrial Commission, "Report by the Industrial Commission on the Relations and Conditions of Capital and Labor Employed in Manufactures and General Business, Vol. 2," 57th Cong., 1st sess., House Document No. 183, p. 418 (hereafter cited as Industrial Commission Report).

110. Ibid., pp. 418–21; *Washington Post,* 18 January 1900.

111. *NYT,* 25 May 1898; Clive Trebilcock, *The Vickers Brothers: Armaments and Enterprise 1854–1914* (London, 1977), pp. 58–64, 135–37. See also Hugh B. Peebles, *Warshipbuilding on the Clyde: Naval Orders and the Prosperity of the Clyde Shipbuilding Industry, 1889–1939* (Edinburgh, 1987), pp. 46–67.

112. *NYT,* 15 and 26 February 1901; *MR,* 3 January 1901; *PI,* 8 and 21 December 1900; Industrial Commission Report, pp. 418–21; Trebilcock, *Vickers,* pp. 137–38.

113. *NG,* 8 February 1900; *PI,* 2 February 1901, 9, 14, 15, 17, 22, 31 May 1901, 16 June 1901; Robert Hessen, *Steel Titan: The Life of Charles Schwab* (New York, 1975), pp. 148, 164–67.

114. Augustus Buell, *Memoirs of Charles H. Cramp* (Philadelphia, 1906), p. 208. On final negotiations, see *PI,* 23 May 1901. On the Turkish cruiser *Medjidia,* see *NG,* 13 June 1901; *MR,* 23 July 1903; "Official Trial and Description of the Imperial Ottoman Cruiser *Medjidia,*" *ME* 9 (1904): 122–26.

115. *MR,* 11 July 1901; *PI,* 6 June 1901. Hessen, *Charles Schwab,* p. 148, argues that "Schwab had purchased Bethlehem for himself; it was an independent investment." According to Hessen, Schwab first discussed the plan to sell Bethlehem Steel to the U.S. Shipbuilding Co. on 12 June 1902, one year after the events discussed here. See, however, *PI,* 16 June 1901, which indicates that Schwab intended to buy Bethlehem to merge it with U.S. Shipbuilding.

116. *NYT,* 18 April 1903.

117. *NYT,* 21 April 1903.

118. *PL,* 28 June 1903.

119. *MR,* 22 August 1901, 5 December 1901, 23 January 1902; *Hours of Labor for Workmen on Public Works* (1900), p. 162.

120. *NG,* 5 June 1902; *PI,* 8, 10, 29 November 1902.

121. Harold U. Faulkner, *The Decline of Laissez Faire, 1897–1917* (New York, 1959), p. 27.

122. *NYT,* 27 June 1903.

123. Ibid.; see also *PI,* 19, 21, 23, 24 April 1903, 1 May 1903.

124. *PL*, 21 April 1903.

125. *PI*, 24 April 1903.

126. *PL*, 1 May 1903.

127. *PI*, 24 April 1903.

128. *NYT*, 3 November 1903; *MR*, 8 October 1903.

129. *NYT*, 31 March 1930; *NG*, 21 February 1907.

130. Quoted in *MR*, 2 June 1904.

131. *Eight Hours for Laborers on Government Work* (1908), p. 209.

132. *NG*, 12 October 1905; U.S. House, Committee on Naval Affairs, "Contracts for Armor Plate," 58th Cong., 3rd sess., House Document No. 351; Friedman, *U.S. Battleships*, pp. 43–47; Albion, *Makers of Naval Policy*, pp. 213–15; Cooling, *Gray Steel*, pp. 169–70.

133. William Cramp & Sons Ship and Engine Building Co., *Annual Reports, 1906–1914* (Philadelphia, 1906–14).

134. *Report of the Merchant Marine Commission . . . Vol. 3*, p. 1355.

135. Dickie, "Can the American Shipbuilder Compete," p. 192; *ITR*, 10 June 1909.

136. *NYT*, 5 January 1912.

137. Henderson B. Gregory, "United States Battleships *Wyoming* and *Arkansas*," *ME* 17 (1912): 397–404; *ME* 16 (1911): 495–98; *ME* 17 (1912): 12–14.

138. *NG*, 17 September 1908; *Report of the Merchant Marine Commission . . . Vol. 3*, pp. 1842–65.

139. *IA*, 15 August 1912; *ME* 19 (1914): 535–45.

140. The most detailed history of the U.S. Shipbuilding Company and the origins of Bethlehem Steel's shipbuilding division is still Arthur S. Dewing, *Corporate Promotions and Reorganizations* (Cambridge, Mass., 1914), pp. 464–509. On the history of Bethlehem Steel in the twentieth century, see Hessen, *Charles Schwab*. See also Schwarz and von Halle, *Schiffbauindustrie*, pp. 180–81.

141. *NG*, 11 November 1908 (quotation); *PI*, 24 October 1898.

142. *NG*, 29 May 1902, 31 March 1904; [Edward D. Swazey], *New York Shipbuilding Corporation: A Record of Ships Built* (New York, 1921), pp. 6–7, 32, 35; De La Pedraja, *Rise and Decline of U.S. Merchant Shipping*, pp. 23–29.

143. Swazey, *New York Shipbuilding Corporation*, pp. 17–18, 22–23; *ME* 17 (1912): 109–12.

144. *NG*, 14 January 1904, 27 August 1908; Swazey, *New York Shipbuilding Corporation*, pp. 20, 39.

145. *NG*, 11 August 1904, 11 January 1906; Swazey, *New York Shipbuilding Corporation*, pp. 14–15.

146. *NYT*, 7 and 14 January 1903, 4 February 1903; *NG*, 8 and 15 January 1903, 22 December 1904.

147. *NG*, 28 June 1906; Swazey, *New York Shipbuilding Corporation*, pp. 44–45.

148. Ibid., p. 47; *NYT*, 26 November 1911; *ME* 15 (1910): 220–21; Albion, *Makers of Naval Policy*, p. 216; Palmer, "Organizing the Shipyards," pp. 109–10.

149. Quoted in *NG*, 27 January 1910.

150. W. Irving Chambers to Secretary of the Navy, 14 May 1909, printed in U.S. Senate, "Battleships for the Argentine Republic," 62nd Cong., 1st sess., Senate Document No. 2., p. 5.

151. Ibid.

152. *ME* 17 (1912): 20–21; Frank Freidel, *Franklin D. Roosevelt: The Apprenticeship* (Boston, 1952), pp. 272–73. New York Ship also built the Chinese cruiser *Fei Hung;* see *ME* 19 (1914): 2627.

153. Tazewell, *Newport News*, pp. 77–78.

Seven: This Machine of War

1. *PB*, 2 June 1941.

2. E. A. Suverkrop, "The Building of the *Tuckahoe,*" *American Machinist* 49 (1918): 279–81.

3. John Russell Smith, *Influence of the Great War upon Shipping* (New York, 1919), pp. 26–48, 244–65; Hugh B. Peebles, *Warshipbuilding on the Clyde: Naval Orders and the Prosperity of the Clyde Shipbuilding Industry, 1889–1939* (Edinburgh, 1987), pp. 88–104.

4. René De La Pedraja, *The Rise and Decline of U.S. Merchant Shipping in the Twentieth Century* (New York, 1992), pp. 47–48; William J. Williams, "Shipbuilding and the Wilson Administration: The Development of Policy, 1914–1917" (Ph.D. diss., University of Washington, 1989), pp. 34–43; Jeffrey Safford, "World War I Maritime Policy and the National Security: 1914–1919," in *America's Maritime Legacy: A History of the U.S. Merchant Marine and Shipbuilding since Colonial Times,* ed. Robert A. Kilmarx (Boulder, Colo., 1979), pp. 116–17.

5. Winthrop Marvin, "American Shipbuilding—A Real Renaissance," *Review of Reviews* 56 (1917): 69–70; Smith, *Influence of the Great War*, p. 187.

6. Smith, *Influence of the Great War*, p. 64; Theodore Frey, "The Renaissance of American Shipbuilding," *Moody's Magazine* 19 (1916): 201–4; John G. B. Hutchins, "History and Development of the Shipbuilding Industry in the United States," in *The Shipbuilding Business in the United States, Vol. 1*, ed. F. G. Fasset (New York, 1948), p. 52; De La Pedraja, *Rise and Decline of U.S. Merchant Shipping*, pp. 47–48.

7. Mike Ratcliffe, *Liquid Gold Ships: A History of the Tanker* (London, 1985), pp. 70–71; Smith, *Influence of the Great War*, pp. 76–77; Rudy Abramson, *Spanning the Century: The Life of W. Averell Harriman* (New York, 1992), p. 119.

8. A. Selwyn-Brown, "The Shipping Boom," *Moody's Magazine* 19 (1916): 357–60; *MR* 46 (1916): 208.

9. Fritz von Twardowski, *Das Amerikanische Schiffahrtsproblem* (Berlin, 1922), pp. 62–63; *MR* 46 (1916): 211; Harry N. Scheiber, "World War I as Entrepreneurial Opportunity: William Straight and the American International Corporation," *Political Science Quarterly* 84 (1969): 486–511.

10. C. J. Stark, "A New American Merchant Marine," *MR* 46 (1916): 40–42; Charles A. Eaton, "Delaware River Shipyards—A Modern Miracle," *Review of Reviews* 58 (1918): 56; *MR* 46 (1916): 187–88.

11. Smith, *Influence of the Great War*, pp. 188–93; De La Pedraja, *Rise and Decline of U.S. Merchant Shipping*, pp. 47–54; Williams, "Shipbuilding and the Wilson Administration," pp. 45–54; Safford, "World War I Maritime Policy," pp. 117–23.

12. C. E. Wright, "America's Great Shipbuilding Development," *IA* 101 (1918): 15; Smith, *Influence of the Great War*, pp. 273–84; Safford, "World War I Maritime Policy," p. 124.

13. Smith, *Influence of the Great War*.

14. Newspaper clipping, 30 September 1915, Cramp File, Urban Archives, Temple University, Philadelphia; *Annual Report of the William Cramp & Sons Ship and Engine Building Co. to the Stockholders for the Year Ending April 30, 1916* (Philadelphia, 1916); *ME* 21 (1916): 422–23. On plant improvements in the wartime shipbuilding industry, see Hutchins, "History and Development," pp. 54–55.

15. Edgar C. Smith, *A Short History of Naval and Marine Engineering* (Cambridge, 1937), pp. 324–39; *ME* 22 (1917): 93–95.

16. Newspaper clippings, 29 December 1916, Cramp File, Urban Archives; *NYT*, 12 and 25 June 1915, 31 March 1930; *Annual Report of the William Cramp & Sons Ship and Engine Building Co. to the Stockholders for the Year Ending April 30, 1917* (Philadelphia, 1917).

17. U.S. Senate, Committee on Commerce, *United States Shipping Board Emergency Fleet Corporation*, 65th Cong., 2nd sess. (Washington, D.C., 1918), p. 133 (hereafter cited as Shipping Board Report).

18. John D. Alden, *Flush Decks and Four Pipes* (Annapolis, Md., 1965); Norman Friedman, *U.S. Destroyers: An Illustrated Design History* (Annapolis, Md., 1982), pp. 39–47.

19. *Cramp's Shipyard War Activities* (Philadelphia, 1919), pp. 17–19.

20. Ibid.; *Activities of the Bureau of Yards and Docks, Navy Department: World War, 1917–1918* (Washington, D.C., 1921), p. 217.

21. *Cramp's Shipyard War Activities*, pp. 15–17; *MR* 49 (1919): 351.

22. *ME* 26 (1921): 209–10; Friedman, *U.S. Destroyers*, p. 41.

23. New York Ship also booked contracts for the slightly larger *Gulfqueen* class, featuring 436-foot hulls, as well as 395-foot *Plymouth*-class colliers; [Edward Swazey], *New York Shipbuilding Corporation—A Record of Ships Built* (New York, 1921), pp. 22–24.

24. *Annual Report of the New York Shipbuilding Corporation—Year Ended December 31, 1918* (New York, 1919), pp. 8–10; *Fifty Years, New York Shipbuilding Corporation, Camden, N.J.* (Camden, N.J., 1949), p. 32.

25. *NYT*, 10 April 1924, 25 October 1927; *Annual Report of the New York Shipbuilding Corporation: Year Ended December 31, 1917* (New York, 1918), p. 2.

26. *Annual Report of the New York Shipbuilding Corporation: Year Ended December 31, 1917*, pp. 5–6; *ME* 25 (1920): 243–45.

27. Shipping Board Report, pp. 137–38.

28. *ME* 25 (1920): 245–51; *War Activities of the Bureau of Yards and Docks*, pp. 217, 224–27.

29. *War Activities of the Bureau of Yards and Docks,* p. 227; *ME* 25 (1920): 254–57; Shipping Board Report, p. 645; *YN,* May 1920.

30. *MR* 47 (1917): 200.

31. Eaton, "Delaware River Shipyards," pp. 56–57; Shipping Board Report, p. 1958; R. H. Robinson, "Fabricated Ships," *ME* 22 (1917): 549.

32. Robinson, "Fabricated Ships," p. 550.

33. Ibid.; *EFN,* 1 January 1919. See also Wright, "America's Great Shipbuilding Development," p. 13; *IA,* 31 August 1916; Abramson, *Spanning the Century,* pp. 115–16.

34. *ME* 23 (1918): 177; *MR* (1916): 220; *ENR* 82 (1919): 57–61; Eaton, "Delaware River Shipyards," p. 57; Robert Haig, "Sun Shipbuilding & Dry Dock Company," in *Historical Transactions,* ed. Society of Naval Architects and Marine Engineers (New York, 1943), p. 236.

35. Shipping Board Report, pp. 140–41.

36. *IA,* 21 September 1916; Eaton, "Delaware River Shipyards," pp. 57–58; Shipping Board Report, pp. 137–39.

37. *War Activities of the Bureau of Yards and Docks,* p. 239.

38. Ibid., pp. 184–89, 242–44; "The Philadelphia Navy Yard," in *Historical Transactions,* p. 25.

39. R. E. Bakenhus, "Development of Shipyards in the United States during the Great War," *TSNAME* 27 (1919): 29; "American Shipyards and Marine Repair Plants," *ME* 21 (1916): 113–44; *IA,* 23 August 1917, p. 441.

40. W. H. Rigg, "Standardization as Affecting the Shipbuilding Industry in the United States," *TSNAME* 30 (1922): 218.

41. R. D. Gatewood, "Pre-Assembly in Ship Construction," *American Machinist* 52 (1920): 1–6; Shipping Board Report, p. 1403.

42. Rigg, "Standardization," p. 219.

43. Ibid., p. 209.

44. Ibid., p. 217.

45. *IA,* 19 September 1918.

46. W. H. Blood, "Hog Island, the Greatest Shipyard in the World," *TSNAME* 26 (1918): 243–44. Abramson argues that the EFC assembly project was outlined in a plan for prefabricated freighter construction conceived by Harriman and his chief advisor Richard H. Robinson; Robinson himself believed that the credit belonged to Charles Jack. See Abramson, *Spanning the Century,* pp. 116–18.

47. *IA,* 14 February 1918; see also Blood, "Hog Island," pp. 244–45.

48. Blood, "Hog Island," p. 118; Robert E. Kline, "Who Will Build the Fabricated Ships?" *ME* 23 (1918): 55–56.

49. Shipping Board Report, p. 1961.

50. Ibid.

51. Quoted in Smith, *Influence of the Great War,* p. 226; see also *ME* 24 (1919): 71–74.

52. Shipping Board Report, pp. 245–58.

53. *IA,* 11 April 1918. For the list of contractors, see *MR* 48 (1918): 411; Leyburn

Fishach, "Inland Ship-Steel Fabricating Plants of the Emergency Fleet Corporation," *ENR* 82 (1919): 332–36. See also *ENR* 81 (1918): 5–12.

54. Blood, "Hog Island," pp. 246–50; *MR* 48 (1918): 277–79.

55. U.S. Department of Justice, *Report of the Investigation of the Hog Island Shipyard* (Washington, D.C., 1918), pp. 11–12. On railroad congestion, see also Smith, *Influence of the Great War*, pp. 205–8.

56. Suspecting excessive profiteering and fraud, Congress and the Justice Department launched investigations but failed to detect criminal wrongdoing. See U.S. Senate, Committee on Commerce, *Hearing before the Committee on Commerce, Part 8*, 65th Cong., 3rd sess. (Washington, D.C., 1919) (hereafter cited as Hog Island Hearing); U.S. Department of Justice, *Report of the Investigation of the Hog Island Shipyard*.

57. Quoted in Hog Island Hearing, p. 385.

58. "Fabricated-Ship Construction in One Year's Experience," *ENR* 82 (1919): 16–17.

59. Shipping Board Report, p. 285.

60. Hog Island Hearing, p. 270; Blood, "Hog Island," p. 247.

61. Blood, "Hog Island," pp. 224–38; *EFN*, 11 March 1918.

62. Shipping Board Report, p. 1740.

63. Ibid., p. 1410.

64. Contract reprinted in Shipping Board Report, pp. 763–75. On dredging, see ibid., pp. 1597–99. See also *ENR* 80 (1918): 17–19; *ME* 23 (1918): 538–39; Abramson, *Spanning the Century*, pp. 118–21. On Westinghouse's Essington works, see *MR* 48 (1918): 349–52.

65. Contract reprinted in Shipping Board Report, pp. 747–63. See also *ME* 22 (1917): 551; *ME* 23 (1918): 9; *MR* 49 (1919): 151.

66. Hog Island Hearing, pp. 267–70.

67. Shipping Board Report, p. 619.

68. U.S. House, Committee on Naval Affairs, *Cost of Naval Preparedness Program*, 64th Cong., 2nd sess. (Washington, D.C., 1917), p. 1091.

69. Smith, *Influence of the Great War*, p. 271.

70. *Cost of Naval Preparedness*, p. 1084; *IA*, 21 December 1916; *War Activities of the Bureau of Yards and Docks*, p. 501. See also David Palmer, "Organizing the Shipyards: Unionization at New York Ship, Federal Ship, and Fore River, 1898–1945" (Ph.D. diss., Brandeis University, 1990), p. 198.

71. *Cost of Naval Preparedness*, p. 1091.

72. Palmer, "Organizing the Shipyards," p. 152.

73. Shipping Board Report, p. 646.

74. *EFN*, 21 November 1918; *YN*, 15 April 1919; Palmer, "Organizing the Shipyards," pp. 199–202. New York Ship launched an Americanization campaign prodding foreigners to learn English and apply for U.S. citizenship; see *YN*, December 1919, February 1920.

75. Shipping Board Report, p. 467.

76. Ibid., p. 646.

77. Ibid., p. 813.

78. Ibid., p. 172.

79. *PL*, 17 January 1921. See also David Montgomery, *Workers' Control in America* (Cambridge, England, 1979), p. 98.

80. S. M. Evans, *A Discussion of Conditions Affecting Ship Production, April to December, 1918* (Washington, D.C., 1918), p. 52.

81. National Industrial Conference Board, *Works Councils in the United States* (Boston, 1919), pp. 87–93, 131; *PL*, 17 January 1921.

82. William Hotchkiss and Henry Seager, *History of the Shipbuilding Labor Adjustment Board, 1917 to 1919* (Washington, D.C., 1921), p. 29.

83. Douglas and Wolfe, "Labor Administration," p. 312.

84. Shipping Board Report, pp. 2190–98; Hotchkiss and Seager, *Shipbuilding Labor Adjustment Board*, pp. 24–28, 96–97.

85. Shipping Board Report, p. 1802.

86. *EFN*, 6 May 1918; *YN*, 30 April 1919, December 1919; *Annual Report of the New York Shipbuilding Corporation 1918*, p. 7; Richard S. Childs, "First War Emergency Government Towns for Shipyard Workers: Yorkship Village at Camden, N.J.," *Journal of the American Institute of Architects* 6 (1918): 237–44, 249–51; *War Activities of the Bureau of Yards and Docks*, p. 501. Despite appalling housing conditions in wartime Philadelphia, the federal government did not finance similar projects in the city. This foreshadowed federal housing policy during the 1930s, which redlined old urban centers and facilitated suburban expansion; see Kenneth T. Jackson, *Crabgrass Frontier: The Suburbanization of the United States* (New York, 1985), pp. 190–218.

87. *YN*, August 1919 and passim; David Brody, "The Rise and Decline of Welfare Capitalism," in *Workers in Industrial America: Essays on the Twentieth-Century Struggle*, ed. David Brody (New York, 1980), pp. 48–81.

88. *EFN*, 10 June 1918.

89. *NYT*, 21 September 1918; see also Douglas and Wolfe, "Labor Administration," pp. 325–26.

90. Shipping Board Report, p. 1624. To be fair, it should be noted that Hog Island was probably better off than the fabrication yard at Newark Bay, which had an estimated rat population of more than 1 million.

91. Dudley R. Kennedy, "Employment of Labor," *Journal of the American Society of Mechanical Engineers* 40 (1918): 1030–31.

92. *ARCN* (1919), p. 13.

Eight: What Next?

1. *PI*, 5 October 1927.

2. Philip Scranton, "Large Firms and Industrial Restructuring: The Philadelphia Region, 1900–1980," *PMHB* 116 (1992): 438.

3. For a statement of "technological pessimism," see the classic work by Joseph Schumpeter, *Business Cycles: A Theoretical, Historical and Statistical Analysis of the Capitalist Process* (New York, 1939).

4. *Engineering and Contracting* 50 (1918): 295.

5. *ME* 24 (1919): 313–14.

6. *EFN*, 5 December 1918.

7. *ARCN* (1919), p. 19.

8. Cited in René De La Pedraja, *The Rise and Decline of U.S. Merchant Shipping in the Twentieth Century* (New York, 1992), p. 60.

9. *Fifth Annual Report of the United States Shipping Board* (Washington, D.C., 1921), pp. 130–32; see also U.S. Senate, Committee on Commerce, *United States Shipping Board Emergency Fleet Corporation*, 65th Cong., 2nd sess. (Washington, D.C., 1918), pp. 1993–94.

10. John H. Kemble and Lane C. Kendall, "The Years between the Wars," in *America's Maritime Legacy: A History of the U.S. Merchant Marine and Shipbuilding since Colonial Times*, ed. Robert A. Kilmarx (Boulder, Colo., 1979), p. 151.

11. John M. Keynes, *The Economic Consequences of Peace* (London, 1920), p. 61.

12. Günter Leckebusch, *Die Beziehungen der deutschen Seeschiffswerften zur Eisenindustrie an der Ruhr in der Zeit von 1850 bis 1930* (Cologne, 1963), pp. 95–111.

13. De La Pedraja, *Rise and Decline of U.S. Merchant Shipping*, pp. 59–62.

14. Ibid.

15. On Harriman's maritime enterprise, see V. G. Iden, "W. A. Harriman," *MR* 51 (1921): 121–27, 175–81.

16. Ibid., pp. 177–80; *MR* 24 (August 1919): 567; newspaper clipping, 16 July 1919, Cramp File, Urban Archives, Temple University, Philadelphia. Rudy Abramson, *Spanning the Century: W. Averell Harriman, 1891–1986* (New York, 1992), pp. 123–25, provides a detailed account of Harriman's merger strategy.

17. Abramson, *Spanning the Century*, pp. 125–30; Iden, "Harriman," p. 126; Frederick E. Emmons, *American Passenger Ships: The Ocean Lines and Liners, 1873–1983* (Newark, Del., 1985), pp. 37–38.

18. Emmons, *American Passenger Ships*, pp. 37–38; Abramson, *Spanning the Century*, pp. 131–33.

19. Abramson, *Spanning the Century*, pp. 136–38; *MR*, September 1926; Emmons, *American Passenger Ships*, pp. 37–39. One may speculate that the HAPAG management saw UAL from the beginning as a useful but expendable instrument to gain access to the North Atlantic trade until its new German liners were ready for service. Moreover, the German line was the original owner of the *Resolute* and *Reliance*, which had been launched as HAPAG vessels in 1914 and then transferred to a Dutch line that later sold them to Harriman; the sale of UAL, which returned these liners to HAPAG's fleet, was in effect a return to the prewar status quo.

20. De La Pedraja, *Rise and Decline of the U.S. Merchant Marine*, pp. 32–33; Abramson, *Spanning the Century*, p. 134.

21. *ARCN* (1921), p. 5 (emphasis in original).

22. Kemble and Kendall, "The Years between the Wars," p. 151; *ARCN* (1923), p. 3.

23. Mike Ratcliffe, *Liquid Gold Ships: A History of the Tanker* (London, 1985), pp. 70–72; *MR*, April 1927, p. 32.

24. Kemble and Kendall, "The Years between the Wars," p. 156.

25. Christopher Hall, *Britain, America and Arms Control* (New York, 1987), pp. 1–35; *MR* 52 (1922): 1–4; *MR* 54 (1924): 330–32.

26. A. Slaven, "A Shipyard in Depression: John Browns of Clydebank 1919–1938," *Business History* 19 (1977): 192–217; Jonathan Zeitlin, *Between Flexibility and Mass Production: Strategic Debate and Industrial Reorganization in British Engineering, 1830–1990* (New York, forthcoming), chap. 4. After the war HAPAG launched a ship assembly yard at Hamburg in cooperation with the Gutehoffnungshütte steel corporation and the Allgemeine Electricitäts Gesellschaft engineering corporation. Like Hog Island, it failed because the builders were unable to coordinate ship fabrication and assembly: the structural steel shops in the Ruhr area were located several hundred miles from the assembly yard at Hamburg. See Leckebusch, *Die Beziehungen der deutschen Seeschiffswerften*, pp. 95–111.

27. *PL*, 5 February 1921.

28. Silas Bent, "Hog Island Goes on the Remnant Counter," *NYT Magazine*, 23 August 1925, pp. 4–5; *Seventh Annual Report of the United States Shipping Board* (Washington, D.C., 1923), pp. 11–12; *Ninth Annual Report of the United States Shipping Board* (Washington, D.C., 1925), p. 8; *Fourteenth Annual Report of the United States Shipping Board* (Washington, D.C., 1930), pp. 4–5.

29. *ME* 52 (1922): 93–99.

30. *ME* 51 (1921): 491.

31. William Hotchkiss and Henry Seager, *History of the Shipbuilding Labor Adjustment Board 1917 to 1919* (Washington, D.C., 1921), p. 25.

32. Ibid.; *NYT*, 6 June 1919.

33. *ME* 52 (1922): 272.

34. *MR* 54 (1924): 283–84; *ME* 27 (1922): 383–85.

35. *ME* 26 (1921): 419. See also *MR* 51 (1921): 281.

36. *NYT*, 2 January 1923; Abramson, *Spanning the Century*, p. 131.

37. *PL*, 21 February 1921; William Collins, "History of Bethlehem's Wilmington Plant," in *Historical Transactions*, ed. Society of Naval Architects and Marine Engineers (New York, 1945), p. 212. On other closures, see Kemble and Kendall, "The Years between the Wars," p. 174.

38. *Annual Report of the William Cramp Ship & Engine Building Company for the Year Ended 1919* (Philadelphia, 1920).

39. *PL*, 17 January 1921 (quotations). On discharges, see *MMJ*, March 1921, p. 264; *BMISBJ*, February 1921, p. 56.

40. *MR* 51 (1921): 128; Hotchkiss, *Shipbuilding Labor Adjustment Board*, pp. 78–86; David Palmer, "Organizing the Shipyards: Unionization at New York Ship, Federal Ship, and Fore River, 1898–1945" (Ph.D. diss., Brandeis University, 1990), pp. 224–27; David Montgomery, *Workers' Control in America* (Cambridge, England, 1979), p. 99.

41. *MMJ*, March 1921, p. 264; *BMISBJ*, July 1921, p. 275; Howell Harris, "Employers' Collective Action in the Open-Shop Era: The Metal Manufacturers' Association of Philadelphia c. 1903–1933," in *The Power to Manage? Employers and Industrial Relations*

in Comparative-Historical Perspective, ed. Steven Tolliday and Jonathan Zeitlin (London, 1991), pp. 134–36.

42. *PL,* 4 February 1921.

43. *BMISBJ,* April 1921, p. 174.

44. *PL,* 20 February 1921; see also *MMJ,* April 1921, p. 337.

45. *MMJ,* May 1921, p. 420 (quotation). See also *PL,* 10, 20, 21 February 1921.

46. *MMJ,* March 1921, p. 264.

47. *MMJ,* April 1921, pp. 317–18, 336; *MMJ,* July 1921, pp. 588–89.

48. *BMISBJ,* July 1921, p. 275.

49. *MMJ,* October 1921, p. 822.

50. Palmer, "Organizing the Shipyards," p. 241; David Montgomery, *The Fall of the House of Labor: The Workplace, the State, and American Labor Activism, 1865–1925* (Cambridge, Mass., 1987), pp. 450–52.

51. *MMJ,* September 1921, p. 771.

52. *MR* 51 (1921): 464.

53. Ibid.

54. *Annual Report of the William Cramp Ship & Engine Building Company for the Year Ended December 31st, 1921* (Philadelphia, 1922). The Muscle Shoals project had been established in 1916 to provide electrical power for government-owned nitrate works and was a model for the Tennessee Valley Authority.

55. *NYT,* 26 March 1923; *Annual Report of the William Cramp Ship & Engine Building Company for the Year Ended December 31st, 1922* (Philadelphia, 1923).

56. *Annual Report of the William Cramp Ship & Engine Building Company for the Year Ended December 31st, 1924* (Philadelphia, 1925).

57. *NYT,* 17 April 1927.

58. *MR* 55 (1925): 110, 213–14, 261, 374; *MR,* July 1926, pp. 36–37; Emmons, *American Passenger Steamers,* p. 59.

59. *Annual Report of the William Cramp Ship & Engine Building Company for the Year Ended December 31st, 1925* (Philadelphia, 1926); *PL,* 30 April 1926; U.S. Congress, *Munitions Industry: Naval Shipbuilding,* 74th Cong., 1st sess. (Washington, D.C., 1935), p. 21.

60. *PI,* 17 April 1927.

61. Ibid.; see also newspaper clippings, 16 and 20 April 1927, Cramp File, Urban Archives.

62. *ME* 32 (1927): 247.

63. Ibid.

64. *Annual Report of the New York Shipbuilding Corporation—Year Ended December 31, 1918* (New York, 1919), pp. 8–10; *NYT,* 18 March 1923; *Fifty Years, New York Shipbuilding Corporation, Camden N.J.* (Camden, N.J., 1949), pp. 35–36.

65. Norman Friedman, *U.S. Aircraft Carriers: An Illustrated Design History* (Annapolis, Md., 1983), pp. 31–41; Robert Stern, *The Lexington Class Carriers* (Annapolis, Md., 1993), pp. 13–30.

66. Stern, *The Lexington Class Carriers,* pp. 30–35.

67. *Dictionary of American Naval Fighting Ships, Vol. 4* (Washington, D.C., 1976), pp. 339–42.

68. *NYT,* 19 March 1924, 3 and 4 April 1924, 31 March 1925; *Fifty Years New York Shipbuilding Corporation,* p. 35.

69. *NYT,* 22 August 1925.

70. *NYT,* 27 January 1925, 31 March 1925, 24 September 1925.

71. Charles Bardo to unknown correspondent, 18 October 1934, printed in *Munitions Industry,* p. 148.

72. *MR,* March 1927, p. 19.

73. *Munitions Industry,* p. 21.

74. American Brown & Bovery to Andrew Mellon, 15 April 1927, printed in *Munitions Industry,* p. 27.

75. Ibid., p. 21.

76. U.S. Senate, Committee on Naval Affairs, *Alleged Activities at the Geneva Conference,* 71st Cong., 1st sess. (Washington, D.C., 1929). Shearer's contribution to the failure of the Geneva Conference involving the United States, Britain, and Japan was probably marginal; a more important factor was the refusal of the American delegation to agree to Britain's demands for a relatively large cruiser force. See Hall, *Britain, America and Arms Control,* pp. 36–58, 75–76.

77. On lobbying, see *Munitions Industry,* p. 7.

78. Kemble and Kendall, "The Years between the Wars," pp. 160–61; Hutchins, "History and Development," p. 56.

79. *Munitions Industry,* p. 149.

Epilogue

1. Newspaper clipping, 1939, Cramp File, Urban Archives, Temple University, Philadelphia.

2. H. E. Gould, "History of Bethlehem's Fore River Yard," in *Historical Transactions,* ed. Society of Naval Architects and Marine Engineers (New York, 1945), p. 203; Ron Chernow, *The House of Morgan: An American Banking Dynasty and the Rise of Modern Finance* (New York, 1990), pp. 66–67; Lothar Gall et al., *Die Deutsche Bank, 1870–1995* (Munich, 1995), pp. 26–52.

3. Lars U. Scholl, "Shipping Business in Germany in the Nineteenth and Twentieth Centuries," in *Business History of Shipping: Proceedings of the Fuji Conference,* ed. Tsunehiko Yui and Keiichiro Nakagawa (Tokyo, 1985), pp. 193–205.

4. Ibid.

5. "Production System Bethlehem-Fairfield Yard," *ME* 47 (October 1942): 178–97; "Fabricating Shop Operations at Bethlehem-Fairfield Shipyard," *ME* 49 (February 1944): 140–51. William Chamlein, *Shipbuilding Policies of the War Production Board, January 1942–November 1945* (Washington, D.C., 1947).

6. Newspaper clippings 1940–67, Cramp File, Urban Archives; *Fifty Years, New York Shipbuilding Corporation, Camden, N.J.* (Camden, N.J., 1949); *NYT,* 25 March 1967, 3 September 1967, 11 May 1967.

7. *PI,* 12 April 1991.

8. *PI,* 27 January 1990, 14 April 1991, 24 May 1991, 23 June 1991.

This essay provides an overview of the most important primary and secondary sources. It is intended as a guide for further research and does not include all sources cited in the notes.

The possibilities for new scholarship in shipyard studies are exciting. Bethlehem Steel's shipbuilding division, whose extensive archives are now open for research, still awaits its historian. Specialists in African American history and the history of technology should examine Newport News Shipbuilding, the first major employer of black industrial labor in the New South, which is today the nation's only shipyard equipped to build nuclear-powered aircraft carriers. Anyone interested in mass-production technology will find a rewarding subject in the World War II Liberty-ship program. Once we have all the pieces, we may be able to put the puzzle together in a comprehensive history of the American iron and steel shipbuilding industry.

Manuscript Collections

Reflecting the prominent role of government contracting, the National Archives in Washington, D.C., holds the most important manuscript collections on American shipbuilding. These records are indispensable for anyone researching the history of private shipyards, navy yards, and warship construction. Most material is indexed in *Preliminary Inventory of the National Archives* (Washington, D.C., 1940) by record group (RG) number. Detailed correspondence between the Navy Department and private shipbuilders, armor producers, and ordnance contractors can be found in RG 19 (Records of the Bureau of Ships). In addition to documenting naval construction, this material provides nuggets of information on private shipbuilding firms with scanty company records. Material on navy yards is held at the National Archives facility in Suitland, Maryland, under RG 71 (Records of the Bureau of Yards and Docks). It can be supplemented by material from RG 181, maintained by regional divisions of the National Archives. The National Archives Architectural and Cartographic Division in Alexandria, Virginia, holds a large collection of construction drawings and a few hull specification ledgers in RG 129.

The "Record of Metal Vessels Built in the U.S." (National Archives, Washington, D.C., RG 41, Entry 129) is an invaluable source for historians of iron and steel shipbuilding. This ledger—which I have not seen cited anywhere in the secondary literature—contains information on every commercial metal ship built and registered in the

United States from 1825 to 1919, including name, rig, gross tonnage, year built, place of construction, and home port. Unlike any other source, the "Record" consistently lists the *builder* in every entry. Anyone trying to compile a complete, year-by-year hull construction list for a particular iron and steel shipyard through World War I—a critical but often frustrating task because even the best company records are usually incomplete—will be able to do so using this source.

The National Archives, Mid-Atlantic Region, Philadelphia, has an important collection of U.S. Shipping Board records, including a monumental and well-documented study of the Hog Island assembly yard conducted during the 1920s. U.S. District Court records held at these branch archives include bankruptcy files pertaining to Neafie & Levy and other local firms. There is also a microfilm copy of the Manufacturing Census for Philadelphia County; the 1850 and 1880 returns provide the most reliable data.

The best collection of company records, hull construction ledgers, engineering drawings, and photographs is the Cramp Collection at the Independence Seaport Museum. In addition to material cited in this study, it contains hitherto unused sources on Cramp's World War II shipbuilding record. For a concise introduction to the collection, see *Shipbuilding at Cramp & Sons: A History and Guide of the William Cramp & Sons Ship and Engine Building Company (1830–1927) and the Cramp Shipbuilding Company (1940–1946) of Philadelphia,* ed. Gail E. Farr (Philadelphia, 1991). Moreover, the Independence Seaport Museum holds a collection of photographs of the New York Shipbuilding Company and some material on the Philadelphia Navy Yard.

Other collections are held by Philadelphia-area archives, including the Hexamer Insurance Records at the Free Library of Philadelphia; the Pennsylvania Railroad Collection at the Urban Archives, Temple University, with business records of the American Steamship Company; and company records pertaining to local shipbuilding firms and steamship lines, held by the Historical Society of Pennsylvania, Philadelphia. The Hagley Museum and Library in Wilmington, Delaware, holds the important Philadelphia & Reading Railroad Company Collection that contains material on colliers and shipping operations. The Marine Historical Society at Mystic Seaport, Connecticut, has some Neafie & Levy company records as well as manuscript material on other nineteenth-century shipbuilding firms. The largest collection of photographs of naval vessels and shipyards involved in naval construction is maintained by the U.S. Naval Historical Institute at the Washington Navy Yard, Washington, D.C., which also holds an extensive collection of secondary literature on warships, naval shipbuilding, and the merchant marine.

Published Government Reports

The best executive-branch report on nineteenth-century shipbuilding is Henry Hall, *Report on the Shipbuilding Industry of the United States* (Washington, D.C., 1882), analyzing the 1880 Manufacturing Census in the context of long-term trends. Comprehensive, year-by-year overviews of commercial shipping and shipbuilding were published in the *Annual Report of the U.S. Commissioner of Navigation,* first issued for fiscal year

1884. Information on naval contracting may be obtained from the *Annual Report of the Secretary of the Navy*, with statistics and special reports by bureau chiefs. The Pennsylvania Department of the Interior published an excellent study of Delaware Valley shipbuilding in *Annual Report of the Bureau of Industrial Statistics (for 1891), Part C.*

The federal legislative branch reviewed maritime and naval policy. Congressional committees—notably the committees on naval affairs, the merchant marine, commerce, and labor—frequently invited shipbuilders, steamship managers, and shipyard employees to hearings where stenographers recorded their testimony. Most committee reports were published in the vast Congressional Hearings Series and are listed in *CIS U.S. Congressional Committee Hearings Index*, 42 vols. (Washington, D.C., 1981–85).

Major hearings pertaining to commercial shipping and shipbuilding are U.S. House Select Committee, *Report of the Select Committee on the Causes of the Reduction of American Tonnage*, 41st Cong., 2nd sess., House Report No. 28 ("Lynch Report"); U.S. House Committee on Merchant Marine and Fisheries, *American Merchant Marine in the Foreign Trade*, 51st Cong., 1st sess., House Report No. 1210 ("Farquhar Report"); and U.S. Congress, *Report of the Merchant Marine Commission, Together with Testimony Taken at the Hearings*, 3 vols., 58th Cong., 1st sess., 1905. World War I government shipbuilding programs are discussed in the monumental (though rarely used) hearing, U.S. Senate Committee on Commerce, *United States Shipping Board Emergency Fleet Corporation*, 65th Cong., 2nd sess., 1919. The origins of American battleship construction are detailed in U.S. House Committee on Naval Affairs, *The Vessels of the New Navy: Hearing on the Subject of the Policy of Naval Reconstruction*, 51st Cong., 1st sess., 1890. The rarely used material printed in U.S. Congress, *Munitions Industry: Naval Shipbuilding*, 74th Cong., 1st sess., 1935, collected during the Nye Committee investigation of the World War I munitions industry, contains valuable information on wartime contracting, price fixing during the 1920s, and profiteering in naval shipbuilding.

Work on government contracts raised the question of federal labor standards, discussed during "Eight-Hour Hearings," which contain interesting facts on capital-labor relations, work at the shop-floor level, and shipyard trade unions. The most interesting hearings are: U.S. Senate Committee on Education and Labor, *Eight Hours for Laborers on Government Work*, 57th Cong., 2nd sess., Senate Document No. 141; and U.S. Senate Committee on Education and Labor, *Eight Hours for Laborers on Government Work*, 58th Cong., 2nd sess., 1904.

Company Publications

Most major shipyards issued their own publications. Books and booklets used for this study include *The Neafie & Levy Ship and Engine Building Company* (New York, 1896); *Cramp's Shipyard Founded by William Cramp* (Philadelphia, 1902); *Cramp's Shipyard War Activities* (Philadelphia, 1920); *New York Shipbuilding Corporation—A Record of Ships Built* (New York, 1921); and *Fifty Years New York Shipbuilding Corporation, Camden, N.J.* (Camden, 1949). See also the detailed *Semi-Centennial Memoir of the Harlan & Hollingsworth Company* (Wilmington, Del., 1886).

From 1903 to 1926, Cramp printed annual statements to shareholders, which included balance sheets and reports on business activities. New York Ship published its first annual report in 1916. (When these were unavailable, I consulted *Iron Age* and the *New York Times* for short summaries of directors' reports at shareholders meetings.)

To improve labor relations during World War I, some yards published short-lived company newspapers. New York Ship's *Yorkship News,* available at the Library of Congress, contains detailed recollections of older employees and reports on plant development, shop equipment, and corporate welfare policies.

Newspapers, Periodicals, and Journals

Since shipbuilding received more newspaper coverage than most other industries, scanning reels of newspaper microfilms is often quite rewarding. For labor and business historians, the most useful local daily is the Philadelphia *Public Ledger,* which published frequent reports on shipbuilding and other Philadelphia industries; researching the post-1900 period is comparatively easy using an index available at the Free Library of Philadelphia. Other dailies consulted for this study include the *Philadelphia Inquirer, Philadelphia Press, Philadelphia Record, Philadelphia Bulletin,* and *New York Times.* For the post-1900 period, an extensive collection of newspaper clippings is available in the Urban Archives at Temple University.

The most valuable weekly publication for the period from 1871 to 1900 is the *Nautical Gazette,* which printed summaries of construction activities in wooden shipbuilding and iron shipbuilding districts, reports on steamship trial trips, and detailed descriptions of major yards. *Marine Review,* sporadically published as a weekly after the turn of the century, concentrated on Great Lakes matters but also reported on seaboard yards and steamship lines. Toward the end of World War I, the Shipping Board published the weekly *Emergency Fleet News,* which gave detailed reports on construction of noncombat vessels, shipyards, and industrial relations.

Marine Engineering is the best monthly shipyard engineering journal available for the period after 1900. Articles examine technical aspects of the shipbuilding process, practical experiences with new shipyard equipment, trial trips, and new marine technologies. Devoted to general engineering, *Cassier's Magazine* and *Engineering Magazine* published summaries of recent developments in marine engineering and naval architecture. Shorter and more readable articles in *Harper's New Monthly Magazine* provide good introductions to shipyard engineering and craftsmanship.

The most important labor periodicals used in this study are the *Boilermakers and Iron Shipbuilders Journal* and the *Machinists Monthly Journal.* Together with conference reports of annual trade union conventions, they provide vital information on labor politics and union locals.

No maritime historian can do without the yearly *Transactions of the Society of Naval Architects and Marine Engineers,* which published papers presented at the annual meeting of the society beginning in 1893, including an important series on the history of

American iron and steel shipbuilding written by Charles Cramp. Also useful but very technical is *Proceedings of the United States Naval Institute.*

Nineteenth- and Early Twentieth-century Books

Although few nineteenth-century books deal extensively with American shipbuilding, some information may be gleaned from publications on shipping, marine engineering, and public policy. These include William W. Bates, *American Marine: The Shipping Question in History and Politics* (Boston, 1892); Frank Bennett, *The Steam Navy of the United States* (Pittsburgh, 1896); and J. D. Kelley, *The Question of Ships: The Navy and the Merchant Marine* (New York, 1884). Samuel W. Stanton's *American Steam Vessels* (New York, 1895) includes handsome illustrations of famous American steamships. British studies are much more detailed, especially John Grantham's classic work *Iron Ship-Building, With Practical Illustrations* (London, 1858).

Books on local and regional industries often yield good information on individual firms. For the Delaware Valley, see especially Charles Robson, *The Manufactories and Manufacturers of Pennsylvania in the Nineteenth Century* (Philadelphia, 1875). Industry directories and handbooks provide useful listings of smaller firms; these include *The Philadelphia Maritime Directory* (Philadelphia, 1890); and *The Philadelphia Shipping Manual* (Philadelphia, 1880).

The period from 1900 to the 1920s produced several important books. Augustus Buell, *The Memoirs of Charles H. Cramp* (Philadelphia, 1906), provides a general overview of Delaware Valley iron and steel shipbuilding. It consists mainly of articles written by Charles Cramp, which are usually reliable, but some of Buell's own comments are factually incorrect. Somewhat useful is Edward Hurley's account of World War I shipbuilding, *The Bridge to France* (Philadelphia, 1927), but readers should keep in mind that the author tried to whitewash his record as chairman of the U.S. Shipping Board.

Industry studies written during the early twentieth century are generally reliable. Tjark Schwarz and Ernst von Halle, *Die Schiffbauindustrie in Deutschland und im Auslande* (Berlin, 1902), an analysis of German, British, and American shipbuilding, contains detailed information on Delaware Valley yards. Another excellent comparative study is John R. Smith, *The Influence of the Great War upon Shipping*, which examines American and British maritime economics, commercial shipping, and wartime shipbuilding programs. Smith's book should be read together with S. M. Evans, *A Discussion of Conditions Affecting Ship Production, April to December, 1918* (Washington, D.C., 1918). Fritz von Twardowski, *Das Amerikanische Schiffahrtsproblem* (Berlin, 1922), is a critical study of American wartime shipping and shipbuilding containing useful statistics.

The labor process is described in meticulous detail in Roy W. Kelly and Frederick Allen, *The Shipbuilding Industry* (New York, 1918). The authors examine skill requirements and worker training for virtually every shipyard trade as well as most trades in subcontracting industries. Wartime industrial relations and collective bargaining structures are discussed in William Hotchkiss and Henry Seager, *History of the Shipyard Labor Adjustment Board, 1917 to 1919* (Washington, D.C., 1921).

Modern Studies

There are many fine shorter studies of various aspects of the industry, which are not listed here but are cited in the notes to the text. John G. B. Hutchins's monumental *American Maritime Industries and Public Policy, 1789–1914: An Economic History* (Cambridge, Mass., 1941) is still essential for anyone interested in maritime history and economics. Unsurpassed in scope and detail, it examines the rise and decline of wooden shipbuilding, the origins of iron and steel shipbuilding, federal maritime policy, and the history of American shipping. Along the way, Hutchins provides comparisons to Britain, Germany, and France; analyses of naval architecture and marine engineering; and evaluations of public policy. Hutchins's later work in maritime history is less well known but essential for the period from 1914 to 1944 not covered in his book. See especially his "History and Development of the Shipbuilding Industry in the United States, 1776–1944," in *The Shipbuilding Business in the United States of America, Vol. 1,* ed. Frederick G. Fassett, Jr. (New York, 1948), pp. 14–60.

Apart from Hutchins's work, a good overview is David Tyler's short book *American Clyde: A History of Iron and Steel Shipbuilding on the Delaware from 1840 to World War I* (Wilmington, Del., 1958). Tyler's book should be read with more recent studies of major shipyards, including Leonard Swann, Jr.'s meticulously researched *John Roach, Maritime Entrepreneur: The Years as Naval Contractor, 1862–1884* (Annapolis, Md., 1965); William Tazewell, *Newport News Shipbuilding: The First Century* (Newport News, Va., 1986); and Ralph L. Snow, *Bath Iron Works: The First Hundred Years* (Bath, Maine, 1987). The early history of Bethlehem Steel's shipbuilding division is covered in Robert Hessen, *Steel Titan: The Life of Charles Schwab* (New York, 1975).

Unfortunately, there is no recent American study to match Sidney Pollard and Paul Robertson's superb *British Shipbuilding Industry, 1870–1914* (Cambridge, Mass., 1979), which is required reading for students of production technology, business organization, plant layout, the labor process, and capital-labor relations in iron and steel shipbuilding. See also Hugh B. Peebles, *Warshipbuilding on the Clyde: Naval Orders and the Prosperity of the Clyde Shipbuilding Industry, 1889–1939* (Edinburgh, 1987); and Fred M. Walker, *Song of the Clyde: A History of Clyde Shipbuilding* (Cambridge, 1984). Two useful books on German shipbuilding are Günter Leckebusch, *Die Beziehungen der deutschen Seeschiffswerften zur Eisenindustrie an der Ruhr in der Zeit von 1850 bis 1930* (Cologne, 1963); and Marina Cattaruzza, *Arbeiter und Unternehmer auf den Werften des Kaiserreichs* (Stuttgart, 1985).

Industrial relations and shipyard unions are analyzed in David Palmer's "Organizing the Shipyards: Unionization at New York Ship, Federal Ship, and Fore River, 1898–1945," 2 vols. (Ph.D. diss., Brandeis University, 1990). See also Keith McClelland and Alastair Reid, "Wood, Iron and Steel: Technology, Labour, and Trade Union Organization in the Shipbuilding Industry," in *Divisions of Labour: Skilled Workers and Technological Change in Nineteenth-Century England,* ed. Royden Harrison and Jonathan Zeitlin (Brighton, England, 1985), pp. 151–84; and Alastair Reid, "Employers' Strategies and Craft Production: The British Shipbuilding Industry 1870–1950," in *The Power to Manage? Employers and Industrial Relations in Comparative Historical Perspective,* ed. Steven Tolliday and Jonathan Zeitlin (London, 1991), pp. 35–51.

In addition to industry and labor studies, there are several important works on naval architecture and marine engineering. On nineteenth-century developments, see Donald L. Canney, *The Old Steam Navy, Vol. 1: Frigates, Sloops, and Gunboats, 1815–1885* (Annapolis, Md., 1990); and *The Old Steam Navy, Vol. 2: The Ironclads, 1842–1885* (Annapolis, Md., 1993). Norman Friedman has written major studies covering later periods, including *U.S. Destroyers: An Illustrated Design History* (Annapolis, Md., 1982) and *U.S. Battleships: An Illustrated Design History* (Annapolis, Md., 1985). See also Ivan Musicant, *U.S. Armored Cruisers: A Design and Operational History* (Annapolis, Md., 1985). Mike Ratcliffe's *Liquid Gold Ships: A History of the Tanker* (London, 1985) is an excellent study of tanker design and operation. Edgar C. Smith, *A Short History of Naval and Marine Engineering* (Cambridge, 1937), provides information on developments in British, American, and German marine technology.

The American carrying trades have received more attention than shipbuilding. I have learned much from Robert Kilmarx, ed., *America's Maritime Legacy: A History of the U.S. Merchant Marine and Shipbuilding since Colonial Times* (Boulder, Colo., 1979); Lewis Fischer and Gerald Painting, eds., *Change and Adaptation in Maritime History: The North Atlantic Fleets in the Nineteenth Century* (St. John's, Newfoundland, Canada, 1985); René de la Pedraja, *The Rise and Decline of U.S. Merchant Shipping in the Twentieth Century* (New York, 1992); and Pedraja, *A Historical Dictionary of the U.S. Merchant Marine and Shipping Industry since the Introduction of Steam* (Westport, Conn., 1994). American steamship fleets are listed in Frederick Emmon's extensively illustrated *American Passenger Ships: The Ocean Lines and Liners, 1873–1983* (Newark, Del., 1985). Case studies of major American steamship companies include James P. Baughman, *Charles Morgan and the Development of Southern Transportation* (Nashville, Tenn., 1968); and Vivian Vale, *The American Peril: Challenge to Britain on the North Atlantic, 1901–1904* (Manchester, 1984), on the International Mercantile Marine.

Page numbers in italic denote illustrations.

Fairview, N.J., 193
Farragut, David, 35
Federal Ship shipyard, 179, 205
Federal Steel Cast Company, 138–39, 159
Federation of Shipbuilders and Engineers, 95
Ferguson, Homer, 189, 197–98, 216
ferryboats, 8, 51, 105, 120
financial markets. *See* banking
Finland (passenger liner), 125, 152
First Bank of the United States, 11
First National Bank of New York, 155, 171
"502"-Class (troopships), 198
"535"-Class (troopships), 180, 198
Florida trade, 79, 126
Florida East Coast Railway, 126
Folger, William, 116
Ford, Henry, 182
Fore River Shipbuilding Company, 123, 136,
    160, 163, 164, 183, 203, 213, 221
forges / forging, 38, 40, 41, 42, 142
Fortuano (wooden steamer), 77, 78
Fortune, William B., 184
foundries, 37, 38, 46, 52, 61, 62, 63, 171, *173*,
    179
"407"-Class (tankers), 174
Fourth Street National Bank of Philadel-
    phia, 155
France, 101, 103
Franklin, Benjamin, 10
Franklin, Philip, 174
freighters, 50, 69, 80–81, 126, 152, 159, 161,
    165–68, 183, 186–89, 197, 199, 201, 202,
    204, 210, 219, 223
Frick, Henry Clay, 132, 174
Frostburg (collier), 84
Fulton, Robert, 14
furnaces, 63
Furness Shipbuilding Company, 203–4

Gallaher, F. B., 184
General Armero (wooden passenger
    steamer), 25
General Electric, 184, 197, 221
Geneva Naval Disarmament Conference,
    216–17
George Blake Manufacturing Company, 115
George W. Clyde (freighter), 53, 54
Georgia (steamship), 80
German Bank. *See* Deutsche Bank
German workers, 190
Germania shipyard, 160
Germany, 197; empire, 101; navy, 166, 170,
    213, 222; and shipbuilding, 46, 160, 163,
    166, 204, 222; and shipping, 32, 166–67,
    199, 204, 222; and submarines, 166

Gilmer, Thomas, 16
Girard, Stephen, 11
Gloucester, N.J., 179, 206, 209
Goethals, George, 169, 200
Gold Rush trade, 12
Gold trade, 28
Goldsboro (wooden steamer), 80
Gompers, Samuel, 145, 147
Goodrich Rubber Company. *See* B. F. Good-
    rich Rubber Company
Gorringe, Henry, 84
Gowen, Franklin, 59, 67, 68
Governor (passenger liner), 161
Grace, Joseph P., 174
Grange, John W., 150
Grantham, John, 63
Great Britain (iron passenger ship), 25
Great Britain, 186, 101, 221; engine building,
    53–54, 86, 103, 129, 218; iron and steel
    shipbuilding, 22, 25, 30–32, 46, 57, 60, 63,
    69, 74, 78–79, 95, 123, 129–30, 163, 198–99,
    203–4, 222; labor organizations, 95–96,
    135–36; Royal Navy, 10, 30, 36, 72, 112, 123,
    129, 166, 170, 182, 188, 203; shipping, 9–10,
    12, 14–15, 30, 54, 62, 63, 69, 70, 74, 78, 79,
    198, 202; wooden shipbuilding; 10, 30
Great Depression, 197, 217, 218
Great Lakes Engineering Works, 168
Great Lakes shipbuilding, 69, 82, 95, 180
Great Lakes shipping, 69, 203
Great Northern (passenger liner), 127, *159*,
    159–60, 210
Great Northern Railroad Company, 127, 159
Great Western (paddle-wheel steamship), 16
Great White Fleet, 156, 163
Greece, 167
Gregory, Francis H., 43
Griscom, Clement A., 57, 109, 125, 126
Grove, Henry S., 155, 156, 171, 191
Guadalcanal, battle of, 215
Gulf of Mexico trade, 79, 127
Gulf Oil Company, 127–28, 161, 167
Gulflight (tanker), 161, 174
Gulfoil (tanker), *128*, 161
Gulfstream (tanker), 161
gunboats, 102, 158
Guzman Blanco, Antonio, 78

H. F. Dimock (freighter), 80, 83
Haddon Township, N.J., 193
half-models, 22, 86
Haitian navy, 72
Hamburg American Line. *See* Hamburg
    Amerika Paket Aktien Gesellschaft
    (HAPAG)

Library of Congress Cataloging-in-Publication Data

Heinrich, Thomas R.
    Ships for the seven seas : Philadelphia shipbuilding in the age
of industrical capitalism / Thomas R. Heinrich.
        p.   cm. — (Studies in industry and society ; 12)
    Includes bibliographical references and index.
    ISBN 0-8018-5387-7 (alk. paper)
        1. Shipbuilding industry—Pennsylvania—Philadelphia—
History.   I. Title.   II. Series.
VM299.6.H45   1997
338.4′762382′0974811—dc20   96-27104
                                                           CIP